MW01121505

MANAGING THE USE OF
FORCE INCIDENT

ABOUT THE AUTHOR

Howard Webb is the executive director of the American Council on Criminal Justice Training (ACCJT), a 501(c)(3) nonprofit public safety training institution. Prior to founding the ACCJT, Howard was the Director of the Montana Law Enforcement Academy. A nationally and internationally recognized use of force expert and criminal justice trainer, he has developed over seventy training courses, instructor development programs, and academy training curriculums. As a Lieutenant for the Oregon Department of Public Safety Standards and Training, Howard developed the National Police Corps academy curriculum and managed the first Police Corps Academy. He was an original member of Macho Products' Redman Advisory Board. As the director of training for DHB Armor Group, Howard developed the Hitman simulation-training suit. He is a police liability consultant and expert witness, who has testified in over three hundred excessive force and officer misconduct lawsuits in state and federal courts.

MANAGING THE USE OF FORCE INCIDENT

For Criminal Justice Officers, Supervisors, and Administrators

By

HOWARD WEBB

CHARLES C THOMAS • PUBLISHER, LTD.
Springfield • Illinois • U.S.A.

Published and Distributed Throughout the World by

CHARLES C THOMAS • PUBLISHER, LTD.
2600 South First Street
Springfield, Illinois 62704

© 2011 by CHARLES C THOMAS • PUBLISHER, LTD.

ISBN 978-0-398-08657-2 (hard)
ISBN 978-0-398-08658-9 (paper)
ISBN 978-0-398-08659-6 (ebook)

Library of Congress Catalog Card Number: 2011011093

With THOMAS BOOKS *careful attention is given to all details of manufacturing
and design. It is the Publisher's desire to present books that are satisfactory as to their
physical qualities and artistic possibilities and appropriate for their particular use.*
THOMAS BOOKS *will be true to those laws of quality that assure a good name
and good will.*

Printed in the United States of America
MM-R-3

Library of Congress Cataloging-in-Publication Data

Webb, Howard, 1956–
   Managing the use of force incident : for criminal justice officers,
supervisors, and administrators / by Howard Webb.
      p. cm.
   Includes bibliographical references and index.
   ISBN 978-0-398-08657-2 (hard) – ISBN 978-0-398-08658-9 (pbk.) –
ISBN 978-0-398-08659-6 (ebook)
   1. Tort liability of police–United States. 2. Police brutality–United
States. 3. Police–United States–Handbooks, manuals, etc. I. Title.

   KF1307.W43 2011
   345.73'052–dc22
                                          2011011093

This book is dedicated to the late Bruce Combs, former lieutenant of Oregon Department on Public Safety Standards and Training. Lieutenant Combs is an Oregon law enforcement-training icon. He was my mentor and good friend. His devotion to excellence lives on through the dedication and service of Oregon's law enforcement officers.

INTRODUCTION

The Los Angeles Police Department is considered one of the most progressive law enforcement agencies in the United States. The L.A.P.D. developed D.A.R.E. and created the first police S.W.A.T. team. It has been the law enforcement muse for countless television dramas and blockbuster movies. However, because of an improperly managed use of force incident, the public primarily remembers the Los Angeles Police Department for the Rodney King incident.

A Google news search of the phrase "police excessive force" identified 1,199 newspaper articles that mentioned lawsuits involving the alleged use of excessive force by police or corrections officers. Keep in mind, these are only the lawsuits that the news media deemed noteworthy. According to a study conducted by the U.S. Department of Justice, law enforcement agencies annually receive, on average, 430,000 complaints of excessive force. Do you think law enforcement agencies are having a problem managing their use of force incidents?

Managing the Use of Force Incident reveals a new and innovative approach to law enforcement liability management. Rather than recite the traditional reactive remedies to department and officer liability, the novel solutions presented in this tome underscores the proactive strategies that officers, trainers, supervisors, and administrators can implement to prevent lawsuits and create an effective preemptive defense against citizen complaints and excessive force litigation.

This proactive liability management philosophy is the product of a professional career spanning over two decades reviewing use of force incidents, consulting with police defense attorneys, and defending criminal justice officers as a use of force expert. The insights into the pitfalls, trends, and strategies explained in this book were developed from an analysis of over nine hundred use of force incidents as a litigation consultant and a defense expert witness, who has testified in over three hundred civil and criminal trials alleging the use of excessive force by police and corrections officers.

As a result, *Managing the Use of Force Incident* addresses excessive force litigation with four inventive strategies:

1. *Understand Causation.* To minimize excessive force litigation, officers, supervisors, and administrators must develop an understanding of the underlying causes of police misconduct lawsuits. An officer's use of sarcasm, vulgarity, or his inability to properly manage perceptions at the scene promotes civil rights litigation by creating a negative perception of the officer's use of force. A supervisor's failure to address an officer's lack of professionalism, poor work performance, or abusive behavior creates liability that could have been prevented. An administrator's inability to predict the negative consequences of a newly written use of force policy, the failure to clearly define management's expectations regarding the use of force to department personnel, or the implementation of a new use of force option without first considering its possible consequences bring about litigation through a lack of administrative foresight. These are just a few examples of the causative issues that are addressed.

2. *Focus on Prevention.* If litigation is predictable, then it may be preventable. It is a given that criminal justice officers will use force. The question is whether the force is objectively reasonable. If a department employs an officer who is reluctant to "go hands on" with a suspect, that officer will eventually overact and use excessive force. If the same department, employs an officer who is hyperaggressive, that officer will eventually use too much force for the circumstances. Both these situations are predictable. And, therefore, preventable with the proper training and supervision.

The historical evidence shows that when cops are given new use of force tools without the proper forethought regarding the consequences of their implementation, it is like giving Donald Duck the atom bomb. The Taser is a classic example. The Ninth Circuit Court of Appeals restricted the use of the Taser because of law enforcement's inability to conclude, on our own, that shocking passively resisting people with a 50,000 volt electronic stun device is excessive force. Who could have predicted that? Chapter 10 provides the information necessary for officers, trainers, supervisors, and administrators to objectively evaluate the potential liability of less-than-lethal force options. Also, Chapter Ten will offer recommendations for the development of performance, training, and administrative solutions to prevent officer and department liability.

3. *Create a Proactive Defense.* Sun Tsu states, "If you know yourself and you know your enemy, even in a thousand battles you will never be in peril." It is impossible to prevent every lawsuit, but an officer and his department can approach every use of force incident expecting a lawsuit to be filed. Chapters 1 and 2 provide examples of the mistakes officers, supervisors, and administrators make that plaintiffs' attorneys look for and exploit in the use of force incident. With this information, you will get to know your enemy. Conse-

quently, you will learn tactics and strategies that build powerful preemptive defenses to excessive force litigation. Rather than play a reactive role against accusations of excessive force and misconduct—as an officer at the scene—you will learn to proactively manage witness and juror perceptions of the use of force incident. As a supervisor or administrator, you will learn to predict potential liability problems and make the necessary changes in policy, supervision, or training to prevent lawsuits. In addition, you will come to understand the importance of a proactive defense, in the event that a lawsuit is filed.

4. *Effective Use of Force Training.* Training does not prevent liability. Effective use of force training, which is well-thought-out, prevents liability. Officers are not sued for using a specific force option; officers are sued for making poor use of force decisions. A classroom use of force lecture does little to enhance an officer's use of force decisions-making abilities. Only a scenario-based use of force training program can effectively minimize officer and department liability. Accordingly, Chapter 12 provides you with a comprehensive overview of the Confrontational Simulation program. This program was the first nationally recognized scenario-based use of force training model.

Moreover, Chapter 12 explains the benefits of an integrated use of force training program. Customarily, training in the use of nondeadly force options (arrest and control tactics, baton, less-lethal impact munitions, pepper spray, and electronic control devices) occur in separate unrelated training modules. This disjointed approach to less-than-lethal and less-lethal force training can unintentionally create officer and department liability. The proactive solution to this liability problem is to implement an integrated approach to less-than-lethal force training. In an integrated use of force program, officers practice the transition from one nondeadly force option to another. This innovative training methodology circumvents a panic-induced overreaction. A panic-induced deployment of nondeadly and deadly force is a major cause of wrongful death litigation.

Managing the Use of Force Incident is the first treatise written that addresses the real world causes of excessive force litigation and provides real world proactive solutions. I will be the first to admit that the observations and recommendations presented in this book are vastly different than those offered in other publications or seminars regarding the use of force by criminal justice officers and liability management strategies for supervisors and administrators. What makes my perspective unique is that it does not originate from a solely academic, administrative, or theoretical understanding of the use of force. It is a culmination of over twenty years of professional experience as a liability consultant, expert witness, law enforcement officer, criminal justice manager, and use of force instructor.

Consequently, this book was written by a cop for cops. As such, the manner and tone in which the information is presented originates from a cop's perspective. This is not to say that the information contained within these pages will not benefit noncriminal justice professionals. The liability management concepts discussed in the following chapters will assist anyone who has a vested interest in minimizing criminal justice civil liability: attorneys, insurance authorities and companies, public administrators, and risk managers.

However, be forewarned, the examples and the dialogues used in my narratives are realistic representations of what occurs on the street and in the correctional facility. Cops are not saints, but they do spend their entire professional lives dealing with sinners (metaphorically speaking). As a result, *Managing the Use of Force Incident* was not written to be a children's bedtime storybook. Some of the examples contained herein may seem a little salty to the civilian reader or the reader expecting a purely academic experience. With that said, as you move forward into the following chapters, if you encounter an example that causes you to raise an eyebrow, I apologize in advance for offending your sensibilities, but not for the context or the purpose for which the example is given.

While preparing to write this book I was actually told by a book publisher (not the publisher of this book) that cops do not read books and their departments buy very few publications. At first this statement offended me. Then, after some reflection on the comment, I came to the conclusion that cops do read books. We just don't read romance novels, self-help books, or fiction. Mainly because cops believe that we have the romance thing nailed down, that we're OK—but everyone else has a problem, and that the real world is crazy enough without reading someone else's distorted fantasies. So, in step with that insightful observation, I would like to thank you for purchasing my book. You are living proof that cops do read, and you will be relieved to know that my next book will not be a romance novel, a self-help book, or fiction.

The concepts explained in the following chapters may take you out of your managing the use of force incident comfort zone. This is a good thing. Because the status quo of liability management research and understanding has failed to successfully address the underlying causes of excessive force litigation. Conventional wisdom may be conventional, but it can be neither wise nor effective. If you contemplate the admonishments, concepts, strategies, and tactics offered in *Managing the Use of Force Incident,* you just might become a little wiser and more enlightened regarding the prevention of officer and department liability.

ACKNOWLEDGMENTS

This book was made possible by the direct and indirect contributions of the following individuals and institutions:

Attorneys Joseph Diaz, Robert Franz, Jr., Steven Kraemer, Lou Kurtz, Steven Sherlag, Robert Wagner, Miles Ward, and Leonard Williamson: Their insights into criminal justice liability and managing the use of force incident form the foundational core of this text.

The Oregon Public Safety Academy: The academy afforded me the professional opportunities that made this treatise possible. Further, the Oregon Academy's progressive training environment cultivated the conceptualization, implementation, and refinement of the proactive liability management strategies that grace these pages.

Captain William Garland (retired) of the Oregon Department of Public Safety Standards and Training: Bill's courage, leadership, and vision were instrumental in my professional development, of which this treatise is based.

Montana Law Enforcement Academy: The MLEA was the proving ground for the leadership, supervisory, and management concepts presented in this text.

Deborah Butler: Deb's editorial skill, guidance, and wisdom were invaluable in the development of this book. As an attorney and a law enforcement trainer, she brought two very important perspectives to this project.

Nick Flores, my lifelong martial arts instructor: Sensei Flores taught me to see the strategic and tactical strengths and weaknesses in all things.

Michael Payne Thomas, my publisher: Michael acutely recognized law enforcement's need for a comprehensive text that addresses the proper management of the use of force incident and the causation of police and corrections liability.

My wife Kelly (an author's widow) and sons Coleman (Spike) and Case: Their unwavering faith in me provided the focus and motivation to start and finish this important project.

LETTER OF RECOMMENDATION

Northland Insurance Companies
400 Country Club Road, Suite 200
Eugene, Oregon 97401

To Whom It May Concern:

RE: Howard R. Webb—Police Liability Expert

Dear Sir or Madame:

I am the Assistant Vice President of Claims for an insurance company that has a significant public entity business. We provide first dollar coverage for liability exposures of Cities and Counties nationally. Police liability is a significant part of that exposure.

We try a high percentage of our police liability claims because of the nature of the business.

Over the last several years we have sought out the expertise of Howard Webb to assist in the evaluation of these difficult cases and to serve as an expert for us in State and Federal Court trials. We have found Mr. Webb to be extremely helpful in the evaluation stage because of his tremendous knowledge of the area and his ability to identify and analyze the issues.

In addition, we have found his expert testimony at trial to be crucial to our success rate in defending police misconduct charges. It is clear from the results that the juries and judges have found his testimony to be credible and convincing. He has demonstrated the ability to adeptly explain to the juries the basis for officers' actions and the training that supports the actions.

I would highly recommend Howard Webb to anyone in need of a trial expert or to merely review a case for liability analysis.

Sincerely yours,

James R. McWilliams, CPCU
Assistant Vice President
Branch Claims Manager

CONTENTS

MANAGING THE USE OF
FORCE INCIDENT

Part I

UNDERSTANDING THE
USE OF FORCE INCIDENT

Chapter 1

LAWSUITS ARE PREDICTABLE, PREVENTABLE, AND WINNABLE

Lawsuits are a fact of life for the criminal justice officer. There are only two strategies that you can implement to prevent a lawsuit. Strategy # 1: Don't go to work. Strategy # 2: If you do go to work, don't talk to anyone, don't touch anyone, and don't drive anywhere. Of course, these are not realistic strategies for the prevention of lawsuits, but they make a point. If you are doing your job, the odds are that you will be—at some point in your career—a defendant in a lawsuit. In fact, the more enthusiastically you do your job, the more likely it is you will be sued. I am not suggesting that you go about your duties in a state of paranoia and fretting about being sued. However, I am recommending that you start every official action with the expectation that it will end with you being a defendant in a lawsuit. Or worse, with you being criminally prosecuted.

Gordon Graham, former California Highway Patrol Lieutenant, lawyer, and police liability expert, states in his seminars that if a lawsuit is predictable, it is preventable. I believe this strategic truth can be taken one step further: If a lawsuit is predictable, it is winnable. It is true that if you can predict officer or department liability; then you can take the necessary steps to prevent the actions, behaviors, or circumstances that create that liability. However, you can do everything within your power to prevent a lawsuit and still get sued. The best strategy for managing law enforcement liability is a two-pronged proactive defense. First, develop the power of foresight. To cultivate the ability to foresee the liability in a given situation is easier than you may think. As Oscar Wilde said, "The power of accurate observation is often called cynicism by those who do not have it." If you can accurately identify a potential liability problem, you can establish the policies or training programs to help prevent it. The second defensive prong emphasizes properly managing the use of force incident at the officer's level. An officer who properly manages the use of force incident does so proactively with the knowledge of how to positively influence the witnesses' and the jurors' perception of his use of force.

The traditional defense to a criminal justice lawsuit starts when the plaintiff's attorney files the civil complaint in state or federal court. At this point, your city, county, or insurance company attorney goes into evaluation mode. Your attorney reviews your written report and the reports of the other officers involved in the incident. He also reviews all witness statements. From the written reports and witness statements, your attorney evaluates the winnability of the case. At this point, the die has been cast. What you have done, said, and written is what your attorney has to work with. Next, your attorney moves into damage control mode. In damage control mode, your attorney seeks your justification for what you did or did not do, what you said or did not say, and what you wrote or did not write in your report. This is the traditional, after-the-fact, reactionary defensive strategy. You have done it. Now, you and your attorney have to defend it.

A more effective strategy is a proactive defense. A proactive defense consists of six components:

PROACTIVE MINDSET. You go into every situation with the expectation that you will be sued or prosecuted for your actions or reactions. If you go into a situation knowing that in the end you must explain and justify your actions to a jury, your actions will be–more often than not–appropriate and defensible.

UNDERSTAND THE OPPOSITION'S MINDSET. Plaintiffs' attorneys are inherently mistrustful of criminal justice officers. This mistrust originates from the anti-police biases of their liberal law school professors. This bias was demonstrated by President Barack Obama's public response to the arrest of Henry Louis Gates Jr., an African American Harvard University professor. Professor Gates was arrested for disorderly conduct during the investigation of the reported break-in of his residence. President Obama, a former president of the Harvard Law Review, publicly denounced the officers' actions without the knowledge of all the facts. In a press conference following the Gates' arrest, President Obama lamented that the officers acted "stupidly." In addition to their law school indoctrination, plaintiffs' attorneys often start their careers as public defenders or practice as criminal defense attorneys in addition to practicing civil rights law. Their evaluation of officers' investigations, tactics, written reports, and testimony from a criminal defense viewpoint reinforces their commonly-held belief that police officers are abusive, dishonest, cover-up for each other, and adhere to the "Blue Code of Silence." Consequently, plaintiffs' attorneys see a police conspiracy in most excessive use of force cases.

UNDERSTAND THE OPPOSITION'S OFFENSIVE STRATEGY. In the majority of lawsuits, a plaintiff's attorney cannot win based on his client's account of the incident. In order to prevail, the plaintiff's attorney must attack your credibility and professional image. The attorney must convince the jury that you are abusive, careless, dishonest, inept, insensitive, negligent, poorly trained, and/or you failed to follow your training or department policy.

KNOWLEDGE OF STANDARDS AND PRINCIPLES. You must gain a working knowledge of the standards that govern the use of force and the principles of use of force justification. Then, you must properly apply these standards in the field and effectively articulate the use of force justification in your written use of force report, deposition, and recorded statements.

PROPER PERCEPTION MANAGEMENT. Possessing the knowledge necessary to properly manage the perceptions of the witnesses at the scene and the jury's perception of your actions during the civil or criminal trial is invaluable to your defense.

PROPERLY WRITTEN USE OF FORCE REPORT. A properly written use of force report includes the collection of the supporting evidence: photographs, physical evidence, logs/records, and audio/video recordings. And, in the event of an officer-involved shooting, a defensible investigative interview with your attorney present.

MAJOR CATEGORIES OF CIVIL LITIGATION

Citizens who believe their constitutional rights have been violated have a civil remedy in the form of financial compensation for their emotional, mental and physical injuries that have been allegedly inflicted by an officer. In addition to being monetarily compensated for their injuries, pain, and suffering, the civil court system has a financially punitive component (punitive damages) to punish officers who apply force sadistically or maliciously.

Civil rights lawsuits brought against criminal justice officers can be divided into four main areas:

Unlawful Entry

The Fourth Amendment of the U.S. Constitution prevents police officers from entering a citizen's home without a valid search warrant. There is an exception to this rule. When the circumstances exist, an officer can make an immediate entry into a residence to protect life or prevent the destruction of evidence. This legal exception to the search warrant requirement is termed "exigent circumstances." It is the officer's responsibility to articulate the circumstances that make obtaining a search warrant for the entry unreasonable. To claim an exigent circumstance exception to the search warrant requirement has become more difficult with the adoption of cellular phones as standard issue equipment by police departments and the almost universal ownership of cell phones by officers. In the pre-cell phone era, an officer had to drive back to the police station to use a landline to call a judge to obtain a telephonic search warrant. Now, an officer can make the call for a telephonic search warrant from the scene.

Consequently, when deciding to make an "exigent circumstance" entry without a search warrant, the officer must identify all the factors that make obtaining a telephonic warrant unreasonable. These factors may include the immediate risk of injury to the occupants, the escape of a dangerous suspect, a lack of law enforcement personnel necessary to adequately secure the building, or to prevent the destruction of evidence involving a serious crime. Lastly, a commonly occurring factor to consider is the "hot pursuit" of a fleeing suspect. The hot pursuit of a suspect is often used as a reason for entering a building without a search warrant, and it is a valid reason for an exigent circumstance entry. However, officers often have a difficult time articulating the justification for a hot pursuit entry, after the fact. Why? Because the officer initiates the hot pursuit not expecting to be sued. You must clearly understand the circumstances that allow you to pursue a suspect into a building or residence before you make the decision to enter without a warrant. There are two concerns that justify an entry without a warrant in pursuit of a fleeing suspect. The first concern: The suspect will harm the occupants of the residence and/or take them hostage. The second concern: The suspect is entering his home to obtain a weapon to harm the officer, himself, and/or another person.

When it comes to entering a home without a search warrant, officers often enter under the concept of community caretaking. With a community caretaking entry, there are no known reasons to enter the residence for the protection of another person from immediate harm. The officer enters the residence to check on the welfare of the resident. When the concern for the resident's safety/welfare is legitimate, the courts and jurors have found the entry into a residence without a warrant lawful.

In contrast, officers often gain entry into a residence through the "Arm's Reach Doctrine." This doctrine is not a legal concept. It is a generally accepted police practice. With the Arm's Reach Doctrine, officers believe that if they can stick their foot between the edge of the door and the doorframe to prevent the door from being closed and grab the suspect a warrant is not required to enter the residence or to extract the suspect. Needless to say, this practice does not meet the requirements for an "exigent circumstance" or community caretaking entry. Consequently, when used, it creates liability for the officer and his department.

Excessive Force

Officers can use objectively reasonable force to protect themselves and others, make a lawful arrest, detain a suspicious person, and to prevent damage to property or the destruction of evidence. This all sounds pretty straightforward, right? Unfortunately, the guidelines for determining whether the officer's use of force was excessive are academic and conceptual. To further complicate the issue, the correctness of an officer's use of force is a matter of perception. Not the officer's perception. Not the suspect's or inmate's perception. But, ultimately, it is the jury's perception. A jury comprised of members of your community. In Chapter 2, the importance of managing witness and juror perceptions will be explained in detail. In addition to the importance of perception management, the U.S. Supreme Court's guidelines for the use of nondeadly and deadly force will be explained in Chapter 4. Explained not from an attorney's perspective (which is a theoretical point of view), but from an officer's perspective (which is a practical point of view).

False Arrest/Imprisonment

An officer can lawfully arrest a person and physically take that person into custody when the officer reasonably believes probable cause exists that the person has committed a crime. "Probable Cause" is a lesser standard of proof than "Proof Beyond a Reasonable Doubt." Although many times an officer develops proof beyond a reasonable doubt (in his mind) before the arrest is made, the officer needs only probable cause for the arrest to be lawful. Consequently, officers often use probable cause arrests to resolve community problems. When this happens, frequently, the prosecutor drops the charge because the level of proof does not reach the required "proof beyond a reasonable doubt" standard for a conviction. This failure to prosecute leads the suspect to believe that he or she was unlawfully arrested and encourages a false arrest and/or excessive force lawsuit.

In many lawsuits, the suspect alleges multiple civil rights violations. It is common for an officer's initial action to create a "domino effect" of alleged civil rights violations. The following is an actual incident where one officer's action set in motion the domino effect that resulted in an allegation of multiple civil rights violations and a monetary judgement against the officer.

Pistorius v. Medford: A mother reported to the police department that her teenage son had run away from home with her small truck. Furthermore, she stated her son was staying with his aunt, and the aunt had concealed the truck in her garage.

Two officers responded to the Pistorius residence. The officers found no one at home. However, they observed the pickup partially concealed in the garage. The truck was covered with a tarp, but the license plate was visible. As the officers were looking through the garage window, Mrs. Pistorius (the aunt) pulled into her driveway in a van. Mrs. Pistorius owned a floral shop, and she used the van to deliver flowers. For protection on her deliveries, she took an attack-trained Doberman Pinscher guard dog with her.

Mrs. Pistorius exited the van and walked toward the front door of her residence with the Doberman in tow. One of the officers called out to her saying, "Ma'am, I would like to talk to you about the pickup in your garage." "There is no pickup in my garage," she relied. As she walked to the door, the officers followed her. Mrs. Pistorius opened the front door and entered the residence. As she attempted to close the door, the senior officer put his foot in the doorway, preventing Mrs. Pistorius from closing and locking the door. As she pushed to close the door, the officer reached through the gap between the door and the doorframe and grabbed her arm. As Mrs. Pistorius fought to escape the officer's grasp, she pulled him into the residence (Arm's Reach Doctrine).

Now at this point, there are two officers in the living room with a very upset Mrs. Pistorius and a growling guard dog. Unknown to the officers, the Pistorious' teenage daughter was in her bedroom and overheard her mother yelling at the officers. The daughter frantically telephoned her father at work (he owned a woodstove store) and asked him to come home. Within minutes, Mr. Pistorious arrived at his residence. Mr. Pistorious told the officers that they were trespassing and demanded they leave. The officers refused to leave, stating they were there to investigate the theft of the pickup. Mr. Pistorious telephoned the police department and demanded to speak to the Chief of Police. The chief was unavailable, so Mr. Pistorious was transferred to the patrol captain. A very irate Mr. Pistorious explained to the captain that two of his officers entered his house illegally, and he demanded that the captain order the officers to leave.

The captain asked to speak with the senior officer. When the officer was put on the telephone, the captain asked for a summary of the situation. The officer explained that they were at the Pistorious residence investigating a report of a stolen vehicle. The captain, forgetting he was on a recorded line, replied, "Pistorious, those people are f . . king nuts! Arrest them, or get the hell out of there!" A recording of that conversation was played for the jury at the civil trial.

As Mr. and Mrs. Pistorious argued with the officers, the Doberman growled and showed his teeth. The senior officer told Mrs. Pistorious "Ma'am, put the dog away, if it attacks I'll shoot it." In response, Mr. Pistorious asked the officer, "How would you like it if I went to my bedroom, got my rifle, and placed you under citizen arrest?" "I will have to shoot you too," the officer replied. Mr. Pistorious turned and walked toward the bedroom. Fearing that he would obtain a rifle, the officers tackled Mr. Pistorious and forced him into handcuffs. He was arrested and taken to jail. During the struggle, Mr. Pistorious' shoulder was injured. Mr. Pistorious sued the officers in federal court for unlawful entry, excessive force, and false arrest.

At the conclusion of the trial, the jury found that when Mr. Pistorious threatened to get his rifle the officers were justified in using force to protect themselves. Also, the jury decided that the threat to get his rifle was an attempt to place the officers in fear of serious physical harm, constituting a criminal act. Therefore, Mr. Pistorious' arrest was lawful. However, the jury determined that the officers did not have "exigent circumstances" that justified an entry into the residence without a warrant.

Police Vehicle Pursuits

Lastly, the fourth-major category of police lawsuits involves the pursuit of a suspect vehicle. Although, litigation involving police pursuits occur much less frequently than the other three categories of lawsuits, when they do occur, the financial settlements and jury verdicts can be extraordinarily large. The larger payoff is primarily due to the category of the people who are injured or killed in the vehicle crash. A large percentage of the people killed in police chases are not directly involved in the pursuit. They are innocent drivers and passengers who are lawfully using the roadway. An additional factor in jury awards and out-of-court settlements is the reason why the officer was pursuing the suspect vehicle. The majority of police pursuits involve a suspect who has committed a traffic violation. When a police pursuit causes serious injury or a fatality, it is much easier to convince a jury that the pursuit was necessary if the officers are chasing a vehicle driven by a dangerous suspect.

If you are one of those officers who argue that "If we don't chase traffic violators that will encourage drivers to run," you need to seriously consider the consequences of that position. In an ideal world, this argument has merit. If we stop pursuing drivers who flee to avoid getting a traffic ticket, some drivers will more likely flee, especially younger drivers. However, the world we police is neither perfect nor ideal. The decisions we make as police officers have life-altering consequences when it comes to police pursuits. The only counter-argument I can offer is this simple question: "What crime or violation would a suspect have to commit that would justify the accidental killing of your spouse, children, parents, siblings, or best friend in a high-speed vehicle pursuit? The answer: No crime or violation is worth that. On one holiday evening, this philosophical question became a horrible reality for one officer. On Thanksgiving Day, officers engaged in a high-speed pursuit of a driver who was attempting to elude the officer for a traffic violation. The suspect vehicle, traveling at a high rate of speed, ran a stoplight at a busy intersection and collided with a minivan that had the right-of-way. An elderly man and woman were killed in the crash. They were the parents of a police officer.

To offer an unemotional argument for not pursuing traffic violators, I provide you with the following example: After a woman was struck and killed during a high-speed pursuit of a teenage driver who was fleeing the police over a traffic violation, a metro police department implemented a policy against pursuing traffic violators in high-speed pursuits. As a result of the policy, the number of the department's high-speed pursuits were reduced by 75 percent from the previous year. So, what does that tell you?

Criminal Prosecutions for Excessive Force

Prior to 1991, the prosecution of police and corrections officers mainly involved criminal activity that was outside the scope of their professional duties. Throughout the history of American law enforcement and corrections, officers have been prosecuted for criminal acts performed on and off-duty. These acts consisted mainly of driving under the influence of alcohol, bribery, domestic violence, corruption, theft of evidence or private property, and sexual misconduct. Before 1991, the prosecution of law enforcement officers for assault and battery or sexual misconduct for actions directly related to their official duties was nearly nonexistent.

On March 3, 1991, the Rodney King incident and the grainy videotape recording of his arrest by the officers of the Los Angeles Police Department changed the way prosecutors and the public view the use of force by police and corrections officers. Based on the videotape evidence and the testimony of the officers who witnessed the arrest, Sergeant Stacey Koon and Officer Lawrence Powell were convicted of assault in a federal criminal court for the force they used to effect Rodney King's arrest. Prior to the Rodney King incident, officers only worried about being sued civilly in state or federal courts. With Sergeant Koon's and Officer Powell's incarceration in federal prison splashed all over the newspapers and the nightly news broadcasts, officers became acutely aware that the threat of criminal prosecution for allegations of excessive force and misconduct was a frightening reality.

If the possibility of a criminal conviction is not enough to worry about, the criminal prosecution can financially ruin you, even if you are found not guilty. When you are civilly sued as an agent of your department, your employer indemnifies you. In other words, your city, county, or state will pay for your legal defense and any monetary judgement levied against you.

This is not the case when you are criminally prosecuted. A criminal prosecution for a misdemeanor assault/battery or sexual abuse allegation can cost you between $20,000.00 and $250,000.00 dollars in attorney and legal fees. Your legal defense against a felony assault or murder charge may cost much more.

There are people in all professions who commit criminal acts, and the law enforcement and corrections professions are not exempted from hiring people who do not have the temperaments to lawfully perform their duties. In over twenty years of defending police and corrections officers in criminal prosecutions for excessive force or misconduct, I have never reviewed an incident where the officer's actions constituted a criminal act. This does not mean that all officer prosecutions are without merit.

However, in the criminal cases that I have reviewed involving the allegations of excessive force or an inappropriate officer safety search, I believe the prosecutions were brought forward by politically motivated prosecutors or as a misguided attempt to show the public that officers are held to a higher standard of conduct.

The following is an example of a misdemeanor prosecution of a patrol officer for two counts of assault, in two separate unrelated arrests. The officer was successfully prosecuted with only the witnesses' statements; the victims failed to appear at the trial.

State of Oregon v. Jerry Walton: Officer Jerry Walton of the Salem Police Department and his partner were on bike patrol along the Willamette River when they observed a homeless man drinking a beer. The City of Salem had an ordinance prohibiting the consumption of an alcoholic beverage on premises open to the public. Previously, Officer Walton had warned the man about drinking beer in a public place. With this violation, Officer Walton decided to issue the homeless man a criminal citation.

Officer Walton told the man that if he cooperated he would be issued a citation, but if he did not cooperate he would be arrested and taken to jail. The man indicated he would cooperate. Officer Walton asked for his identification. The suspect gave Officer Walton a state issued identification card. When Officer Walton asked the suspect if the information on the card was current, the suspect replied, "You got my ID." Officer Walton asked several more times if the information was current, and each time the suspect answered, "You got my ID." Because the suspect refused to cooperate, Officer Walton placed the suspect under arrest and handcuffed him. Because the arrest occurred on a gravel road along the river, Officer Walton decided to walk the suspect to an adjoining paved road and radio for a patrol car to transport the suspect to jail. Officer Walton walked with the suspect while his partner walked with their bicycles. They had walked about ten feet when the suspect said to Officer Walton, "If you are going to take me to jail, you are going to have to carry me," and he sat down on the gravel road. Officer Walton tried to convince the suspect to stand up, but he refused to cooperate.

Officer Walton radioed for the responding patrol car to come to their location. As they waited for the transport car to arrive, Officer Walton decided to fill out the custody paperwork. Officer Walton asked the suspect to lean forward, so he (Officer Walton) could remove his wallet from his rear pants pocket. Instead of learning forward, the suspect leaned backward preventing Officer Walton access to his wallet. Officer Walton laid the suspect on his side and kneeled across the side of his head to pin him to the ground. Once the suspect was immobilized, Officer Walton asked his partner to remove the suspect's wallet. The Cover Officer removed the wallet without interference, and Officer Walton lifted the suspect up to a seated position. It is important to note that Officer Walton did not forcefully push the suspect over. Officer Walton controlled the suspect's descent to the gravel road. The suspect received a few minor scratches on his face from being pinned against the gravel. Officer Walton retrieved the ID card from the wallet and completed the paperwork. The patrol car arrived at the scene, and the suspect was transported to the county jail.

When Officer Walton and his partner arrived at the police department, his partner (who had limited police experience) told Officer Walton that she felt he had used excessive force on the homeless man. Not wanting to cause tension in their working relationship, Officer Walton appeased his partner by stating that maybe he should not have pinned the suspect's face to the gravel road.

A few days later, Officer Walton was on vehicle patrol when he received a report of an intoxicated man blocking traffic on Lancaster Drive, a busy roadway in the business district of Salem. An intoxicated homeless man, with a large bottle of wine, had wandered into a medical clinic on Lancaster Drive. The clinic's staff escorted the man out onto the sidewalk. He staggered into Lancaster Drive and sat down, stopping traffic for several blocks. Two good samaritans (a husband and wife) pulled their car over, helped the intoxicated man out of the roadway and onto a bus-stop bench, and called the police department for assistance.

Officer Walton arrived at the scene and observed a man sitting on a bus-stop bench drinking from a large wine bottle. Officer Walton contacted and quickly interviewed the good samaritans. After talking with the couple, Officer Walton contacted the intoxicated man, informed him that there was a city ordinance against consuming alcohol in public, and told him to put the bottle down on the ground. The suspect ignored Officer Walton and continued to drink from the bottle. When Officer Walton reached for the bottle, the suspect pulled the bottle way, placed it between his thighs, and clamped down on the bottle with both hands. Officer Walton told the suspect to drop the bottle several more times. The suspect refused to comply. Officer Walton pulled his pepper spray canister and sprayed the suspect in the face. The suspect's large prescription eyeglasses shielded his eyes from the pepper spray, minimizing its effectiveness. In response, Officer Walton angled the pepper spray nozzle over the top of the eyeglasses and sprayed again. This application had the desired effect. The suspect wailed in pain, dropped the bottle, and brought his hands to his face. At this point, the suspect is still sitting on the bench with his heels curled up–locking him in place.

Officer Walton placed a wristlock on the suspect. It was Officer Walton's intention to stand the suspect up and handcuff him. Unfortunately, Officer Walton did not realize the suspect had clamped his heels to the bottom of the bench. As Officer Walton pulled the suspect up and forward, he fell headfirst onto the cement sidewalk. From the impact with the sidewalk, the suspect's eyeglasses were broken, and he received a large bump on his forehead. The suspect was arrested and handcuffed. The couple who had helped the man out of the street witnessed the pepper spraying and the fall off the bench. They become enraged over what they perceived as excessive force. Officer Walton radioed for a supervisor to respond to the scene. As the good samaritans were berating Officer Walton, the patrol sergeant arrived. Officer Walton directed the irate samaritans to his sergeant. The couple continued to express their outrage. The sergeant told the good samaritans that if they wanted to file a citizen's complaint they needed to contact the chief's office, and he handed them a police department business card. The husband and wife not only filed a complaint with the police department, but they also filed a criminal complaint with the district attorney's office.

When Officer Walton's partner from the previous incident learned of the Lancaster Drive complaint, she contacted the Internal Affairs Division and reported that she had witnessed Officer Walton use excessive force on a homeless man during a previous arrest.

Officer Walton, a ten-year police veteran, was convicted of two counts of misdemeanor assault in a jury trial. The homeless suspects failed to appear in court, and Officer Walton was convicted with only the witnesses' testimony. Officer Walton was terminated from the police department, and he amassed approximately $30,000.00 in attorney fees.

Officer Jerry Walton did not use excessive force on either suspect. He did, however, make the same mistake in both arrests; he failed to properly manage the witnesses' and the jury's perception of his use of force. Officer Walton's missteps will be analyzed in Chapter 2. Additionally, examples of how he could have managed the perceptions of the witnesses and jurors will be discussed.

As stated previously, officers are not only prosecuted for allegations of excessive force. They are prosecuted for allegations of sexual abuse in performance of their duties. The following is an example of a misdemeanor prosecution of a state trooper for the alleged inappropriate touching of a female suspect during an officer safety search. The officer was found not guilty in a jury trial. But, the prosecution professionally and financially ruined the trooper.

State of Oregon v. Daniel Beugli: Oregon State Police Senior Trooper Daniel Beugli was on patrol when he observed a woman standing outside the fence of the state prison. Trooper Beugli contacted the woman and asked for her driver's license. She told Trooper Beugli that she did not have a license because her driving privileges had been suspended. After further investigation, the trooper determined the woman had driven to the prison in a vehicle parked nearby and that her driving privileges were revoked. Trooper Beugli issued the woman a traffic citation for driving while suspended, and he told her not to drive her car. The woman asked Trooper Beugli for a ride to a friend's house. He offered to call her a taxi. She declined the offer, stating she could not afford to pay for a cab. He offered to call a friend for a ride. She told the trooper there was no one she could call to give her a ride. As an act of kindness, Trooper Beugli agreed to give the woman a ride to her friend's house in his patrol car.

Trooper Beugli told the woman that before he would give her a ride he needed to perform a pat-down search for weapons. She consented to the search. The trooper lightly ran the palm of his hand around the outside of her waistband, pockets, and the legs of her pants. Also, he used the edge of his hand to search between and under her breasts. Finding no weapons, she was placed unhandcuffed in the back of his patrol car and driven to her friend's home. The next day the woman filed a compliant with the State Police stating Trooper Beugli had sexually abused her during the pat-down search. At the time, it was the State Police's policy and training to search a woman's breast area by tapping her chest lightly with a Kubaton, baton, or flashlight, while listening for the metallic sound of a concealed weapon.

Trooper Beugli was placed on paid administrative leave while Internal Affairs (IA) conducted an investigation. During the IA investigation, he gave an account of the stop. The district court ruled that Trooper Beugli's statements were inadmissible in court. The District Attorney appealed the ruling. During the appeal process, Trooper Beugli was placed on paid administrative leave for seven years. He was required to stay at his residence from 8:00 a.m. to 5:00 p.m., five days a week. Even though he was collecting his full salary, Trooper Beugli was forced to get an evening job to help pay for his legal fees. Finally, the appellate court ruled that his statements were admissible and a trial date was set. At this point Trooper Beugli had amassed $250,000.00 in attorney's fees. He was financially ruined and was forced to have his attorney court appointed.

After hearing all the evidence, the jury found Trooper Beugli not guilty on all criminal charges. He had been on administrative leave for so long that the State Police sent him back through the basic police academy as a training refresher. After completing his academy training, he was assigned to patrol in the county where he had been prosecuted. The district attorney sent a letter to the State Police Superintendent informing him that the district attorney's office would not prosecute Trooper Beugli's arrests. In response, the State Police transferred Trooper Beugli to an adjoining county. The prosecuting district attorney sent a letter to the adjoining county's district attorney stating that Trooper Beugli was not a viable witness, and he should not prosecute Trooper Beugli's criminal cases. Based on that letter, the adjoining district attorney refused to prosecute Trooper Beugli's arrests. Unable to get his investigations prosecuted, the State Police transferred Trooper Beugli to an administrative position at State Police Headquarters.

An allegation of sexual abuse originating from an officer safety search of a female suspect is of serious concern to patrol officers and law enforcement administrators. The common knee-jerk response to such complaints is to compromise the searching procedure when a female officer is unavailable to perform the search. Compromising the searching procedure often leads to missed concealed weapons that would have been otherwise found in a properly performed pat-down of her outer clothing.

In an incident involving an arrest of a female suspect by patrol officers, the male officers performed a "visual frisk" for weapons in lieu of a proper intrusive clothing search. After being transported to the police department, the suspect was taken to an interview room. As the officers questioned her, she reached into the front of her jeans and pulled out a loaded snub-nose 38-caliber revolver and placed it on the table. As she pulled the gun from her pants, she told the officers, "You might want to take this before I go to jail." The next day I received a telephone call from the department's training sergeant, who asked me to provide training on how to properly conduct opposite-gender clothing searches to the members of his department.

In Chapter 2, I will discuss strategies for positively influencing the jury's perception of your opposite-gender search. Furthermore, I will provide guidelines for creating a proactive defense against allegations of misconduct and sexual abuse when conducting an opposite gender pat-down search and intrusive clothing search incident to the arrest.

Causes of Use of Force Liability

The law enforcement and corrections professions have their own version of a Zen koan. A koan is a question of which the meaning cannot be understood by rational thinking, yet it may be accessible by intuition. You're familiar with Zen's most famous koan: What is the sound of one hand clapping? For criminal justice administrators, mid-managers, supervisors, and officers, the koan is much less esoteric, but equally elusive: What are the causes of use of force liability?

I did not have to meditate under a locust tree for forty days and nights to answer that question. But, I did review hundreds of use of force incidents, read thousands of pages of incident reports and depositions, and consulted with dozens of criminal justice civil defense attorneys and a few plaintiffs' attorneys. The following is what experience, not intuition, has taught me about the causes of use of force liability:

HIGH STRESS. Law enforcement and corrections are the only civilian occupations where we intentionally place ourselves in life-threatening situations. When the shots are fired or the blood is flowing most people run away, we run toward the fighting, chaos, and gunfire. Needless to say, our most important decisions are made in a state of high emotional and physical stress.

Psychologists link stress levels to heart rate. When your heart rate elevates to one hundred and forty-five beats per minute you have reached a level of stress where your judgement and decision-making abilities are impaired (Siddle, 1995).

In his law enforcement training seminars, Dave Grossman, author of *On Killing,* explains the cognitive and physiological effects of stress. When you experience high levels of stress, you stop using the frontal lobes of your brain, the intellectual part of your brain. And you start using your mid-brain, the primal and instinctive part of your brain. Grossman refers to the mid-brain as the "animal brain," because you are not thinking–you are reacting. According to Grossman, when officers are under extreme levels of stress they think with the intelligence level of a smart dog. It is the use of the "animal brain" that causes poor use of force decisions and officer and department liability. The following is a narration of an officer's stress-induced shooting of a burned and unarmed suspect and the subsequent multi-million-dollar settlement.

Kaady v. City of Sandy: An officer from the Sandy Police Department and deputies from the Clackamas County Sheriff's Office responded to a motor vehicle accident. The officer and deputies were told by dispatch that the incident involved multiple "Hit and Run" vehicles and that the suspect's vehicle had crashed and was on fire. In addition, the officers were told that the suspect was naked, extremely combative, armed with a gun, high on drugs, and had ran into the woods near the crash site.

The Sandy officer was first to arrive at the scene. Witnesses told the officer that the driver was naked, burned, armed, ran into the woods, and after he entered the woods they heard a gunshot. Also, the officer was told that the suspect had assaulted a man who had stopped to help him. As the officer was talking to the witnesses, two deputies arrived at the scene.

Shortly after the deputies arrived, the officers overheard radio traffic stating that a citizen had reported a naked and bloody man running down the road. One deputy agreed to stay at the crash site while the Sandy officer and the other deputy responded to the man's location. When the officers arrived, they saw a badly burned, bloody, and naked man (Kaady) sitting in the middle of the roadway. Fearing that Kaady may be armed, they initially approached the suspect with their firearms drawn. Not seeing any visible weapons, they transitioned from their firearms to their Tasers.

The deputy ordered Kaady to prone out on the ground several times. Kaady acknowledged the officers, but he refused to comply. The officer deployed his Taser to Kaady's back. When the Taser was deployed, Kaady laid flat on his back and was controlled for the five seconds that the Taser cycled. When the Taser stopped cycling, Kaady sat back up. The deputy told Kaady to comply or he will be shocked again. Kaady started to stand up, looked directly at the deputy, growled, and showed his teeth. The officer shocked Kaady again. Kaady fell on his back, but he is able to fight through the Taser shock and started to get up. The deputy shot his Taser into Kaady. With both Tasers deployed, Kaady was able to stand up and run away from the officers, breaking the Taser wires. When the wires broke, he turned back toward the officers.

The deputy attempted to reload his Taser, but stress had impaired his ability to perform fine motor skills. Kaady screamed at the officers "I'am gonna kill you." The officers retreated to the patrol car in an attempt to use it as barrier. As they reach the patrol car, they saw Kaady closing the distance. As he turned back toward Kaady, the deputy observed Kaady jump up on the roof of the patrol car. On top of the car, Kaady screamed "I'am going to kill you." Believing Kaady was about to leap onto the deputy, both the deputy and officer fired their handguns. Kaady was shot seven times and died at the scene.

Fouad Kaady was twenty-seven years old. He weighed one hundred and fifty pounds and was five foot and nine inches tall at the time of the shooting. He had received third-degree burns to the upper half of his body. Kaady had no history of mental illness. He was not under the influence of alcohol or drugs.

As the attorneys, risk-managers, and the public analyzed the Kaady incident, two use of force questions came to the forefront. First, why did the officers choose to Taser a burnt, naked, passively resisting man? There were two officers. Why didn't they attempt to control Kaady with physical control techniques or overpower him?

Second, why did the officers shoot a burned, five-foot and nine-inch, one hundred and fifty-pound unarmed suspect? Why didn't they attempt lesser force first? A baton may have disabled Kaady. Focused blows made have stunned him. The vascular neck restraint may have rendered him unconscious. All of these options are greater force than the Taser, but lesser force than a bullet.

The answer: The officers were experiencing high levels of stress. Prior to contacting Kaady, the officers were informed that Kaady had rammed several vehicles, he was armed, and he had physically attacked a person who stopped to help him. Plus, factor in a high-speed—Code Three—response in a patrol car and the emotional impact of confronting a badly burned man, who overcomes the effects of the Taser and threatens to kill them. Due to the high levels of stress that the officers are experiencing, their ability to analyze their force options was diminished. The mid-brain had taken over. The officers were reacting in survival mode, not operating in "let's solve this tactical problem mode."

To further complicate the case, in a pretrial ruling, a federal magistrate ruled that the Tasering of Kaady while he passively sat, unarmed, in the roadway was excessive force. As part of the ruling, the judged stated that the officer knew or should have known that the use of the Taser was unlawful. Even if the officer did know that it was unlawful to use the Taser on Kaady, due to the effects of stress, he was unable to access the part of his brain that would enable him to draw that conclusion. The fatal blow to the city's defense came when the Sandy officer pled guilty to identity theft/official misconduct for allowing a minor to use a confiscated driver's license to get into a bar. You will see a related connection to this case when you read the section titled "Stupidity."

After a grand jury review, hundreds of hours of investigation and depositions, and thousands of dollars in attorney and expert witness fees, the City of Sandy, Clackamas County, and the Kaady family came to a $2,000,000.00 out of court settlement.

Being under the effects of stress may not be a justification for using the Taser or deadly force, but it does explain the officer's and the deputy's decision-making process in this incident. Fortunately, through proper training, officers can be inoculated to the effects of stress. In Chapter 12, I will explain how scenario-based use of force training improves an officer's use of force decision making and minimizes liability.

GROUPTHINK. George Santayana opined, "Those who cannot learn from history are doomed to repeat it." You would think that intelligent criminal justice administrators, officers, and trainers would learn from the historical record of the evolution of nonlethal weapons adopted by corrections and law enforcement.

The first technological advancement in nonlethal weapons after the introduction of the expandable baton was pepper spray. Pepper spray was touted by its manufacturers and instructors as a completely safe, biodegradable, aerosol restraint. While attending one of the first pepper spray instructor courses offered by a company instructor, we were told that pepper spray was completely safe, regardless of the fact that it impaired respiration, caused temporary blindness, and felt like a small nuclear weapon had gone off near your face. Furthermore, we were told that the use of pepper spray should be placed above verbalization and below physical contact on the force continuum. In essence, as pepper spray instructors, we were being taught that is was no longer necessary to make physical contact with a resisting suspect or inmate. Just spray him. Consequently, as it was explained, officer injuries would be reduced because our officers were no longer fighting with suspects or inmates.

Now, I am not the sharpest knife in the drawer, but I intuitively knew that this recommendation would, under certain circumstances, constitute excessive force. As I raised that specific issue in class, it became immediately apparent that I was the only instructor in the room who was not a religious convert to the use of pepper spray. In fact, the recommendation of "Spray them, don't touch them" was embraced by criminal justice agencies nationwide. It was even supported by a study conducted by the Federal Bureau of Investigation.

Common sense dictated that it was excessive force for a twenty-five-year-old, six-foot, 200 pound, male officer to pepper spray an intoxicated, seventy-two-year-old, five-foot, ninety-five pound, woman in a bar because she refused to leave. But, apparently when it came to the use of pepper spray, common sense was in short supply. You did not have to be clairvoyant to predict what happened next. As more and more suspects and inmates were sprayed, pepper spray lawsuits involving injuries to the eyes, skin, and respiratory system started to have an impact on law enforcement's use of pepper spray. Consequently, pepper spray was moved up on the force continuum to the physical control category and by some departments to serious physical control.

Always searching for a better mousetrap, law enforcement embraced the deployment of less-lethal impact munitions by the patrol officer. Beanbag munitions had been in use for a number of years by SWAT teams prior to its issue to patrol officers. It was déjà vu. I was sitting in an impact munitions (beanbag) instructor course when I was told by the manufacturer's instructor that a ballistic bag, filled with lead shot, fired from a twelve gauge shotgun was the same level of force as the baton. In fact, the company instructor called it an "extended range impact weapon." Again, I expressed by opinion that a lead-filled projectile fired from a shotgun probably was more injurious than a blow delivered with a twenty-four-inch baton. Again, I was shouted down by my classmates, who were intoxicated with the breathless anticipation of the deployment of a new and completely safe use of force option.

Nationwide law enforcement agencies distributed converted less-lethal shotguns and beanbag ammunition to patrol officers. And the beanbag was used often in lieu of the police baton to control suspects. And then came the lawsuits involving serious physical injury or death. As could have been predicted, the Ninth Circuit Court of Appeals ruled that the use of the beanbag was more force than a bite from a police dog—a level of force much greater than the impact from a police baton.

Then, one day, the gods smiled on law enforcement and gifted us with a powerful and completely safe electronic control device called the Taser. As in days of my youth, I sat in an instructor course where the company instructor told us that this new less-lethal control device was completely safe to use in lieu of "going hands-on" with suspects and inmates. We were told that the use of the Taser would miraculously reduce the number of officer and suspect injuries. My classmates were mesmerized by a video of a bull being disabled by the Taser. As in previous instructor courses, I was the lone voice in the wilderness. I voiced my opinion that suspects and inmates might be seriously injured from a dart hitting an eye or from the impact with a floor from the unprotected free fall. The instructor acknowledged that those were possible scenarios; however, they were highly unlikely and the company had never received a report of a serious injury or death from the deployment of the Taser. And, my classmates were in complete agreement that the Taser was completely safe and I was a misguided naysayer.

Criminal justice agencies worldwide embraced the Taser. The company's stock soared. Police and corrections officers nationwide were shocking suspects and inmates instead of controlling them by the laying of hands. What happened next was completely unexpected by chiefs and sheriffs who were drunk on the group think of Taser Mania. Newspaper articles started to appear reporting officers zapping six-year-olds at school, intoxicated junior high school girls playing hooky, people with no legs in wheelchairs, and a seventy-five-year-old woman who brought cookies to a convalescent home and then refused to leave. Next came the videos. The most memorial is the visual of a gigantic male officer towering over a seventy-year-old great-grandmother who refused to sign the traffic citation just before she hit the pavement after being Tasered. It didn't take long before newspaper articles started to appear with interviews of chiefs and sheriffs explaining how they hoped the revision of their departments' Taser policies would prevent future inappropriate use of the Taser. However, there were newspaper articles where some chiefs and sheriffs stubbornly defended the use of the Taser at its lower level in the force continuum.

What happened next caught the law enforcement masses flatfooted and completely off-guard. The Ninth Circuit Court of Appeals reviewed the traffic stop of a young man, wearing only boxer shorts and tennis shoes, who was Tasered and injured from the impact with the pavement. In their ruling, the Ninth Circuit stated that it is unlawful to use the Taser in probe mode on passively resisting suspects and that the use of the Taser is greater force than pepper spray, physical control holds, or police nunchucks. Who could've seen this coming?

GroupThink is intellectual laziness. It takes less intellectual effort to accept the manufacturer's recommendation at face value than it does to analyze the consequences of implementing a new use of force option. And, as history has demonstrated, Group Think has been and continues to be an underlying cause of lawsuits involving the adoption and implementation of new force options by law enforcement and corrections.

INTELLECTUAL INCEST. Intellectual incest can occur in any size law enforcement agency or department of corrections. However, it manifests itself mainly in large departments who develop an isolationist attitude and create their own instructors. Departments that suffer from this condition believe that they are the wellspring from which all law enforcement knowledge flows for their state and even the nation. Therefore, whatever they teach to their officers is cutting edge and above question. This attitude is passed on from one generation of instructor to the next. Through their teachings, their officers or deputies adopt this attitude. They justify their sense of superiority by telling themselves that their environment is different from that of other cities or counties; therefore, they are in need of specifically developed tactics or philosophies regarding the use of force. Departments suffering from intellectual incest have a higher number of excessive force complaints from citizens and larger out of court settlements and jury verdicts. Because they are unable to admit their training or philosophies are ineffective, outdated, or just plain wrong, they continue to be plagued by excessive force complaints and lawsuits.

I observed the effect that intellectual incest had on an instructor while attending the now defunct American Society of Law Enforcement Trainers' conference. ASLET had made arrangements for the conference attendees and instructors to be transported via school bus from the airport to the conference center. I had boarded the bus and was in the process of selecting a seat when I hear my name being called. I looked back and recognized the person who was calling my name. He was a full-time officer and part-time instructor for his department. The officer was a member of the largest agency in his state, but that was like being the tallest person on a pigmy basketball team. He asked if I had been to an ASLET conference before? I told him I taught at every ASLET conference. Now, keep in mind we are speaking loud enough to be heard throughout the bus. I asked him if he had previously attended an ASLET conference? He had not. Now, in a bus full of criminal justice trainers (big egos) from all over the United States, he goes on to say that other instructors from his agency had attended past conferences, and they had told him it was good to attend this conference so he could observe firsthand how more advanced and progressive their department's training was when compared to that of other agencies.

I was stunned and horrified at the instructor's arrogance. Everyone turned and looked at this instructor. He was unfazed. He truly believed that his department was the wellspring from which all law enforcement knowledge flowed. He did not come to the conference to learn other points of view or different concepts for possible integration into his department's training program; he was sent to the conference to have his superior sense of worth validated.

EGO-CAUSED EMOTIONAL REACTION. No one has a bigger ego than a law enforcement officer. Whether you come from a large or small department, the moment you put on the uniform your ego starts to grow. It is just one of those absolute truths about being a cop. Male or female your ego grows with your experience. This is not necessarily a bad thing, unless you allow it to override your intellect when it comes to using force. The most infuriating affront to a cop's ego is a challenge to his or her authority. No one enjoys having their authority challenged. But, cops hate it. This disdain is not personality based. All cops start out as normal people. What transforms us is the role we play in society. We enforce the rules. In what we do, there is no compromise. An arrest warrant starts with "Greeting to all peace officers. You are hereby commanded to take John Doe into custody. . . ." Not a lot of room for compromise there. A bartender calls the police to remove an intoxicated patron who is causing trouble. The patron must leave—on his own or in handcuffs. Either way, he is gone. No compromise there. So, we become accustomed to having people do what we tell them to do. And, when they don't, it really causes our blood to boil. Again, that's okay. Everyone experiences something in their job that gets under their skin. But, they don't act out in anger. The following is an example of an officer's ego-caused emotional reaction that ended badly for the suspect and the officer.

A police officer stopped a vehicle on a downtown street just after bar closing for driving carelessly. The driver of the vehicle was not from that city and was following the lead car to their destination. The plaintiff was a passenger in the lead car. When the officer stopped the suspect vehicle, the lead car pulled to the curb. The officer issued a citation to the driver, drove away, and parked approximately thirty yards up the street. The suspect vehicle remained stopped on the street where the citation was issued. The plaintiff exited his vehicle and walked back to give the driver directions.

The officer looked over and saw the plaintiff standing next to the driver's door. The officer yelled, "Get out of the street." The officer yelled this command at least three times. By the officer's own account, there were between one hundred and fifty and two hundred and fifty people walking in the street, crossing the street, or standing on the sidewalks. The plaintiff heard the officer yelling, but did not believe the officer was yelling at him. Angry because the plaintiff appeared to be challenging his authority, the officer exited his patrol car and confronted the plaintiff. When the officer confronted him, the officer put his nose three inches from the plaintiff's nose, and said "Do you have something wrong with your ears." The plaintiff responded with a surly "There is nothing wrong with my ears–get out of my face." The officer placed the plaintiff in a wristlock and handcuffed him. When the officer applied the wristlock, he broke the plaintiff's wrist. A schoolteacher was walking by, witnessed what she believed was excessive force, and yelled at the officer. The officer told the plaintiff to stand against the wall and not to move, which he did. Cover Officers were called and the schoolteacher was arrested. She resisted the arrest and the officers struggled to control her.

After the schoolteacher was driven from the scene, the officer contacted the plaintiff, told him that if anyone deserved to go to jail it was the teacher, took off the handcuffs, and un-arrested him. He was released with a broken wrist and no criminal charges. The City settled the lawsuit.

With every arrest, there is one simple question to ask yourself for the prevention of a "Contempt of Cop" lawsuit: Am I arresting this person because it is in the public's best interest, or am I making the arrest as punishment because I am angry with this person? If your answer is only I am making the arrest because I want to punish this person, don't make the arrest. We have previously discussed the negative impact of stress (anger is a form of stress) on your judgement. As illustrated in this case, the officer made an emotional decision to arrest, cooled down, and realized he made a mistake. This mistake was preventable. If the officer would have kept his ego in check, he would not have been sued, and the city would have more money in its budget.

MISINFORMATION. The most expensive mistake that criminal justice agencies make regarding use of force training is they assume that the training their officers receive is current and valid. Criminal justice officers receive training from a multitude of sources: academies, product manufacturers, consultants, and commercial and nonprofit training providers. The problem is that most administrators, training officers, and even department instructors do not know if the information they are receiving is valid. When officers apply use of force formation that is incorrect, outdated, or profit motivated, it creates liability for the officer and his department.

When I accepted a training position at the Montana Law Enforcement Academy, I was given responsibility for the use of force training curriculum and program. As I reviewed the training materials, I discovered that the academy's contract instructor was teaching outdated information regarding the use of nondeadly and deadly force. The instructor, a retired Montana Department of Justice attorney, had retired before the U.S. Supreme Court ruled on *Tennessee v. Garner* and *Graham v. Conner.* Unfortunately for the law enforcement officers, their departments, and the insurance authorities that indemnified their cities and counties, the instructor had not stayed current on the Supreme Court's or the federal appellate courts' rulings on the use of force. To remedy this situation, I replaced the instructor and updated the academy's use of force curriculum.

Later that same year, Montana's municipal and county insurance authorities organized a committee to develop a model use of force policy. I was appointed to the committee. During the orientation of our first meeting, we were told that two years ago the insurance authorities paid out seven million dollars in attorney's fees, settlements and jury verdicts. This year, we were told, the insurance authorities would pay out seventy million. Their solution to this hemorrhaging of money was to develop a statewide use of force policy. The problem was not a lack of uniformity in use of force policies statewide. The problem was that Montana's law enforcement officers had been taught the wrong legal standards for using force for the past twenty years at the state's only training academy. Officers base their use of force decisions on the formal instruction they receive at the academy and during inservice training. The academy's administration and Montana's chiefs and sheriffs assumed the instructor was teaching current use of force information. Unfortunately, for the insurance authorities, it was an expensive assumption.

A LACK OF KNOWLEDGE. Knowledge is information combined with experience. Said in another way, knowledge is the product of the application of information to a successful end. A lack of knowledge, on the officer's part, is the primary reason why criminal justice lawsuits are settled or lost. It is not slick lawyers or a crybaby society of victims. It is the lack of knowledge of how to properly manage the use of force incident at all levels in the chain of command, from the street to the chief's or the sheriff's office.

After being away from the Oregon Public Safety Academy's staff for almost five years, I returned to the academy for a two-week recertification course. I left Oregon to manage the law enforcement training program at the Montana Academy. In doing so, my Oregon peace officer certification expired. Oregon's recertification course consisted of two weeks of legal updates. As a former academy staff member, I told myself I would attend the classes, be a good student, and keep my opinions to myself. My first class was use of force. I felt a great deal of pride when I learned our use of force instructor, for the first half of the class, was someone that I had trained. Even more gratifying, the instructor used the use of force presentation that I had developed; however, I found it disconcerting that the U.S. Supreme Court rulings of *Graham v. Conner* and *Tennessee v. Garner* were absent from his presentation.

The second half of the class was taught by a local deputy district attorney. He did a nice job covering the state laws governing the use of non-deadly and deadly force, but there was no mention of *Graham v. Connor* or *Tennessee v. Garner*. After covering the state statutes, the instructor gave us hypothetical use of force questions.

The first hypothetical was a deadly force scenario: Officers respond to a noise complaint in an apartment complex. They knock on the door. When the door opens, they see a naked man covered in blood holding a knife and a bleeding body on the floor behind him. The naked man drops the knife and runs out of the apartment and down the hallway. An officer shoots the unarmed fleeing suspect in the back. "Is the shooting justified?" The instructor asked.

There was a long silence. My classmates either didn't know or were afraid to give a wrong answer. So, I raised my hand and answered with a confident, "yes!" "No it's not," the instructor replied. "Yes it is," I said with a slight tone of defiance. "No it's not," he said with a glare. We went back and forth like an Abbott and Costello comedy routine, but we were not trying to be funny.

Finally, I told him that I had developed the academy's use of force training program and taught this class at the academy for eleven years. I went on to explain that *Tennessee v. Garner* allowed for the use of deadly force when the officer reasonably believed that the suspect had committed a crime involving the use or threatened use of serious physical harm. Furthermore, I stated that the Portland Police Bureau had a real-life shooting under similar circumstances ten years go and the shooting was deemed lawful. "If you did that in my county you would be prosecuted," he stated with conviction. "That's why I don't work in your county," I snapped back. It was clear that, as a criminal prosecutor, the instructor was unfamiliar with the federal guidelines for using force. Needless to say, my participation during the remainder of his presentation was subdued to say the least.

After completing the academy's two-week recertification course, I met with Robert Franz Jr. to consult as a use of force expert on an excessive force lawsuit. Robert is one of Oregon's premiere criminal justice civil defense attorneys and was Northland Insurance Company's primary police liability attorney.

After discussing the case at hand, I asked Robert what percentage of his cases involved an allegation of police excessive force. He said approximately 60 to 70 percent. Robert went on to say that back in the 1980s police excessive force cases made up 90 percent of his legal defense work. Then in the 1990s it dropped to 10 percent. Now, it was back up to 60 percent and raising. I asked him what he thought was causing the increase in excessive force lawsuits? Robert's conclusion: Oregon's officers lack the knowledge necessary to make proper use of force decisions.

POORLY DESIGNED TRAINING. Training does not minimize liability. Properly designed training minimizes liability. Criminal justice trainers must understand that the training they develop and conduct can have unforeseen consequences for their officers and their departments when the training is poorly designed or improperly conducted.

I was conducting a scenario-based use of force instructor course at a large police department's academy when I was asked to review a video of a use of force incident during the break. The academy commander had setup the patrol car's video recording of the incident in another training room for me to view. The car's video camera recorded a very slow speed pursuit of a Lexus driving through a neighborhood of expensive homes. The pursuit was occurring during daylight hours, so I couldn't see the flash of the patrol car's emergency lights, but I could hear wail of the siren. Slowly, the Lexus pulled into a driveway of a residence that was more expensive than any home I could ever afford.

The driver's door opened and out stepped a young man in his twenties dressed in an expensive suit. As the driver stepped out of the car, he said to the officer, "This is my house." At this point, the officer was not visible in the video. However, I did hear a deep, booming, male voice say: "Get on the ground!" The driver pointed to the residence and said again, "This is my house." From the left side of the television screen, I saw a huge, male, officer come into view. He had an extended expandable baton cocked back over his shoulder. The officer gave another command to the driver to get on the ground. The driver stood in an open stance with questioning body language. Then, the officer started to deliver baton blows and verbal commands to the driver. The driver danced, bobbed, and ducked as the officer delivered baton blow after baton blow. I timed the incident. From the time the first baton blow was delivered until the driver went to the ground was seventy-three seconds. As I watched the video, the incident seemed like it lasted fifteen minutes. It was a visually ugly use of force incident. The Academy Commander told me the driver had been stopped for a traffic violation and he received two broken arms from the baton blows. The Commander asked me what I thought of the use of force?

I looked around the training room. The room was ringed with new baton striking shields leaning upright against the walls. Laying at the foot of each striking shield was a foam practice baton. "Did this officer have baton training prior to this incident?" I asked. "Ya, he went through baton training about a week before this incident," the Commander replied. "Do you guys do a Three Minute Drill during your baton training?" I asked. The Commander nodded in the affirmative. I pointed to the television and said, "That looks like a Three Minute Drill to me." The Commander's blood drained from his face.

In the "Three Minute Drill," the officer delivers strikes with a training baton to an instructor in a protective suit for three minutes. The instructor does not go to the ground and assume a prone handcuffing position. Nor does the officer practice transitioning to another force option. The instructor advances, retreats, and circles the officer as the officer delivers baton blows for the full three minutes. The officer in the video had done exactly what his department had trained him to do.

IMPROPERLY EXECUTED TRAINING. Criminal justice trainers have the best of intentions, but sometimes their well-intended instruction causes liability for their students. When officers participate in training scenarios that require them to demonstrate their knowledge, they cannot be allowed to make a mistake without the error being corrected. If the officer is not corrected, the improper technical execution is validated and reinforced as being acceptable. When improper behaviors are unintentionally reinforced, they will–more likely than not–be replicated by the officer in the field.

I was hired by the Oregon Board on Police Standards and Training and assigned to the Oregon Police Academy to manage the academy's defensive tactics and use of force training programs. I had been a full-time academy staff member for approximately three months when I was called to the Director's Office. The Director told me that a metro sheriff's department had just settled a lawsuit involving an unlawful warrantless entry by two of their deputies during a domestic violence investigation. When asked why they made the warrantless entry into the residence, the deputies stated that they had followed the training they had received at the academy. At that time, the academy's domestic violence investigation class consisted of a classroom presentation and a series of training scenarios.

The domestic violence instructors were well qualified to teach the subject. One was a former prosecutor, two were ten-year police veterans from a major police department, and the fourth was a deputy who would later became sheriff.

The Director told me that the instructors had videotaped the training scenarios. He handed me a box of fifty videotapes and told me to review the tapes and determine if we had taught the deputies to make the unlawful entry. I retreated with the box to an unoccupied classroom and plugged a videotape into the VCR. I had gotten lucky. The first tape I selected involved the deputies. The scenario took place in a simulated apartment. There was music playing in the background and a woman dressed in a bathrobe sitting on the couch. I heard a knock at the door, and the woman in the robe opened the door. I heard the deputies tell the woman that a neighbor had called 911 and reported hearing a man and women arguing in her apartment. The woman had no visible signs of abuse and there were no signs of violence in the apartment. The deputies asked if they could come in and speak with her and her husband. The woman said they couldn't and closed the door.

Without an invitation, the deputies opened the door and walked into the apartment. A shouting and shoving match erupted between the deputies, the woman in the robe, and two other men. The situation escalated into full-blown anarchy: people being thrown to the ground, struggles over batons, and guns being drawn. It was not what I expected to see in a domestic violence investigation-training scenario. After the instructors became tired of struggling with the deputies, the scenario ended. Much to my surprise, there was no debrief of the officers' performance by the instructors. The deputies were sent out of the room, and the instructors prepared for a new scenario. I reviewed all the videotapes. The scenarios varied in script, but the format was the same: the entry (sometimes lawful and sometimes not), an out of control struggle, and no debriefing of the students. I show this video in my instructor development courses as an example of how not to conduct scenario-based training.

I met with the Director and told him that by not correcting the deputies when they made the unlawful entry in their training scenario that the academy did infer that their entry was lawful. The academy's improperly conducted training had unintentionally created liability for the two deputies and their department.

LACK OF OR POOR SUPERVISION. First-line supervisors are responsible for quality control of their teams. Knowledgeable first-line supervision is a cornerstone to minimizing excessive force complaints and winning the lawsuits that are filed against their officers.

An officer's use of force report is reviewed and approved by the shift supervisor. And, often, supervisors see firsthand their officers' use of force at the scene of an arrest. Consequently, it is the supervisor's responsibility to correct an officer's improper use of force. A supervisor's evaluation and oversight of an officer's use of nondeadly and deadly force can only be as effective as the supervisor's knowledge in managing the use of force incident. If the supervisor's understanding of the use of force is limited, outdated, or simply wrong, the officers that are mentored by that supervisor are not well served and the department is exposed to liability. The following example illustrates this point.

I was sitting in my office when a recent academy graduate appeared in my doorway. He rapped on my open door and asked if I had a minute to talk. I invited him to come in and take a seat. The young officer had questions about two use of force incidents that he had witnessed, both involving his field training officer (FTO). But, he was more concerned about his sergeant's attitude regarding the use of force. In the first incident, he and another young officer had chased down a fleeing suspect. By the time his FTO had caught up, the suspect was on the ground, handcuffed, and not offering any resistance. When the panting FTO made contact with the younger officers, he grabbed the suspect by the hair and ran his face into the corner of a building several times. When the trainee questioned his FTO regarding his use of force, the FTO explained: "You have to teach these sh . t-heads not to run from the police."

About a week later, the officer and his FTO were engaged in a very slow speed pursuit of a suspected drunk driver. The officers followed the suspect vehicle for several blocks before it came to a stop. When it stopped, his FTO jumped out of the patrol, pulled the driver out the vehicle by the hair, and kicked him in the face three times. The driver was so intoxicated he could not offer any resistance. Five other officers and a patrol sergeant witnessed the FTO's use of excessive force. After the suspect was in custody, the officer questioned the sergeant about his FTO's use of force. "I know I don't have a lot of experience, but is this the way we do business?" The trainee asked. In a nutshell, the sergeant explained that his FTO should not have kicked the driver in the face with so many witnesses around.

Fortunately, the trainee had been a reserve officer for another law enforcement agency before being hired by his current department; consequently, he had a fundamental understanding of what constituted reasonable and excessive force. But, after receiving his supervisor's critique of his FTO's use of force, he started to doubt what he had been previously taught regarding the proper use of force. As we discussed the incidents, I validated his belief that the FTO used excessive force. Further, I pressed the point that the FTO's actions constituted a criminal assault and recommended he contact the internal affairs division. About six months after our discussion, I learned the city settled the driver's excessive force lawsuit.

BASING FORCE OPTION APPLICATION ON THE MANUFACTURERS' RECOMMENDATIONS. As explained in GroupThink, the vast majority of excessive force complaints and lawsuits can be linked to administrators, officers, and trainers following–without question–the manufacturers' recommendations on usage and/or training for newly developed force options. Because of lawsuits, workman's compensation claims, and negative media attention, law enforcement is always on the lookout for the "Magic Bullet." A new, safe, and technologically improved method to control a resisting suspect without injury to the suspect or the officer–like the Phaser on stun mode used by the crewmembers of the Star Ship Enterprise. This may be a surprise to some of you Trekies, but *Star Trek* is fiction. In the real world, any device or substance that impairs or incapacitates a human being will cause, directly or indirectly, serious physical injury or death.

So, how did administrators, officers, and trainers come to the conclusion that pepper spray, impact munitions, and electronic control devices were safe to use at the lowest levels of the force continuum? That's what they were told by the makers of these less-than-lethal and less-lethal weapons. The manufacturing of less-lethal products is a business. Businesses exist to make money. Putting a product's best foot forward to promote its sales is called marketing. When marketing a product, a company emphasizes the product's positives and intentionally fails to mention any possible negatives. That's good business sense. Businesses who manufacture less-lethal products know that only the officer using their product can be sued for excessive force. Only the government or its agent can violate a citizen's civil rights. So, there is no incentive for the company to disclose the possible negative consequences from the use their product.

When pepper spray was introduced to us as a suspect control device, we were told by its manufacturers oleoresin capsicum was not a chemical weapon–OC was a harmless food additive. Then, suspects received third-degree chemical burns to their skin, eye injuries, and died from respiratory failure after being pepper sprayed. The injured suspects sued the officers and their agencies. Settlements were paid. Lawsuits were lost. And law enforcement reevaluated pepper spray as a force option.

When beanbag projectiles were introduced to us as a suspect control device, we were told by the manufacturers of impact munitions that the beanbag–fired from a 12-gauge shotgun–was no more injurious to a suspect than the impact with a standard police baton. Then, suspects had their hearts stopped, eyes removed, abdomen's punctured, and testicles crushed from being shot with a beanbag round. The injured suspects sued the officers and their agencies. Settlements were paid. Lawsuits were lost. And law enforcement reevaluated beanbag projectiles as a force option.

When plastic ball projectiles (filled with oleoresin capsicum or water) were introduced to us as a suspect and crowd control device, we were told by its manufacturer that it was safe to shoot directly into groups of people for crowd control. Then, a ball projectile killed a college student when officers fired into a rowdy crowd after a Red Sox game. And law enforcement reevaluated plastic ball projectiles as a force option.

When Taser was introduced to us as the ultimate suspect control device, we were told by the M26's manufacturer that it was perfectly safe. And company videos and the shocking of officers during training sessions demonstrated its safety and effectiveness. In company-sponsored training classes, we were initially told the entire body, except for the head and groin, were target areas. Later, Taser's training program promoted the shocking of the suspect's neck in "Drive Stun" mode. Then, without warning, Taser changed its recommended target areas. No longer was the neck or the chest recommended targets. A Taser International's memo to its law enforcement instructors stated shocks to the chest area might cause heart failure. This memo was issued with dozens of wrongful death lawsuits pending against officers who deployed the Taser probes to the chests of the deceased suspects. Finally, the Ninth Circuit Court Appeals ruled that the Taser was not a completely safe subject control device. And law enforcement was forced to reevaluate electronic control devices as a force option.

You probably noticed a pattern in more than just my prose. With every new introduction of a commercially developed subject control product, administrators, officers, and trainers blindly adopted the manufacturer's deployment recommendations like lemmings mindlessly hurtling themselves off a cliff. I am not suggesting that the use of pepper spray, impact munitions, or the Taser has not saved the lives of suspects or officers. Nor do I say that they're not highly valuable tools for use by criminal justice officers. I do, however, believe it is a tragedy that cities, counties, and states have needlessly paid out millions of dollars in lawsuits that could have been prevented had administrators not taken at face value the company deployment and training recommendations in their initial policy development when adopting new use of force measures.

STUPIDITY. The definition of insanity is doing the same thing over and over again and expecting a different result. If an officer is not insane, but continues to make bad use of force decisions, he is just plain stupid. It may not be kind or politically correct to say so, but all of us have worked with intellectually diminished officers. All of us have done dumb things on duty. We all have made honest mistakes. Competent officers learn from their mistakes. Intellectually challenged officers fail to understand the relationship between the cause and the effect of their bad use of force decisions. You can send cognitively defective officers to training. You can give them more tools. You can more closely supervise them. But, as comedian Ron White explains in his comedy routine, "You can't fix stupid." And officers who do stupid things on-duty or off-duty are a liability to your department.

Recently, I reviewed a use of force case involving the tasering of a handcuffed suspect. The suspect was taken to the ground and handcuffed by three officers in a bar. As the suspect laid face down on the floor, he yelled insults and threats at the officers. One officer pulled his Taser and shot the probes into the handcuffed suspect to silence him. When the attorney representing the city interviewed the officers, the two officers and the sergeant who witnessed the incident stated they thought the tasering was unjustified. When the attorney asked the four officers individually how many times they had used the Taser in the past twelve months, the three officers who witnessed the incident stated they had used their Tasers between two to six times each. The officer who tasered the handcuffed suspect reported he had deployed his Taser in probe mode twenty-seven times. The lawsuit was settled out of court. The tasering officer is still employed by the department and does not believe he did anything wrong.

However, I do believe, when it comes to being stupid, this incident wins hands-down. The headline says it all: "Surgeon to City Council: Jailing wasn't warranted for expired tags." In the state where the doctor resides, traffic violations are classified as misdemeanors. Consequently, when the on-call neurosurgeon was stopped for driving a car with expired license plate tags, he was arrested, handcuffed, and taken to jail–as his patients waited and his pager beeped. His wife posted his bail. The officer did have the option of issuing a written citation, but chose not to. During a city council review of the incident, the doctor told the council he felt that the police reaction was out of proportion with his offense. Ron White is right: You can't fix stupid.

An Officer's Actions and Tactics Can Facilitate the Need to Use Force

In *Tennessee v. Garner,* the United States Supreme Court stated the correctness of an officer's use of deadly force can only be judged at the moment the officer administers the deadly force. The officer's tactics are not to be considered. In simple terms, if the officer's tactics facilitated the shooting, the poor tactics are not to be factored into the reasonableness calculus. The only issue to be considered is whether the suspect posed an immediate threat of serious physical harm or death to the officer or others at the moment that the deadly force was used.

Tennessee v. Garner is the–after the fact–constitutional standard for lawfully using deadly force. However, proper police tactics can sometimes prevent the need to use deadly force. If you can prevent a shooting through the use of proper tactics, you can proactively prevent the wrongful death lawsuit.

I first learned how proper tactics can minimize police liability from a southern California Range-Master. I was conducting a Confrontational Simulation Instructor Course hosted by the Burbank Police Department when I was given the opportunity to participate in the department's in-service high-risk vehicle stop training. The Burbank Police Department integrated a live fire exercise into their vehicle stop training. After the training exercise, I asked the Range-Master, "How many shootings has Burbank PD experienced in the last five years?" "None," he replied. I was surprised by his answer. With the vast number of people who live or work in Burbank, I expected the number to be much greater than what we experienced in the Northwest, not smaller. "What do you contribute that to?" I asked. "We train our officers that when someone yells gun–you take cover and hide. Our officers are trained not to put themselves in situations where they have to shoot–if it's possible," he answered.

In contrast with the Burbank Police Department's tactical philosophy, many officers approach an armed suspect knowing full well they may be required to shoot. In the police involved shooting of a woman threatening to commit suicide, the officers responded to a call for help from a downtown phone booth. When the officers arrived, they found the booth unoccupied and a blood trail leading toward the rear of a concrete building. As the officers rounded the corner of the building, they saw a woman sitting against a cement wall. She was bleeding from her wrists and holding a bloody box cutter in one hand. Even more problematic, the officers saw the butt of a handgun sticking out from under her leg.

The officers took cover behind several concrete planters that were approximately thirty feet from the woman. From behind the hard cover, the officers had an unobstructed view of the woman and the handgun. The officers ordered the woman to drop the box cutter and move away from the gun. The woman ignored the officers' commands and started to slash her wrists. With the intention of stopping the woman from cutting her wrist further, the officers left the protection of their cover–with their guns drawn–and advanced toward the woman. The officers advanced on the woman knowing full well, that if she made a move for the handgun or lunged with the edged weapon they would shoot her. When the officers came within twenty feet, she grabbed the handgun and pointed it in the officers' direction. The three officers fired twenty-seven rounds–hitting the woman twenty-one times. She died at the scene. During the examination of the woman's handgun, the officers discovered it was a pellet gun. Even though the shooting was lawful, the news media had a field day with the incident. The local newspaper covered the story with a half-page illustration of the sequence of the events that led up to the fatal shooting. And, there was public outcry lamenting that the woman had called the police department for help, not to be shot twenty-one times.

An Officer Who is Reluctant to Physically Engage a Suspect Will Eventually Overreact

Psychologist and former Army Ranger Dave Grossman in his book, *On Killing,* asks and then answers the question "Why can't Johnny Kill?" Mr. Grossman goes on to explain the moral and cultural influences that create an innate aversion that man has to the killing of his fellow man. Over the past twenty years, each subsequent generation of law enforcement officers has developed an ever-increasing aversion to physically engaging resisting suspects. The origin of this growing reluctance to go "hands-on" with a suspect is rooted in the pacification of Americans and is enabled by advancements in less-lethal technology.

This reluctance to go hands-on with a suspect is primarily based on fear. A fear that is often objectively unreasonable. When an officer's use of force overreaction is panic induced, suspects are unnecessarily injured, lawsuits are filed, and out of court settlements and large jury verdicts are the result.

I observed the beginning of this trend as an instructor at the Oregon Public Safety Academy in the early 1990s when American law enforcement embraced the concept of community policing. Law enforcement agencies across the nation were no longer advertising for police officers or deputy sheriffs. In the new era of policing, law enforcement recruitment advertisements were posted in local newspapers as "Community Police Officer" positions. Not the outdated, hard-nosed cop, but a new kinder and gentler officer. The problem with this new enlightened approach to policing is that the world had not gotten kinder and gentler. I guess career criminals, drug dealers, gang members, rapists, spousal abusers, and terrorists don't read the "Jobs" section of the newspaper or attend career days at college campuses.

I witnessed a large influx of people hired as community police officers who had no idea that the job had changed in title only. I was disturbed by the number of academy students who told me that they did not join the department to be a police officer; they joined the force to be a "community police officer." Many of these new community police officers were middle-aged professionals who left successful careers.

In the previous decades, 75 to 90 percent of police recruits had served in the military. With the bloom of community policing, we were getting accountants, dentists, engineers, computer programmers, psychiatric nurses, nannies, and yuppie soccer moms as police recruits. Over a five-year period, the Oregon Academy surveyed the basic police students regarding their experience with confrontation and their willingness to use force. The results were mind-blowing. Ninety percent of the basic police students had never experienced a physical confrontation. Only 25 percent had played contact sports. Fifty percent stated they were unsure if they were capable of using deadly force on a suspect, even if the suspect was attempting to use deadly force against them. The results of this study changed the way the academy conducted survival skills training. One such change was the integration of a boxing exercise into the defensive tactics program. We integrated a two-minute sparring session to expose the students to the pain and shock of being hit and to build their confidence in the ability to defend themselves.

After one boxing session, I had a middle-aged female police student come to me after class and comment on the exercise. The student told me that she found the boxing exercise interesting. But, because of her twenty years of experience as a psychiatric nurse, her educational background, and her well-honed interpersonal communication skills, she would never need to use physical force on a suspect. I looked into this student's big blue eyes and it was like looking into an aquarium with no tropical fish. This student was void of any understanding of what police officers did on the street. I wish I could tell you that I was surprised by her naivete, but I had grown accustomed to these unrealistic assumptions made by new community policing officers. So, I responded by giving her a hypothetical situation. "Let's assume what you say is true–based on your experience, education, and interpersonal communication skills that you will never have to use force to control a suspect. But, your patrol partner (Bob) is a flaming jerk, he has incited a suspect to riot, and he is getting the crap kicked out of him. How are you going to help Bob?" I asked. She looked at me for several moments with those vacant aquarium blue eyes and then said, "I never thought about that." Need I say more?

By the new millennium, community policing had become a term only used in college criminal justice courses, city council meetings, and as the butt of jokes in patrol briefings. Departments had reverted back to advertising and recruiting for police officer and deputy sheriff positions. However, in response to the pacification of American society, law enforcement administrators had to revise their employment applications. When I entered the law enforcement profession—a time when officers were steel and ships were wood—the application asked these questions: Are you willing to work weekends, nights, and holidays? Are you willing to work by yourself or with little or no backup? Now, in the twenty-first century, most major police department applications ask the applicant: Are you capable of using deadly force on a person? It is unbelievable to me that an agency has to ask a police applicant that question. Why is this question necessary? The answer: Many of today's police applicants suffer from a sheltered and extended adolescence.

Over the past ten years I have encountered numerous defendant officers in lawsuits who tell me: "I don't get paid to fight with suspects." Well, if you are one of those officers, I have a rude awakening for you: Fighting with a suspect is what a law enforcement officer is paid to do. You are the only person in society that when someone yells fight, gun, or help you run toward him—everyone runs away. The time of the naïve, middle-aged, community-policing officer is over.

The new generation of officers are products of guilt-ridden, permissive parents who send their children to college on their dime and then allow them to live at home until they are thirty. They have not played contact sports like boxing, football, and wrestling. They played safer sports like chess and soccer. When they were children, they could not play outside for fear that the neighborhood child molester would steal them, so they were forced to become couch potatoes and spend endless hours playing video games in the safety of their latch-key home. They have been taught by their permissive parents and progressive college professors that they don't have to excel to succeed in life, are special for just existing, and entitled to employment, health care, and unencumbered happiness. The absence of an education in warrior ethos culminates in an officer who puts his law enforcement profile on Facebook, thinks it is professional to display body art in uniform that you previously had to pay an admission fee to view at a carnival, expects his work schedule to be adjusted to accommodate his childcare conflicts, won't attend training unless he's paid overtime, takes breaks in a public coffee house with his nose buried in a laptop computer (completely unaware of his surroundings), is hyper-fearful of physical confrontation, and when he overreacts and uses excessive force out of panic he claims victim status.

I know you think this sounds a little harsh, but every police civil defense attorney that I have consulted with over the past ten years shares this observation.

Now, I want to acknowledge—in all fairness—that the majority of twenty-first century law enforcement officers are dedicated and courageous public servants who truly believe it is their calling to "Protect and Serve" the members of their communities. However, there are a substantial number of officers, who by not being emotionally and psychologically prepared for the stresses of physical conflict, overreact and cost their departments substantial amounts of money in lawsuits and public goodwill.

To make my point, I give you the facts regarding a wrongful death lawsuit where the deputy shot an unarmed suspect. Rather than give you my opinion, I will let you review the incident and draw your own conclusions.

On a fall evening, the suspect consumed hallucinogenic mushrooms in his apartment. Afterward and under the influence of the hallucinogen, the suspect left his apartment and entered the apartment of another tenant uninvited. The tenant, a petite woman, was sleeping on her sofa when she was awakened by the suspect standing over her. The suspect leaned over her with his arms extended and stated, "I can feel your aura." The woman stood up and asked if he was alright? "I took srooms," he replied.

The woman took refuge in a bedroom with her daughter and called the police. A struggle ensued between the suspect and the woman. When an officer arrived at the apartment, he found the suspect lying face up on the floor with the woman holding him down. The woman released the suspect and left the bedroom with her daughter. The officer struggled with the suspect, but he is unable to handcuff him. The suspect ran out of the apartment and through a grassy area with the officer in pursuit. The officer called for assistance and a second officer arrived at the scene. The cover officer was armed with a beanbag shotgun. As the officers pursued the suspect, they shocked him several times with the Taser and shot him several times with beanbag munitions. Each time the suspect was shocked and shot he became stunned, but he was able to recover. At no time did the suspect attack or threaten the officers, he was simply attempting to flee. Further, the officers had no reason to believe the suspect was armed.

A deputy pulled up in a patrol car near where the suspect was sitting on the ground with the two police officers standing close to him. The deputy exited his car and left the driver-side door open. The suspect looked over at the deputy, stood up, and started walking toward him. As the suspect moved toward the deputy, the officers told the deputy that the Taser would not control him. As the deputy took verbal control of the suspect, the other two officers assumed cover-officer roles.

When the suspect got within ten feet of the deputy, he tasered the suspect seven times within a minute and ten-second time span. Each time the Taser was activated the suspect fell to the ground and rolled back and forth. After the seventh shock, the Taser malfunctioned. The deputy believed the suspect had pulled out the darts. The suspect stood up and walked toward the open patrol car door. The deputy pulled his handgun and issued verbal commands. The deputy had no reason to believe that the suspect was armed. The suspect moved through the open driver's door and into the interior of the car. The deputy fired six forty-caliber rounds at the suspect. Five rounds hit the car, and one round struck the suspect in the chest. The wounded suspect fell to the ground and sat next to the doorframe of the patrol car. The deputy continued to give the suspect verbal commands. The wounded suspect sat on the ground for about two minutes; then, he turned toward the car and started to crawl inside passenger's compartment. The deputy shot the suspect in the back of the head–killing him.

All three officers are male, between twenty and thirty years-of-age, at least six feet tall, and weighed approximately two hundred pounds. The suspect was twenty years-old, five feet and eleven inches tall, and weighed one hundred and twenty-eight pounds. All three officers were armed with an expandable baton, Taser, pepper spray, and a handgun. One officer was additionally armed with a beanbag shotgun.

The two officers stated that they did not transition to their batons, physical control holds/takedowns, pepper spray, strikes and kicks, or the neck restraint because they believed those other tools would not be effective, since the beanbag and Taser were not completely effective in incapacitating the suspect.

The deputy stated he did not transition to other force options for the same reason the cover officers chose not to deploy them. Both officers and the deputy stated they were afraid to go "hands-on" with the suspect because the Taser was not completely effective.

Further, the deputy stated he shot the suspect both times because he believed the suspect would gain access to the MP5 forty-caliber carbine that was secured in a steel Tuflock electronic gunlock that was bolted between the front seats and use it against him. The gunlock's release switch was located on the floorboard next to the parking brake. Furthermore, the deputy stated he did not direct the two cover officers to control and handcuff the suspect when he was under partial control by the seven Taser cycles or after he had been shot because officers from different departments cannot work together as a team to control a suspect.

As you evaluate this incident, you may want to consider theses questions: Was the deputy's use of deadly force justified? Was the officers' belief that the other force options would be ineffective in controlling the suspect valid? Have you experienced similar Taser and/or beanbag failures? If so, did you react differently than the officers did in this incident? If you did, why? Based on your own experience, why do you think the officers reacted the way they did?

So, what do you think? How well did the officers and the deputy handle the incident?

An Officer Who is Overly Aggressive Will at Some Point Use Excessive Force

The best law enforcement officers are aggressive. They aggressively seek out criminal activity on patrol. They aggressively follow-up on investigations. They aggressively take control of crisis situations. However, there is a fine line between being aggressive and being excessive when it comes to using force.

The overly aggressive officer has an abnormally high number of citizen complaints, when compared to other officers. These complaints are generated from his hard-edged, in your face, communication style and his use of offensive physical touching: shoving, slapping items out of a suspect's hands or mouth, jerking on clothing, etc. This officer pushes his physical dominance over people to the limit. And, if not properly supervised, will likely use excessive force.

Plaintiffs' attorneys find something troubling in an officer's abnormally high number of citizen complaints. A high number of complaints, alone, is not necessarily proof that the officer is abusive. Aggressive officers almost always lead the department in the issuance of traffic citations, investigations conducted, and arrests made. Statistically, the more negative interaction (citations and arrests) an officer has with the members of the community the more complaints he will receive. This is just a common sense conclusion. The important issue in evaluating the number of citizen complaints is whether the officer received formal discipline based on the complaint. The overly aggressive officer's problem is personality based. Like the Rottweiler that bites unprovoked, an overly aggressive officer's use of excessive force is in his nature. Active supervision, immediate discipline, and employment termination are the keys in preventing lawsuits with an overly aggressive officer.

An officer who is constantly being counseled for overly aggressive behavior is a liability to your department. An administrator who keeps an officer with a history of excessive force lawsuits that were settled out of court has set the stage for a financial catastrophe for the city, county, or state and a public relations nightmare for the department.

The financial ramifications of keeping an overly aggressive officer on a department are illustrated by the lawsuits that plagued one Sheriff's department. The newspaper headline said: "Sheriff's Deputy has a history of being sued over force–Deputy has cost the county hundreds of thousands." In total, the deputy had cost the county over $400,000.00 in settlements from lawsuits alleging the use of excessive force.

In his first lawsuit, the deputy's police dog attacked an innocent bystander. Within the same year, the deputy assaulted a suspect at the county fair. When a bystander tried to intervene, the deputy knocked the bystander to the ground. The deputy denied using excessive force, but two independent witnesses stated the deputy's version of the events was untrue. A year later, the deputy falsely arrested a woman and menaced her with his handgun. Ten months after that, while in foot pursuit of a suspect, the deputy confronted a driver at gunpoint, tasered the driver, dragged him from his car, and arrested him. The driver was sitting in his driveway. And, he had no connection to the fleeing suspect. In his latest round of legal problems, the deputy was charged with domestic abuse for shoving his wife against a wall in the sheriff's office while on-duty. You do not have to be Nostradamus to predict that this deputy will continue to make bad use of force decisions, and the county will continue to settle or lose lawsuits if his employment is not terminated.

In this chapter, I explained that if a lawsuit is predictable it may be preventable, but it is certainly winnable if you utilize a proactive defensive strategy in the management of the use of force incident. In the next chapter, we will explore the role that witness and jury perceptions play in preventing and winning excessive force lawsuits and the criminal prosecutions of officers.

Chapter 2

THE IMPORTANCE OF PERCEPTIONS

There are three perceptions that win police lawsuits: The jury's
perception of the officer, the jury's perception of the plaintiff,
the jury's perception of the witnesses.
–Lou Kurtz, Attorney at Law
(Personal communication, 1990)

Lou Kurtz was the police defense attorney who was hired to defend the Medford Police Department and the Jackson County Sheriff's Office against twelve federal court lawsuits. A local plaintiff's attorney had placed an advertisement in the newspaper asking people who believed that the police department or the sheriff's office had violated their civil rights to contact him. Shortly afterward, the attorney filled all twelve lawsuits in federal court on the same day.

I testified as Mr. Kurt's use of force expert at trial in those lawsuits. The night before our first trial was to begin Lou and I were discussing my testimony. During our discussion, I asked Lou what he believed won police and corrections lawsuits? "The single most important element in winning a lawsuit is perception," Lou replied. "How so?" I asked. "There are three perceptions that win police lawsuits: The jury's perception of the officer, the jury's perception of the plaintiff, and the jury's perception of the witnesses," he explained. I wrote that quote down in my Franklin Planner; I still have that handwritten quote. For the past twenty years, Lou's explanation of what wins lawsuits has been the foundation of my use of force training. And, as you have probably noticed–as you read through Chapter 1, it is the foundation for this book.

Manage the Perception and You
Positively Influence the Outcome

I touched on this strategy briefly in Chapter 1. In a lawsuit where there is no smoking gun regarding an officer's use of excessive force, a plaintiff's attorney cannot win the lawsuit when the facts are in dispute, unless he damages the officer's credibility. Fortunately for you, jurors have an inherent trust of criminal justice officers and an innate dislike of lawbreakers. To prove my point, I have included a summation of a newspaper reporter's interview with attorneys who specialize in litigating civil rights violations against criminal justice officers.

"Lawyers: Public Doesn't See Police in the Role of Bad Guys" was the newspaper article's headline in the metro section. The reporter interviewed several metro area attorneys who specialized in suing criminal justice officers. During their interviews, the attorneys made several observations that I feel are important to properly manage the use of force incident.

People Do Not Want to Believe that Police Lie

It is a professionally accepted truth among attorneys who defend cops and those who sue them that when an officer takes the witness stand, raises that right hand, and swears to tell the truth, jurors want to believe that the officer will be truthful. There aren't any empirical studies that explain why cops have inherent credibility with jurors. They just do. However, after twenty-five years of consulting on police and corrections excessive force lawsuits, I have developed a theory about the source of this inherent credibility.

In a country where its citizens rely more and more on the government for their personal safety and well-being, the average citizen—for his or her own peace of mind—wants to believe that the agents of our government are capable of keeping them safe. When a woman dials 911 for help, she wants desperately to believe a professional and well-trained police officer is coming to her aid. When that person sits on a jury, her belief in that responding officer's professionalism and competence is projected onto every criminal justice officer who takes the witness stand. As an example of this, in an incident where the officer shot and killed an unarmed suspect, the federal court trial ended in a hung jury. When the plaintiff's attorney questioned the jurors, three women jurors told the attorney that they believed that whatever level of force a police officer used it would be justified.

The Nature of the Injuries, Backgrounds of Their Clients, and Even What People Watch on Television Makes it Hard for the Plaintiff's Attorney to Win

NATURE OF THE INJURIES. Very few excessive force lawsuits involve serious physical injury or death. Most lawsuits involve observable injuries that are no more severe than the bruises, scrapes, and cuts that you received as a child rough-housing with your siblings. Moreover, injuries to the soft tissue are not visible to the naked eye and difficult for a jury to evaluate. Jury awards are based on loss, pain, and suffering. In lawsuits where the plaintiffs have injuries no more serious than those received in a playground scuffle or where there is no observable injury at all, juries find it difficult to believe the force was excessive.

BACKGROUND OF THEIR CLIENTS. When plaintiff attorneys lament about how difficult it is to win a lawsuit because of their client's background, they are referring to their client's criminal background.

Jurors are not sympathetic to criminals, and the more disturbing the crime the less sympathy the plaintiff will receive. Almost everyone has been directly or indirectly affected by crime, and the resentment of being a crime victim or knowing one can prejudice jurors.

I understand why from personal experience. While conducting a training course, I mistakenly left my briefcase on the front seat of my vehicle as it was parked overnight at the hotel. When I came out the following morning, I discovered my driver's door window broken and my briefcase stolen. If that was not bad enough, the portable drive containing my PowerPoint presentation was in my briefcase. I had to give my presentation from memory without the professionalism and polish of computer-generated visual aides. To add insult to injury, I had to drive back to Montana with a piece of clear plastic shower-curtain ducktaped to my driver's door window.

Was I angry that some Crack Head (I am sorry, I mean some morally challenged drug addict) damaged and stole my property and diminished the professionalism of my presentation? You bet I was. In fact, I am still angry. Does being a crime victim affect me as a potential juror? Well, let me put to you this way: If I were summoned for jury duty, I could listen objectively to all the evidence, weigh the credibility of the witnesses, find the suspect guilty, and then personally pull the switch on the electric chair. Of course, I am not serious about the execution. But, I would find it difficult to be an objective juror. And, according to the attorneys interviewed, I am the norm and not the exception.

WHAT PEOPLE WATCH ON TELEVISION. Where do civilians learn about police use of force? The movies and television, and cop movies and television programming have gotten increasing more violent over the years.

It all started with *Dirty Harry*–the first real cop film. I watched *Dirty Harry* as a teenager in a packed movie theater. I have a fond memory of Detective Calhoun shooting a psycho–who had buried a little girl alive–in the leg with the most powerful handgun in the world. Then, Harry stepped on the suspect's gunshot wound to extract the little girl's whereabouts. No one in that theater shed a tear when Harry tortured the little girl's burial site out of that psycho. But, we were incensed when the judge suppressed the suspect's confession. As a result, I overheard the man sitting next to me tell his wife: "We don't have a criminal justice system; we have a legal system. Where is the justice in that ruling?"

Next, came the *Lethal Weapon* series. LAPD Detectives Martin Riggs and Roger Murtaugh shot and fought their way through four action-packed movie sequels. I was in a crowded multiplex theater when I watched *Lethal Weapon 2.* The movie climaxes with a scene where a corrupt South African diplomat shoots Detective Riggs, throws down his gun, and tells Detective Murtaugh he is entitled to diplomatic immunity. Detective Murtaugh has the diplomat at gunpoint, rotates his neck in his taking aim ritual, and revokes his diplomatic immunity by shooting him between the eyes. The audience went wild with approval.

America's fascination with police use of force culminated with two television series: the *Shield* and *24.* These law enforcement dramas brought the most violent depictions of police use of force that I have ever seen into America's living rooms. Who can forget the scene in the *Shield* where Detective Vic Mackey beats a confession out of a sex offender with a telephone book. The scene in *24* was equally as shocking when Jack Bower shoots a suspect in the chest during an interview at CTU (Counter-Terrorism Unit) headquarters and then cuts off his head with a tactical folding knife for use to infiltrate a terrorist cell. Television networks create these programs for a reason: People watch them.

There is a common theme in all-violent law enforcement action-movies and television dramas: The end justifies the means. This theme's premise is based on a commonly held belief that the criminal justice system is broken, so the cops are entitled to break the rules to save the lives of the innocent– even if it means using murder and torture. I believe this message has a real impact on the way the average juror views the use of force by corrections and police officers. Apparently, so do plaintiffs' attorneys.

Now, I am in no way implying that the use of excessive force is ever acceptable. It is not. The point I am trying to drive home is that jurors are predisposed to believe your version of the use of force incident. The jurors' predisposition to believe you on the witness stand gives you an edge in an excessive force lawsuit or during your criminal prosecution—an edge that is easily lost if you have poorly managed the use of force incident. Keep in mind, that jurors bring to your trial expectations of you as a criminal justice professional. If you have not followed the game plan for properly managing the jurors' perception of your actions on and off-duty, you will lose your advantage and possibly the trial.

In defending yourself against allegations of misconduct and excessive force, perception is everything. If the perception that the jurors have of you is professional, truthful, self-controlled, knowledgeable, caring, tolerant, and polite, you are almost guaranteed a favorable verdict. If the perception that the jurors have of your department's policies, training records, and training programs is that they are current, well-established, and not in conflict with each other, your actions are more easily defended. With most negative verdicts, the plaintiff's attorney does not win the lawsuit nor does the prosecutor build a successful case. In most negative verdicts, the officer loses the lawsuit or convicts himself by not positively managing the perceptions of the witnesses at the scene or the perceptions of the jurors at trial.

As you read further in this chapter, you will find a discussion of the actions, circumstances, and evidence that diminishes your credibility with the witnesses at the scene and the jurors at trial. Furthermore, we will discuss how to positively influence perceptions while conducting an opposite gender clothing search. Lastly, a detailed analysis of the *State of Oregon v. Jerry Walton* will be presented with an explanation of what Officer Walton could have done to properly manage the witnesses' and the jurors' perceptions.

Actions and Evidence that Damage an Officer's Credibility

Any officer and citizen interaction can result in an excessive force lawsuit or a misconduct complaint. In his best-selling book, *The Seven Habits of Highly Effective People,* Stephen Covey tells his readers to "Begin with the end in mind." Good advice for all criminal justice officers when using force. Beginning each citizen contact knowing that you may be sued will assist you in managing witness and jury perceptions of the incident, and it will build a foundation for your defense against an allegation of excessive force or misconduct. In the majority of excessive force lawsuits, it is not the level of force that concerns civil defense attorneys; it is the wide variety of dumb things officers say or do before, during, or after using force on the suspect or inmate. The following are the most common officer blunders that lose lawsuits or promote out of court settlements:

PROFANITY. Damages your professional image. The use of profanity in what would otherwise be considered appropriate verbal commands hurts your case. Popular verbal commands like: "Get the f . . k on the ground!" "Don't you f . . king move!" And of course the very popular: "I will f . . k you up" tarnishes your professional image. The use of these and similar vulgarities in your verbal commands create the impression with witnesses and jurors that you are out of control or acting out in anger. I have heard over and over again the tired old justification that officers give for using profanity in verbal commands: "I speak in terms that the suspect can relate to." I agree that most criminals do have an incredibly profane vocabulary. However, not many criminals make it through the jury selection process, but grandmothers and Sunday schoolteachers do. Food for thought.

SARCASM. It may feel good at the time, but it makes you look like a jerk to witnesses and jurors. To win an excessive force lawsuit, the jurors have to like you; no one likes a jerk with a badge. It is tough standing there and taking a suspect's nasty comments, personal attacks, racial slurs, and vulgar rants. So, you hit back with the only weapon you can use–cutting sarcasm. Just like the time you tasered the drunk brother-in-law in front of his relatives at the family reunion. His family called you a bunch of not so nice names and demanded to know why he was the only one going to jail? Your answer: "I only arrest the ugly ones." That stinging retort may give you some satisfaction, but it is not the explanation you want recited to a jury when you're being sued for a million dollars.

POLICY VIOLATION. A violation of your department's policy may not necessary constitute a civil rights violation. Your department can implement a policy more restrictive than the Supreme Court's guidelines on the use of nondeadly and deadly force, but not more permissive. However, the plaintiff's attorney will try to convince the jury that you are an incompetent for not knowing or following your department's policy. Policies that are of the greatest concern:

- the use of nondeadly/deadly force
- documenting/reporting the use of force
- opposite gender searches
- collection of evidence after using force
- entry without a warrant
- traffic stops
- ramming or shooting at vehicles
- high-speed pursuits.

Not long ago, I reviewed an incident that involved the ramming and shooting of the vehicle of a fleeing drunk driver. Although it could be argued that the shooting was justified, the case was damaged by numerous department policy violations: vehicle pursuit, vehicle ramming, and shooting at a moving vehicle. So egregious were the violations, the chief of police publicly admitted his officers made serious mistakes during the incident.

EMOTIONAL OUTBURST. The emotional shouting at a suspect or inmate has the same negative impact on witnesses and jurors as the use of profanity. Proper verbal commands are authoritative, clear, and direct the person to do something: Get on the ground! Don't move! Show me your hands! An emotional outburst is high pitched, emotes stress, and asks a question: What the f . . k are you doing? What the hell? Do you want your ass kicked? As described previously, the officer had an emotional outburst when he went nose-to-nose with the plaintiff and asked him, "Do you have something wrong with your ears?" The display itself is not excessive force. But, it gives witnesses and the jury the impression that the officer is out of control and using excessive force. Remember in that incident, the teacher who witnessed the arrest became upset because she believed the force being used was excessive.

RUDE COMMENTS BETWEEN OFFICERS. Cops develop a unique sense of humor. We do so because it helps us relieve stress. If we didn't find humor in the odd things that people do, we would go out on stress retirements. Cops are only people, and people like to share experiences they find funny. The key is to share the stories and comments in private. Dark comments said between officers that are recorded on your car's video camera, sent via department email, or overheard by citizens makes you appear unprofessional and insensitive. This is a perception that the plaintiff's attorney will exploit. In an excessive force lawsuit involving a welfare check, a man was shot in the back with a Taser after he opened his front door. The man fell face down and was injured. In an audio recording of the moments following the tasering, the officers are heard using profanities while speaking with each other about how the welfare check went awry. Because of the officer's insensitive comments and profane language, the city settled the case.

HIGH FIVES BY OFFICERS. Athletes do it. Fathers and their kids do it. Buddies do it. Cops should not do it in public. A video of officers giving each other high-fives over a handcuffed suspect looks bad. It gives the impression you enjoy using force on people. If the exuberant behavior is not videotaped, jurors will hear it described by witnesses and family members. The plaintiff's attorney will make the point that you view using force as some twisted sport to be celebrated. There is nothing wrong with being proud of a job well done. But, when it comes to using force, it is best not to succumb to the urge to display an outward expression of triumph. During an arrest of a man on a street corner, the patrol car video camera recorded officers standing over the handcuffed suspect giving each other "high-fives." Further, during the witnesses' depositions, they reported seeing grinning officers giving each other "high-fives" around the injured handcuffed suspect. The city settled the lawsuit.

BRAVADO. Not keeping your ego in check will come back to bite you. No one likes the puffed-up, full of himself, cop. Needless to say, coming across as a pompous ass does not endear you to jurors. In a lawsuit involving an injury to an intoxicated woman at a restaurant, the officer hung himself during his deposition. The officer had responded to a complaint of an intoxicated woman who refused to pay for her meal. When the woman refused the officer's commands to step outside, the officer placed the woman in a wristlock. The jointlock broke her wrist. As a result, she sued the officer for excessive force. In the officer's deposition, the plaintiff's attorney asked the officer if he had used similar force in his former position as a deputy sheriff? The exchange went like this:

Question: In your former position as a deputy, did you use force?
Answer: Yes, sir.
Question: When you used force, was it similar to this incident?
Answer: No, sir.
Question: That's something different?
Answer: Yes, sir.
Question: What was that?
Answer: Courtesy.
Question: You challenged a guy to a fight?
Answer: No, he challenged me.
Question: You took him up on it?
Answer: I gave him the opportunity to fulfill his wishes.

At the trial, the plaintiff's attorney asked the officer to explain to the jury when it was appropriate to use force? The officer gave the standard answer: to protect life and property, to effect a lawful arrest, to overcome a suspect's resistance. Then, the attorney asked if an officer could ever use force on a suspect out of courtesy? Forgetting what he had said in his deposition, the officer stated courtesy was not a valid reason to use force. In response, the attorney read the previously listed part of the officer's deposition to the jury. His recorded bravado had come back to bite him. The jury ruled that the officer used excessive force.

POSTING OFFENSIVE COMMENTS ON "FACEBOOK." Very few things surprise me anymore, but I almost fell out of my chair when I learned what officers post on their "Facebook" pages would be used against them in a lawsuit. Be aware that what you post on the Internet can negatively impact you professionally. In a lawsuit alleging the use of excessive force, officers kicked in the front door of a residence, tackled a man, and arrested him on two misdemeanor warrants. Unfortunately, the man arrested was not the man named on the warrants. To make matters worse, the arresting officer had posted comments on his Facebook page about "messing with people" and suggesting that laws were needed to send "stupid" people to jail. "His statements on the site indicate a callous disregard for the importance and seriousness of his profession and a practice of intimidating and belittling citizens with whom he has even minimal contact," the plaintiff's attorney stated in the civil rights complaint. The officer resigned two weeks after the plaintiff's attorney discovered the posting. Of course, you guessed right; the lawsuit was settled.

THREATS OF ARREST OR VIOLENCE. Officers commonly use threats of arrest or violence to control and intimidate suspects and inmates, but it is a bad practice. I am not saying I have not done it. But, after reviewing hundreds of lawsuits, I stopped doing it. Using a veiled threat by presenting the options to a suspect or inmate is a valid control technique; the use of direct threats is a completely different matter. Presenting the suspect's options by telling him, "You can leave on your own, or be arrested for trespassing" will not hurt you in a lawsuit. Telling a suspect to "Shut your pie hole, or I will take you to jail" will hurt your professional image with a jury. In a lawsuit that was settled out of court for $270,000.00, the officer is heard saying–on a video recording taken by the plaintiff's neighbor–"Be quiet. Don't you get in my face, pal. I will knock your teeth into the ground." In the process of being arrested, the plaintiff received four broken ribs and a punctured lung. The recorded threat was the reason the lawsuit was settled.

DEMEANING COMMENTS DIRECTED AT THE SUSPECT. Making demeaning comments to arrested suspects is unprofessional and loses lawsuits. You should be happy with your personal victory over a resisting suspect, but there is no need to add insult to injury after using force. It makes you look small and petty, and the jurors do not like it. The truth is always stranger than fiction.

While investigating a bad check case, a detective received a suspect description that was similar to that of his ex-wife–it smells bad already doesn't it? The detective ran his ex-wife for wants and discovered she had warrants for failure to pay traffic fines. If you have ever had an ex-spouse, you know this is a fantasy come true. The detective notified two deputies and provided them with the warrant information.

The deputies arrived at the ex-wife's residence, informed her of the warrants, and placed her under arrest. The ex-wife reentered the residence to get her purse and the deputies followed. The ex-wife's boyfriend stopped the deputies in the hallway and a fight ensued. The boyfriend was physically controlled and handcuffed. As the ex-wife was being handcuffed, the boyfriend became upset and kicked at the other deputy. The deputies pounced on the handcuffed boyfriend.

At some point during the second struggle, a deputy pepper-sprayed the boyfriend in the eye at pointblank range. The eye immediately swelled and appeared as if it is going to pop out of its socket. The boyfriend complained about the intense pain. In response, the deputy who deployed the pepper spray told him, "Don't be a pussy." To make matters worse, on their way to the jail, the deputy called the detective and gave him a blow-by-blow account of the arrest on a cellular phone. A citizen overheard the conversation on a police scanner and tape recorded the deputy's conversation.

The citizen was disturbed by what he heard; consequently, he sent copies of the audiotape to the State Attorney General, Governor, Sheriff, District Attorney, and Circuit Court Judge. During the civil trial, the federal judge ruled that the conversation was unlawfully recorded and not admissible as evidence. However, the plaintiff's attorney was aware of the conversation on the audiotape; consequently, the deputy—during the civil rights trial—had to admit that he made demeaning comments to the injured, handcuffed boyfriend. The jury concluded the deputy's use of pepper spray was excessive force.

VIOLATION OF TRAINING. Just like violating your department's policy, violating your training does not necessarily create a constitutional violation. Often, however, jurors view your actions as inappropriate when you violate your training. As an example, a group of protesters in the northwest had camped out in trees that were to be cut down. The department's tactical plan involved approaching the tree-clinging protesters with a bucket truck, attach a nylon strap to the protester, and lower the protester to the ground. Once on the ground, the protester would be handcuffed and transported to the jail. With the first protester, the tactic worked very well. However, the protesters were resourceful. After observing one of their brethren being plucked from a tree, they strapped themselves to the tree trunks with their belts.

The bucket with two officers in it advanced to the next tree. When they approached the next protester, the officers realized the protester had used his belt to tie himself to the tree trunk. After a short discussion, the officers decided to cut the protester's belt with a pair of medic's shears. When the belt was cut, the protester's pants fell to his ankles, but he still clung to the tree. Because the protester was facing away from the officers, they could not pepper spray his face. So, the officers chose an alternative target; they sprayed his genitalia. In the aftermath of the protester removal, a lawsuit was filled against the officers for excessive force. The issue that caused the city attorney the most distress was that the department's pepper spray training manual listed the target areas for pepper spray application as the eyes, face, nose, and mouth. Nowhere in the manual was genitalia listed as a target area. The lawsuit was settled.

CRIMINAL CONVICTION. Officers who make bad use of force decisions, often, make bad life choices. I am not talking about the officer who uses force lawfully, but gets prosecuted by an overzealous district attorney. I am referring to the officer who intentional violates the laws he or she has sworn to uphold. Officers who break the law fall into the "stupidity" category. Ask any civil defense attorney what damages an officer's defense the most. The attorney will tell you a criminal conviction on the officer's record. Since use of force incidents take approximately three years to go to trial, the defendant officer's criminal conviction usually comes after the use of force incident. A criminal conviction destroys any credibility the officer may have had with a jury. Consequently, it is a major factor in deciding whether the case goes to trial or settles.

While booking the plaintiff at the police station, the officer slammed the plaintiff's head into a wall, threw him to the floor, and drove his knee into the plaintiff's back. As a result, the plaintiff became a quadriplegic. The officer claimed the force was necessary because he believed the plaintiff was about to take a swing at him. In the three million dollar out-of-court settlement, the officer's criminal conviction for insurance fraud was the primary reason the case settled. The city attorney said in a press release, "The officer's disciplinary record would have led to questions about his credibility if he had to testify before a jury." The city attorney was concerned that a jury might award the plaintiff more than the three million if the lawsuit went to trial.

FORCE APPLIED TO PUNISH. In *Graham v. Connor,* the U.S. Supreme Court stated because an officer has to make split second decisions on how much force to use, the officer must be given some leeway when determining if the force was excessive. Consequently, when an officer uses force in good faith and without malice, courts and juries have historically been supportive of the officer. Conversely, when a jury determines that the officer's force was applied as "Street Justice," the officer is punished. In a case involving the beating of a sixty-seven-year-old man by a police officer, a federal judge determined the $360,000 jury award was neither excessive or did it "shock the judicial conscience." The jury found the officer civilly liable for using excessive force by repeatedly striking the plaintiff in the face with his fists while the plaintiff was handcuffed. The jury awarded the plaintiff $60,000 in compensatory damages and $300,000.00 in punitive damages.

REACTING OUT OF ANGER. Restraint is what separates cops from criminals. Criminals act out in anger. Good officers manage their anger. Anger is an emotion that officers cannot allow themselves to be highjacked by. I am not saying that you are a bad cop if you get angry on duty. The point I am trying to make is that you can't let your emotions dictate your use of force decisions. When you act out in anger, you open yourself up to criminal prosecution and civil liability. In the criminal prosecution of an officer who struck a handcuffed suspect in the face out of anger, the Assistant Attorney General for the Civil Rights Division stated in a press release, "It is simply unacceptable for a police officer to beat up a handcuffed arrestee. A badge is a sacred trust, not a license to bully." The officer pled guilty to excessive force and causing bodily injury. He faced up to ten years in federal prison for the civil rights violation.

In a jail use of force incident, the booking area video camera captured a corrections deputy strike an inmate multiple times in the face and head with his fist as another deputy pulled the inmate to the floor. The deputy stated the inmate hit him in the nose with his elbow as the deputy attempted to push the inmate onto the booking counter. But, the video showed the inmate's arm missed the deputy's nose by a few inches; then, the deputy flailing on the inmate. The video was the most damaging video recording of an officer's use of force I have ever viewed. It was an ugly use of force. A federal jury determined the deputy used excessive force.

POORLY WRITTEN POLICY. Use of force policies that are outdated or poorly written damage an officer's defense against allegations of excessive force or misconduct. If you are an administrator, risk manager, or policy wonk, you may be offended by what I am about to tell you: Policies are completely overrated when it comes to eliminating or minimizing liability. Use of force policies do not effectively minimize department or officer liability; properly developed use of force training effectively minimizes liability. With that in mind, an administrator should never substitute policy in lieu of use of force training. Unfortunately, administrators do this frequently.

Use of force policies keep attorneys up at night, give bureaucrats something to do, and are often misunderstood by officers. From a defense point of view, a well-written use of force policy is benign at its best. In contrast, a poorly written policy gives the plaintiff's attorney an opportunity to portray the officer as an incompetent. In the worst case scenario, a poorly written use of force policy can be used as evidence to support the plaintiff's attorney's assertion that the officer used excessive force.

In a lawsuit alleging that jail deputies used excessive force on an inmate who was resisting being placed in a restraint chair, the department's use of force policy inferred that the deputies used deadly force.

A male suspect was booked into jail on a misdemeanor charge. Based on the suspect's behavior, it was believed he was under the influence of a controlled substance. After completing the booking process, he was placed in an isolation cell. Almost immediately, the suspect started to act out: yelling, hitting and kicking the cell door, and banging his head on the walls. For his safety, the jail staff decided to place him in a restraint chair. Three deputies entered the cell and struggled with the inmate to get him handcuffed and shackled. After he was restrained, they removed the inmate from the cell to place him in a mobile restraint chair. Their plan was to confine the suspect to the restraint chair and roll him back into his cell.

As a deputy controlled each of the suspect's arms, the third deputy slide the restraint chair up to him. The handcuffed and shackled inmate resisted being placed in the chair by stiffening his body. The third deputy placed a neck restraint on the inmate and rendered him unconscious. The inmate collapsed into the restraint chair. As the deputies were securing the chair's straps, the inmate regained consciousness and started to struggle. A deputy applied a neck restraint and rendered the inmate unconscious a second time. The deputies strapped down the unconscious inmate. As the deputies were rolling the inmate back into his cell, one deputy warned, "Hey, he is not looking too good." The suspect had stopped breathing and had turned a bluish color. He was removed from the chair and given CPR. The inmate was resuscitated, but suffered permanent brain damage.

There were a number of subtle issues that hurt the deputies' defense, but the most damaging blow came from the department's use of force policy. Per their department's policy, a deputy could only use deadly force to protect the deputy or another person from death or serious physical harm. In the neck restraint section of the use of force policy, the policy classified the application of the neck restraint as deadly force. During the trial, the plaintiff's attorney claimed that the deputies, as defined by their own department policy, had used deadly force to place a handcuff and shackled inmate into a restraint chair. Fearing the jury would award the plaintiff the full two million dollars, the county settled the case on the last day of trial for $900,000. When the plaintiff's attorney questioned the dismissed jury, the jurors told him they were ready to award the plaintiff four million dollars in general and punitive damages. In Chapter 11, we will discuss recommendations for the construction of defensible use of force policies.

POORLY KEPT TRAINING RECORDS. An effective defense against accusations of excessive force or misconduct is to state that you followed your training. Knowing that, the first place the plaintiff's attorney will look for weaknesses to exploit is in your department's training records. The more detailed your training record the better your defense. The Plaintiff's attorney will compare the documented number of training hours regarding the action being litigated to other, but unrelated, skills.

As an example, in a lawsuit alleging the use of excessive force on a mentally ill man, the plaintiff's attorney compared the number of training hours the officer had in dealing with mentally ill people with the number of his firearms training hours. The officer's training record consisted of a combination of specific topics and generally titled units of training. The officer's training record specifically listed every firearm-training course the officer attended. As a twenty-year veteran, the officer had hundreds of firearms training hours documented. However, there was no specific training hours recorded in dealing with the mentally ill. The department's training officer insisted that the officer received training in dealing effectively with mentally ill people in the forty-hour block listed as "inservice training" on the officer's training record. But, there were no lesson plans or performance objectives to prove it.

At trial, the plaintiff's attorney claimed that if the officer had received as much training in dealing effectively with mentally ill citizens as he had in shooting them his client would not have been injured. Although the lack of documented training in the area of recognizing the mentally ill had nothing to do with the correctness of the officer's use of force, the plaintiff's attorney used the officer's lack of specifically documented training to portray the officer as being poorly trained.

DAMAGING VIDEOTAPE EVIDENCE. If a picture is worth a thousand words, then, a video recording of a use of force incident can be worth millions of dollars to a plaintiff. A graphic video portraying an officer in a negative light will be used by the plaintiff's attorney as leverage to force a settlement in lieu of litigating the incident. If you appear abusive, emotionally out of control, insensitive, rude, or vulgar on the video, your city or county will settle the case fearing that a jury will award the plaintiff a larger sum in general and punitive damages. Even if your force is justified, your bad behavior caught on video will severely damage your defense.

In a wrongful death lawsuit involving the arrest of a drunk driver, the patrol car's video camera recorded the driver's pleas to call for an ambulance as he was dying at the scene. The video showed the officers standing over the handcuffed suspect for over twenty minutes as he told the officers he was dying—his voice becoming weaker with every plea for help. Even though the medical examiner stated that if the injury had occurred in a hospital parking lot the driver would not have survived, the lawsuit was settled out of court for millions of dollars. The recorded officers' indifference and the driver's fading pleas for help overshadowed the scientific evidence, making an effective defense of the officers' use of force impossible.

If the video does not support your version of what occurred, the jury will conclude you are not being truthful. In the largest excessive force verdict in the United States, the jury awarded the plaintiff over sixteen million dollars in damages and over two million dollars in attorney's fees. According to the lawsuit, deputies responded to a loud noise complaint at a Samoan wedding shower. The deputies claimed that the incident turned into a riot. The plaintiff claimed the deputies overreacted because Samoans are big people, and they have a reputation for being combative. Unfortunately for the deputies, a neighbor recorded the incident with his video camera. The video supported the plaintiff's version of the incident. The jury, believing the deputies were being dishonest in their testimony, punished the deputies with a sixteen million-dollar verdict.

DAMAGING AUDIOTAPE EVIDENCE. Almost as damaging as an officer's unprofessional behavior caught on videotape is an audio recording of an officer's profane, insensitive, or rude comments regarding the injured suspect or how the incident had gone tragically wrong.

In a lawsuit involving a loud noise complaint, the officers tasered a naked and intoxicated man, eleven seconds, after he answered his door. The man fell face down onto his outside deck and crushed his skull. He underwent three brain surgeries and suffers from memory loss, slurred speech, and vision problems. The officers claimed that they used the Taser in self-defense when the man suddenly attacked them—a legitimate justification for the use of the Taser. However, there was a problem. The patrol car's video camera wireless microphone recorded the officers using profanities while discussing how the routine call had gone wrong. The plaintiff's attorney cited the audio recording as evidence that the officers' used excessive force. The lawsuit was settled out of court.

NEGATIVE NEWSPAPER PHOTOGRAPHS. Although they don't have the same level of impact on a jury as a graphic video or audio recording, still photographs accurately portray an attitude regarding the officer's use of force. If the photograph portrays the officer's use of force negatively, it damages the officer's defense.

In a lawsuit alleging the use of excessive force against passively resisting protesters, the local newspaper published two photographs in their front-page article of the incident. The first quarter page photograph was a frontal, close range, picture of an officer—clad in riot gear—spraying the newspaper photographer with pepper spray. The officer sprayed directly into the camera.

To enhance the image's impact, the newspaper highlighted the cone-shaped cloud of pepper spray in fluorescent green. The caption under the picture read: "Officer sprays newspaper photographer during Monday's protest." That image really helped the city with the subsequent lawsuits alleging excessive force by their officers—not!

In the second quarter-page photograph, you see three large officers—clad in riot gear—standing over three protesters (two men and a woman) sitting on the ground. Two of the officers have their hands on their hips. The third officer is pointing a pepper spray canister at the protesters. In her deposition, the female protester testified that before they were sprayed she looked up and told the officers "I forgive you for what you are about to do us." Further, the three protesters alleged that after being sprayed, they were left to wander (unprotected) through the downtown streets blinded by the pepper spray. Needless to say, the city settled the lawsuit.

Counter-independent Witness Statements. Independent witnesses can make or break an officer's defense. Because independent witnesses have no connection to the officer(s) or the plaintiff, they have tremendous credibility with jurors. When an independent witness supports the plaintiff's version of what happened, you lose the lawsuit. That is exactly what happened when two independent witnesses testified at in federal civil rights lawsuit.

The driver testified that the lead officer punched him three times and told a passenger in the backseat: "Shut up. And, if you say another thing, I am going to shoot you." The officers denied punching the driver or making the threat. However, two independent witnesses contradicted the officers' version of the event. The witnesses testified that they were so unnerved by the officers' actions they dropped their car seats back so they could watch without being detected. The jury determined the officers used excessive force. "Those witnesses were a key to the jury's verdict," the jury foreman told a newspaper reporter.

Although I can't state with absolute certainty, my experience suggests that if the officers had followed Stephan Covey's admonishment to "begin with the end in mind" they would have made different choices and consequently experienced more positive results.

Just Because You Can—It Doesn't Mean You Should

There is an old adage: "When you have a hammer, the whole world looks like a nail." When an officer is asked why he or she arrested the suspect, the most common reply is, "I could." Citizen legislators write criminal laws with the best of intentions. However, most criminal laws are not written with their specific law enforcement application in mind.

The law that allows you to seize an uninsured motorist's car is a classic example. Do you seize the car of every driver who fails to provide proof of his automobile insurance coverage? No. What criteria do you use to determine which car gets impounded? Probably, the main criterion is whether the driver has gotten under your skin. The law allows you to tow his car, so you use the law to give out a little legal payback. I don't think the legislature had that application in mind when they wrote the law.

So, if it is legal—what's the problem? The problem occurs when your emotional enforcement of a law creates a negative jury perception. Said another way, the jury believes you took the enforcement action because the driver ticked you off. The U.S. Supreme Court recognized in *Graham v. Conner* that there is a continuum of criminality—when determining whether an officer's use of force is reasonable the severity of the crime must be considered.

The following lawsuit is a classic example of how arresting someone because you can creates liability for you and your department. A recent academy graduate and his field training officer (FTO) were on patrol one evening when they observed a car roll through a stop sign. When the trainee activated the emergency lights, the driver did not pull over and a very low speed pursuit ensued. After following the violator's vehicle for several blocks, it pulled over next to the curb. The trainee contacted the driver at the driver's door. The driver rolled down her window and asked, "Why did you stop me?" "Let me see your driver's license," the officer replied. Again, the driver asked, "Why did you stop me?" Again the officer replied, "Let me see your driver's license." "I am not going to give you my license until you tell me why you stopped me," the driver said adamantly. "Ma'am, if you don't give me your driver's license, you will be arrested for failure to present your license," the officer warned. "I am not giving you my license until you tell me why I was stopped," she insisted.

Now, in the proactive management of a jury's perception of the incident (begin with the end in mind), the smart thing to do is tell the driver why she was stopped. Although the law allows the officer to arrest a driver who fails to carry or display a driver's license, it doesn't mean he should. The subsequent arrest, use of force, driver's injury, and the lawsuit could have been avoided if the officer had explained his justification for the stop. Even if after the officer answered the driver's question and she did not cooperate, the act of answering her question positively influences the jury's perception of the officer's subsequent use of force.

The trainee informed the driver she is under arrest, opened the driver's door, and pulled her out of the car. When he grabbed her left arm, he noticed something small in her left hand. He placed the object in his waistband and handcuffed the driver. She is placed in the back of his patrol car. With the driver secured, the trainee pulled the object from his waistband and discovered it is her driver's license.

The trainee and his FTO searched the driver's car (the reason is unclear), and they find medication that indicated she suffered from a mental illness. Because it was a cold night, the driver was wearing a heavy coat. The heavy coat concealed the driver's badly deformed right arm. While the officers were searching her car, the driver yelled to get the officers' attention. The officers contacted the driver. She told them that the handcuffs were hurting her right arm. The FTO told her that if she agreed to get back into his car he would take off the handcuffs. "Your car! Your car! Your car . . ." the mentally ill driver said several times. The FTO looked at his trainee, shrugged his shoulders, and slammed the door closed–leaving the driver handcuffed until she was issued a citation. Consequently, the strain of the handcuffs injured her deformed arm.

At the civil trial, the driver wore a sleeveless blouse that accentuated her badly deformed arm. The driver, a woman in her mid-forties, was barely over five feet tall. The officers were male and both over six feet. On the witness stand, the trainee's justification for the arrest was that the driver had broken the law. He did not have an effective explanation for his unwillingness to explain the reason for the stop to the driver. During his testimony, the senior officer explained that the driver was handcuffed for his and the trainee's safety. However, when pressed by the plaintiff's attorney, the senior officer admitted that at no time did he fear for his or his trainee's safety during the traffic stop. The jury was unimpressed. The jury determined the officers used excessive force. The case took seven years of appellate litigation to come to a resolution. The appeal process cost the city hundreds of thousands of dollars in attorney fees, and in the end, the city lost the lawsuit.

This incident is not an anomaly. Use of force cases every year across the United States are tried and lost or settled because the officers made the arrest because they could, not because it was the best possible solution to a challenging situation.

Perceptions and Opposite Gender Searches

Regardless of which "pat-down" or intrusive clothing search technique is used, you cannot prevent an allegation of sexual abuse when performing an opposite-gender search. You can, however, proactively manage the perceptions of your search by the suspect, witnesses, and jurors.

As you learned in *State of Oregon v. Daniel Beugle,* an opposite-gender search of a person can have destructive criminal, financial, and professional consequences. However, not searching a person for weapons can have fatal consequences.

Oregon State Trooper Brett Clodfelter made that fatal mistake. Trooper Clodfelter was shot three times in the back of the head by a passenger in the car of an arrested drunk driver. Not wanting to leave the two passengers stranded alongside the road, he placed the handcuffed suspect and the other passengers in the back of his patrol car. Although, he searched the suspect, he did not search the passengers. As Trooper Clodfelter sat behind the steering wheel, one of the passengers pulled a handgun and shot and killed him. To make this needless loss even more tragic, his wife (a deputy sheriff) committed suicide over the grief of losing her husband a year later.

The Trooper Clodfelter assassination is evidence that regardless of the potential risk of criminal or civil litigation a "pat-down" for weapons must be conducted before a person is placed in your vehicle.

The proper procedure for conducting opposite-gender "pat-downs" and intrusive clothing searches incident to an arrest is no different than the method you use for the same gender searches. With that being said, there are specific things you can do to protect yourself against accusations of misconduct during an effective opposite-gender search. Not to beat a dead horse, but I want to emphasize it is always better to have the same gender officer conduct the search. But, if that is not possible, the following procedures will help protect you against allegations of misconduct and create a proactive defense of your search.

EXPLAIN THE SEARCH PROCEDURE TO THE SUSPECT. Prior to conducting the search, tell the suspect how the search will be conducted and what areas will be touched. Inform the suspect that you are going to use the inside of your hand to touch her waistband, pockets, chest area, legs, and the inside and outside of her thighs. Letting a female suspect know how and what you are going to touch minimizes the shock and surprise of being touched in a way that most people find offensive. An additional advantage of explaining the search procedure is that it creates the impression, with the suspect and witnesses, that the search is standard police procedure and not sexual in nature. Lastly, explaining the procedure aids in your defense against allegations of inappropriate touching. Perception is everything to a jury. A jury is more likely to believe your search was conducted properly if they hear you had explained the procedure to the suspect before you conducted the search.

HAVE A COVER OFFICER WITNESS THE SEARCH. As previously discussed, jurors want to believe what you say occurred is the truth. As in most sexual harassment complaints, an allegation of improperly searching a female suspect becomes a "he said versus she said" situation—that is what happened in Trooper Beugle's prosecution. Having another officer witness what you told the suspect and how you conducted the search protects you from allegations of inappropriate behavior.

HAVE A NEUTRAL CIVILIAN WITNESS THE SEARCH. Having an independent civilian witness your opposite-gender search is better than having a cover officer witness the search. Independent witnesses have no reason to lie or cover up for you; therefore, they have tremendous credibility with investigators and jurors. Make sure you explain the search procedure, the areas to be touched, and why the search is important to the witness before you conduct the search. Explaining the procedure prior to conducting the search prevents misperceptions or misinterpretations of your actions by the civilian witness.

VIDEOTAPE RECORD THE SEARCH WITH YOUR CAR-MOUNTED VIDEO CAMERA. Seeing is believing. The best defense against any allegation of misconduct is a videotape recording demonstrating what you did and how you did it. Keep in mind, a video recording of your actions can work for you or against you. When using video to document your search, make sure your search procedure is approved by your department. I have reviewed more than a few car camera and jail video recordings that hurt the officer's defense more than it helped him.

AUDIO-TAPE YOUR INSTRUCTIONS AND THE SUSPECT'S REACTIONS TO THE SEARCH. A small, cassette, tape recorder is a piece of equipment that every officer should carry on-duty. Only second to videotaping an opposite-gender search is audio-recording it. Again, it goes back to a jury's perception of your search. It is one thing for you to tell the investigator or the jury how you performed the search and how the suspect reacted. It is another to have the jury or the investigator hear it for themselves. An important strategic point about audio recording your opposite gender search is to make sure that you use the tape recorder every time the other three options are not available. This is especially important if the suspect is complaining about how she is being touched. On the audiotape, the jury will hear the suspect objecting, and you explaining how you are searching. Because there is no visual record, the jury will have to decide whom to believe based on their perceptions of you. If you don't audio record every opposite-gender search—when the use of the patrol car's video camera or having someone witness the search is not an option— you will be accused of using the audio recording, this one time, to cover up your abuse of the suspect.

We will close Chapter 2 with a review and analysis of Officer Jerry Walton's mismanagement of the witnesses' perception of the arrests and the jury's perception of him during the trial. As previously explained, Officer Walton was convicted of two counts of assault (battery in some states) on two transients in two separate arrests, without the victims appearing at trial. He was convicted with only witness testimony. Officer Walton did not use excessive force on the suspects. He did, however, mismanage the witnesses' perceptions of his use of force and the jurors' perceptions of his honesty. Furthermore, the responding supervisor did not properly manage the witnesses' perceptions after he arrived at the scene.

In the first incident, Officer Walton mismanaged the Cover Officer's perception of his use of force. When his partner accused him of using excessive force at the police department, Officer Walton self-destructed: He agreed with her. I consulted on this case and testified on his behalf. Officer Walton did not use excessive force. When being accused of using excessive force and your force was not excessive, stand your ground and justify your use of force to the accuser. Capitulation is not a defense. Stating your justification is properly managing the use of force incident.

Officer Walton should have looked his partner in the eye and said: "I didn't use excessive force. I did not knock him over. I did not push him over. I controlled his descent as I laid him on his side. The suspect was being uncooperative. I placed my knee across the side of his head to keep him from rolling over and kicking you in the teeth as you reached to remove his wallet. So, for future reference, I would like to know if you would rather be kicked in the teeth than have me control the suspect? Just let me know how you want to handle these situations." Even if she did not believe his justification, she is going to give this account of his response to the internal affairs investigators.

In her statement to internal affairs, she told the investigators she confronted Officer Walton about his use of force, and he admitted the force was excessive. If Officer Walton would have given his partner the explanation that I recommended, the investigators would have had to prove excessive force based on the evidence. There was no physical evidence. The suspect had no injuries. In fact, the investigators did not have a victim—he had left town. The only evidence the investigators had was his admission. Officer Walton had unintentionally shot himself in the foot. He was wounded, but not dead. The fatal shot was to come, and again, it would be self-inflicted.

In the second incident, Officer Walton did not properly manage the perceptions of the witnesses at the scene. If you have reviewed my narrative of the Lancaster Drive incident, you are aware that the two people who witnessed Officer Walton's use of force are the same two people who initially stopped to help the suspect. This distinction is important. The witnesses are not neutral. They have an emotional connection to the suspect. The witnesses stopped to help him out of the street, and they called the police to get him assistance. In fact, the witnesses told the internal affairs investigators: "We feel so bad. We called the police to help him—not kick his ass." That's the problem: their perception of Officer Walton's use of force is that it was an "ass kicking." Officer Walton did not use excessive force. The suspect's fall off the bench was an accident, but to the witnesses—who were not told differently—it was perceived as an intentional infliction of pain.

As the suspect was being treated by the EMTs, Officer Walton should have contacted the witnesses and (without becoming defensive) listened to their concerns, complaints, and objections. Then, Officer Walton should have told them: "I know this incident looks really bad. The reason I used pepper spray was because I was concerned that the suspect would hit me with the wine bottle. About two months ago a Salem officer was injured by a hit in the face with a glass bottle. Further, it was not my intention to take the suspect to the ground. My plan was to stand him up and handcuff him. I did not realize he had locked his feet up under the bench. So, when I pulled him up off the bench, he accidentally fell forward onto the sidewalk. I feel really bad about his injuries."

I realize that explaining what happened to angry and upset witnesses at the scene is a challenge. There will be interruptions, emotional outbursts, and accusations from the witnesses. None of that matters. Either they believe your explanation and they are appeased, or they don't and a complaint is forthcoming. You can't force the witnesses believe you. The purpose of your on-scene explanation is to properly manage the jury's post-incident perception of your use of force. Jurors are more likely to accept your testimony if they hear you made an effort at the scene to address the witnesses' concerns and objections.

In the improved version of the incident, when the witnesses talk to the internal affairs' investigators, what do they say when asked, "Did the officer say anything to you at the scene?" Their answer: "Yes, he said he was concerned about being hit with the bottle. And, he did not intend for the guy to fall headfirst on the ground." It does not matter if the witnesses believe Officer Walton's explanation. It is the perception of the investigators, prosecutor, and the jurors that matter. By taking the time and effort to explain what happened to the witnesses at the scene, Officer Walton has created the perception that he cares. He cares about the suspect. He cares about the witnesses. He cares about the citizens of his community. Why would an abusive officer take the time to explain what happened to the witnesses and apologize for accidentally injuring the suspect? An abusive officer wouldn't. And, that's my point.

As you know, in the criminal prosecution, the prosecutor must prove that Officer Walton intended to use excessive force beyond a reasonable doubt. It would be tough for the most accomplished prosecutor to get a conviction after the jury hears the witnesses testify how the officer took the time to explain his justification for the use of the pepper spray and his explanation for the headlong fall off the bench. The jury's perception of Officer Walton is that he cares. Caring officers do not intentionally use excessive force. The perception of caring equals "reasonable doubt."

Lastly, the supervisor did not properly manage the perceptions of the witnesses at the scene. The witnesses went through all the effort to file criminal charges against Officer Walton with the district attorney's office because they believed the police department would not take their complaint seriously. What would you think if you told the sergeant at the scene you wanted to file a complaint and he gave you a business card and said call the chief's office? How confident would you be that the police department would investigate your complaint? The purpose of properly managing the use of force incident is to reduce citizen complaints. The sergeant should have listened to their concerns, assured them that the department takes citizen complaints seriously, explained the investigative process for complaints, and then write down in front of them their personal information and statements. In closing, the sergeant should have told the witnesses that he would personally investigate the incident and forward his report to the patrol lieutenant for review. If the sergeant had used this process, would the witnesses still have gone to the District Attorney's Office? We will never know. However, what we do know is that the approach the sergeant used didn't defuse their anger with Officer Walton.

My involvement in Officer Walton's case started with a telephone call from his attorney. The attorney informed me of the criminal complaint and he asked if I could meet with them to discuss a possible defense. About a week later, I met with Jerry and his attorney at the Academy. Jerry explained what had happened during both arrests. The force Jerry used in both arrests seemed justified to me. I told Jerry and his attorney that we taught officers at the academy that a suspect's close proximity to a weapon is justification for the escalation of force. Therefore, I had no problem with him pepper spraying the suspect. I asked Jerry if he was concerned about the glass wine bottle the suspect possessed? Jerry stated he was afraid that if he got too close to the suspect he would be hit with the bottle. That's why he pepper sprayed the suspect in lieu of going hands-on. Jerry went on to say that two months prior to this incident a Salem officer was hit in the face with a glass Snapple bottle and received a serious facial injury. His attorney believed that Jerry's concern about being hit with the bottle and his knowledge of a previous assault were key issues in Jerry's defense. I agreed.

The attorney asked if I would testify as an expert witness at Jerry's criminal trial. I told them I was more than willing to help any way I could. I asked to receive copies of Jerry's police reports regarding both arrests and the internal affairs investigator's report. The attorney told me that he believed my testimony would be straightforward, so he didn't think I needed to review the reports.

The day of the trial came. I took the witness stand and did my best to explain to the jury what officers are taught at the academy and how Officer Walton's actions were commensurate with what the academy taught regarding the proper use of force. The jury seemed very receptive. When I was done testifying, the court recessed for twenty minutes. I met with Jerry and his attorney during the recess. They were pleased with how the trial was preceding. Jerry was to take the stand when the jury returned from the afternoon recess. I had been released as a witness, which meant I could watch the remainder of the trial. So, I decided to stay and observe Jerry's testimony.

Jerry took the witness stand. He was doing a great job explaining what he did and why. It appeared to me that he had a not guilty verdict in the bag. Then, the deputy district attorney started his cross-examination. Jerry, a ten-year veteran, was doing a good job keeping the prosecutor at bay. The prosecutor, who had done most of his cross-examination standing up, sat down and opened a three-ringed binder. I did not know it at the time, but it was the internal affairs investigator's report. Because the District Attorney's Office requested the investigation, the Oregon State Police had been asked to conduct Jerry's internal affairs investigation. The prosecutor stood up and asked Jerry, "You testified that you were concerned about the wine bottle being used as a weapon, didn't you?" Jerry answered that he did. Jerry went on to explain about the Salem officer who had been hit with the Snapple bottle. The prosecutor reached down, snapped open the three-ring-binder, and removed a sheet of paper. The prosecutor asked Jerry if he remembered being interviewed by the State Police. Jerry said he did. Next, the prosecutor asked, " Do you remember this–Question: Were you concerned about the wine bottle? Answer: No." My heart sank. I looked over at the jury, and their entire body language changed. It would not matter what Jerry said from this point forward. His credibility with the jury was destroyed. Jerry had failed to properly manage the jurors' perception.

After all the testimony and closing arguments, the jury was released to deliberate. They came back with a guilty verdict of assault on both counts. The jurors believed Jerry had been untruthful with his testimony, and they punished him for it.

Chapter 3

STANDARDS GOVERNING
THE USE OF FORCE

As a criminal justice officer, you are regulated by two governmental standards regarding the use of force: Your state's statutory guidelines and the United States' Constitution as interpreted by the Supreme Court and the applicable Court of Appeals for your district. An individual state can establish a more restrictive requirement governing the use of force, but not more permissive. In fact, it was the more permissive Tennessee state law governing the use of deadly force by police that gave us the definitive United States Supreme Court ruling of *Tennessee v. Garner*.

For the purpose of our discussion, I will only address the federal requirements for lawfully using deadly and nondeadly force. Although you can be sued in state court for a state constitutional violation or for simple negligence, the vast majority of civil rights lawsuits are filed and heard in federal courts.

Previously we discussed the proper management of witness and juror perceptions, now I would like to take a moment to explain how to positively influence the plaintiff attorney's perception of you as an officer. You may find this surprising, but many plaintiff's attorneys think cops are dumb. Most have respect for what we do, but let's be honest, it does not take seven years of college to be a police officer, not even to be a really good cop. So, naturally, based on their educational credentials they are going to look down on us as a profession. Because they spend seven years in college, their orientation is academic in nature: legal theory, conceptual rules, and well-established standards. It is for this reason.

QUOTING THE USE OF FORCE STANDARD IN YOUR JUSTIFICATION ENHANCES YOUR CREDIBILITY

Your written report is the first document the plaintiff's attorney will review in an incident involving the use of nondeadly force. At the Academy, it was pounded into you that your written report creates the first and most lasting impression of you as an officer. Unfortunately, that admonishment doesn't stay with most cops after they graduate. Further, in a deadly force incident, the first document the plaintiff's attorney will review is a written transcript of your audio/video recorded internal affairs' interview. With either document, the attorney will use the content of your information to evaluate how knowledgeable you are regarding the use of force and how effective your testimony will be on the witness stand.

Consequently, by quoting the legal standard in your report, during your internal affairs interview, and in your deposition, you create the perception that you are very knowledgeable regarding the use of force. The more knowledgeable you appear to the plaintiff's attorney the less likely he or she is to pursue the lawsuit. And if the attorney does continue to press the litigation, the more likely he or she will settle the case for a pittance. The following are examples of quoting the use of force standard in a written report and during a recorded internal affairs' interview:

Nondeadly Force (Written Report)

As Mr. Jones continued to ignore my verbal commands to "Stop! Get on the ground," he advanced toward me, at a faster than normal pace, with his fists clenched. I pulled my Taser, issued another verbal command to "Stop, get on the ground!" and deployed my Taser in probe mode. Mr. Jones fell to the ground incapacitated by the Taser shock. As per *Graham v. Conner,* an officer can use nondeadly force if the suspect poses an immediate threat to an officer or others. Furthermore, per Graham, an officer must take into account the severity of the crime the suspect has committed, and whether the suspect is actively resisting arrest. I deployed my Taser because Mr. Jones presented an immediate threat of serious physical harm to me through his superior size and strength—he is six feet and five inches tall, weighs two hundred and forty-eight pounds, and has a body builder's physique. Further, I feared for my safety because Mr. Jones had previously committed a violent crime by punching and kicking another patron in the bar—causing a serious head injury. Lastly, he resisted arrest through a verbal threat to assault me. I told Mr. Jones he was under arrest for battery. When I did, he glared at me and said, "I am not going to jail and if you try to take me I will kick your ass." Then, he advanced toward me to carry out his threat.

Deadly Force (Transcript of the recorded IA interview)

Detective: Did you intentionally shoot Mr. Jones?

Officer: Yes, I did.

Detective: Why?

Officer: *Tennessee v. Garner* allows a police officer to use deadly force to protect himself when he reasonably believes the suspect poses an immediate threat of death or serious physical harm to the officer. Mr. Jones refused to drop the knife that he held in his right hand. He held the knife out in front of him and made thrusting motions toward me. After refusing to obey my verbal commands to "Drop the knife," he continued to advance toward me. I could not retreat any further because of a wall. When he was within twenty feet of me, I shot him twice in the chest. I did so because, as per *Tennessee v. Garner,* he presented an immediate threat of serious physical injury or death to me as he advanced toward me with the knife.

As you can see, if you know the legal standards for using nondeadly and deadly force, they are easily included in your written report or oral explanation. In doing so, you will positively influence the plaintiff attorney's perception of you as an officer. If the plaintiff's attorney believes you are knowledgeable regarding the use of force; then, the attorney is more likely to believe you did not use excessive force on his client. Positively influencing the plaintiff attorney's perception of you is an important element of a proactive strategy for managing the use of force incident.

Origin of "Killing a Fleeing Felon"

The American legal premise for allowing an officer to kill a fleeing felon dates back to medieval England. During that period of time, there were two rules of law: the monarchy (King) and the Church. The Church's biblical law regarding crime and punishment was more lenient: "An eye for an eye, a tooth for a tooth, the punishment should fit the crime." When laws were first established in England by the Crown, all crimes were classified as felonies, and there were only a few: high treason, treason, murder, robbery, rape, burglary, assault, and theft.

As a commoner (peasant), if you were charged with a crime almost always you were convicted. If you were convicted—more likely than not—you were executed (hanged). So, as a practical matter, the moment you were placed under arrest you were headed to the gallows. Consequently, if you were killed trying to escape, it just saved the trouble of holding a trial. This archaic concept of allowing law enforcement officers to kill any fleeing felon remained in the American legal system until 1985. In that year, the U.S. Supreme Court ruling of *Tennessee v. Garner* restricted the use of deadly force by the police.

Constitutional Standards Governing the Use of Deadly Force

Tennessee v. Garner (471 U.S. 1-1985) is the definitive U.S. Supreme Court decision on the use of deadly force by police. The facts of the shooting are as follows:

On October 3, 1974, Memphis police officers Elton Hymon and Leslie Wright responded to a residential burglary in progress. As Officer Hymon entered the backyard, he saw a young (15 years old) male burglar (Edward Garner) exit the house and crouch beside a six-foot chain link fence. Garner had stolen less than twenty dollars and a purse.

After illuminating Garner with his flashlight, Officer Hymon identified himself as a police officer and gave the command to "Halt!" As Garner attempted to escape by climbing the fence, Officer Hymon fired at the upper part of the Garner's body. The bullet struck Garner in the back of the head; he died of the gunshot wound at the hospital.

Officer Hymon was "reasonably sure" that Garner was unarmed, and he shot the burglar to prevent his escape. At that time, Tennessee state law allowed deadly force to be used on any fleeing felon. The Memphis Police Department had a more restrictive policy, but it allowed for the use of deadly force on a fleeing burglar. Therefore, the officer's actions were justified under an existing state fleeing felon statue and department policy.

Garner's father filed a lawsuit in federal court following the incident. The Sixth Circuit Court of Appeals concluded that the officer's actions (shooting Garner) amounted to a seizure, and thus, was governed by the Fourth Amendment. Prior to the appellate court's ruling, the primary constitutional standard that was applied to a police shooting was the Fourteenth Amendment. The Fourteenth Amendment guarantees citizens the right to due process.

The Supreme Court adopted the Sixth Circuit Court of Appeals interpretation. The High Court ruled that the officer had used excessive force; therefore, he was liable for his actions when he "seized" Garner by gunshot. In *Tennessee v. Garner,* the Supreme Court introduced a new standard for determining police liability. The courts are to balance the nature of the intrusion (death or serious injury) on the person's Fourth Amendment rights against the governmental interests (protection of the community or the officer) alleged to justify the intrusion.

Though this balancing act may seem difficult to apply, it is really quite intuitive. When the interest of the government (to protect the members of the community) outweigh the interest of the suspect to be free from harm (seriously injured or killed), you can use deadly force to end his dangerous behavior or to prevent his escape and his opportunity to seriously harm others.

The Supreme Court ruled that an officer may seize the suspect (with deadly force) only when the officer reasonably believes the suspect poses a threat of serious physical harm to the officer or others. Serious physical harms occurs when:

- There is an immediate danger to the officer or others.
- When the suspect demonstrates dangerousness by the previous use of or threatened use of force.

In addition, an officer may use deadly force when he or she reasonably believes that the suspect has committed a crime involving the use or threatened use of serious physical harm. Under these circumstances, an officer may use deadly force in the absence of an immediate threat.

Furthermore, an officer must issue a verbal warning before using deadly force, when it is reasonable to do so.

As you can clearly see, in *Tennessee v. Garner,* the Court established standards for using deadly force in two separate, but potentially related, circumstances:

First, when the person is an immediate threat (of serious physical injury or death) to you or someone else–immediate indicates the dangerous action is occurring or is likely to occur momentarily. In practical terms, you can use deadly force to protect yourself or another person from a suspect using or threatening to use force that is likely to cause serious physical injury or death. The mechanism of that force can be a weapon, superior strength, and/or superior skill.

Second, to prevent the suspect's escape–if you reasonably believe the suspect has committed a crime involving violence (threatened or applied). This knowledge can be firsthand or conveyed through the receipt of an arrest warrant or other official communications source. In practical terms, you can use deadly force to prevent the escape of a suspect who has committed an assault (that caused serious physical injury), a menacing act with a weapon, robbery involving the threat or use of force, forcible rape, attempted murder, murder, forcible kidnapping, intentional arson that threatens life, and any other crime that involves the intentional infliction or threat of serious physical injury or death to the victim.

The following hypothetical scenarios are designed to test your knowledge and understanding of *Tennessee v. Garner.* As you ponder each question, analyze each scenario by balancing the community's interest against the suspect's interest to be free from harm.

- An officer makes a traffic stop. As he approaches the violator's vehicle, the driver exits and points a gun at him. Can the officer use deadly force? *Yes,* the suspect is an immediate threat to the officer. Ok, that was a no-brainer; I will give you that one. We have gotten the easy one out of the way, now move on to the more challenging scenarios.
- An officer responds to a report of a criminal trespass in a residence. He arrives at the scene, and the resident tells the officer she came out of her bedroom and found a strange man sleeping on her sofa. She wants him removed. The officer is male, approximately five feet and ten inches tall and weighs one hundred and seventy-five pounds. The suspect is male, six feet and four inches tall and weights two hundred and thirty pounds. As the officer shakes the suspect to wake him, he grabs the officer and pulls him to the ground. As the officer struggles with the suspect, the suspect straddles the officer's body and chokes the officer with both hands.

    Can the officer use deadly force? *Yes,* due to the suspect's size and strength, the officer is in immediate danger of serious physical injury or death.
- Officers respond to a report of a domestic conflict at a residence. As the officers approach the open front door, they hear the husband threatening to kill his wife. The primary officer peers inside the residence and he sees the husband threatening his wife with a large kitchen knife. Can the Officer use deadly force? *Yes,* the suspect is an immediate threat to the wife. Further, the suspect has demonstrated dangerousness through the threatened use of serious physical harm.
- Officers respond to a report of a domestic conflict at an apartment complex. As the officers approach the apartment's bedroom window, they hear a person gasping for air. The primary officer peeks between the bedroom curtains, and he sees a man choking a woman on the bed. As the officers enter through the apartment's unlocked front door, a man holding a pair of scissors confronts them. They order the man to drop the scissors and to get down on the floor. The man advances toward the officers with the scissors held in an ice-pick grip.

    Can the officers use deadly force? *Yes,* the suspect is an immediate threat to the officers, and he has demonstrated dangerousness through the previous use of force (choking the woman).

In the previous scenarios, the use of deadly force was straightforward. Common sense dictates that you could use deadly force to protect yourself or another. Now, the following hypotheticals will become less black and white and more gray.

- An officer responds to a complaint of a homeless man bothering employees of a fast food restaurant. The manager confronted the man, and he threatened the manager. The manager wants the homeless man removed from the store's property. It is noon and the restaurant is full of local high school students.
  The officer drives her patrol vehicle around the building. As she does, she sees the suspect standing in the dumpster looking through the trash. The officer stops her vehicle twenty feet in front of the dumpster, exits her vehicle, and asks the suspect to step out of the dumpster. The suspect crawls out of the dumpster, pulls a fixed blade knife from his pocket, and threatens to kill her. The officer pulls her handgun, retreats to use her car as cover, and orders the suspect to drop the knife. The suspect refuses to drop the knife and threatens to gut her like a fish, but does not advance on the officer. After ordering the suspect to drop the knife and get on the ground several times, the suspect drops the knife and starts to walk toward the restaurant's side entrance. Can the officer use deadly force? *Yes,* the suspect has committed a crime involving the threatened use of serious physical harm and therefore is an immediate danger to the patrons in the restaurant. The interest of the patrons to be protected from a man who has, moments before, threatened a police officer with a knife outweighs the man's interest to be free from harm.

Remember, when the protection of the community outweighs the interest of the suspect to be free from harm, you can use deadly force. Do you know if the suspect has another weapon? Keep in mind the "One Plus Rule." If the suspect possesses a weapon, assume he possesses another of the same or more lethality. A suspect who threatens an officer with a knife, will in all probability, seriously harm or kill another person. You have a duty to protect the innocent people in the restaurant.

Those of you who say "I wouldn't have shot the suspect, your decision is not wrong. When it comes to using deadly force, the question is not **would you shoot?** The million-dollar question is **could you shoot**. *Tennessee v. Garner* is the legal standard for the use of deadly force by police; it is not a moral standard. As an officer, you must know the difference between **could** and **would** to properly manage the use of force incident. As my favorite professor in college told me, it is okay to break the rules of english when you write, if you know you are doing it. The law enforcement application: It is okay to say you would not shoot, as long as you know you could.

- A man walks into a bar (no, this is not the start to a joke), orders a drink, and tells the bartender "If anyone messes with me—I will take care of them" as he displays the handgun in his waistband. The bartender calls the police. Before the officers can arrive, the man leaves the bar. The bartender notifies the police that the armed man has left and gives the 911 call-taker a description of the suspect. An officer responding to the call observes a man fitting the suspect's description walking on the street near the front of the bar. The officer draws his handgun and performs a High Risk Stop on the suspect. The suspect refuses to obey the officer's verbal commands. At some point during the stop, the suspect shows the officer his handgun and says, "My gun is bigger than yours." It is summertime and a city park with children is next to the street where the suspect has been stopped. Without warning, the suspect turns and walks toward the park. Can the officer use deadly force? *Yes,* the suspect has demonstrated dangerousness through the threatened use of deadly force in the bar. Furthermore, the suspect—by being armed with a handgun—is an immediate threat to the children in the park. The safety of the children outweighs the suspect's interest to be free from harm.
- An officer responds to a report of a suspicious person looking into parked cars in a shopping mall's parking lot. The officer contacts the suspect and asks for identification. The suspect hands the officer an Arizona driver's license. The officer runs the suspect for wants and warrants via his portable radio. Dispatch informs him that the suspect has a felony warrant for forcible rape out of Maricopa County, Arizona. As the officer starts to draw his handgun, the suspect turns and runs. The suspect possesses no visible weapons.
Can the officer use deadly force to prevent his escape? *Yes,* the officer can use deadly force to prevent the escape of a suspect who he reasonably believes has committed a crime involving the use or threatened use of serious physical harm. In fact in this scenario, the officer has more than a reasonable belief; he has probable cause. An arrest warrant is based on probable cause, a higher standard of proof than reasonable belief. The interest of the officer's community to be free from the danger of a violent rapist outweighs the suspect's interest to be free from harm.

Plaintiff's attorneys find it puzzling that *Tennessee v. Garner* allows for the use of deadly force at a lower legal standard–reasonable belief–than is required to make a misdemeanor arrest–probable cause. The Supreme Court took into account that officers must make split-second deadly force decisions when they established the reasonable belief standard. A standard that is reality based and not founded on an academic legal theory.

The previous hypothetical scenarios are based on actual shootings where a judge determined that, based on the law, the use of deadly force was justified. Although it is impossible to present every situation where you may be forced to make a deadly force decision, the previously discussed scenarios will give you an understanding of the real world application of *Tennessee v. Garner*. The following appellate court ruling will clearly define the use of deadly force as outlined in Garner.

Plakas v. Drinski, 19 F. 3d 1143 (1994) addresses (in your favor) many of the claims a plaintiff's attorney will argue regarding your use of deadly force. The facts of the incident are as follows:

On February 2, 1991, at 9:30 p.m., members of the Newton County, Indiana, Sheriff's Department responded to the scene of a vehicle accident. When Sergeant Buddy King arrived, he found an unoccupied car in a water-filled ditch. When Sergeant King requested assistance, Corporal David Koby and two paramedics (Glen Cain and Steven Whitt) responded. While enroute, Glenn Cain saw Konstantino Plakas, wet from the waist down, walking along State Road 10–a mile from the accident scene. Cain stopped Plakas and transported him back to the scene of the accident.

As he interviewed Plakas, Corporal Koby smelled alcohol on his breath. Thereupon, he asked Plakas to go to the Sheriff's Department to take an intoxylizer breath test. Plakas volunteered to take the sobriety test. Corporal Koby frisked, handcuffed Plakas with his hands behind his back, and placed him in the rear-caged passenger compartment of his patrol car. For an unknown reason, the rear door handles of Corporal Koby's patrol car had not been removed.

While en route to the Sheriff's Department, Plaskas opened the rear car door. Corporal Koby heard the road noise and slowed his vehicle. As the vehicle slowed, Plakas jumped from the vehicle and fled into the snow-covered woods. Corporal Koby reported the escape and called for assistance. Sergeant King, Deputy Jeffrey Drinski, Indiana State Police Trooper Lucien Perras, and paramedic Glen Cain responded.

Plakas ran to his fiancé's house. The fiancé's father convinced Plakas to surrender to the police. Corporal Koby and Glen Cain were the first to contact Plakas at the residence. As they spoke with Plakas, he became "hysterical, slipped his handcuffs to the front of his body, and backed into a corner near a set of fireplace tools. Plakas picked up a fireplace poker with a hook end and a two to three-foot shaft. Gripping the poker with both hands, he rushed at Corporal Koby and struck him on the wrist, injuring him. Plakas exited through the front door of the residence followed by Deputy Drinski and Trooper Perras—with their guns drawn.

Deputy Drinski and Trooper Perras gave chase, shouting "Stop, Police." They followed Plakas into a clearing surrounded by thick hedges. Plakas turned and faced them. Deputy Drinski blocked the opening. For between fifteen to thirty minutes, Deputy Drinski and Trooper Perras attempted to talk Plakas into surrendering.

When the negotiations failed, Plakas pointed the poker at Deputy Drinski and said, "Either you're going to die or I am going to die here." Then, Plakas attempted to break through the hedges. Being unable to push through, Plakas turned back toward Drinski, raised the poker over his head, and charged. At the moment he charged, Plakas and Deputy Drinski were approximately fifteen feet apart. Deputy Drinski attempted to back away, but a tree and a near stumble stopped his retreat. When Plakas was two arm lengths away, Deputy Drinski fired one shot into Plakas' chest. Plakas died after he arrived at the hospital.

The attorney representing Plakas' Estate filed a federal excessive force lawsuit against Deputy Drinski and Newton County. A federal judge for the District of Indiana granted summary judgement to Deputy Drinski finding that he had lawfully used deadly force under the guidelines established in *Tennessee v. Garner.*

Plakas' attorney appealed the District Court's ruling to the Seventh Circuit Court of Appeals. In his brief to the court, the attorney claimed that Deputy Drinski and Newton County had a constitutional obligation to do more to preserve Plakas' life than they did. The attorney argued to the Appellate Court that:

- Deputy Drinski knew Plakas' identity; consequently, he should have let Plakas go, procured a warrant, and arrested him later when he was in a more rational state of mind.
- Deputy Drinski had a duty to use alternative control methods short of deadly force to resolve the situation.
- Deputy Drinski should have used all available alternatives before exercising deadly force.
- Deputy Drinski should have maintained a safe distance from Plakas and kept some form of barrier between them to eliminate the need for deadly force.

- Deputy Drinski should have deployed pepper spray to incapacitate Plakas or used a police dog to disarm him in lieu of deadly force.
- Newton County was liable because it failed to equip its sheriff's deputies with less-lethal weapons and train Deputy Drinski in unarmed self-defense tactics that would enable him to protect himself from a blow to the head with the fireplace poker.

The three judge appellate court panel ruled in favor of the District Court's summary judgment. In doing so, they stated:

- Officers are not required to use alternatives to avoid creating a deadly force situation.
- When deadly force becomes necessary, officers are not mandated to employ nondeadly alternatives.
- Law enforcement agencies are not constitutionally required to supply officers with less-than-lethal alternatives to use in lieu of deadly force.
- Officers are not required to be trained in the use of less-than-lethal options "beyond the acceptable training program already mandated" (P.O.S.T. standards).
- Officers are not required to maintain a specific distance or use a barrier to eliminate the need for deadly force.
- Officers are not required to retreat or "just walk away" in lieu of using deadly force.

Plakas v. Drinski more specifically defined when deadly force can be used under *Tennessee v. Garner*. Clearly, when an officer uses deadly force, he or she is only to be judged at the moment the officer pulls the trigger. And, the plaintiff's attorney cannot muddy the officer's decision to use deadly force with accusations that if only the officer would have, could have, or should have, the suspect would be alive and unharmed today.

Lastly, in discussing the Supreme Court's guidelines on the use of deadly force, I want to include *Brosseau v. Haugen*. Although, this case has no direct impact on the practical application of deadly force, it is a positive ruling that protects officers from "the sometimes hazy border between excessive and acceptable force." In Brosseau, the Supreme Court stated, "If the law at that time did not clearly establish that the officer's conduct would violate the Constitution, the officer should not be subject to liability or, indeed, even the burdens of litigation."

Brosseau v. Haugen, 35 F .3d 372 (2003), is the first U.S. Supreme Court ruling on an officer's use of deadly force since *Tennessee v. Garner*. The facts of the case are as follows:

Officers of the Puyallup, Washington, Police Department responded to a fight between Kenneth Haugen and two of his criminal cohorts at Haugen's mother's residence. The responding officers were aware that Haugen had an arrest warrant for possession of a controlled substance (nonviolent crime). When Haugen attempted to flee the scene in his Jeep, Officer Rochelle Brosseau smashed the driver's door window out with her handgun and hit Haugen several times in the head with the barrel and butt of her gun. As the Jeep pulled away, Officer Brosseau fired one round through the Jeep's rear-side window striking Haugen in the back. Officer Brosseau shot Haugen because she was "fearful for the other officers on foot who she believed were in the immediate area and for the occupied vehicles in Haugen's path and for any other citizens who might be in the area." So, in summary, Officer Brosseau shot Haugen to protect the other, unseen officers who were participating in the neighborhood canvas for Haugen and any unseen citizens who may be in the area.

The Supreme Court granted Officer Brosseau qualified immunity for the following reasons:

First, in order for an officer to violate a suspect's rights through the use of deadly force, there must be clearly established law stating that the use of force (under the specific circumstances of the incident in question) is unlawful. At the time of this shooting, there was not clearly established case law preventing an officer from shooting a suspect under these circumstances.

Second, *Tennessee v. Garner* is a general standard for the use of deadly force by police. Consequently, the evaluation of whether the use of deadly force violates a suspect's rights must be determined by the examination of the particular facts of the specific incident.

As I mentioned earlier, this ruling—for your application—has very little impact, if any, on *Tennessee v. Garner's* requirements for the use of deadly force. However, from a technically legal perspective, it is of great importance to your defense attorney in the event you use deadly force in the sometimes "hazy border between excessive and acceptable force."

A consideration that is very seldom discussed in use of force training is the moral component of using deadly force. The intentional taking of another person's life should not be viewed only through the prism of jurisprudence. The lawful killing of a human being is allowed under generally defined circumstances. Consequently, in the real world, an officer should not only act lawfully when using deadly force, but the officer should also act according to his or her own conscience and values. A use of force incident that involves the use of lawful and moral force is less likely to result in civil rights litigation. Do not misinterpret "moral force" as a religiously established standard, although for some officers it is. An officer does not need religious conviction to know intuitively when a use of force is "righteous" as well as lawful. The following incident illustrates my point:

A victim of domestic violence walked into the lobby of the police department to report the assault. When the officer interviewed the victim, he observed redness and swelling to the victim's eye. When asked about the condition of her boyfriend, she told the officer that he was under the influence of both heroin and meth. As the officers were preparing to leave the station, an officer warned that the suspect was a known drug addict, that he had AIDS, and during previous contacts he had made threats about stabbing officers with a dirty needle to infect them.

When the primary officer and his sergeant arrived at the suspect's residence, they announced their presence at the front door. The suspect yelled to the officers to "Come in." The officer ordered the suspect to come to the door several times. The suspect refused. After several failed attempts to get the suspect to open the door, it became apparent that they would have to enter on their own. Further, they speculated that the suspect probably had set up an ambush. When the officers attempted to open the front door, they discovered it was barricaded.

The officers forced the door open, searched the residence, and found the suspect in a small bedroom. The suspect was sitting on the bed with his back against the wall, with a pillow on his lap. The officer was concerned that the suspect had concealed a weapon under the pillow. Fearful that the suspect may be armed, he pulled the bedroom door closed, so that it was only open eight to ten inches. The gap gave the officer enough room to communicate with the suspect, maintain a good visual, and shoot the suspect if necessary. Further, if the suspect sprang off the bed without a weapon, the door could be closed and used as a barrier to impede the suspect's attack.

The officer negotiated with the suspect for several minutes. Then, without warning, the suspect threw the pillow off his lap, grabbed a large kitchen knife and a syringe full of AIDS infected blood (that had been concealed under the pillow), and stood up on the bed. The officer narrowed the gap in the door, used the door as cover, put his sights on the center of the suspect's chest, and took the slack out of the trigger. At that point, the officer made the decision that if the suspect made even the slightest movement forward he will kill him. The officer ordered the suspect to drop the weapons. The suspect backed up and placed his back against the wall near an open window. He held a large knife in one hand and the syringe in the other. The suspect warned that if the officer tried to make an arrest he would give the officer AIDS.

While the officer was negotiating with the suspect, the sergeant exited the residence to cover the open window. As the sergeant was covering the window, additional cover officers arrived and secured the inner perimeter. One of those officers was armed with a less-lethal shotgun.

Then, suddenly and without warning, the suspect jumped through the window. When he did, the primary officer heard his sergeant give the suspect verbal commands. When the primary officer exited the residence, he observed the suspect sitting on the ground with the weapons in his hands and the sergeant and the officer with a beanbag shotgun covering him at a distance of thirty feet.

The sergeant ordered the suspect to drop the weapons and lay face down on the ground, several times. The suspect refused to comply. Just when it appeared the suspect was going to prone out on the ground, he stood up and backed away from the officers. Then, as suddenly as he backed away, the suspect moved forward toward the sergeant. In response, the sergeant retreated, maintaining the thirty-foot reactionary gap. Suddenly, the suspect stopped his advance and retreated. At that point, the less-lethally-armed officer and the primary officer engaged the suspect. The officer with the beanbag shotgun ordered the suspect to stop and get on the ground. The officer's verbal commands caused the suspect to focus and advance on him. When the suspect was within twenty feet of the less-lethal officer, he fired a beanbag round that struck the suspect in the face. The projectile lodged in his jaw.

When the less-lethal projectile hit the suspect, he spun away from the officers and ran. The suspect was hit in the back with two additional beanbags. The third shot dropped the suspect face down. The suspect was taken into custody and transported to the hospital. After all the dust had settled, it was the general consensus of the emergency room doctor and nurses, the district attorney, the judge, and the officers who were not at the scene that the suspect should have been shot and killed.

In the post-use of force debriefing, the officers discussed why they did not shoot the suspect, even though they knew they were justified in doing so. The primary officer who had first confronted the armed suspect in the bedroom stated that he was fully prepared to kill the suspect, but he had a physical barrier between the suspect and himself, which offered him some protection. Further, the primary officer stated that he felt that if he had shot the suspect as he backed away toward the wall it would have been an execution and not a righteously justified shooting. Moreover, the officer explained that he had no moral aversion to killing the suspect and that he believed the world probably would be a better place without a drug addicted, spousal abusing, career criminal. But, he found no personal honor in shooting the miscreant, just because it was lawful.

The sergeant stated that his decision not to shoot was predicated on the reactionary gap and the mental "line in the sand" that he had drawn through it. If the suspect had crossed that line, he would have shot the suspect. For the sergeant, the act of crossing the imaginary line was the factor that changed the potential shooting from an execution to a righteous shooting.

In this incident, I believe there are two perspectives that are pertinent to the discussion of an officer's personal values and the use of deadly force. First, the primary officer's moral distinction between what he considered a lawful execution and a righteous shooting. Through personal introspection, the officer came to the conclusion that the use of deadly force (for him) requires more than just legal authority. It must fall within the perimeters established by his personal code of honor. Throughout history, the mores that regulated the use of deadly force have been formalized by codes of honor. In Europe, the medieval knights' actions during combat were dictated by the code of chivalry. In Japan, bushido was the samurai's code of honor that influenced his conduct in battle.

The second perspective is the mental "line in the sand" that the sergeant established as a determinant as to when to use deadly force. At any point during the confrontation, the sergeant would have been legally justified in using deadly force. But he chose not to shoot. Instead, the sergeant established a tactical and morale distinction between a lawful execution and a righteous shooting. Unlike the primary officer's completely moral reason for not shooting, the sergeant's decision not to shoot was based on a combination of distance, perceived threat, and conscience.

So, how does an officer's belief system effect liability? I believe the officer's reasons for not shooting support my previous admonishment: "Just because you can use force; it doesn't mean you should use force." For whatever reason each officer had for not shooting, the officers prevented a civil rights lawsuit by deciding to wait to use deadly force until it was necessary, not just legally justified.

Constitutional Standard Governing the Use of Nondeadly Force

Graham v. Conner, 109 S. Ct. 1865- (1989) defined the legal standard used in nondeadly force litigation. Further, in this ruling, the Supreme Court established the "Objective Reasonableness Standard," which is to be applied to both deadly and nondeadly use of force litigation. The facts of the incident are as follows:

On November 12, 1984, Dethorne Graham, a diabetic, felt the onset of an insulin reaction. He asked a friend, William Berry, to drive him to a convenience store to purchase orange juice to counteract the reaction. When Graham entered the store, he observed several people ahead of him in the checkout line. Concerned about the delay, he hurried out of the store and asked Berry to drive him to another friend's house to obtain the juice. Officer M. S. Connor–a member of the Charlotte, North Carolina, Police Department–observed Graham rush into the store, wander around, and quickly exit. Believing Graham's behavior was suspicious, Officer Conner followed Berry's car for about half a mile and then made an investigative stop. Although Berry told Officer Connor that Graham was suffering from a "sugar reaction," the officer ordered Berry and Graham to wait in their car while he determined what, if anything, had occurred at the store. When Officer Connor returned to his patrol car to call for backup, Graham exited the car, ran around it twice, sat down on the curb, and passed out.

At Officer Connor's request, other police officers arrived on the scene. While ignoring Berry's pleas to give Graham sugar, an officer rolled Graham over on the sidewalk and cuffed his hands behind his back. In response to Berry's request for sugar, another officer said: "I've seen a lot of people with sugar diabetes that never acted like this. Ain't nothing wrong with the mother f . . ker but drunk. Lock the son of the bitch up." Then, several officers lifted Graham up from behind, carried him over to Berry's car, and placed him face down on its hood. Regaining consciousness, Graham asked the officers to check his wallet for a diabetic decal that verified his medical condition. In response, one of the officers told him to "shut up" and shoved his face down against the car's hood. Then, four officers grabbed Graham and threw him headfirst into the passenger compartment of a caged police car. A friend of Graham's brought orange juice to the scene, but the officers refused to let Graham have it. Finally, Officer Connor received word that Graham had done nothing wrong at the convenience store. Thereupon, Officer Connor drove Graham home and released him.

From the officers' actions, Graham received a broken foot, cuts to his wrists, a shoulder injury, a bruised forehead, and suffers from an incessant ringing in his right ear. Graham filed a Section 1983 lawsuit accusing the officers of using excessive force during the investigatory stop. The Fourth Circuit Court of Appeals affirmed a lower court ruling that the force was not excessive. The Supreme Court overturned the decision and stated that the lower courts had applied the wrong legal standard (due process under the Fourteenth Amendment). The Supreme Court made it clear that all future claims of excessive force (deadly or nondeadly) during an arrest, investigatory stop, or other seizure of a free citizen are to be analyzed under the Fourth Amendment's "Objective Reasonableness Standard." The Objective Reasonableness Standard has two parts:

First, liability decisions are to be made only from the objective facts, as they are known at the time, from the perspective of a reasonable officer at the scene. The benefit of "20/20 hindsight" is not to be used in determining the reasonableness of the officer's force.

Second, an officer must consider the reasonableness of the seizure. This is accomplished by weighing the government's interests (to protect the community) against the individual's interests (to be free from harm or government intrusion). While the Supreme Court stated that "Reasonableness is incapable of precise definition or mechanical application," the Court identified four specific factors or circumstances to be considered when determining liability:

- Whether the suspect poses an immediate threat to the officer or others.
- Whether the suspect is actively resisting arrest.
- Whether the suspect is trying to escape.
- The severity of the crime.

Furthermore, the Supreme Court wrote in their opinion: "The calculus of reasonableness must embody allowance for the fact that police officers are often forced to make split-second judgements (in circumstances that are tense, uncertain, and rapidly evolving) about the amount of force that is necessary in a particular situation." Under *Graham v. Conner,* an officer is not required to use the least amount of force necessary to control the suspect or inmate. The force used needs only to be reasonable, giving consideration to the totality of the circumstances. However, keep in mind that a jury (consisting of members of the general public) determines whether your force was reasonable or excessive. Consequently, the least amount of force necessary to control the suspect or inmate is always objectively reasonable and easier to justify to a jury.

Graham v. Connor is the definitive standard regarding the proper use of nondeadly force. So, what does that mean? When detaining, handcuffing, and/or arresting a suspect or when defending yourself or another against nondeadly force, you must consider the following when deciding what level of nondeadly force is objectively reasonable:

- The "Officer versus Threat Factors" and "Influential Circumstances" that define when a suspect or inmate is an immediate threat to you or another. These factors and circumstances are explained in detail in Chapter 4.
- The severity and dangerousness of the crime the suspect is committing or has committed. The federal courts have ruled that traffic violations, passive resistance, minor disorderly conduct offenses, and lesser property crimes do not justify the use of serious levels of force, on their own merit.

- How rigorously or violently the suspect is resisting arrest or trying to escape. The level of force you can use to overcome a person's resistance is directly related to the type and intensity of the resistance that the person is offering. The courts have ruled that some forms of resistance: emotional outburst, bizarre behavior, and nonthreatening behavior only justifies lower levels of force. The Ninth Circuit Court of Appeals ruling in *Bryan v. MacPherson* explains this issue very well. Bryan is the next case we will discuss. In addition, the federal courts consider a force option's potential for injury in determining whether the use of nondeadly force was excessive. This question has been an important criterion in evaluating the reasonableness of an officer's use of an electronic control device (Taser) and the extended range impact weapon (beanbag). The following are the appellate court rulings that address the deployment of these force options.

Carl Bryan v. Brian MacPherson, 590 F. 3d 767 (2009) is the federal appellate court ruling that restricted the dart deployment of the Taser. The facts of the case are stated below:

In the summer of 2005, at a stoplight, Officer Brian MacPherson of the Coronado, California, Police Department stepped in front of Carl Bryan's vehicle and signaled to him not to proceed–Bryan was not wearing his seatbelt. Bryan immediately realized he had not buckled his seatbelt after receiving a speeding ticket from an earlier traffic stop. Becoming angry with himself over the prospects of another ticket, Bryan hit the steering wheel and yelled expletives to himself.

Without being told to exit, Bryan stepped out of his vehicle clad in only boxer shorts and tennis shoes. As Bryan stood outside his car, he appeared agitated, yelled gibberish, and hit his thighs with his hands. However, he did not verbally threaten the officer, nor did he attempt to flee. Bryan was standing twenty-five feet away from the officer when, without any warning, Officer MacPherson shot Bryan with his Taser. Immobilized by the Taser, Bryan fell face first onto the pavement. From the impact, he fractured four teeth and suffered facial contusions. Bryan was transported to the hospital by ambulance where a dart was removed with a scalpel.

Bryan filed an excessive force lawsuit against Officer MacPherson and the City of Coronado. As part of his force justification, Officer MacPherson stated he shot Bryan with the Taser because Bryan took a step toward him. Bryan denied taking a step. The physical evidence (the location of the darts and the direction that he fell) indicated that Bryan was facing away from the officer when he was tasered.

The District Court concluded that a reasonable jury could not find that Bryan presented an immediate danger to Officer MacPherson. Further, the court ruled that a reasonable officer would have known that the use of the Taser would cause pain and the resulting fall could cause injury. The court found that under the circumstances, it would have been clear to a reasonable officer that shooting Bryan with a Taser was unlawful. The Ninth Circuit Court of Appeals concurred with the lower court's ruling that Officer MacPherson's use of the Taser was excessive force.

Bryan v. MacPherson is an interesting ruling. The Ninth Circuit's opinion is well-thought-out and their position is thoroughly explained. I encourage you to review it for yourself. A summary of the Ninth Circuit's restrictions on the dart deployment of the Taser is as follows:

- Because of the high level of pain and the foreseeable risk of injury, the dart deployment of the Taser is a higher level of force than other less-than-lethal methods.
- Because the Taser's pain is far more intense, not localized, not gradual, and not within the victim's control, it is a greater level of force than pepper spray or mechanical pain compliance.
- The probe deployment of the Taser is classified as an "intermediate level of force."
- The probe deployment of the Taser cannot be used on drivers who only have committed a traffic violation.
- The probe deployment of the Taser cannot be used to control nonviolent misdemeanors or nondangerous mentally ill persons.
- The probe deployment of the Taser cannot be used for "passive resistance" or "minor resistance."
- An officer must issue a verbal warning and give the person an opportunity to comply before deploying the Taser, when reasonable to do so.
- Officers are required to consider what other tactics are available, if any, to resolve the situation before deploying the Taser in probe mode.
- An unarmed, stationary, suspect facing away from the officer at a distance of twenty feet is not an "immediate threat."

In the Bryan ruling, the Ninth Circuit issued a two-part ruling: First, Officer MacPherson used excessive force when he tasered Carl Bryan. And second, Officer MacPherson was not entitled to qualified immunity for his use of excessive force. Stated more simply, Officer MacPherson was civilly liable for his use of excessive force.

After their first ruling, the Ninth Circuit Court of Appeals agreed to reconsider their ruling on the Bryan case. In doing so, the Ninth Circuit reversed their denial of Officer MacPherson's summary judgement. In the Ninth Circuit's reversal opinion, they wrote:

Two other panels have recently, in cases involving different circumstances, concluded that the law regarding tasers is not sufficiently clearly established to warrant denying officers qualified immunity. *Mattos v. Agarano,* 590 F.3d 1082, 1089-90 (9th Cir. 2010); *Brooks v. City of Seattle,* 599 F.3d 1018, 1031 n.18 (9th Cir. 2010).

[21] Based on these recent statements regarding the use of tasers, and the dearth of prior authority, we must conclude that a reasonable officer in Officer MacPherson's position could have made a reasonable mistake of law regarding the constitutionality of the taser use in the circumstances that Officer MacPherson confronted in July 2005. Accordingly, Officer MacPherson is entitled to qualified immunity. *See Ctr. For Bio-Ethical Reform v. Los Angeles County Sheriff Dept.,* 533 F.3d 780, 794 (9th Cir. 2008).

CONCLUSION

Viewing the facts, as we must, in the light most favorable to Bryan, we conclude, for the purposes of summary judgment, that Officer MacPherson used unconstitutionally excessive force. However, a reasonable officer confronting the circumstances faced by Officer MacPherson on July 24, 2005, could have made a reasonable mistake of law in believing the use of the taser was reasonable. Accordingly, we REVERSE the district court's denial of summary judgment on the basis of qualified immunity.

In their reversal opinion, the Ninth Circuit reaffirmed their previous ruling that Officer MacPherson's use of the Taser on Carl Bryan was excessive force for all the previously stated reasons. Even though it is not specifically stated, it appears that (in their reversal ruling) the Ninth Circuit followed the opinion of the U.S. Supreme Court in BROSSEAU v. HAUGEN: "If the law at that time did not clearly establish that the officer's conduct would violate the Constitution, the officer should not be subject to liability or, indeed, even the burdens of litigation."

In *Bryan v. MacPherson,* the Ninth Circuit failed to specifically address the difference between being shocked with a probe deployment and being Drive Stunned. A few months after the Bryan ruling, the Ninth Circuit addressed the difference between the two methods of Taser deployment in the following case:

Brooks v. City of Seattle, 599 F .3d 1018 (2010) is the federal court ruling that determined the electronic control device (ECD) Drive Stun is a lesser use of force than a probe deployment. Here are the specifics of the case:

On November 23, 2004, Officer Juan Ornelas stopped Malaika Brooks for speeding in a school zone. As Brooks sat in her car, she refused to sign the traffic citation. In an effort to resolve the situation, Officer Jones arrived at the scene and unsuccessfully tried to convince Brooks to sign the citation. At Officer Ornelas' request, Sergeant Daman arrived and asked Brooks to sign the citation. When Brooks refused, Sergeant Daman told the officers to arrest her.

The officers told Brooks she was under arrest and ordered her to step out of her car. When she refused to exit her car, Officer Jones showed Brooks his Taser, displayed its arc in Drive Stun mode, and told her it would hurt "extremely bad" if she were shocked with it. In response, Brooks told the officers that she was pregnant and she needed to use the restroom.

As Brooks sat in the car, the officers discussed among themselves what area to Drive Stun–deciding to shock Brooks on the thigh. Prior to applying the Taser, Officer Ornelas applied a pain compliance control hold by bringing Brooks' left arm behind her back. Brooks reacted by stiffening her body and clutching the steering wheel with her free hand. Because the control hold was ineffective in removing Brooks, Officer Jones Drive Stunned Brooks' thigh through her sweat pants. She yelled and honked the car's horn, but she refused to exit. Officer Jones Drive Stunned Brooks on the shoulder and neck. The Drive Stuns caused Brooks to release the steering wheel and move to the right, which allowed the officers to pull her from the car. Brooks was arrested for refusing to sign the notice (citation) and resisting arrest.

Brooks filed an excessive force lawsuit in federal court. The district court ruled that the officers violated Brooks' constitutional rights. The City of Seattle appealed the lower court's ruling. The Ninth Circuit determined that the officers did not use excessive force when they Drive Stunned Brooks. In forming their opinion, the Ninth Circuit stated:

- Because the "Drive Stun" mode involves touching the body (not firing darts) and causes only temporary, localized pain (not neuromuscular incapacitation), the Drive Stun is less force than a probe deployment.
- The Drive Stun is equivalent to pain compliance techniques that cause bruises, pinched nerves, and broken wrists.
- Drive Stun burn marks and scars are far less serious than a dart penetrating the flesh, incapacitating muscle contractions, and injuries from an impact with objects from a Taser induced free fall.
- Before Drive Stunning Brooks, the officers gave multiple warnings that a Taser would be used, explained its effects, and demonstrated its electrical arc. Consequently, Brooks had control over the amount of pain she experienced from the Drive Stun(s).
- When the officers discovered Brooks was pregnant, they took steps to employ a localized type of force away from her stomach. This indicated that the officers considered other force options prior to tasering Brooks.

In *Brooks v. City of Seattle* the appellate court formally established what should have been determined by common sense–the Drive Stun is a lesser use of force than a probe deployment.

Deorle v. Rutherford, 272 F, 3d 1271 (2001) is the appellate court ruling that restricted the use of impact munitions. The details of the incident are as follows:

On September 9, 1996, Richard Deorle–upset at being diagnosed with Hepatitis C, having consumed a half-pint of vodka, and ingested Interferon–began behaving erratically. He threatened suicide, screamed, and banged on the walls of his house. Concerned that her husband might harm himself, Mrs. Deorle called the police for help and then left the residence with her children.

When the officers arrived, they found Deorle outside of his house. Though verbally abusive, he was physically compliant and generally followed all the officers' instructions. From his position on the outer perimeter, Officer Rutherford did not observe Deorle touch or attack anyone. Nor, did he receive any report of any such action on Deorle' s part. Officer Rutherford did, however, hear Deorle yell that he would "kick his ass."

After wandering around his property, Deorle walked with a steady gait toward Officer Rutherford with a can or bottle in his hand. When Deorle reached a predetermined point (a mentally drawn line in the sand), Officer Rutherford shot Deorle with a beanbag projectile. Prior to shooting Deorle, Officer Rutherford did not order him to stop or drop the bottle or can. Further, Officer Rutherford did not warn Deorle that he would be shot if he did not stop. The cloth-cased projectile struck Deorle in the face, knocked him off his feet, and lodged "half out of his eye." As a result, Deorle suffered multiple fractures to his cranium, loss of his left eye, and had lead shot embedded in his skull. Subsequently, he filed a civil rights lawsuit against Officer Rutherford. The Ninth Circuit Court of Appeals ruled that Officer Rutherford used excessive force when he shot Deorle with the less-lethal round. In forming their opinion the Court stated:

"The force applied through the use of the cloth-cased shot can kill a person if it strikes his head or the left side of his chest at a range of under fifty feet. Such force is much greater than that applied through the use of pepper spray, or a painful compliance hold (Orcutt Police Nunchakus or using wrist and arm-twisting and pressure-point holds) and more likely to cause a life-threatening injury than most dog bites." Furthermore, the Ninth Circuit stated that before using an extended range impact weapon (beanbag), the officer must give a verbal warning, if reasonable.

It should not be a surprise to anyone that the courts have found that a ballistic bag filled with lead shot fired from a 12-gauge shotgun could cause serious physical injury or death. Even the makers of impact munitions describe their products as less-lethal and not less-than-lethal. Common sense dictates that we should have come to this conclusion on our own, but as lawsuits illustrate common sense is often not so common.

Constitutional Standard Governing the Stop and Frisk of a Suspect

An issue that surfaces quite often in police excessive force cases is the stop and frisk of a suspect for officer safety. Ask most officers why they stopped and searched a suspect and they will tell you: "Officer Safety." When you ask an officer to expound on why he stopped and searched the suspect, he will say "OFFICER SAFETY" louder. As if after saying it louder, you're supposed to say, "Oh, yeah, I completely understand the reason—now." I watched an officer on the witness stand do just that as a defendant in a lawsuit. He lost the litigation. As you have learned, perception is important in winning lawsuits.

In a recent lawsuit, two officers used force to remove an intoxicated patron from a bar. In the primary officer's deposition, the plaintiff's attorney asked the officer for his justification for frisking the suspect. The following is an excerpt from the officer's deposition:

Question: Did you do a search of Mr. . . . ?

Answer: I did a frisk to make sure he didn't have any weapons.

Question: What were the exigent circumstances that justified the frisk?

Answer: A frisk that I am allowed to do for my safety to make sure they don't have any weapons.

Question: What were the circumstances that made you believe that was possible?

Answer: He was wearing clothing, and the clothing had pockets, I believe, and people keep weapons in their pockets. And, also, he had a waistband on his pants, and people tuck weapons and things of that nature in their pants and shoes.

Question: I think we all have waistbands on our clothes. Does that mean that you have exigent circumstances to pat us down?

Answer: Yeah. Anytime I have contact with people at work as a police officer, and they are a suspect or even sometimes a bystander in a situation, I frisk them just for my safety. It's . . . you know, especially if they're wearing baggy clothing or loose clothing. You just always frisk people for weapons to be safe. And, from my training, what I've been trained and what I've been taught, I'm allowed to do that with or without consent.

Question: To just anybody?

Answer: If I have—if I'm able to articulate that I believe they might have weapons on them, and from my training that I receive.

At the time of the deposition, the officer had less than three years of law enforcement experience. Based on his explanation for frisking the suspect, what is your perception of the officer? Do you believe he is knowledgeable regarding the basic legal requirements of a "Stop and Frisk?" What is the plaintiff attorney's perception of this officer? And you wonder why attorneys think we are dumb? The city settled the lawsuit.

Possessing the knowledge to explain your justification to a jury for the "stop and frisk" is equally as important as having the legal authority to detain and search. Consequently, in this section, we will discuss the Supreme Court ruling of *Terry v. Ohio.*

Terry v. Ohio, 392 U.S. 1-(1968) outlines the lawful authority of a police officer to stop and frisk a suspect for officer safety. However, keep in mind, the standard applied to determine if the force used to conduct the stop and frisk was reasonable is *Graham v. Conner.* The facts of the case are as follows:

On October 31, 1963, at approximately 2:30 p.m., Detective Martin McFadden—in plain clothes—was patrolling the downtown area of Cleveland, Ohio. Detective McFadden had been a police officer for over 39 years, a detective for 35 years, and had been assigned to patrol the downtown area for shoplifters and pickpockets for 30 years.

Detective McFadden observed two suspicious men (Terry and Chilton) on a street corner. He watched the men proceed alternately back and forth along an identical route, pausing to stare into the same store window. They did this a total of 24 times. After each pass, the two would confer at the street corner. During one of these passes, they were joined by a third suspect (Katz)—who hurried off.

Detective McFadden, believing they were "casing a job—a stickup," followed the two men and watched them rejoin the third suspect in front of a store a couple of blocks from the cased store. Detective McFadden approached the three suspects, identified himself as a police officer, and asked their names. The men "mumbled something." Fearing the men may be armed, he spun Terry around, patted down the outside of his clothing, and found a handgun in an overcoat pocket. Due to the design of the pocket, McFadden was unable to remove the gun. He ordered all three suspects into the store. Detective McFadden removed Terry's coat and retrieved a revolver. Then, Detective McFadden ordered the suspects to face the wall with their hands raised. When he patted Chilton down, he found a revolver in his outside overcoat pocket. No weapons were found on Katz. When Detective McFadden patted down the three suspects, he did not put his hands under their outer garments until after he felt the guns.

All three suspects were taken to the police station; Terry and Chilton were charged with carrying concealed weapons. In a pretrial hearing, the judge denied the motion to suppress and admitted the weapons into evidence. The weapons were admitted on the grounds that Detective McFadden had cause to believe that Terry and Chilton were acting suspiciously; therefore, their interrogation was warranted. Thereupon, Detective McFadden for his own protection had a right to pat down their outer clothing, having reasonable cause to believe that the suspects might be armed. The court identified a difference between an investigatory stop and an arrest. Furthermore, the court identified the difference between a "frisk" of the outer clothing for weapons and a full search for evidence of a crime.

Terry and Chilton were convicted. The state appellate court affirmed the conviction, and the State Supreme Court dismissed the appeal. On June 10, 1968, the U.S. Supreme upheld Terry's and Chilton's convictions. In the Supreme Court's opinion, the justices stated "Officer McFadden, on the basis of his experience, had reasonable cause to believe that the defendants were acting suspiciously. . . . Purely for his own protection, the officer had the right to pat down the outer clothing of these men, who he had reasonable cause to believe might be armed. . . . The frisk was essential to the proper performance of the officer's investigatory duties, for without it the answer to the police officer may be a bullet."

In *Terry v. Ohio,* the Supreme Court ruled that a police officer may "stop and frisk" a suspect for officer safety if based on the officer's training and experience:

- The officer reasonably believes the person has committed a crime or is about to commit a crime.
- The officer reasonably believes the lawfully stopped person poses a threat to the officer's safety and/or the safety of others.
- The search is limited to the exterior of the person's outer clothing.
- A search for weapons in the absence of probable cause to arrest must be strictly based on the exigencies of the situation.

Here are guidelines for positively influencing a jury's perception of your "Officer Safety Search" and the handcuffing of a suspect for officer safety:

- If you are going to use your experience as justification for the "Stop and Frisk," you need have an impressive number of years of service (McFadden had thirty-nine). If you have less than five years of police experience, be humble, and emphasize your training for the justification for the stop and frisk. When using your training as a justification, you must specifically state what training you have received and why it is relevant to this particular situation. Additionally, if you are going to use statistical information in your justification, you must be able to explain how it applies to your specific "Stop and Frisk." Boldly stating on the witness stand, "Based on my training and experience . . . ," and then not having much of either does not support your search.

• Be able to intelligently articulate the reasons why the person to be searched and/or handcuffed is an immediate threat to your and/or a third person's safety. Do not rely on just the general reason of "Officer Safety." "Officer Safety" is a term and a state of being; it is not a defendable justification.

• Tell the person he is not under arrest and that he is being searched and handcuffed for your and his safety. Telling the suspect that he is not under arrest, is the first step in building your proactive defense against a false arrest lawsuit.

• Conduct an exterior search of the person's outer clothing for weapons prior to handcuffing the person for "Officer Safety" to illustrate the concern you have for your personal safety.

Law Enforcement officers detain, search, and handcuff people routinely for their safety. Because this police practice is performed so frequently, it often becomes a meaningless habit–you do it without any forethought as to why. For police officers, meaningless habits are bad habits. Every action you perform regarding the stop, detention, search, and arrest of a suspect should be done deliberately with the justification for the action in mind and with the expectation that you will be sued.

Use of Force and the Americans with Disabilities Act

In the past decade, plaintiff attorneys have discovered an additional area of police liability. The American with Disabilities Act is being used more and more to sue criminal justice officers for their actions involving the detainment, restraint, and confinement of suspects and inmates.

AMERICANS WITH DISABILITIES ACT of 1990 (Public Law 101-336) enacted by the 101st Congress of the United States requires that public entities make reasonable accommodations for people with disabilities. Title II of the ADA act specifically authorizes enforcement under the terms of the Rehabilitation Act of 1973. In doing so, an injured suspect or inmate is entitled to a jury trial, compensation for damages, and attorney's fees. You, as a criminal justice officer, are an agent of a public entity. And therefore are required to modify your procedures to accommodate a suspect's or inmate's disability when reasonable and safe to do so. ADA lawsuits filed against criminal justice officers and their agencies include the failure to make a reasonable accommodation for people with sight and hearing impairment, drug addiction, mental illness, and physical disabilities. By far, the most common ADA lawsuit filed against criminal justice officers involves the physical restraint of a detained or arrested suspect.

The following are examples of two ADA lawsuits filed against criminal justice officers and their agencies. The first incident involves the arrest of a disabled suspect on a warrant. The second incident involves a hearing impaired man who was arrested and lodged in the county jail.

A municipal police officer stopped a vehicle for a traffic violation. When the officer ran the driver for wants and warrants, the dispatcher informed the officer that the driver had a warrant for "Failure to Appear" for a misdemeanor crime. The officer told the driver that he was under arrest for a warrant regarding his failure to appear in court. The officer told the driver to turn around and place his hands behind his back. Before the driver turned around, he told the officer that he was a former minor league baseball player, and he had suffered an injury to his elbow. Further, he stated that a surgery was performed to repair his elbow, and it left his arm unable to be bent. Additionally, the driver told the officer that if he would look at his elbow he would see a large surgical scar.

The officer ignored the driver's warning about his physical disability, forced his arms behind his back, and handcuffed him. As he was being handcuffed, the driver complained of extreme pain in his elbow and forearm. The driver was placed in the patrol car and transported to the county jail. The driver filed two lawsuits against the officer: An excessive force lawsuit and a lawsuit under ADA. During the discovery process, the officer's attorney received color photographs of the driver's large scar–it ran from his triceps, down the outer forearm, and ended a few inches above his wrist. The city settled the lawsuit.

In the second example, a hearing impaired man with mental illness issues was arrested for domestic violence. As the officers responded to the scene, the city's dispatch center failed to inform the officers that the suspect was hearing impaired and mentally ill. The suspect fought with the police officers who, in response, shocked him several times with a Taser and used a takedown technique to control him. The suspect received an injured shoulder during the struggle. The suspect was arrested and lodged at the county jail.

At the jail, the deputies failed to give the suspect an American sign language interpreter or otherwise inform him "of his rights as a disabled person." The suspect filed a lawsuit against the officers for excessive force, a lawsuit against the city dispatch center for negligence, and an ADA lawsuit against the county jail.

A federal jury determined that the officers did not use excessive force. However, the jury did find the dispatch center liable for negligence and the county liable for violating the American with Disabilities Act. The county was ordered to pay $100,000.00 in punitive damages and $7,500.00 in actual damages. The city was ordered to pay $50,000.00.

The majority of ADA lawsuits involve an injury to a pre-existing condition, injury, or limitation. The most common areas of injury are the neck, spine, shoulder, elbow, forearm, wrist, hip, or knee. The most common activity that causes the injury is cooperative or high-risk handcuffing. Fortunately, you can minimize the potential for an ADA lawsuit and positively influence the jury's perception of your actions with a little common sense and sensitivity. The following are a few things you can do to prevent or win an ADA lawsuit:

- Before you handcuff a cooperative person, ask if he or she has any pre-existing conditions or limitations that will impair his or her ability to be handcuffed with the arms behind his or her back. This not only prevents injury to the person; it makes you appear caring to the jury.
- If the person or another informs you of a preexisting condition/injury, check the person for scars, limited mobility, and/or medication. Yes, criminals do lie. So, you never take the person's statement regarding a preexisting condition or injury at face value. Always, evaluate his or her condition for yourself.
- If the person has a physical limitation, modify the handcuffing procedure if reasonable: use a waist-chain or multiple pairs of handcuffs. If you don't carry more than two pairs of handcuffs or a waist-chain in your equipment bag, buy them. A minor personal investment in equipment can save you from the burdens of a lawsuit and your city, county, or state the cost of ADA litigation.

When dealing with ADA issues, keep in mind it must be reasonable under the circumstances to make the accommodation. If an accommodation will threaten your safety or the safety others, it is not reasonable to make the accommodation. Also, if the person is physically resisting arrest, it may be impossible to make a reasonable accommodation. Ultimately it is your responsibility to justify why an accommodation was unreasonable in your written report.

Corrections' Use of Force

The use of force by corrections deputies and officers is defined by two constitutional standards: the Fourth Amendment as established by *Graham v.*

Conner for pretrial detainees and the Eighth Amendment as defined in *Whitley v. Albers* and *Hudson v. McMillian* for convicted inmates.

Using a police nondeadly use of force standard in a correctional setting can be hard to get one's head around, but that is the standard used for pretrial detainees–inmates arrested, held for trial, but not yet adjudicated. The legal theory behind this odd marriage is that the inmate is innocent until proven guilty and, therefore, entitled to the protections of the Fourth Amendment to be free from unnecessary government intrusion. In theory, when you use force on a pretrial detainee, it is a seizure under the Fourth Amendment, even though it occurs inside a correctional facility and the inmate is not free to leave. Therefore, all four elements of the "Objective Reasonableness Standard" under Graham apply.

The Eighth Amendment protects convicted inmates from cruel and unusual punishment. In the Supreme Court rulings of *Whitley v. Albers* (and, then more clearly defined in *Hudson v. McMillian*) the Court ruled that force which is applied maliciously and sadistically–not for a legitimate correctional objective–is excessive. The corrections profession defines its operational mandates as "legitimate correctional objectives." The legitimate correctional objectives for jails and prisons are to maintain control, order, health, safety, and security of their correctional facility. These objectives ensure the safety of the community, correctional staff, and the inmates.

Because a convicted inmate is not entitled to all the civil protections of a pretrial detainee, the burden of proof for excessive force under the Eighth Amendment is higher than that of the Fourth Amendment.

Whitley v. Albers, 475 U.S. 312-(1986), is the Supreme Court ruling that changed the standard for determining excessive force under the Eighth Amendment's "cruel and unusual punishment" clause. Whitley changed the standard from the "deliberate indifference" test to the "unnecessary and wanton infliction of pain and suffering applied maliciously and sadistically for the very purpose of causing harm" standard. The facts of the incident are as follows:

On June 27, 1980, at about 8:30 P.M., inmates of Cell Block "A" at the Oregon State Penitentiary rioted over what they perceived as mistreatment by Officers Kemper and Fitts. As a result, Officer Kemper was assaulted, but he was able to escape. Officer Fitts was taken hostage and held in a cell on the second tier. The inmates barricaded themselves in the cellblock and warned the penitentiary staff that if they attempted a rescue the officer would be killed.

At about 10:30 P.M., Captain Harol Whitley made the decision to breach the barricade and rescue the officer. Captain Whitley armed his officers with shotguns and told them to shoot any inmate that climbed the stairs to the second tier, since that inmate would be climbing the stairs to kill Officer Fitts. As Captain Whitley and the other officers cleared the barrier, Officer Kennicott fired two warning shots. Then, he saw Inmate Albers run up the stairs. Officer Kennicott shot Inmate Albers in the knee. Another inmate was shot on the stairs and several more inmates were shot and wounded on the lower tier. Captain Whitley made his way to the second tier and rescued Officer Fitts. Inmate Albers sued, claiming the shooting was excessive and it violated his right to be free from cruel and unusual punishment.

The Supreme Court disagreed and established the following considerations for determining if the force used on an inmate was excessive:

- A corrections officer's use of force cannot be held to violate the Eighth Amendment unless the force was applied "maliciously and sadistically for the very purpose of causing harm."
- The EighthAmendment forbids the "unnecessary and wanton infliction of pain."
- Corrections officers must balance the need to maintain or restore discipline through force against the risk of injury to the inmate(s).
- Was the force used in good faith to maintain or restore discipline or "maliciously and sadistically for the very purpose of causing harm?" "When corrections officers maliciously and sadistically use force to cause harm, contemporary standards of decency are always violated."

With this ruling, there was considerable discussion and disagreement within the corrections community as to whether Whitley applied only to riot situations or all situations where force was used by corrections officers. The question was finally answered by the Supreme Court with *Hudson v. McMillian.*

Hudson v. McMillan, 962 F .2d 522 (1992) clarified the requirements under "Whitley" and made it clear "Whitley" applied to all use of force situations, not just to prison riots. The facts of the case are as follows:

On October 30, 1983, Keith Hudson was an inmate at the state penitentiary in Angola, Louisiana. During the early morning of the 30th, Inmate Hudson and Officer McMillian argued. As a result, Officers McMillian and Woods handcuffed and shackled Hudson to move him to the "administrative lockdown" area.

On the way to the lockdown area, Officer McMillian punched Hudson in the mouth, eyes, chest, and stomach, while Officer Woods held him from behind. Then, Officer McMillian held Hudson, and Officer Woods kicked and punched him. To make the situation even more outrageous, Supervisor Mezo—who told the officers "not to have too much fun"—witnessed the beating and did not intervene. As a result of the beating, Hudson suffered minor bruises and swelling of his face, mouth, and lip. His teeth were loosened, and his partial dental plate was cracked–making it unusable for several months.

Hudson sued the three officers in federal court alleging a violation of the Eighth Amendment's protection against cruel and unusual punishment. Hudson agreed to have his case heard before a federal magistrate, who found the officers had used excessive force. The case was appealed, and the appellate court overturned the magistrate's ruling. The Court of Appeals for the Fifth Circuit held that an inmate alleging the use of excessive force in violation of the Eighth Amendment must prove:

- Significant injury.
- The injury was directly and only inflicted from the use of force that was clearly excessive to the need.
- The action constituted an unnecessary and wanton infliction of pain.
- The force was objectively unreasonable.

The Court of Appeals determined that the officers' use of force was objectively unreasonable because Hudson's action required no force. Furthermore, the actions by the officers were clearly excessive force and constituted unnecessary and wanton infliction of pain. However, because Hudson's injuries were minor and required no medical attention, his claim of excessive force did not meet the "significant injury" component of the Court's four-part test. Therefore, the Court concluded there was no Eighth Amendment violation, and overturned the lower court's finding of excessive force.

The U.S. Supreme Court accepted three components of the Fifth Circuit Court's four-part test for determining excessive force. However, the High Court ruled that the force used by a corrections officer need not cause "significant injury" to an inmate to be deemed "cruel and unusual punishment" under the Eighth Amendment.

In *Hudson v. McMillian,* the Supreme Court reaffirmed the standards set previously in *Whitley v. Albers.* Furthermore, the Court makes clear their stand on the relationship between the level of injury an inmate receives and its relationship to the claim of excessive force. The Court stated "When prison officials maliciously and sadistically use force to cause harm, contemporary standards of decency always are violated. This is true whether or not significant injury is evident. Otherwise, the Eighth Amendment would permit any physical punishment, no matter how diabolic or inhuman, inflicting less than some arbitrary quantity of injury."

The important points in *Hudson v. McMillian* are:

- The guidelines established by "Whitley" apply to all claims of excessive force under the Eighth Amendment, not just to riot or hostage situations.
- Force use by corrections officers need not cause a "significant injury" to be cruel and unusual under the Eighth Amendment.
- In order for an inmate to prove an excessive force case under the Eighth Amendment, he or she must prove: The action constituted an unnecessary and wanton infliction of pain. The injury must be directly and only the result of the use of force that was clearly excessive to the need. The excessiveness of the force was objectively unreasonable–as defined by *Graham v. Connor's* objective reasonableness standard.

In addition, the federal and state courts have recognized that corrections deputies and officers can use reasonable force to:

- Protect themselves, other correctional staff, and inmates from violence.
- Maintain the order, safety, and security of the correctional facility.
- Protect an inmate from self-injury.
- Prevent damage to facility property.
- Prevent an escape.

Failure to Train

A criminal justice agency can incur liability for more than excessive force or an ADA violation. When a department deliberately chooses not to provide training to its officers and that decision causes harm to a person, the "deliberate indifference" to that training need can violate a person's civil rights.

City of Canton v. Harris, 489 U.S. 378-(1989) is the Supreme Court's ruling that established that an agency's deliberate indifference to a training need that causes an injury to a person can violate that person's civil rights. The following is an account of the events that led to this unique court ruling:

In April 1978, officers of the Canton, Ohio, Police Department arrested Geraldine Harris. Harris was brought to the police station in a patrol wagon. When she arrived, Harris was found sitting on the floor of the vehicle. The officers asked her if she needed medical attention, and she responded with an incoherent remark. After she was brought inside the station, Harris slumped to the floor on two occasions. Fearing she would fall again, the officers left Harris lying on the floor. The officers never summoned medical attention for her. After about an hour, Harris was released to family members, and taken by an ambulance (provided by her family) to a nearby hospital. Harris was diagnosed as suffering from several emotional ailments and was hospitalized for one week. After being discharged from the hospital, Harris received subsequent outpatient treatment for an additional year.

Per the Canton Police Department's policy, the shift commanders were authorized to determine, in their sole discretion, whether a detainee required medical care. However, the shift commanders were not provided with any specialized training to make a determination as to when to summon medical care for an injured detainee. The Supreme Court upheld the Sixth Circuit Court of Appeals' ruling that the city's "deliberate indifference" to the training that was required for a shift commander to determine if a detainee required medical attention, and the city's decision not to provide it, violated Harris'constitutional rights.

"Deliberate indifference" is a very high standard to prove. The plaintiff's attorney must prove that your department required you to perform a specific task or function, and the department made a deliberate decision not to provide you with the training necessary to properly perform that task or function. Then, the plaintiff's attorney must prove that your department's "deliberate indifference" to that need for training caused the plaintiff's injury or death. The following is a classic example of "failure to train" liability:

A mentally ill man had an altercation with police officers on a street corner in his neighborhood. In front of a growing crowd of his neighbors, the officers used their batons to pummel the suspect into submission. After the suspect was controlled and handcuffed, the officers laid the suspect facedown on the sidewalk. As the officers stood around the handcuffed suspect, he went into respiratory failure. Unfortunately, for the suspect, the police department's command staff had previously made the decision not to provide CPR and first aid training to their officers to save money in their training budget. The command staff based their decision on an erroneous belief that the paramedics' response time to the scene was so short that there was no need for their officers to receive CPR and first aid training.

Consequently, the untrained officers stood by (as the onlooking neighbors pleaded with the officers to help him) as the suspect died on the sidewalk for all to see. Of course, the local newspaper had a full-page article describing the incident, complete with a large photograph of his elderly parents in mourning. As a result, the city settled the lawsuit for $380,000.00.

Tragically, this is what happens when criminal justice administrators lack the foresight to recognize the potential liability in their decisions, and their officers fail to properly manage the use of force incident: lawsuits get settled and the departments gets bashed publicly for being indifferent to the needs of the community.

You may not be able to prevent all failure to train lawsuits, but you can implement a proactive defense against them. To create a proactive defense, your department must provide current and relevant training that is conducted by qualified instructors. The training must be directed by performance objectives and the officer's performance must be recorded on lab sheets. The content of the training classes must be documented with current lesson plans. In addition, the officer's attendance must be documented in a training record that lists the date, course title, and the number of hours per course/topic.

In this chapter, we explored the U. S. Supreme Court's requirements for the use of nondeadly and deadly force by criminal justice officers. In that exploration, we discovered that the Supreme Court requires a person to be an immediate threat to you or others before you can lawfully use nondeadly and deadly force. In the next chapter, we will discuss the factors and circumstances that define when a person is an immediate threat to you and others. I will explain the principles of use of force justification and the criteria for the justification for the escalation of force.

Chapter 4

THREAT ASSESSMENT

USE THE TERM "THREAT"–NOT
SUSPECT, INMATE, OR WORSE

The Supreme Court identified an immediate threat to the officer or others as a lawful reason for the use of nondeadly and deadly force. However, the Court did not define the factors or circumstances that constitute an immediate threat. In this chapter, we will discuss those factors and circumstances. But first, I would like to address the benefits of using the term "Threat" instead of "suspect" or "inmate" in your use of force justification. Using the term "Threat" has three distinct benefits.

First, by using the term "Threat" in your defensive tactics and use of force training, it reinforces to your officers that they are only justified in using force when the inmate or suspect is an immediate threat to the officer or others. As you have learned, properly managing perceptions is an important strategy in managing liability. By using the term "Threat" in lieu of inmate or suspect, it demonstrates to the plaintiff's attorney that your use of force training is in accordance with the Supreme Court's guidelines on the use of nondeadly and deadly force. The more credible your use of force training appears the less likely the plaintiff's attorney is to follow through with the lawsuit.

Second, using the term "Threat" in your use of force explanations and training discourages the use of "pet names" that officers develop for inmates and suspects. Pet names such as dirtbag, hairball, puke, asshole, or worse. Even though some pet names may be humorous and even actuate, they are inappropriate law enforcement vernacular. The use of these derogatory terms gives the impression that you are callused and insensitive. Their use will taint a jury's view of you and your use of force. I know you are wondering when did he get all warm and fuzzy? When I learned I could be prosecuted for not positively managing the perceptions of witnesses when using

101

force on a suspect or inmate–that's when.

Jurors have an innate respect and trust of criminal justice officers. As an example of this deeply rooted trust, in a lawsuit involving the shooting of an unarmed suspect, the jury deliberated for several days only to come to an impasse on a verdict. When the plaintiff's attorney questioned the jurors as to why they could not reach a verdict, one juror stated that he believed that whenever an officer uses force it is justified regardless of the circumstances. As this example illustrates, the credibility deck is stacked in your favor, so don't diminish the natural support that jurors have for you by using derogatory terms.

Third, I have found substituting "Threat" for suspect or inmate is beneficial in explaining an officer's use of force to jurors. In federal court, expert witnesses are often not allowed to testify to the reasonableness of the officer's use of force–some judges feel that is only a question for the jury to answer. But an expert can testify about the training an officer receives. Jurors have no actual experience in using force on an inmate or suspect; consequently, they form a conceptual understanding of the use of force through the oral explanations of the officer and the expert witness. The terms you use can have a positive impact on a jury's perception of your use of force. When jurors learn that the term "Threat" is used to instill that force is only justified when the person is an "immediate threat" to the officer or others, the jurors often conclude that the officer's use of force was in accordance with his training, and therefore, reasonable. As you can see, managing a jury's perception of the use of force starts with a training program that positively influence perceptions.

Immediate Threat

The United States Supreme Court stated criminal justice officers may use nondeadly and deadly force when a person is an immediate threat to the officer or others. Unfortunately, the court did not define the elements that are required to establish an inmate or a suspect as an "immediate threat." Accordingly, we must look elsewhere in the law for guidance. Under common law, a prosecutor must prove a suspect's intent, means, and opportunity to get a criminal conviction of an intentionally committed crime. There is no more appropriate legal concept to use in establishing when an inmate or suspect is an immediate threat to the officer or others. As a result, in a civil excessive force lawsuit, you must prove the suspect or inmate demonstrated the intent, possessed the means, and had the opportunity to inflict harm to you or another to be considered an "immediate threat." The following is an explanation of each element as they apply to the use of nondeadly and deadly force.

INTENT. The person must demonstrate his/her intent to resist being controlled or to inflict physical injury, serious physical jury, or death. The intent can be demonstrated physically (menacing body language or aggressive/violent behavior) or indicated verbally. Or, a combination of the two demonstrative behaviors. The physical demonstration of the Threat's willingness to engage in combat with an officer can range from subtle challenging body language to overt rage. Taking a step back, blading his body, and giving you that "thousand yard stare" is an example of challenging body language. Although the Threat is making no verbal threats, his body language indicates that a physical assault is imminent. Consequently, this is not the time to get all warm and fuzzy and tell the Threat: "It looks like someone needs a hug." Based on the Threat's communicated intent to fight, the escalation of force is justified.

MEANS: The person must have the physical capabilities to carry out the articulated or perceived aggression. The mechanism for inflicting injury, serious injury, or death can be through superior size and strength, by the use of a weapon, multiple assailants, or superior fighting skill. For example, a six-foot and six-inch tall officer who weights two hundred and eighty pounds, with a body builder's physique, confronts a five-foot tall and one hundred and twenty-pound Threat in a bar and orders him to leave. The wee Threat blades his body, raises his clenched fists, glares at the officer, and threatens the officer by saying "I stand on your feet, twist off your head, and poop down your throat." Is the officer justified in escalating to an intermediate level of force? *No.* The Threat has indicated his intent to engage in combat with the officer, but he does not have the physical means to carry out the communicated violence.

OPPORTUNITY. The person must have access to the officer, another person, and/or the object (weapon) to carry out the articulated or perceived aggression. As often happens, you respond to a fight at a bar. When you arrive at the scene, you observe two males subjects fighting near the entrance. There is a group of bar patrons ringed around the combatants. You and the cover officers pull the combatants apart and they resist arrest. As you struggle to control the suspects, the crowd turns ugly and starts to yell obscenities at you. After the suspects are controlled and handcuffed, you turn to the crowd and order them to disperse. The unruly mob files back into the bar, with one exception. One obnoxious patron runs across the parking lot, turns, and yells to you: "You, bastard. I will kick your ass!" There are forty yards between you and the obnoxious patron. Are you justified in racing across the parking lot and using force on him? *No.* He has verbalized his intent. He has the physical capabilities to carry out the assault. But, due to the distance between you and the Threat, he lacks the opportunity to carry out the threatened violence.

Now, let's change the scenario. The obnoxious patron tells you that he is going to retrieve a gun from his car and shoot you; then, he starts to move toward the car. Can you use force on him? *Yes.* He has the opportunity to access the gun in his car.

As the examples illustrate, an inmate or a suspect must meet all three requirements to justify your use of nondeadly or deadly force.

Continuum of Criminality

Of the four elements identified by the Supreme Court in *Graham v. Conner* for determining if an officer's force was objectively reasonable, the "severity of the crime" is the least considered element by officers. In fact, often it is completely ignored. In most incidents where officers use force, they focus on the immediate threat and the resisting arrest elements for their justification. In spite of this, the courts apply equal weight to the severity of the crime when considering the reasonableness of your force.

Stated in practical terms, the courts recognize that there is a Continuum of Criminality. Not all crimes are considered equal in severity. When officers include the severity of the crime in their force justification, most of the time it is a crime on the violent end of the continuum. Many officers lose sight of the fact that if a crime involving violence is justification for using greater levels of force; then, traffic violations, nonviolent property crimes, and crimes involving passive disobedience only justify the use of lower levels of force.

The federal courts' position on this issue is expressed in *Bryan v. McPherson.* As you are aware from reading Chapter 3, the officer shocked Mr. Brian with a Taser during a traffic stop for not wearing his seatbelt. Mr. Brian was severely injured from the free fall and the subsequent impact with the asphalt. In ruling that the use of the Taser was excessive force, the Ninth Circuit Court of Appeals stated the following:

> Bryan's initial crime was a mere traffic infraction–failing to wear a seatbelt– punishable by a fine. Traffic violations generally will not support the use of a significant level of force. . . . Officer MacPherson also claims that he reasonably believed Bryan had committed three misdemeanors and that these constitute serious–dangerous–criminal activity. We disagree. . . . While the commission of a misdemeanor offense is not to be taken lightly, it mitigates against finding the force used to effect an arrest reasonable where the suspect was also non-violent and posed no threat to the safety of the officers or others.

Clearly, the severity of the crime that Mr. Brian had committed factored heavily into the Court's decision in determining that the officer used excessive force.

In another incident where the severity of the crime became an issue, a city attorney contacted me to discuss a lawsuit involving the arrest of a young woman for roller blading on a city street. The eighteen-year-old woman was roller blading down a residential street, accompanied by three male friends on bicycles. As she skated down the street, an officer pulled up next to her in a patrol car. The officer informed her that the city had an ordinance against roller blading on the street, and she needed to move onto the sidewalk. Being youthfully irreverent, the young woman replied, "If this cheap city would repair the cracks in sidewalks I would gladly roller blade there." The officer stated he was not going to debate the issue, and again, he told her to move out of the street and onto the sidewalk. Thereupon, he drove away.

Regardless of the warning, the young woman continued roller blading down the street. The officer looked back in his rearview mirror and saw the woman defying his order. According to a witness, the officer violently whipped a U-turn in the street–dragging his rear bumper as he turned around in the witness' steep driveway. The officer stopped, dragged the woman to his car, placed her in the back seat, and slammed the car door. Unfortunately for the woman, the officer did not realize her roller blades were not in the car when he slammed the door, and the door slammed on her shins. The woman let out a shriek in pain. The officer picked up her feet, tossed them in the car, and slammed the door.

Her three male friends disapproving of the officer's behavior voiced their objections. "Shut up or you all will go to jail," the officer threatened. In spite of the warning, the young men continued to call for the woman's release. The officer called for back-up. When the cover-officers arrived, the three young men were arrested for disorderly conduct.

After hearing all the details, I told the city attorney, "Let's apply *Graham v. Conner* to this incident. The young woman was not an immediate threat to the officer. She violated a city ordinance against roller blading in the street– not a very serious offense. In fact, it appears to me she was really arrested for "Contempt of Cop." She did not resist arrest or attempt to escape. I think you have real problems with this case." The city attorney agreed and the lawsuit was settled.

With an understanding of the importance of the severity of the crime in an officer's use of force decision, we will next examine the levels of a Threat's physical resistance.

Levels of Resistance

Use of force training programs offer definitions for the escalating levels of physical resistance a criminal justice officer will encounter on the street or in the correctional facility. As important as using the term "Threat," the terms you use to define the levels of resistance are equally as important in managing the jury's perceptions of your use of force.

The following terms and their definitions have been proven to be effective in both the courtroom and the classroom in explaining the necessity and justification of the use of force.

STATIC RESISTANCE. The Threat refuses to comply with your verbal commands and/or attempts to gain physical control by balking, becoming dead weight, and/or grasping a solid structure.

Static resistance is the most often incurred form of physical resistance that officers encounter. Frequently termed "passive resistance" by use of force instructors, I discourage the use of that term. The term passive resistance is an oxymoron. Passive implies the person is inert. Telling a jury that you used force on a passively resisting Threat does not create a positive mental image of your use of force in the jurors' minds. The Threat is not inert (powerless to move); he or she is actively resisting your verbal commands and attempts to gain physical control by balking, becoming dead weight, or holding on to another person, a steering wheel, cell bars, or other solid object.

Static resistance is the only level of resistance where an officer can effectively apply joint manipulation techniques and pressure points. To successfully apply a joint manipulation technique, the Threat must allow you to touch and manipulate his or her fingers, hand, and/or arm. When the Threat tenses his or her arm or pulls the arm away, you lose the ability to apply the technique.

ACTIVE RESISTANCE. The Threat physically resists your verbal commands and/or attempts to gain physical control by pulling away, attempting to escape, or powering through a control hold.

With active resistance, the Threat is dynamically resisting your attempt to gain physical control: As you touch the Threat's arm to apply an escort hold, he or she jerks the arm away. As you approach the Threat, he or she moves away to create distance from you or the Threat flees. Or after applying a physical control hold to Threat's wrist, he is strong enough to twist out of the hold. This more dynamic level of resistance justifies a higher level of force to gain control.

OMINOUS RESISTANCE. The Threat demonstrates the willingness to engage in combat through verbal challenge and/or aggressive behavior. Or, the Threat attacks (bites, pushes, kicks, strikes, chokes, etc.) or attempts to attack.

The *Merriam-Webster Dictionary's* definition of ominous is "threatening or impending doom." An appropriate word and definition for this level of resistance. With ominous resistance, the person demonstrates his willingness to use force against you through his body language, words, and/or actions. His intent can be nonverbal: a bladed body, "thousand yard stare," or clenching of fists. Verbalized: threats of violence or the raised pitch and tone of the voice. Animated: pacing, rocking back and forth, forward movement, or finger pointing. Acted out: a successful or unsuccessful assault.

This serious level of resistance justifies the use of intermediate force: baton strikes, pepper spray, focused blows, probe deployment of the Taser, neck restraint, dog bite, extended range impact weapon.

LETHAL RESISTANCE. Any force under the circumstances in which it is used is readily capable of causing death or serious physical injury. The mechanism of the force can be a weapon, superior strength, or superior fighting skill. A person does not necessarily need a weapon to kill you. Powerfully strong people can beat and choke you to death. People with martial arts skills, regardless of their size and strength, can seriously injury or kill you without a weapon.

When developing terms and definitions for describing the levels of resistance to officers and jurors, keep in mind that the bulk of your audience is not going to have doctorates in nuclear physics. Because of this, you don't want to use elaborate terms or complex definitions. On the other hand, most cops and jurors are educated people and/or have a great deal of life and work experience. Consequently, you don't want to insult their intelligence with primary school terms: hard hands, soft hands, etc. Your explanation of the levels of resistance must accurately, professionally, and understandably represent the escalating behaviors exhibited by resisting inmates and suspects.

In Chapter 5, we will match the levels of resistance with the correlating use of force options.

Prerequisites of Force Escalation

The escalation of the force is based on the "Totality of the Circumstances." The totality of the circumstances is a concept generally defined as the dangerous, emotional, environmental, harmful, mental, physical, and/or tactical circumstances that justify a specific action or level of force. Now, doesn't that concept help you make better use of force decisions? The concept of the totality of the circumstances is so vast and nebulous it is impossible to specifically define. The working definition of the totality of the circumstances is in a sense like the working definition of pornography—you may not be able to define it, but you know it when you see it. Fortunately, included in the concept of the totality of the circumstances are two specific categories of attendant conditions that define when an inmate or a suspect is an immediate threat to you: "Officer versus threat factors and influential circumstances.

Officer versus Threat Factors

Officer versus Threat Factors are identifiable differences between the officer and the Threat (inmate or suspect) that justifies the initial escalation of force due to the increased risk of jury, serious physical injury, or death to the officer. These differences are divided into six distinct factors. Because these factors justify your use of force, they must be properly explained in your report, recorded statements, deposition, and trial testimony. To help you incorporate these factors into your use of force justification, I have included an example narration for each officer versus threat factor.

OFFICER'S VERSUS THREAT'S COMBATIVE SKILL LEVEL. An officer can initially use more force to protect the officer or others and to effect an arrest against a Threat who has a combat skill that the officer does not process. Combat skills such as boxing, wrestling, martial arts, firearms expertise, tactical training, and military experience give the Threat a serious advantage in a physical confrontation and increases the risk of serious physical injury or death to the officer. To compensate for a combat skill disadvantage, an officer can initially use more force to control the Threat. The following incident illustrates the danger that a Threat with a superior combative skill level can pose to an officer who lacks equivalent skill.

When a deputy arrived at a MIP party out in the rural countryside, the juveniles fled the scene. The deputy pursued a truck containing two suspects down a gravel road. When the road dead-ended, the truck stopped and the driver and passenger fled on foot. The deputy chased after the driver. The deputy's patrol car dash video camera captured the incident. As you watch the video, nothing but the parked truck can be observed for several minutes. Then suddenly, the driver appears, throws an unidentified object into the bed of the truck, and drives off. The video continues to show only darkness and the patrol car's headlights for several more minutes. Then, the movements of the headlights indicate the deputy has entered the patrol car, and the patrol car starts to make a slow wide turn.

What you cannot determine from the video is that the deputy had football-tackled the driver. Unfortunately for the deputy, the driver is a former state high school wrestling champion. Because the driver had a combat skill that the deputy did not have, he severely beat the deputy, disarmed the deputy of his handgun, and attempted to execute him. The deputy's handgun had an external safety, so when the driver pulled the trigger the gun did not fire. Believing the gun had been damaged in the struggle, the driver threw it into the back of the truck. To inflict additional injury to the deputy, when the driver drove away, he intentionally ran over the deputy–breaking his leg. The deputy crawled to his patrol car and drove to a location where he could call out for medical assistance.

The following is an example narration of the "officer's v. the threat's combative skill" level as a justification for the use of force:

> When I contacted Mr. Johnson at the north end of the bar, I informed him that the bartender wanted him removed from the lounge. "I am not going anywhere until I finish my beer," he replied. I told Mr. Johnson that he needed to leave the lounge now, or he would be arrested for criminal trespass. In response, Mr. Johnson slammed his beer bottle down on the bar, stepped back in a bladed martial arts stance, and raised his clenched fists. As he assumed this fighting stance, he told me: "I have a black belt in Tae Kwon Do. If you touch me, I will beat your ass."
>
> I took several steps backward, pulled my Taser, put the laser sight on his torso, and ordered him to turn around and kneel on the ground. Mr. Johnson took a step toward me and I deployed my Taser. The probes hit him in the lower abdomen. Mr. Johnson fell forward incapacitated. When he made contact with the tile floor, Mr. Johnson received a facial injury. Officer Dague handcuffed Mr. Johnson while I maintained tethered control of him with my Taser.
>
> I deployed my Taser in probe mode because Mr. Johnson had a combative skill level that neither Officer Dague nor I have. As a result, I was afraid that if we came within Mr. Johnson's striking distance he would severely injury Officer Dague or me with his martial arts skills.

OFFICER'S AGE VERSUS THREAT'S AGE. An older officer can initially use more force to protect him or herself, protect others, and effect an arrest against a younger Threat. Older officers are physically weaker, more injury prone, less aggressive, and generally less aerobically fit than younger Threats. The greater physical strength and fitness level gives the younger Threat a serious advantage in a physical confrontation and increases the risk of serious physical injury or death to the officer. Consequently, an older officer can initially use more force to control the younger Threat.

I have personally experienced the injury potential of getting older. Here is my experience with the aging process:

I have a martial arts background. And I taught the martial arts professionally before and after I became a police officer. Back in my younger martial arts days, we did not use training mats. When we trained, we threw each other down on cement and wood floors. So, in my twenties and thirties when teaching defensive tactics to officers, I had nothing but contempt for older officers who would come to class with physical limitations. The older cops would complain that the application of control holds hurt their bad wrists, elbows, and shoulders. Their bad knees, hips, and backs limited their mobility and made it painful for them to get up and down on the mat. I would listen to their moans and groans and say to myself: "These old farts need to retire and let a healthy body have their job." Then, I turned forty.

Shortly after I turned forty, I was laying on the sofa watching television with the kids. I rolled over and pinched a nerve in my back that disabled me for a week. In my mid-forties, I stepped out of my patrol car and my right hip locked up. As I felt down my hip, I located a sore spot under my wallet. Sitting on my wallet pinched a nerve in my hip. When I was fifty, I injured my shoulder from a fall on foot patrol. When I tripped and fell forward, I used my right arm to soften my impact with the ground. The pressure to my arm tore my rotator cuff. When I went to the orthopedic surgeon, I asked him: "Hey, doc, I workout. How did this happen?" "Well, your fifty, things just wear out," was his not-so comforting answer.

Now, I am a lot more sympathetic to the limitations of older officers during defensive tactics training. Further, as an older officer, if I had to fight with a twenty-something male suspect–I would still win, but we would both go to the hospital on gurneys. Needless to say, when confronted with a resistive younger male Threat, it would be safer for him and me if I initially escalated my level of force to overcome the Threat's resistance quickly.

The following is an example narration of the "officer's age versus threat's age" as justification for the use of force:

> After the dispatcher informed me that Mr. Samson had an outstanding warrant for "failure to appear" for DWI, I contacted Mr. Samson at his driver side car door and asked him to step out of his vehicle. He refused to exit his car. I told Mr. Samson that he had an outstanding warrant for failure to appear in court and that he was under arrest. "I can't go to jail; I will lose my job," he told me. I opened his car door and ordered him to "get out of the car." In response, he grabbed the steering wheel with both hands and looked straightforward. I ordered him to exit the car three more times. He refused to comply with my lawful orders. I pulled my pepper spray canister from its holster and showed it to him. As I displayed my pepper spray, I warned Mr. Samson that if he did not exit the vehicle he would be sprayed. He refused to exit the car. In response, I sprayed Mr. Samson's face with pepper spray. As I sprayed Mr. Samson, I ordered him to get out of the car and get on the ground.
>
> Mr. Samson released the steering wheel, put his hands to his face, and exited the car. I gave Mr. Samson two more commands to get down on the ground or I would spray him again. After the second command, he laid face down on the ground. I ordered Mr. Samson to place his hands

out to his sides (palms up), cross his ankles, look away from me, and not to move unless ordered to do so. He complied. I handcuffed Mr. Samson with his hands behind his back. I checked his handcuffs for the proper tightness, and activated the double locking mechanism. I placed Mr. Samson in the back of my patrol car. Mr. Samson complained of a painful burning sensation to his eyes and face. I told Mr. Samson that the painful effects of pepper spray are only temporary. To ease Mr. Samson's discomfort, I obtained moist towelettes from my equipment bag and wiped the pepper spray from Mr. Samson's face.

I sprayed Mr. Samson with pepper spray rather than attempting to remove him from his car with a pressure point tactic or joint manipulation technique because of our age difference. Mr. Samson is an athletic twenty-five-year-old Threat and I am a fifty-four-year-old officer. Because I am an older officer, I lack the physical agility, stamina, and strength to effectively control a younger stronger Threat. Consequently, I was afraid that if I attempted to extract Mr. Samson from his car with a physical control technique he would overpower me, wrestle me to the ground, disarm me of my handgun, and kill, or seriously injure me.

OFFICER'S GENDER VERSUS THREAT'S GENDER. A female officer can initially use more force to protect herself, protect others, and effect an arrest against a male Threat. Generally, men are physically stronger than women. In fact, women only have 60 percent of the upper body strength of that of men. It is for this reason that the Cooper Standards (the scientifically developed fitness standards used by the U. S. military and law enforcement) have a lesser repetition requirement and a slower run time for women than men of the same age. Because of the strength difference, the female officer is at a dangerous disadvantage in a physical confrontation. As a female officer, do not confuse being different with being inferior. Because of force options such as pepper spray, Taser, baton, police K9, less-lethal munitions, and the firearm, a female officer's ability to control a male Threat is equal to that of her male counterpart. Because of her ability to initially use a higher level of force to protect herself, others, and effect an arrest, she has a tactical advantage.

In contrast, in a situation that involves a male officer and an unarmed resistive or combative female Threat, the male officer should be more conservative in his initial use of force than he would be with a male Threat. Often, jurors believe that a male officer can control an unarmed female Threat without the use of an intermediate level of force. Consequently, the majority of excessive force lawsuits where a jury finds the officer used excessive force involve a male officer and a female Threat.

The following is an example narration of the "officer's gender versus threat's gender" as justification for the use of force:

> After the dispatcher informed me that Mr. Ochoa had a warrant for theft, I contacted Mr. Ochoa and placed him under arrest. When I told Mr. Ochoa he was under arrest, he turned and ran away. I chased Mr. Ochoa through the park. When I caught up with him, I grabbed Mr. Ochoa by the collar of his shirt. When I pulled back on his shirt, he turned and punched me in the face, knocking me to a seated position on the ground. I landed approximately six feet away from Mr. Ochoa.
>
> As he started to move toward me, I pulled my handgun and told him that if he came closer to me I would shoot him. I ordered Mr. Ochoa to get on the ground–face down. He complied. I scrambled to a standing position, held Mr. Ochoa at gunpoint, and radioed for "Code Three Cover." I ordered Mr. Ochoa to put his arms out to his sides (palms up), cross his ankles, look away from me, and not to move. Because I was informed that cover officers were close to my location, I chose to wait for the cover officers to arrive to handcuff Mr. Ochoa.
>
> When Officer Henderson arrived at my location, he kneeled down on Mr. Ochoa to handcuff him while I covered Mr. Ochoa with my Taser. When Officer Henderson placed his knee on Mr. Ochoa's back, Mr. Ochoa turned toward Officer Henderson and pulled him onto the ground. Mr. Ochoa was able to roll up onto Officer Henderson as they wrestled. I deployed my Taser in probe mode to Mr. Ochoa's back. The Taser shock caused Mr. Ochoa to fall off Officer Henderson. When the Taser finished cycling, Officer Henderson handcuffed Mr. Ochoa.
>
> After being knocked to the ground by Mr. Ochoa's punch, I pulled by handgun and threatened to shoot Mr. Ochoa if he continued to advance toward me because as a female officer I am aware that a male Threat has at least 40 percent more upper body strength than I do. Consequently, I was afraid that if Mr. Ochoa attacked me he would overpower me, disarm me of my handgun, and kill me with it. Furthermore, I chose to deploy my Taser in probe mode to Mr. Ochoa's back while he grappled with Officer Henderson because of our size and strength difference. I knew I could not effectively control Mr. Ochoa with lesser physical control techniques. As a result, I was afraid that if I physically engaged Mr. Ochoa he would overpower me, disarm me of my handgun, and use it against Officer Henderson and me.

SIZE AND STRENGTH. Regardless of the officer's age, gender, or skill level, a smaller and weaker officer is at a serious disadvantage in a physical confrontation with a larger and stronger Threat. It is for this reason professional combat sports (boxing, wrestling, martial arts, mixed-martial arts) have weight divisions. Weight divisions are mandated for the fairness of the competition and the safety of the participants. Do you know what they call a lightweight boxer who fights a heavyweight boxer? An organ donor. The larger size and greater strength gives the Threat an advantage in a physical altercation and increases the risk of serious physical injury or death to the smaller officer. To compensate for the size and strength disadvantage, a weaker officer can initially use more force to control the stronger Threat.

The following incident illustrates the impact that a Threat's size and strength can have on excessive force litigation:

An officer responded to a report of a domestic assault occurring in a vehicle that was parked in the downtown area. When the officer contacted the vehicle, he observed a very large male suspect choking a small female victim. As the suspect choked the victim, he banged her head off the roof of the car.

The officer opened the car door and ordered the suspect to exit. As the suspect stepped out of the car, he got bigger and bigger and bigger. The suspect was six feet and five inches tall, weighed over two hundred and thirty pounds, and had a body builder's physique. He was a massive human being. The officer described him as looking like "Conan the Barbarian." The officer, who was less than six feet tall and had an average build, told the suspect he was under arrest. The suspect stepped back in a fighting stance. In response, the officer pulled his side-handle baton, and wailed on the suspect.

When the suspect got tired of being hit, he stopped fighting and ran down the street, with the officer in foot pursuit. When the suspect tired of running, he turned and assumed another fighting stance. The officer responded with more baton blows. This run and fight sequence went on for five separate episodes. During the last encounter, finding that the normal baton blows were ineffective, the officer turned the baton over and (while holding it like a war club) hit the suspect. As a result of these hatchet-like blows, the suspect surrendered. After being released from jail, the suspect contacted an attorney and filed a civil rights excessive force lawsuit against the officer.

During the suspect's deposition, the officer's attorney asked the plaintiff this question: "You look like a pretty strong guy. How strong are you?" "I am strong enough that if I would have got that baton away from that officer I could have broke it in half," he replied with a haughty tone. Immediately, his attorney asked for a recess and the attorney and the plaintiff left the room. Ten minutes later, the attorney returned to the deposition room and informed the officer and his attorney that her client was dropping the lawsuit.

The plaintiff my have filled out a size 58 jacket, but he wore a size 2 hat. His attorney knew that with the plaintiff's physical size and strength combined with his stupid admission that they could not convince a jury that the officer used excessive force.

The following is an example narration of "size and strength" as justification for the use of force:

The truck had just came to a stop when the driver's door opened and a very large and enraged man exploded out of the truck. Because of the short time frame between the truck stopping and the driver exiting, I had just enough time to exit my patrol vehicle–without notifying dispatch of my location. I had not intended to execute a vehicle stop on the truck. However, it suddenly pulled to the side of the road and slid to a stop. It appeared to me that the driver might be having a medical problem, so I pulled in behind it.

The driver ripped his shirt off and threw his cell phone on the pavement. As he did, he glared at me and yelled, "I am a warrior and I will deal with you myself." At this point, we were approximately twenty feet part. I pulled my expandable baton from it holster and extended it. I indexed it over my right shoulder and ordered the driver to "Get on the Ground." In response, the driver yelled, "I am tired of you cops picking on me and I am not taking it anymore." Then, he advanced toward me. I ordered him to "Stay back!" and "Get on the ground!" three times. When the driver was within six feet of me, I delivered a baton strike to the side of his left knee. As I delivered the baton strike, I ordered him to "Get on the ground!" When the baton made contact with his knee, it buckled and he fell forward onto the pavement.

I ordered the driver to place his hands out to the sides of his body. He refused and instead raised up to a crawling position on his hands and knees. Again, I ordered him to lay flat on the ground. As he started to push himself up from the ground, I delivered a baton strike to his left forearm. This strike motivated him to flatten out on the ground. I ordered the driver into a high-risk handcuffing position, and I handcuffed him with his arms behind his back. He was placed in the rear passenger compartment of my patrol vehicle. Because the driver had received baton strikes to his arm and knee, I requested that medical respond to my location to examine the driver.

The driver is six feet and five inches tall and weights two hundred and fifty-five pounds. I am five feet and eleven inches tall and weigh two hundred pounds. Because the driver is substantially larger and stronger than I am, I was afraid that if I attempted to apply a lesser level of force that it would fail to control the Threat; consequently, he would wrestle me to the ground, overpower me, and disarm me of my handgun and seriously injure or kill me with it.

MULTIPLE THREATS. Interacting with two or more people (Threats) is inherently more dangerous than confronting, controlling, or arresting a single person. The main reason is obvious, two or more people can more easily distract, overwhelm, disarm, and kill an officer. As seen in the Darrell Lunsford video, Constable Lunsford was taken to the ground, disarmed, and killed by three smaller, unarmed, drug dealers on a traffic stop. His death was recorded on his patrol car video camera.

In addition to the danger of being swarmed, your risk is increased by the lengthening of your reaction time. When the number of stimuli you must process doubles, your reaction time doubles. As an example, a state trooper stopped two hitchhikers on the shoulder of a freeway. While running both hitchhikers for wants, it was discovered that one had a warrant. While the trooper was handcuffing the wanted suspect, the other hitchhiker pulled a handgun from his pocket and shot the trooper. The trooper was killed because his reaction time had been lengthened by the increased amount of information he was processing: handcuffing one suspect and trying to control the other suspect's movement.

As these examples illustrate, interacting with more than one Threat increases the danger to an officer. Therefore, an officer can initially use more force to control multiple Threats.

The following is an example narration of using the presence of multiple Threats as justification for the use of force:

> After Mr. Evans failed the series of field sobriety tests, I told him that he was under arrest for driving under the influence of intoxicants. When I did, the two male occupants (later identified as Marcus and Martin Evans) exited the suspect vehicle. I ordered the two men to get back in their vehicle. The two men refused to obey my verbal commands. Further, the men told me they were not going to allow me to arrest their brother. As the two moved toward Mr. Evans, I stepped back and pulled my pepper spray canister from its holster. I told the other two men that they were under arrest for interfering with a police officer, and I ordered all three men to "Get on the Ground!" They refused. I gave this order four times. When the men had advanced to within six feet of me, I sprayed all three men in the face with my fogger pepper spray. As I sprayed them, I ordered the men to "Get down on the ground!"
>
> The pepper spray stopped their advance and impaired their eyesight and breathing; however, they refused to lay on the ground. As a result, I knocked Mr. Evans to the ground with front kick to the groin. I told the

other two men that I would apply the same force option to them if they continued to resist arrest. They voluntarily laid face down on the ground. All three suspects were handcuffed with their hands behind their backs and placed in the back of my patrol car.

I pepper sprayed all three suspects because I was afraid that if they were not all physically impaired at the same time they would overpower me and seriously injure or kill me with my duty handgun. When the pepper spray failed to force their complete compliance, I feared that, even though they were somewhat impaired, all three suspects would fight through the effects of the pepper spray and attack me.

When I attended the police academy, I watched a video of Constable Lunsford being overpowered and killed by three suspects on a traffic stop. Fearing that would happen to me, I escalated to focused blows to control the Threats.

MENTAL STATE. People with an altered mental state–intoxicated (drugs or alcohol), angry, emotionally disturbed, fearful, mentally ill, or under the influence of adrenaline–have a higher pain tolerance. Moreover, a person with an altered mental state behaves irrationally. A person who does not respond to pain and/or who is not thinking rationally is more dangerous to an officer.

In the training video "Deadly Effects," Dr. Martin Fackler–a physician and an expert on wound ballistics–states that the reason why people fall down after they have been shot is psychosomatic: what people watch on television and the movies conditions them to fall down after being shot. Furthermore, Dr. Fackler goes on to explain that when a person has an altered mental state the psychological processes are not in place to tell him or her to fall down. As a result, the person keeps on fighting.

If a Threat with an altered mental state is not going to respond to being shot with a firearm, what makes you think that joint locks, pepper spray, electronic control devices, and less-lethal impact munitions will be 100 percent effective? They may not be. Therefore, an officer can initially use more force to control a Threat with an altered mindset.

The following incident illustrates the impact that a Threat's altered mindset can have on an officer's ability to stop an attack and physically control the Threat.

Two probation officers conducted a home visit of a violent, mentally ill, sex offender who had stopped taking his medication. It was a condition of his probation that the offender stay on his psychotropic medication.

The sex offender lived by himself in a basement apartment. The probation officers contacted the offender at the bottom of a set of cement stairs in the basement. They told the offender that he was under arrest for the probation violation. When they did, the offender bolted up the cement stairs. The male officer gave chase, and he caught the offender midway up the stairs by his long hair. The officer forced the offender up against the wall. With the officer pushing him up against the wall with two hands full of hair, the offender pulled his head away, leaving large patches of hair in the officer's hands.

As the offender ripped his head away, the female officer sprayed both the offender and male officer with pepper spray. The pepper spray had no effect on the mentally ill offender, but it impaired the male officer's ability to breathe. The male officer, a former college wrestler, grabbed the offender and after a brief struggle they rolled down the stairs in a grapple.

The officers scrambled to the top of the stairs in attempt to obtain fresh, nonpepper spray contaminated, air. After the officers had gulped several breaths of fresh air, they turned and looked back into the basement. When they did, they observed the offender climbing the stairs with an object in his hand.

The male officer moved to the top step and ordered the offender to drop the weapon and get down on the floor. The offender continued to climb the stairs. The officer, who had a brown belt in karate, waited for the offender. When the offender reached the top step, he swung the object at the officer's head. The officer blocked the object and delivered a full-power palm heel strike to the offender's chin. His head snapped back, he fell backwards, and rolled back down the stairs. To the officers' surprise, the offender sprung to his feet and climbed the stairs with the object.

Again, the officer waited for the offender to reach the top step. When he did, the offender swung the weapon again. The officer blocked the strike and this time delivered a pull power forearm strike to the offender's head. His head snapped back and down the stairs he rolled. When the offender hit the floor at the bottom of the stairs, he stood, threw the object down, and ran up the stairs.

This time the officer waited for the offender's head to reach approximately waist level to the officer. When the offender's head was in range, the officer delivered a full-power front snap kick to the offender's chin with the heel of his shoe. The offender rolled backwards down the stairs. When the offender landed on the basement floor, he stood up. To the officer's amazement, the offender was completely uninjured. The offender ran to an open basement window, crawled through it, and walked down the street.

The male officer exited the basement entryway and gave chase. The officer followed him for several blocks ordering the offender to get on the ground. Then, just a suddenly as the altercation started, the offender sat down on the ground, looked up at the officer, and said: "You don't give up do you? Ok, I'll go." With that, he put his hands behind his back. The officer handcuffed the offender and transported him to jail.

When they arrived at the jail, the officer told the jail deputies that the inmate was a violent sex offender, he was mentally ill, and he was off his medication. In addition, the officer told the deputies that he had fought with the inmate and hit him with several focused blows to the head, which had no effect. Because of the offender's violent behavior, the officer recommended that the deputies leave the offender in handcuffs while he was being kept in the holding cell.

As the probation officer stood by, the deputies chose to ignore the recommendation and removed the handcuffs. The moment the second handcuff came off the inmate's wrist he attacked the deputies. The deputies emptied six cans of pepper spray on the inmate, with no effect. Finally, it took five large corrections deputies to hold the inmate down and handcuff him.

As the officer relayed his story to me, he said: "It was like a horror movie where the monster couldn't be stopped. When we were done fighting, he did not have a mark on him—he was not even breathing hard."

The following is an example narration of using the Threat's altered mental state as justification for the use of force:

> When I contacted the bartender, he told me that Edward Barnes was causing problems in the bar, and he wanted Mr. Barnes arrested for criminal trespass. Further, the bartender told me that Mr. Barnes was intoxicated, angry at being denied more beer, and was threatening other patrons.
>
> I contacted Mr. Barnes at his table near the north wall of the dance floor. I told Mr. Barnes that he could either leave the bar or be arrested for criminal trespass. "I am not leaving and you f . . king can't make me leave," he replied. I attempted to persuade Mr. Barnes to exit the bar with me, but I was unable to convince him to leave on his own. Consequently, I told Mr. Barnes that he was under arrest and ordered him to place his hands behind his back. His whole body language changed. The muscles in his neck, shoulders, and arms tensed. He clinched his teeth and glared at me.
>
> Since my presence in uniform and attempts at verbal persuasion were ineffective in getting Mr. Barnes to leave the bar or submit to being arrested, I applied an arm bar to his right arm and took him to the floor. Once on the floor, Mr. Barnes was placed in a high-risk handcuffing position and handcuffed. After Officer Hanson and I lifted Mr. Barnes off the floor, he complained of pain in his right shoulder and elbow. As a result of his complaining of shoulder and elbow pain, I requested medical re-

spond to our location to evaluate Mr. Barnes.

The EMTs determined Mr. Barnes' shoulder and elbow may be injured. Subsequently, he was transported to the hospital for further evaluation. At the hospital, the ER doctor diagnosed Mr. Barnes with a possible torn rotator cuff and fractured elbow joint. Mr. Barnes was issued a citation for criminal trespass and released.

I applied an arm takedown to Mr. Barnes because he had an altered mental state. The bartender had told me that Mr. Barnes was intoxicated and angry. I know from my defensive tactics training that people with an altered mental state are unpredictable, irrational, have a higher pain tolerance, and pose a greater danger to officers. Consequently, I was afraid that if I applied a pain compliance comealong technique it would be ineffective in controlling Mr. Barnes because of his higher pain tolerance, and he would assault me.

Influential Circumstances

In addition to the "officer versus threat factors," there are eight distinct circumstances that justifies the greater initial use of force on a Threat (inmate or suspect) due to the immediate threat to the officer.

CLOSE PROXIMITY TO A WEAPON. An officer can use more force initially to control the Threat when the person is in close proximity to a weapon. A weapon is defined as any object within the Threat's control that can inflict injury to an officer. These objects include, but are not limited to: a glass bottle, glass mug, pencil/pen, syringe, construction/automotive tools, baseball bat, lumber, chain, rope, knife, firearm, rocks/stones, vehicle–the list is endless. The point is not to limit your recognition of a weapon to only knives or firearms.

Further, the Threat does not have to possess the weapon. Remember the three elements of an immediate threat: intent, means, and opportunity. A weapon in close proximity provides the Threat with the opportunity to inflict serious physical injury or death. The fear of being injured by the weapon justifies an escalated use of force, even though the Threat does not have physical possession of it.

The purpose of escalating your initial use of force is to quickly take control of the Threat, effectively denying him or her access to the weapon. By quickly controlling the Threat, it minimizes the need to escalate to a more injurious level of force i.e., deadly force.

For example, officers respond to a loud noise complaint at a residence. The neighbors report hearing yelling from the residence. The officers arrive at the scene and contact a woman at the front door with a fresh red mark on the side of her face.

As the officers enter the residence, they observe a man sitting on the sofa in the front room. Two officers stay with the man on the couch, while the third officer interviews the woman. The two officers attempt to question the man on the couch, but he refuses to speak to them.

The third officer returns and tells the man on the sofa he is under arrest for domestic assault. Further, the officer orders the man to stand up and place his hands behind his back. The man refuses to cooperate. As the two officers move forward to take the man into custody, he shifts his position on the sofa. As he shifts his weight, a used syringe falls from his clothing and onto a sofa cushion, just beyond his reach. The officers move back and draw their handguns. At no time does the suspect reach for the syringe. The officers order him to get on the floor. He refuses to move.

The primary officer holsters his handgun, draws his Taser, and issues one final command to get on the floor. The Threat refuses to move. The officer deploys his Taser in probe mode to Threat's the lower abdomen. When he is shocked, he falls forward to the floor. While under power of the Taser, the two cover officers control and handcuff the suspect.

Even though the suspect is only passively resisting the officer's verbal commands is the use of the Taser justified? Answer: *Yes.* The key question is why? The justification is threefold.

First, the nature of the crime: The suspect is under arrest for committing a violent crime. As a result, the officers know the suspect has a potential for violent behavior. Second, the suspect is in close proximity of a weapon, the used syringe. A stab with a dirty needle can be a death sentence. Third, the officers have a legitimate fear that if they attempt to apply a lesser use of force the suspect could defeat the physical control technique, grab the syringe and stab an officer.

The following is an example narration of using the "threat's close proximity to a weapon" as justification for the use of force:

> When I observed the syringe fall from the Mr. Adams' clothing and land on the sofa's cushion, I pulled my handgun and ordered Mr. Adams to lay down on the floor. The reason why I covered Mr. Adams with my handgun was that I feared he might grab the syringe and stab the other officers or me. I ordered Mr. Adams to "Get down on the floor!" three times. Because the display of my handgun and my verbal commands were ineffective in convincing Mr. Adams to move away from the syringe, I holstered my handgun and deployed my Taser to Mr. Adams in probe mode. I escalated to the Taser because of Mr. Adams was in close proximity to the syringe. I was afraid that if I attempted to apply a phys-

ical control technique to Mr. Adams' arm he would stab me with the syringe.

OFFICER EXHAUSTION. The two main reasons for a referee stoppage of a mixed martial arts match are an injury to a fighter or the fighter's inability to intelligently defend himself. If the fighter is physically exhausted to the point he simply covers up and allows his opponent to pummel him, the referee will stop the fight for the exhausted fighter's safety. A referee and safety rules are what separates a combat sport from real combat.

In a combat sport, the loser goes home with a lesser monetary prize. In a struggle between an officer and a Threat, if the officer loses, he or she may be hospitalized or–even worse–transported to the morgue. A physically exhausted officer cannot (through physical strength) effectively control a resisting Threat or defeat a combative one. Consequently, an exhausted officer can use more force to control a Threat or protect himself or herself.

When I managed the defensive tactics program at the Oregon Academy, I implemented a boxing exercise for the basic police and corrections students. One reason was to expose the little cosmic oatmeal cookies (that we were getting as officers) to a controlled fight. The second reason was for the officers to experience the effect that being physically exhausted had on their ability to defend themselves. In addition, I wanted the officers to experience for themselves how long they could effectively fight. The method to my madness was quite simple: If an officer was forced to escalate his or her force due to being exhausted, I wanted the officer to be able to testify before the jury that officer had learned his or her effective physical limit at the academy.

It was an exercise that produced some surprising results. When I first implemented boxing, I had the students spar for three minutes. How many students out of fifty-five do you think could put up an effective fight for three minutes? You guessed it. None. So, I reduced the sparring time to two minutes. How many students could spar for two minutes effectively? Nope. You're wrong. Not a student. The average student could only effectively fight for ninety seconds. And for safety reasons, I limited the actual boxing to a one-minute cycle and then had the students finish the exercise with a one-minute continuous punching cycle on a striking shield.

The final results of the Oregon Academy's boxing exertion exercise (fourteen hundred and thirty corrections and police students participated): 35 percent of the students could not fight for longer than sixty seconds. The remaining 65 percent of the students could not fight for longer than ninety seconds.

The following is an example narration of using the officer's physical exhaustion as justification for the use of force:

I told Mr. Tillman that he was under arrest, to turn around, and to place his hands behind his back. He complied. When I grabbed his right hand to apply the handcuff, Mr. Tillman spun and tackled me. We fought on the shoulder of the roadway for several minutes. The longer we struggled the more physically exhausted I became. Suddenly, I felt a tug on my handgun holster. I reached down with my right hand and felt Mr. Tillman's hand on my handgun. Because I did not have the strength to prevent Mr. Tillman from removing my handgun from its holster, I drove my left thumb into his right eye as deeply as I could. Mr. Tillman released my handgun, and he covered his face with both hands. As a result, I was able to push him off of me, get to a standing position, and pull my handgun. I gouged Mr. Tillman's eye to prevent him from disarming me. Due to our prolonged struggle, I did not have the physical strength to prevent Mr. Tillman from taking my handgun and killing me with it.

TERRAIN/ENVIRONMENT. There is one deficiency in the way we conduct defensive tactics training. Defensive tactics training is conducted in a gym on mats. Are you ever going to struggle with an inmate or suspect in a gym on mats? Probably not. The reason why we conduct the training on mats is obvious—the safety of the trainees. Nevertheless, practicing control techniques on mats does not give you a complete understanding of how the terrain or the environment can impair your ability to apply control techniques or defend yourself.

A wet cell floor, beer spilled on a barroom floor, subdued light, snow/ice/mud, blowing dust or rain, glass, blood, obstructions, protrusions, stairs, railed walkways, etc. are examples of terrain or environments that create a higher level of danger when physically controlling or fighting with a Threat. Consequently, an officer can initially use more force to control a Threat or to protect him or herself when the terrain or the environment impairs the officer's ability to effectively apply force.

The terrain and the environment were factors in Deputy Drinski's decision to shoot Konstantino Plaskas. As you remember, Deputy Drinski followed Plaskas into an area that was ringed with hedgerows. As Plaskas advanced toward Deputy Drinski with the fireplace poker, Deputy Drinski retreated with his handgun drawn. Deputy Drinski's retreat was stopped after he stumbled on the uneven ground and backed into bushes. The terrain and the environment prevented Deputy Drinski's further retreat, forcing him to shoot Plaskas in self-defense.

In an incident where three escaped convicts were able to overwhelm an officer on a traffic stop, the terrain and the environment worked against the officer's ability to fight off the convicts and use deadly force. In a rural area, a police officer stopped a vehicle for speeding. What the officer did not know was that the driver and two passengers were escaped dangerous convicts from a prison in a neighboring state.

The vehicle had been stopped previously by a state trooper. But, because of spotty radio coverage, the trooper was unable to run the driver for wants or the driver's status before issuing a traffic citation for speeding. When the convicts were released from the stop, they decided that the next time a cop stopped them they would kill him.

When the officer was just feet from the driver's door, the three convicts sprang out and attacked him. As the officer fought with the convicts they fell over a guardrail and into a water-filled ditch. The officer fought with the convicts in the ditch for several minutes. At one point during the struggle, the officer was able to pull his handgun. Unfortunately, the handgun was so full of mud from fighting in the ditch that it would not fire.

The convicts subdued the officer and dragged him to his patrol car. Once at the patrol car, they held the officer's arm against the driver's side door jam and slammed the door closed on his arm several times, breaking the bones in his arm.

By the grace of good patrol tactics, the officer had informed dispatch of the stop and his location. A competent dispatcher had status-checked the officer several times while he fought with the convicts in the ditch. Being unable to receive a response, the dispatcher sent Code-Three-Cover to his last known location. When the convicts heard the sirens of the responding cover officers, they dropped the officer and drove off in their stolen vehicle. The officer was left severely injured at the scene, but alive. The convicts were apprehended in the next county.

In the first incident, the terrain (rough ground) and the environment (brush) were important elements in the justification of Deputy Drinski's use of deadly force. In the second incident, the location's terrain (muddy ditch) and environment (guardrail) were responsible for the officer's fall into the ditch, the malfunction of his handgun, and his subsequent injuries.

The following is an example narration of using the incident's terrain and environment as justification for the use of force:

> The Dispatcher informed me that Mr. Blake's driving privileges had been felony revoked as a habitual traffic offender. I asked Mr. Blake to exit his car. He complied. I told Mr. Blake that he was under arrest for driving while his driving privileges has been revoked. Subsequently, I asked him to turn around and to place his hands behind his back. "I can't get arrested. It will violate my probation," he said. Then, he turned and

ran north into a snow-covered field. I followed his footprints in the snow. They led to an old truck that was parked on the north edge of the field. I found Mr. Blake hiding in the bed of the truck. He had covered himself with loose hay. I removed my Taser from its holster and ordered Mr. Blake to exit the truck. When Mr. Blake climbed out of the truck, I ordered him to "Get down on the Ground!" "If you're going to arrest me–then, arrest me. But, I ain't laying in the wet snow," he said. "If you don't get on the ground, now, I will deploy my Taser," I warned. He refused to lay down on the ground. I deployed my Taser to Mr. Blake in probe mode. The probes hit him in the lower abdomen, and he fell forward into the snow. I deployed my Taser to Mr. Blake for the following reasons:

When I initiated the traffic stop, I observed a National Rifle Association sticker in the left rear corner of his truck window. This made me fearful that Mr. Blake may have a weapon concealed in his clothing. It was a cold, dark, and moonless night. The darkness of the night and the limited illumination that my flashlight provided made it impossible for me to perform an effective visual frisk of Mr. Blake for weapons. As a result, I was afraid that if I attempted to control Mr. Blake with a physical control technique he would access a weapon concealed in his clothing and stab, strike, or shoot me with it.

Further, the field was covered with approximately six inches of wet snow that concealed roots, vegetation, and uneven ground. Moreover, the wet snow had turned the dirt into slippery mud. These adverse ground conditions impaired my ability to move quickly and maintain my balance. Based on these environmental conditions, I was afraid that if I physically struggled with Mr. Blake I would fall and be injured. Or, because of the additional weight of my uniform and equipment belt, I would lose my balance enabling Mr. Blake to overpower me and use my baton, pepper spray, Taser, or handgun against me.

PREVIOUS EXPERIENCE. An officer's previous experience in controlling large, intoxicated (alcohol or drugs), mentally ill, emotionally disturbed, armed, resistive, or combative inmates and suspects can justify the use of an escalated level force. The offer of employment as a criminal justice officer is not a suicide pact. If an officer has previous experience in using levels of force that were ineffective in controlling or stopping an inmate or a suspect, the officer is not obligated to use the same level of force under similar circumstances.

For example, if you apply a wrist lock to a large and intoxicated male suspect and he pulls away and assaults you, the next time you encounter a large, intoxicated male suspect you can escalate your use of force based on your previous experience with the technique failure. Your experience with the failure of a lower level force is justification for initially using a higher level force under similar circumstances.

In the evenings at the Montana Academy, I offered two hours of extra counter-assault tactics training to the students to enhance their skill level and to keep them out of trouble: bars, taverns, and lounges. In this particular class, there was the largest and most powerfully-built human being I had ever met. He had recently graduated from the Montana State University, where he had played football as a lineman. Brian was at least six feet and five inches tall and weighed three hundred and fifty pounds. He was solid muscle. Brian's biceps were so large that they required fence posts to hold up his barbed wire tattoos.

Brian had been hired by a sheriff's office and sent to the academy. During the first week of Brian's academy class, I conducted counter-assault tactics sessions, after hours, in the gym. The students were practicing focused blows on striking shields when I observed Brian deliver a forearm strike that would have dropped an elephant. No offense to the PETA members.

Brian and his partner were practicing their techniques in the middle of a full court gym. His partner was no midget–six feet and two hundred pounds. When I gave the command to strike, Brian delivered the blow. When Brian's forearm hit the striking shield his partner went vertical at least two feet, flew horizontal four feet off the floor the entire width of the gym, landed on the floor, and slid into the wall headfirst. It was the most impressive display of raw power I have ever witnessed.

From that experience I learned three things that justify an initial escalation of force: One, I cannot control a threat of that size and strength with physical control techniques. Two, a threat that size could easily kill me with his bare hands. Three, a threat with Brian's physical strength could easily disarm me and kill me with my own handgun. It is similar previous experiences which you have had that justify your escalation of force.

The following is an example narration of using your previous experience as justification for the use of force:

> Mr. Jackson had stopped taking his medication two days ago. As a result, he told his mother that the voice in his head was telling him to kill his family. She immediately called the police department for assistance. When I told Mr. Jackson that he was being taken into protective custody because I believed that he was a danger to himself and others, he looked at me with a blank stare as he stood in the bedroom. I asked Mr. Jackson to turn around and place his hands behind his back. "No. I am not going

to the hospital again," he replied.

I have had previous experience with mentally ill people who have fallen off their medication. It has been my experience that a mentally ill person who hears voices telling him to act out violently can be dangerous to physically control. More specifically, I have previous experience with Mr. Jackson when he has stopped taking his medication. It has been my experience that Mr. Jackson will strike, kick, and bite at officers when being taken into custody on a mental health peace officer hold. It is for these reasons that when Mr. Jackson refused to place his hands behind his back that I deployed my Taser in probe mode to his rear torso to incapacitate him and take him into custody.

SPECIAL KNOWLEDGE. The special knowledge category is divided into two areas: First, the knowledge that the officer personally possesses regarding the dangerousness of the Threat. Second, the statistical knowledge that the officer possesses regarding the dangerousness of the circumstances or call for service.

An officer can use more force initially to arrest a suspect who the officer knows has a history of assaulting officers or committing violent crimes. Similarly, officers can initially use more force to control suspects during the execution of a narcotics search warrant because the officers have special knowledge that most drug dealers possess and carry weapons. It is the special knowledge the officer has regarding the suspect's potential for violent behavior and/or the possession of weapons that makes the suspect an immediate threat to the officer.

In addition, the statistical information you receive through formal training classes or personal research regarding the dangerousness of specific circumstances or calls for service can justify the use of an escalated level of force. The following are examples of statistical information that has been used successfully by officers to justify the escalation of force:

Officers Killed During Suspicious Person Calls (Aims Media)
40% - killed immediately on contact with the suspect(s).
45% - killed interrupting a crime in progress.
33% - killed investigating suspicious vehicles.
20% - killed during the initial conversation with the suspect(s).
20% - engaged in a foot pursuit.
20% - killed when the suspect realized he was under arrest.

Officers Killed Responding to Burglaries in Progress (Aims Media)
21% - killed during their approach of the building.

50% - killed by a lookout while making their approach.
66% - killed responding to an alarm.
59% - killed in burglaries that involved more than one suspect.
30% - killed searching inside the building.
70% - of the burglars were armed with a firearm.
21% - killed taking the suspect into custody.
26% - killed in a foot pursuit with the fleeing burglar.
44% - observed suspicious behavior but did not use the appropriate tactics.
20% - were faked out: the suspect pretended to be an employee, janitor, family member, manager, owner, or bystander.

Officers Killed On Traffic Stops (Aims Media)
88% - killed on one-officer traffic stops.
45% - killed during the early stage of the stop.
60% - of suspects had predetermined to kill the officer if given the opportunity.
25% - killed during an argument or a struggle.
25% - killed with their own handgun.

Officers Killed On Man With Gun Calls (Aims Media)
25% - of suspects were armed with a rifle of .223 caliber or larger.
70% - of suspects had made the decision to kill the officer at first opportunity.
25% - killed by a suspect hiding outside of the residence.
33% - killed using insufficient Hard-Cover.
63% - of suspects were over forty years old.

Officers Killed Handling Prisoners (Aims Media)
43% - killed with their own handgun.
49% - killed after the prisoner was in physical custody.
27% - killed controlling the prisoner prior to taking into custody.
24% - killed while handcuffing the suspect.
38% - officer did not handcuff the suspect.
27% - officer conducted a poor search or no search.

The following is an example of the use of statistical information as a justification for the use of force. The incident involved the investigative detention of three burglary suspects. Early in the afternoon, a woman witnessed three young men open and crawl through a window in the back of her neighbor's house. The woman called the police department and reported the burglary. Further, the witness told the police that she knew her neighbor was at work and the house was unoccupied prior to the entry.

Five police officers arrived at the scene and secured the outer perimeter of the residence. An officer called to the suspects in the house to come out. Three men exited through the front door. The first suspect to exit told the officers that his mother owned the house and he had permission to be there. The suspects were controlled at gunpoint, ordered to prone out on the ground, and were handcuffed. When an officer telephoned the homeowner, she told the officer that one of the suspects was her son and he had permission to be in the home, but she did not know the other two suspects and they did not have permission to be there. The suspects were unhandcuffed and released. A few days later, the suspects contacted an attorney and sued the officers for excessive force.

During their testimony, the officers stated that the reason they took the burglary suspects down at gunpoint and handcuffed them—even though one suspect claimed his mother owned the house and he had permission to be there—was because 20 percent of the officers who are killed investigating burglaries in progress are faked out by the killer. The jury deliberated just long enough to have lunch and take their first vote. The jury concluded the officers did not use excessive force.

The following is an example narration of using "special knowledge" as justification for the use of force:

> I responded to a man with a gun call on the corner of Brooks Street and Tenth Avenue. The dispatcher informed me that the suspect was a white male (20 to 30), approximately six feet tall, average build, wearing a black coat. As I was responding to the scene, I observed a person fitting the suspect's description walking northbound on Tenth Avenue, between Brooks Street and Jennings Street.
>
> I drove past the suspect, turned around, activated my emergency lights, and parked approximately twenty-five feet to the rear of the suspect. As I exited my vehicle, I pulled my handgun and pointed it at the suspect. I identified myself as a police officer, told him to "Stop! Put your hands in the air! Face away from me!" The suspect complied. I ordered the suspect to walk back toward my voice. As the suspect was walking backward, Officer Jenkins arrived at my location. When the suspect was about ten feet in front of my patrol car, I told him to get on the ground. He complied. Officer Jenkins handcuffed the suspect and searched him for weapons. No handgun or other weapons were found. The suspect (Robert Earp) was placed in the back of my patrol car.
>
> I drove Mr. Earp to the corner of Brooks Street and Tenth Avenue, so the reporting person (Ralph Middleton) could positively identify Mr. Earp as the person who had the gun. Mr. Middleton stated that Mr. Earp

was not the person who had fired the shots. I removed Mr. Earp's handcuffs, apologized for detaining him, and explained my justification for handcuffing him at gunpoint.

I stopped and detained Mr. Earp at gunpoint because I am aware that 70 percent of the suspects that kill law enforcement officers, who are investigating "man with gun calls," have made a predetermined decision to kill the officer if given the opportunity. Consequently, I was afraid that if I used insufficient caution when I stopped and detained Mr. Earp, who was suspected of possessing a handgun, I would be killed.

Officer Disability. A physical impairment is justification for the use of an escalated use of force. An officer can have a physical disability that impairs his or her ability to control a resisting Threat or defeat a combative one and still be approved by a physician for full duty.

A heart problem will impair an officer's ability to win a prolonged struggle. Chronic knee and hip pain limits an officer's ability to move quickly and restricts balanced movement. Elbow and shoulder pain reduces the flexibility and the strength required to deliver effective baton strikes, focused blows, and apply joint manipulation control techniques and leverage takedowns. Fused or deteriorating spinal disks limit the officer's range of motion and lessens his or her ability to bend, turn, twist, lift, push, and pull—all movements necessary to physically control a Threat.

Simply stated, because of the disability, the officer fears that he or she will be overpowered and seriously injured or killed. A reasonable fear, since 83 percent of officer assaults are committed with the Threat's hands, fists, or feet.

In the following wrongful death lawsuit, the officer successfully used his disability as justification for his use of deadly force. On a warm summer afternoon, a deputy responded to a complaint of a man bothering patrons at a mini-mart. The middle-aged deputy had just returned to full duty after having a pacemaker placed in his heart. The deputy pulled into the store's parking lot and immediately identified the panhandler. The suspect was nineteen years old, over six feet tall, and weighed a lean one hundred and ninety pounds.

The deputy entered the mini-mart and was told by the store manager that she wanted the panhandler off the store's property. The deputy exited the store and told the suspect that he needed to leave or he would be arrested for criminal trespass. The suspect pulled a large knife from the rear waistband of his pants. The deputy pulled his handgun and backed away from the armed suspect. The deputy ordered the suspect to drop his knife several times. The suspect dropped his knife and told the deputy, "I don't need a knife to kill you." Then, he advanced on the deputy. The deputy backed across the parking lot to the edge of the busy street. As the suspect walked toward the deputy, his shirt blew open exposing his well-defined chest and abdomen muscles.

When the suspect was within ten feet, the deputy fired one round. The suspect died at the scene. At the civil trial, the deputy testified that he shot the suspect because he feared that–because of this heart condition–he would be overpowered and killed with his own handgun. The jury concluded the deputy's use of deadly force was justified.

The following is an example narration of using a physical disability as justification for the use of force:

> I told Mr. Baker that he was under arrest for an outstanding warrant for failure to appear in court for driving while suspended, to stand up, and place his hands behind his back. He remained seated on the sofa. I ordered Mr. Baker three times to stand up and submit to being handcuffed. "If you are going to take me to jail, you are going to have to come get me. I can beat your ass on my worst day," was his response. At that time, I pulled my Taser, placed the laser sight on his abdomen, and warned him that if he did not get on the floor he would be shocked. He look up at me and said: "F . . k you. Shock me. I will sue your ass."
>
> I deployed my Taser to Mr. Baker in probe mode. The probes hit him in the lower abdomen and the left upper thigh. As a result of the shock, he fell forward onto the floor. While under power of the Taser, Officer Myers handcuffed him.
>
> Mr. Baker is five feet and nine inches tall and weighs three hundred and nine pounds. I deployed the Taser to Mr. Baker in probe mode because I have a previously injured right shoulder. Although my physician has approved my return to active duty, there is a possibility that if I strain my shoulder or if a suspect pulls on my arm my shoulder may be reinjured.
>
> Because of Mr. Baker's size, I feared that if Officer Myers and I applied physical pain compliance holds to Mr. Baker's arms that he would actively resist and reinjure my shoulder. If my shoulder were injured, I would be unable to keep Mr. Baker from disarming me of my handgun during the struggle–my gun is carried on my right side. Consequently, I feared that if I became disabled Mr. Baker would kill me and/or Officer Myers with my handgun.

GROUND LEVEL. There is an old law enforcement adage: "If you are on the ground, you are losing the fight." Mike Espinoza (law enforcement veteran, black belt in Brazilian Jiu-Jitsu who was personally trained by the Gracie Family, and a law enforcement ground-fighting instructor) tells officers in his classes: "The last place you want to be during a struggle is on the ground. You don't want to grapple with a suspect on the asphalt with a gunbelt or on the floor of a bar with the suspect's drunk buddies circled around you." The goal of Mike's law enforcement ground-fighting training is to use Jiu-Jitsu techniques to protect yourself, escape to a standing position, and transition to a more appropriate level of force: baton, pepper spray, Taser, or firearm.

Recently, defensive tactics instructors have become enamored with ground fighting. Yes, basic ground-fighting skills are beneficial, but they should be part of the total training package and not the sole basis of the defensive tactics program.

There is a reason why we order and take suspects or inmates to the ground: They are more easily immobilized, controlled, and restrained. Furthermore, they cannot generate as much power or leverage to resist while on the ground. Lastly, placing a suspect on the ground places him or her in a tactically inferior position. It is for these reasons that an officer, who finds himself or herself at ground level, is at a greater risk of being seriously injured or killed.

On a traffic stop, an officer discovered why it is dangerous to grapple with a suspect on the ground. The officer had stopped the vehicle for speeding. When he ran the driver for wants, dispatch informed him that the driver had a nonviolent misdemeanor warrant. The officer asked the driver to step back to his patrol vehicle. The driver complied. Once at his car, the officer told the driver he was under arrest for an outstanding misdemeanor warrant and to place his hands behind his back. The driver placed his hands behind his back and gave the officer no indication he planned to resist. When the officer grabbed his hand to placed the first handcuff on, the driver spun around and tackled the officer.

The officer and the driver grappled on the ground. The officer had received ground defense training through his department. After wrestling briefly on the ground, the officer found himself on his back with the driver on top of him. The officer wrapped his legs around the driver's torso in a "Closed Guard" position. Further, the officer trapped the driver's head and pulled it to him to control the driver's posture. The officer could hear the sirens of the responding cover officers. He knew back-up was no more than a minute away, so his strategy was to keep the driver held in place until the cover officers could remove and control him.

What the officer did not know was that his back-up pistol had fallen from its ankle holster while he grappled with the driver. The driver had found the weapon and had it pressed against the officer's head, as the driver repeatedly pulled the trigger. By the grace of God, the driver did not know the pistol had an external safety. When the cover officers arrived, they found the driver secured in the officer's Guard, and the driver trying to shoot the officer in the head.

The following is an example narration of using being at ground level as justification for the use of force:

> When I applied the Escort Hold to Mr. Stanley to lead him out of the bar, Mr. Stanley pulled his arm away violently. As he pulled his arm away, I lost my balance and slipped on a puddle of beer that was on the floor. I fell backward and landed on my back on the floor. I was not injured by the fall, but Mr. Stanley was standing over me with his fists clenched. I pulled my Taser and ordered him to back away. Mr. Stanley took two steps back and said: "You are not so tough now, are you?" I deployed my Taser in probe mode to Mr. Stanley's abdomen. As I deployed the Taser, I stood up. When Mr. Stanley was Tasered, he fell to his right–landing first on a table and then on the floor.
>
> I deployed my Taser in probe mode to Mr. Stanley because I feared he would kick me or jump on top of me while I was on the ground. I know I cannot defend myself effectively while sitting or laying on the ground. Being at ground level limits my mobility, places me at a tactical disadvantage, and places me in greater danger of being successfully assaulted and disarmed of my pepper spray, Taser, and handgun. Consequently, I deployed my Taser to Mr. Baker because I was afraid that Mr. Baker or another patron in the bar would assault me.

DISTANCE. In officer survival training, the distance between you and the Threat is referred to as the "reactionary gap." The shorter the distance between you and the Threat, the less time you have to react. This creates more danger for you. To explain this concept, law enforcement developed its own Theory of Relativity: Distance = Time = Options. As this theory illustrates, the greater the distance between you and the Threat the more time you have to evaluate the level of danger and to choose an appropriate defensive response. The "Twenty-one Foot Rule" for defending against an edged weapon attack is a classic example of the application of this theory. Studies have shown that a Threat armed with an edged weapon can bridge a distance of twenty-one feet before an officer can shoot. Of course, there are variables that could lengthen or shorten this reactionary gap. Regardless, the purpose of the study is to illustrate the dangerousness of an edge weapon and the impact distance has on your safety.

The following is an example narration of using distance as justification for the use of force:

I told Mr. Taylor that he was under arrest for DWI. When I did, he tossed his hat on the ground and pushed his sleeves up on his jacket. These behaviors are indications of potentially violent behavior. Fearing that I was about to be assaulted, I applied a hair takedown to Mr. Taylor and took him to the ground.

I applied the hair takedown because Mr. Taylor was less than three feet away from me. At this close distance, I was within his effective striking range. Aware that his action is faster than my reaction, I had to react immediately to prevent Mr. Taylor's imminent attack.

CONFINEMENT. As a criminal justice officer, I have never struggled with a person in the living room of a five thousand square foot house. I have, however, grappled with suspects in small apartments and single-wide trailers, bathrooms, bedrooms, crowded bars, jail cells, restaurants, small living rooms packed with furniture and people, buses, cars, motorhomes, tents, trains, and a U-Haul trailer. A confined space increases the danger to you by placing you too close to the suspect or inmate. An environment that is crowded and/or confined can interfere with your ability to apply control and takedown techniques. Being in a confined space limits your ability to evade the Threat's attack. It increases the risk that you will trip or fall over an object. And just as important, a confined space can prevent your escape or retreat.

Two officers discovered how dangerous dealing with a suspect in a confined space can be when an inexperienced officer took off the suspect's handcuffs to allow him to use the bathroom.

The officers responded to a loud party complaint. When they arrived at the scene, the officers found a house full of underage drinkers. At some point during the round-up of the intoxicated minors, an intoxicated male suspect shoved an officer. He was arrested, handcuffed, and placde on a sofa. As the officers were processing the other minors, the handcuffed suspect told an inexperienced officer that he needed to relieve himself. Not knowing any better, the officer walked him to the bathroom, removed the handcuffs, and stood in front of the open bathroom door as the suspect urinated. When the suspect had finished his business, he refused to come out of the bathroom. The inexperienced officer entered the very small bathroom to retrieve the suspect. When he entered, the suspect punched the officer and a struggle ensued.

The supervisor heard the commotion in the bathroom and responded. The two officers struggled with the suspect in the very confined space. Because the supervisor had no room to maneuver, the suspect was able to kick the supervisor in the groin and the knee (injuring his knee) before the suspect was finally controlled with the Taser.

This example clearly illustrates the danger presented in confronting and controlling a Threat in a confined space.

The following is an example narration of using confinement as justification for the use of force:

> I was issuing citations for minor in possession of alcoholic beverages to the people in the living room when I heard an officer giving verbal commands from the bathroom.
>
> When I reached the bathroom doorway, I observed Officer Bateman struggling with a male suspect. The officer had the suspect pushed up against the sink, and the suspect was swinging his left elbow backward attempting to strike the officer.
>
> I entered the very small bathroom and grabbed the suspect's left arm. The suspect threw a back kick that struck my knee; the pain caused me to release his arm. Before I could recover from the kick to my knee, the suspect kicked backward again and struck me in the groin. This kick pushed me against the wall. When I hit the wall, I observed the suspect spin and punch Officer Bateman in the face.
>
> I pulled my Taser and deployed the probes to the right side of his torso. The suspect fell forward onto the bathroom floor. Officer Bateman handcuffed the suspect under the power of the Taser.
>
> I deployed my Taser in probe mode to the Threat because of the confined space in which Officer Bateman and I were struggling with the Threat. The confinement of the small bathroom prevented me from disengaging from the Threat after I had been kicked twice. In addition, the confined space prevented Officer Bateman from evading the Threat's punches. Further, because of the confined space, there was not enough room to take the Threat to the ground with a takedown technique. As a result of our confinement, the deployment of the Taser in probe mode was the safest and most effective way to control the violent Threat.

SUDDEN ATTACK. When the Threat suddenly attacks an officer, he or she is not afforded the time to evaluate his or her force options and select the least intrusive force option. Subsequently, the officer simply instinctively reacts in self-defense. Action is faster than reaction. Consequently, when a Threat initiates a sudden attack, the Threat has the tactical advantage, and the officer is put on the defensive. As a result, the officer can use more force initially to protect himself or herself.

The following is an example narration of using a sudden attack as justification for the use of force:

The security guard pointed to Mr. Alberton and said: "That's him. I want him removed from the beer garden." I walked over to Mr. Alberton and informed him that security wanted him to leave. "I am not going anywhere. I just bought this beer," he replied. Mr. Alberton's eyes were glassy and his speech was slurred. It was obvious to me based on his appearance, speech, and odor that the beer he had in his hand was not his first.

When Mr. Alberton put his cup on the table, I placed an escort hold on Mr. Alberton's right arm to escort him out of the beer garden. He had reluctantly taken a few steps toward the exit, when he spun toward me and threw a punch at my face with his left hand. I pulled my head back, causing his punch to narrowly miss my face. I released the escort hold, trapped Mr. Alberton's head with both of my hands, and delivered three knee strikes to his abdomen. With each strike, I told him to "Get on the ground." The strikes stunned Mr. Alberton. As a result, I was able to pull him forward and onto the ground. After I had Mr. Alberton controlled, I handcuffed him with his hands behind his back.

I delivered the knee strikes to Mr. Albertson because he suddenly attacked me. Consequently, I had very little time to react to his attack. Mr. Alberton's first punch barely missed my face. I was afraid that if I did not act quickly and decisively Mr. Alberton would throw another punch, knee strike me in the groin, kick my knee, or stomp on my foot.

Criteria for the Justification of Force

The escalation of force is only justified when the application of lesser force is ineffective or inappropriate. There are times when you must react spontaneously, without the luxury of a reasoned response to a situation. However, more often than not, you will have the time to weigh the use of force options and select the appropriate response. During this selection process, ask yourself the following questions:

Is the action (use of force) worth the risk of injury to the Threat or myself? Are you acting on behalf of the public's best interest or because your ego has been bruised? The potential for serious physical injury to the Threat or yourself should always be considered when choosing a force option. However, you also must consider the risk of professional and financial injury to yourself. Is what you are about to do worth the emotional wear and tear of an excessive force lawsuit, the professional devastation of a criminal conviction, or the financial ruin from legal fees? The question applies to both genders, but it especially applies to male officers. The vast majority of excessive force lawsuits involved male officers, for two reasons: Male officers make up a much higher percentage of a police force. Male officers are action driven and product oriented.

In her book, *You Just Don't Understand: Men and Women in Conversation,* Deborah Tannen explains that men are product oriented and women are process oriented. To a man, the outcome is what is most important–how that outcome is achieved is given little if any consideration. In contrast, to a woman, the process that is used to create the outcome is equally as important as the outcome. For an example: An officer tells the driver of a 1960 Ford sedan that he is under arrest and to step out of his car. The driver refuses to exit. In response, a male officer tells the driver: "You can come easy or you can come hard it doesn't matter to me. If I have to recreate your birth by pulling you out through the wing-vent, so be it." Conversely, a female officer will respond by asking, "Why won't you step out of the car? Is there a reason why you can't? If you can, but you won't–I will have to Taser you. You will fall out of the car; it will really hurt. And, you will still go to jail. What do you want to do?" Of the two responses, which officer do you think will probably be sued?

Is this the least amount of force necessary to accomplish my goal (Threat control)? It is easier to sell your use of force decision to a jury when you start with the lowest appropriate force option and escalate up the continuum until you find a level of force that is effective.

Here is an example: "I told Mr. Smith to stand up and put his hands behind back. He refused. Because my presence and verbal commands were ineffective, I applied an escort hold to his left arm and attempted to pull him out of the chair. He balked at my effort to pull him up. Because the escort hold was ineffective, I applied a wrist lock to his left arm. He stiffened his arm and powered out of my wrist lock. Because my attempts to use lesser force were ineffective, I deployed my Taser in probe mode to the left side of Mr. Smith's torso. The Taser shock was effective in controlling Mr. Smith."

As explained in *Graham v. Conner,* you are not required to use the least amount of force necessary to control a suspect or inmate. However, from a lawsuit winnability viewpoint, the least amount of force necessary to control the Threat often appears to be the most reasonable to a jury.

Does the Threat have the opportunity to comply with my commands? People are not born with the innate knowledge to assume a high-risk handcuffing position or to stop resisting when subjected to pain compliance by an officer.

For example, most of the injuries that occur from the use of pepper spray does not come from the pepper spray. The suspect is injured from the takedown that occurs after the suspect has been sprayed. When I ask officers why they physically forced the suspects to the ground? "He didn't go to the ground after I sprayed him," they almost always answer. "Did you tell him to get on the ground?" I ask. "Ah, no," is almost always their reply. If you don't give verbal commands when using force—you can't expect the Threat to comply, a witness to recite them at trial, or convince a jury that the Threat was intentionally resisting your attempts to control him or her.

Is the current course of action accomplishing the desired result? If your force is not working, change it. If what you are doing is not effectively controlling the Threat, you have three options: disengage, escalate the force, or use a different force option.

I don't understand why, but officers have a tendency to continue to use an ineffective force option or stubbornly struggle to apply a control technique that they clearly cannot effectively apply. I see this happen time and time again in defensive tactics training, and I observe it routinely in lawsuits.

For example in one lawsuit, the officers continued to shoot the suspect with beanbag rounds and shock him multiple times with the Taser when the officers knew those force options had proven ineffective to control him. If the officers would have abandoned their use of impact munitions and the Taser and applied the polyester pile, focused blows, baton strikes, or the neck restraint, the incident may not have ended in a shooting. From a managing the use of force incident point of view, if the officers had exhausted all their force options before shooting the suspect, it would have been easier to sell their use of deadly force to the jury.

Principles of Force Justification

While developing the Oregon Public Safety Academy's use of force curriculum, I formulated the following principles to assist officers in understanding the relationship between the Threat's resistance, the officer's application of force to overcome that resistance, and the potential for injury.

If the level of force is justified, the implement or delivery system used is of minimal relevance. This principle provides you with a practical understanding of the admonishment from *Graham v. Connor* that your force needs only be objectively reasonable. In theory, it is the level of force that is evaluated and not the weapon. For example: If you are justified in applying a joint manipulation technique to a Threat, it does not matter which technique you use or whether you apply the lock to the wrist, elbow, or shoulder.

If you are justified in striking a Threat with an impact weapon, it does not matter whether you use a conventional baton, expandable baton, side-handle baton, a flashlight, folding chair, muzzle or butt of a gun, shovel handle, etc.

If you are justified in using deadly force, it does not matter whether you use your gun, a third person's gun, a tactical folding knife, baton, or your patrol car, etc.

If the level of force is justified, the degree of injury the Threat may sustain is determined by the level and intensity of the resistance offered. When an officer applies force, the intensity and frequency of that force is determined by Threat's reluctance to comply. Officers do not apply force proactively; an officer's force is administered in response to the Threat's verbal, nonverbal, and physical resistance.

For example: When an officer applies a wristlock, the pressure to the wrist is graduated until the Threat complies. If the Threat complies after only moderate pressure to the wrist, the pressure is maintained until the handcuffs are applied; consequently, the wrist is not injured. However, if the Threat continues to resist, the officer applies graduated pressure to the wrist until the Threat submits. The increasing pressure may cause a strain or more serious injury before the Threat submits to use of pain compliance.

In this scenario, the Threat is in control of how much force is applied to his or her wrist. At any point, the Threat can comply and stop the increasing pressure to his or her wrist.

The Threat's behavior and actions dictate the degree of force to be used; therefore, the Threat is responsible for any injury that may incur while resisting a lawful application of force. As explained in the last principle, an officer's use of force is reactionary. This does not imply that all force applied in reaction to the Threat's behavior is lawful. However, in the justified reactionary use of force, the Threat is responsible for any injury the Threat receives from his or her failure to comply with the officer's lawful orders.

A Threat has two choices when an officer gives him or her verbal commands: comply or resist. When an officer tells the Threat to stand up and place his hands behind his back, if the Threat complies, the officer's force is minimal and the Threat is not injured. If the Threat resists, the officer is required to apply a greater level of force to overcome his or her resistance. If during the process of overcoming the Threat's resistance he or she is injured, the Threat is responsible for that injury. If the Threat had simply complied with the officer's verbal commands, he or she would not have been injured. This principle applies only to lawfully deployed force.

It is incumbent of the officer to overcome the Threat's resistance as quickly as possible to minimize the possibility (or the degree) of injury to the Threat and/or the officer. Under certain circumstances, it is preferable that an officer deploys a level of force that quickly overcomes the Threat's resistance, even if that level of force causes some degree of injury.

By overcoming the Threat's resistance quickly, the officer limits the Threat's opportunity to assault the officer or access one or more of the officer's weapons. Quickly taking control of the Threat can minimize the need to escalate to a level of force that may seriously injure the Threat.

In every officer and Threat interaction, the Threat has access to a weapon—the officer's. Officers carry as part of their uniform a baton, electronic control device, handcuffs, pens, pepper spray, portable radio, tactical folding knife, and a firearm.

During the officer's attempt to control the Threat, the Threat can gain access to any of these tools and inflict serious injury or death to the officer. Therefore, the officer can be justified in the use of deadly force to protect him or herself.

An officer's decisive application of force does more than limit the Threat's access to the officer's tools; it can prevent the Threat from obtaining objects that can be used as a weapon in the immediate area.

Furthermore, the decisive use of force can prevent a physical assault with the Threat's personal weapons and a subsequent officer disarming. As has been demonstrated in many officer deaths, the Threat initially used personal weapons to disable the officer to gain access to his or her weapon.

In this chapter, we discussed the factors and circumstances that define when a person is an immediate threat. Furthermore, I presented guidelines for the justification for the escalation of force, and I explained how those guidelines can positively influence the outcome of an excessive force lawsuit. In the next chapter, I will offer an explanation of the levels of force and their placement in the continuum of force.

Part II

PREPARING FOR THE
USE OF FORCE INCIDENT

Chapter 5

THE FORCE CONTINUUM–TO USE OR
NOT TO USE THAT IS THE QUESTION

The benefit of using a force continuum to train police officers is that at trial
it shows the jury that there is a reasoned thought process used in making use
of force decisions. It shows that cops are not just a bunch of out of control
cowboys out there using force on people.
–Robert Franz, Jr., Attorney
(Personal communication, 1989)

Recently, a philosophical movement has gained momentum regarding a change in the way use of force is taught to criminal justice officers. A small number of police defense attorneys are recommending that criminal justice agencies abandon the concept of a continuum of force with all its trapping and instruct officers in only *Graham v. Connor's* objective reasonableness standard. This training recommendation is based on the premise that the objective reasonableness standard is so vague that a plaintiff's attorney cannot exploit the discrepancies between the officer's actions and his use of force training.

Here is the flaw with replacing a force continuum model with the objective reasonableness standard: The strategy is myopic and shortsighted; it only provides your attorney with a tactical advantage at trial. Teaching only the objective reasonableness standard does not address the cause of excessive force litigation and all the problems associated with it.

The primary cause of excessive force litigation is poor use of force decision-making by the officer. How does only teaching officers that their use of force must be objectively reasonable based on the totality of the circumstances help them make proper use of force decisions? Hello, pull your head out of the group think tank–it doesn't. It is like telling a fat kid with diabetes to make healthy food choices without providing him with the nutritional information regarding his food options. The secondary cause of excessive force litigation is the mismanagement of the use of force incident. If teaching officers the guidelines outlined in *Graham v. Connor*–a ruling made in 1985– was effective in managing the use of force incident, by now, excessive force complaints would be only faded memories.

Even if you do embrace replacing the force continuum with the objective reasonableness standard, you have to acknowledge the universal truth regarding the use of force: There is a continuum of force that starts with the officer's presence, escalates with increasingly more intrusive force, and culminates with deadly force. So, if the continuum of force exists, why not teach it?

The purpose of the force continuum is to provide an officer with an understanding of which level of force is objectively reasonable in relationship to a specific level of resistance. In addition, the force continuum conveys the department's standards regarding the proper use of force to the officer. How can you expect a new officer to make proper use of force decisions if you don't explain the hierarchy of force? A new officer has little, if any, law enforcement experience to draw from to determine what is an objectively reasonable amount of force to use in any given situation.

Further, how can you expect veteran officers to make proper use of force decisions if you do not provide a use of force blueprint for them to follow? Like the fat kid who will always choose cake over brand cereal without considering the long-term health consequences of his decision. The veteran officer, without a use of force model to guide him, will intuitively make decisions on the amount of force to use without considering the decision's impact on a potential lawsuit.

The main argument against using a force continuum model stems from the plaintiff attorney's ability to effectively challenge a poorly conceived force continuum and the officer's inability to explain the use of force generally. During the discovery process, the plaintiff's attorney will receive copies of the department's use of force training materials. Often included in those materials is a copy of the department's force continuum model. Most criminal justice agencies do not develop their own force continuum. They adopt another department's continuum model with little understanding of how to explain it. Or, if the agency does develop their own model, the developers do so not anticipating it would be used against their officer in an excessive force lawsuit.

The following is an excerpt from an officer's deposition in an excessive force lawsuit. The officer is asked to explain an inconsistency between his use of the Taser and his department's force continuum model. Unfortunately, the officer's department adopted the continuum model with little understanding of how to explain the levels of force:

Question: And was this the use of force continuum that your agency used in 2006?

Answer: Yes.

Question: And is it still your use of force continuum?

Answer: Yes.

Question: Where does the use of the Taser fall?

Answer: Under physical control.

Question: Isn't it listed under serious physical control?

Answer: This is a very old continuum that was adopted from the academy a long time ago.

Question: So the use of OC spray would be deemed more serious than the use of the Taser under this continuum?

Answer: No. If we were to make a continuum for the Taser, the Taser would be right beside OC.

Question: So a Taser can be a serious physical control or a physical control?

Answer: It could be–once it meets physical control, you can use anything below that. So if you are in serious physical control–why it goes up to serious physical control is because it can be–we don't want to deter people from trying lesser options like the Taser or OC even if it gets to where they are impacting–doing impact weapons or focused blows or anything like that. They can still have that option available to them if that makes sense.

Did his explanation make any sense? Do you understand why the Taser is placed in the physical control category? I reviewed the department's force continuum model, and I don't understand what he is trying to say. The officer's explanation is a classic example of what happens when a department adopts another organization's force continuum model without obtaining the necessary knowledge to explain it.

Most of the early use of force training models only illustrated the escalating levels of force. The levels of force were normally represented in a stair-step graphic. Although the "Stair-Step" force continuum effectively illustrates the hierarchy of force, it does not define the relationship between each level of force and the levels of the Threat's resistance.

Consequently at trial, the plaintiff's attorney successfully attacked the officer's use of force by claiming that he was trained to start at "Step One" in the force continuum and escalate through each successive level of force until the inmate or suspect was under control. But because the officer immediately went to "Step Four," he violated his training and therefore used too much force for the situation. Then, to make matters worse for the officer's attorney, the officer could not intelligently explain to the jury why the plaintiff attorney's interpretation of the force continuum was wrong.

Americans in general are plagued by a "victim mentality." "It's not my fault," is the rallying cry when things don't go our way. Criminal justice officers are not exempt from this American malady. The only thing cops hate more than being wrong is being made a fool of on the witness stand. Unfortunately for us, that is what attorneys are trained to do. So, rather than admit that he lacked the knowledge to effectively justify his use of force, the defendant officer blames the loss of the lawsuit on the force continuum model, the slimy plaintiff's attorney, and dumb jurors.

Knowing that law enforcement officers and trainers are reluctant to accept responsibility for the loss of their excessive force lawsuits, a few civil defense attorneys started recommending that academies and departments drop the force continuum model and only teach the "objective reasonableness" standard. As stated previously, a recommendation that helps the trial lawyer, but does nothing to proactively minimize excessive force complaints and lawsuits or effectively manage the use of force incident.

FORCE CONTINUUM MODELS

The force continuum is the full spectrum of force that starts with your presence and escalates to deadly force. It is impossible to include every conceivable force option in a force continuum model. Consequently, only the force options that are taught in defensive tactics, firearms, and other use of force-related classes are included in a use of force training model. Furthermore, a force continuum is based on an ideal model: The Threat and the officer are equal in every way. This is often not the case. Therefore, you must move up or down the continuum based on the Threat's actions, officer/threat factors, influential circumstances, and the totality of the circumstances.

There are five force continuum models that are used to train criminal justice officers. The following is a description of each model accompanied by a discussion of its strengths and weaknesses.

STAIR-STEP CONTINUUM. As was discussed previously, the Stair Step Continuum (Figure 5.1) was the first force continuum model developed, and it was avidly adopted by criminal justice agencies. Illustrated as a set of stairs with each step representing a level of force, the first step was titled "Officer Presence" and the top step was labeled "Deadly Force." Each step in-between was labeled either as a level of force or as a method of force.

This model of continuum has been illustrated as a ladder, a sliding scale, and a pyramid. This continuum effectively demonstrates the hierarchy of

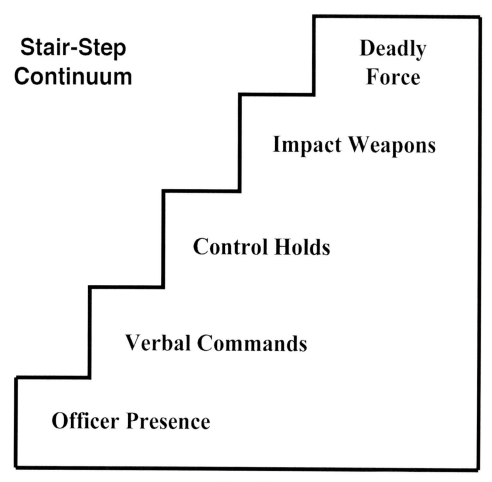

Stair-Step Continuum

Deadly Force

Impact Weapons

Control Holds

Verbal Commands

Officer Presence

Figure 5.1

force. However, as a stand-alone training model, it is incomplete; this model does not represent the relationship between the level of resistance and the appropriate level of force. Consequently, when officers have been trained with this model, plaintiff attorneys have effectively challenged the officer's use of force at trial.

PIE OR WHEEL CONTINUUM. The wheel continuum (Figure 5.2) was developed to prevent a plaintiff's attorney from claiming that the officer had to start at Step One and escalate up through each subsequent level of force. This continuum model resembles a sliced pie with a circle (hub) in the center. The hub is labeled as the "Officer." Each slice of the pie is labeled as a method of force. This model effectively illustrates the methods of force that are available to an officer. However, this model is flawed in that it represents

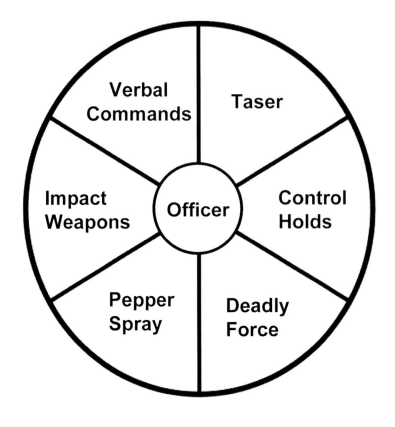

Wheel Continuum

Figure 5.2

all force options as being of equal intrusiveness: Pepper spray is the same level of force as a bite from a police dog. Consequently, this model provides no meaningful guidance in selecting the appropriate force response to a specific level of resistance to inexperienced officers and veterans alike.

INTERLOCKING RINGS CONTINUUM. This model (Figure 5.3) is a stylistic variation of the Pie Continuum. This force continuum is represented by an overlay of five to seven rings that form a circular cluster. The center ring represents the officer. Each overlapping ring is labeled as a level of force or a method of force. This model suffers from the same instructional deficiencies as the Pie Continuum.

MATRIX CONTINUUM. A matrix force continuum model (Figure 5.4) uses a graph consisting of lined columns and rows with the levels of resistance labeled on a horizontal scale and the methods of force on a vertical scale. A

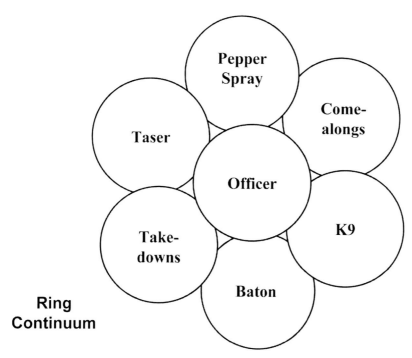

Figure 5.3

check mark or an "X" is used to indicate where the use of force method and the level of resistance intersect. Because this chart links each force option to a method of resistance in a grid, it has an overwhelming appearance and is difficult to interpret. Another form of matrix continuum uses three or more separate graphs that represent the levels of resistance, methods of force, and their definitions. These complicated continuums are often developed by academics. Consequently, the officer must be a doctoral candidate to decipher the continuum. Because of their complexity, these models of continuum–although at first glance look quite impressive–offer very little useful guidance to the average officer.

RELATIVE CONTINUUM. This model is titled the Relative Force Continuum (Figure 5.5) because is illustrates the relativeness between the level of the Threat's resistance and the appropriate force option. I originally developed this continuum model for the Oregon Board on Police Standards and Training. It has been successfully used to defend criminal justice officers' use of force over two hundred times in state and federal court trials and labor relations' hearings. When the officer's use of force was applied in accordance with the guidelines set forth in this model, jurors have found the officer's use of force reasonable in 97.7 percent of the civil trials.

Methods of Force	No Resistance	Passive	Active	Aggressive	Lethal
Deadly Force	●	●	●	●	X
Neck Restraint	●	●	●	X	✓
Less-Lethal	●	●	●	X	✓
Impact Weapon	●	●	✓	X	✓
Counter Strikes	●	●	✓	X	✓
Taser - Probe	●	●	✓	X	
Takedowns	●	✓	X	✓	
Pepper Spray	●	✓	X	X	
Comealongs	●	X	✓		
Pressure Points	●	X	✓		
Verbal	X				
Presence	X				

Matrix Continuum

● - N/A   X - Primary   ✓ - Secondary

Resistance Category

Figure 5.4

The following is an explanation of what sets a Relative Continuum apart from other force continuum models:

Court Defensibility: When the plaintiff's attorney attacks this continuum as he does a stair-step continuum, the attack is countered by explaining that this is a relative continuum model and officers are trained to identify the level of resistance that the Threat is offering in the Level of Resistance column and index to the left to the Method of Force column to determine the appropriate level of force. This explanation immediately neutralizes the plaintiff's attorney's attack.

Clearly Illustrates the Hierarchy of Force: The Relative Continuum not only lists the levels of force, but it also defines the methods of force for each level. For placement in the continuum, the methods of force were evaluated and rated for their injury potential by a cross-section of physicians: orthopedic surgeon, neurologist, internist, optometrist, and a pathologist. Based on the physicians' rating for potential injury, the methods of force were listed in an escalating scale from least injurious to most.

Illustrates the Relationship between Resistance and Force: This model links the Level of Resistance to the Level of Force and not a specific force option. Each Level of Force has contained within it a list of escalating force options.

Relative Force Continuum

Level of Force		Method of Force		Level of Resistance	Threat
VI	**Deadly**	Any force readily capable of causing death or serious physical injury		**Lethal**	**R E S I S T I V E**
V	**Serious Physical Control**	Neck Restraint Less-Lethal K-9 (Bite) Impact Weapon Focused Blows Electrical Stun (Probe Deploy)	*Pain Compliance*	**Ominous**	
IV	**Physical Control**	Hair Takedown Joint Takedown Digital Control Pepper Spray ECD - Drive Stun Joint Comealong Pressure Points		**Active** **Static**	
III	**Physical Contact**	Escort Position Directional Contact		**Verbal**	Undecided
II	**Verbal** Communication	Direct Order Questioning Persuasion			
I	**Presence**	Display of Force Option Body Language Identification of Authority		**None**	Complying

Developed by Howard Webb

Figure 5.5

Therefore, this model operates philosophically within the objective reasonableness standard: The officer is not required to use the least intrusive force option in the Level of Force. The officer may choose any force option in that level of force that the officer can justify as being reasonable.

Easily Understood: This model uses a very simple and straightforward illustration to represent the continuum of force. It was developed by a criminal justice trainer to train criminal justice officers to make proper use of force decisions. The new officer, with limited experience, can easily understand which methods of force would be appropriate for a specific level of resistance. Veteran officers at a glance can use it as a blueprint for using objectively reasonable force. First-line supervisors can use it as a resource in determining if their officers' use of force was appropriate for the level of the suspect's resistance.

The Relative Continuum Model explained in this book is an updated version of my original continuum. The updated model includes the current developments in subject restraint technology. Further, this version reflects the federal courts' rulings that have placed restrictions on the use of these new technologies.

Developing a Force Continuum Model

As with developing any criminal justice training program, the first step in developing a use of force training model is to clearly define its objectives. An effective force continuum model addresses the following training objectives:

To Train New Officers to Use Reasonable Force. How can an inexperienced officer make a proper use of force decision without an understanding of what your department deems reasonable force? In the absence of specific guidelines, the inexperienced officer will use a trial and error approach for determining reasonable force—an approach that can cost your department hundreds of thousands of dollars in lawsuits. Consequently, your force continuum model should establish guidelines for using force that are easily understood by the recruit officer.

To Provide a Blueprint for Veteran Officers' Use of Force. Just as a carpenter cannot properly build a house without a blueprint, an officer cannot properly manage the use of force incident without a schematic explaining the relationship between the proper level of force and the level of resistance. Through your force continuum model, the veteran officer applies the use of force within a framework that your department has sanctioned as reasonable.

To Explain Police Use of Force to Citizens. Your force continuum model may be used to explain the use of force generally to attendees of a citizens' police academy, and justify an officers' specific use of force to a citizen review board, the city council, or county commissioners. Your force continuum, therefore, must be easily understood by the layperson.

To Assist Jurors in Understanding the Officer's Use of Force. A properly developed force continuum model is essential in explaining an officer's use of force to a jury. When properly constructed, a force continuum will illustrate the reasonableness of an officer's use of force. However, the continuum's effectiveness in court is directly linked to the ease in which the jurors can understand it. With that point made, a continuum model that logically explains the levels of force and their relationship to the levels of resistance in common language will assist in the officer's defense against allegations of excessive use of force.

To develop your own continuum model requires a moderate amount of research and a great deal of common sense. The second step in creating a force continuum model is to develop a comprehensive understanding of the use of force in your specific discipline: corrections, law enforcement, or both. Every criminal justice officer has an opinion regarding the proper use of force; however, if you are going to put your model in the classroom and/or courtroom to be challenged, your explanation of the continuum must be informed, reasoned, and defendable.

Your research should start with a review of the U.S. Supreme Court's and appellate court's rulings on the use of deadly and nondeadly force. This can help you to quickly establish the proper placement of a specific force option in the hierarchy of force. For example, the Ninth Circuit Court of Appeals has ruled that a Taser Drive Stun is less force than a probe deployment. Furthermore, the Ninth Circuit ruled that the use of beanbag munitions is a greater level of force than a police dog bite. Research of this nature, not only will save you time, it ensures your model is defensible. When the federal courts evaluate whether the use of a specific force option was reasonable, it ultimately comes down to the severity of the injury the inmate or suspect sustained. Consequently, I strongly recommend that you consult with a cross section of medical experts regarding the injury potential for each specific force option. And base the placement of each force option in your continuum on the potential for injury.

Next, you want to research examples of where specific methods of force have injured inmates and suspects in the field and officers in training. Very few state criminal justice regulating agencies conduct independent research on the effectiveness and injury potential of subject control devices and methods. Consequently, newly developed force options are implemented by criminal justice agencies without a thorough understanding of the device's injury potential. As a result, you are forced to analyze antidotal and not statistical information to assist you in making the determination on a control method's placement in the force continuum.

Lastly, you must consider what level of mastery the officer must possess to effectively apply the control method to a combative or resisting inmate or suspect. As an example, I heard a police tactics expert testify that an officer can effectively defend himself against pugilistic attacks (punches and kicks) with joint manipulation techniques. Well, maybe, if the officer is a world-renowned Aikido or jiu-jitsu master. However, I have never met an officer who had that level of skill. Based on the limited number of hours officers receive in defensive tactics training at the academy and during inservice training, you must realistically consider the average officer's control tactics skill level when correlating the method of force with the level of resistance in your force continuum model.

Levels of Force

To properly manage the use of force incident, you must understand the hierarchy of force. For this reason, we will discuss the levels of force and the force options that constitute each level. The levels of force identified in continuum models vary between five to seven. I have found that by dividing the continuum into six levels officers and jurors quickly develop a practical understanding of the use of force.

The following is an explanation of each level of force and its force options starting with the officer's presence and escalating to deadly force:

Level One–PRESENCE

An officer has an expectation that inappropriate or unlawful behavior will stop upon the officer's arrival. Presence is comprised of three progressive levels:

DISPLAY OF AUTHORITY. A badge, uniform, police identification, and/or a marked patrol vehicle are identifiable symbols of an officer's authority. An officer uses these symbols for psychological control and to deter unlawful behavior. You have observed compliance through a display of authority on the freeway when you encountered a group of vehicles all traveling at the same speed. As you weaved your way through the vehicles, you will find a marked patrol vehicle at the front of the group. The officer's presence encourages compliance with the speed limit.

OFFICER'S BODY LANGUAGE/DEMEANOR. According to body language experts, up to 90 percent of the communication that occurs between two people is nonverbal. Consequently, through your demeanor and nonverbal gestures, you take psychological control of the Threat. A bladed body, extended eye contact, and/or aggressive hand gestures are examples of non-verbal control tactics.

You use body language intentionally or unintentionally as a form of psychological control every time you confront a noncompliant inmate or suspect. When you initially contact the Threat, you assume an open, nonintimidating posture. But, as soon as the Threat says "no" to your requests, you step back with the gun-side of your body into a bladed stance, place your hand on your gun, and steel your gaze. Your body language and demeanor sends a powerful but simple message: "Do you feel lucky, punk? Well, do you?"

DISPLAY OF A FORCE OPTION. The presentation of a pepper spray canister, electronic control device, baton, K-9, firearm, or a display of a numerical superiority of officers is used to intimidate the Threat into complying. The uninformed mistakenly interpret the pointing of a firearm at a Threat as a use of deadly force. The pointing of a firearm is not deadly force; it is a display of a force option, only. Deadly force does not occur until the bullet leaves the barrel and strikes the body. Merely, pointing a gun at the Threat is only an escalated level of presence. The federal courts have ruled that the use of presence alone as a control method is not excessive force.

Level Two–VERBALIZATION

An officer's verbalization consists of three progressive levels of nonphysical control:

PERSUASION. Verbal persuasion is the use of interpersonal communication skills to defuse hostility and gain the Threat's compliance in lieu of using physical force. Law enforcement personnel refer to interpersonal communication as tactical communication.

QUESTIONING. An officer has the lawful authority to stop, detain, and question a person who the officer reasonably believes is about to commit a crime, is committing a crime, or has committed a crime. Because the person is not free to leave while being questioned, this level of verbalization constitutes an escalated level of intrusion into the person's Fourth Amendment's rights.

DIRECT ORDERS. Are clear and concise verbal commands given that direct an inmate or suspect to do something, not to do something, or stop doing something. Effective verbal commands are simple, given by one officer, and void of profanity. The following is an explanation of each component:

Simple: Effective verbal commands consist of no more than three directives given at one time, one directive at a time is the most effective. Research indicates that under stress a person can only hold between three and five pieces of information in the conscious mind (short-term memory). Our inability to remember no more than three to five pieces of information under stress is the reason why the emergency telephone number has three digits: 911. Because of this hardwiring of our short-term memory, a series of single commands (Get on the ground! Put your arms out to your sides! Turn your palms up! Don't move!) will be more effective than a single string of multiple commands: Get on the ground, put your arms out to your sides, turn your palms up, and don't move!

Given by One Officer: When one officer gives the verbal commands, it eliminates the issuance of contradictory orders from other officers. There have been a number of lawsuits where the witnesses have reported that the officer (after giving the order "Don't move!) shot the suspect for doing what the other officer told him to do ("Get your hands up!"). Further, when two or more officers shout commands simultaneously, the Threat and the witnesses hear only garbled noise.

Void of Profanity: Proper verbal commands are free of profanities and void of terms of endearment that officers develop for the people they interact with in the correctional facility and on the street. I am not so naïve to believe that you will not use profanity on-duty. You will. I did. Suspects and inmates spew vulgarities, and we unconsciously integrate that language into our working vocabulary. So penetrating is the emulsion into the vulgar that you could have been abandoned at birth on the front steps of a monastery and raised by priests who had taken a vow of silence. Within thirty days of becoming an officer, a person would believe, based on your use of profanity, that you were abandoned on the wharf and raised by a gang of longshoremen.

I am not making an excuse for the use of bad language. I am pointing out a side effect of working in the criminal justice system. An adverse side effect that will hurt your credibility with a jury if you allow it to go unchecked when using force.

In *Wold v. City of Springfield,* the federal magistrate ruled in a pretrial motion that if an officer makes a verbal threat regarding the use of force and the use of force being threatened is not justified, the threatening verbalization can violate a person's civil rights.

In Wold, a patrol officer and a K9 Unit responded to a report of a possible burglary of a hotel room at a Red Lion Hotel. The hotel had been plagued by a series of break-ins by homeless people trying to escape the cold weather. Accordingly, when a reception desk clerk received an alert that someone had requested a pay-for-view movie in an unoccupied room, she suspected that a homeless person had broken into the room.

When the officers arrived at the hotel, they were met by hotel security. The security officer followed the officers and the police dog to the burglarized room. The officers knocked on the door, announced their presence, and ordered the burglar to open the door. They did this several times, with no response from the person inside the room. The security officer contacted the front desk and requested that the clerk make a telephone call into the room. A few minutes later the clerk notified security that a man had answered the phone in the room. In addition, the clerk told security that she had told the man that the police were outside his door and he needed to speak with them. A moment later the man in the room opened the door a few inches, it was being held closed by the security latch.

The K9 handler told the man that they believed the room was being burglarized and that if he did not open the door they would send in the police dog. The man unlatched the door. When the officers entered the room, they found an angry, middle aged, naked man standing between the beds. The man angrily told the officers that he had rented the room. As the officers attempted to calm the man down, the front desk clerk telephoned the room and told the officers that she had made a mistake—the man had, in fact, rented the room. Instead of being a homeless person, the occupant was a wealthy businessman from out of town.

The businessman hired an attorney and filed an excessive force lawsuit against the K9 officer. The Plaintiff alleged that the K9 officer had threatened him by saying: "Calm down old man or I will sic my dog on you." As a result, the plaintiff suffered from post-traumatic stress disorder: Every time he observed a police officer or a police dog he would have an anxiety attack and break down with fits of uncontrollable sobbing.

The officer, K9 handler, and the security officer stated that the businessman was never threatened with a dog attack. In fact, the dog didn't even bark, growl or snarl. It just sat there by its handler. However, there was one problematic statement made by the K9 handler to the security officer. While the officers were walking to the hotel room, the security officer asked the handler if his dog was aggressive? "He just went on a call where he got to bite someone, so he may be a little jacked up—he still has the taste of blood in his mouth," the handler replied. Remember our discussion about bravado?

In a pretrial motion, the K9 handler's attorney argued before the court that "We are not saying the officer made that threat, but if he had the police dog did not bite the plaintiff. So, no harm no foul." The magistrate disagreed. In his written decision, he stated the following:

> Plaintiff contends that the police officer defendants threatened to unleash the dog to attack him if he did not "shut up." The officers deny this, but at this stage of the case the court must apply its legal analysis to the plaintiff's version of the

event. In oral argument, counsel for the defendant officers took the position that the threat of force should not be deemed unreasonable so long as the force was not used and a reasonable officer could conclude that such a threat would be useful in gaining control of the situation. When asked if the officers could have threatened to shoot the plaintiff if he did not stop talking, counsel replied that such a threat was not actionable under S 1983 so long as it was not carried out.

The court disagrees with this proposition as a matter of law. If the use of excessive force could not be justified, the threat to use such force, coupled with the apparent immediate ability to use it, would seem to fit the classic definition of an assault.

What was once rude or just offensive language is now an actionable civil rights violation.

Level Three–PHYSICAL CONTACT

This force option utilizes the invasion of a person's personal space, a guiding physical touch, and tactical communication skills to control the Threat. Nonoffensive physical contact is often the starting point for the application of a joint manipulation technique. The two elements of physical contact are:

DIRECTIONAL CONTACT. You may find this surprising, but criminals don't like you. Consequently, they have a tendency to move away from you when move toward them. In fact, most people don't like their personal space invaded or to be touched. As a result, people unconsciously move away from an invasion of their personal space and a physical touch.

You can utilize this naturally occurring reaction as a form of Threat control. By invading the personal space and gently touching the arm or shoulder of the Threat, you can control the movement or change the location of the Threat without him or her feeling threatened or manipulated.

ESCORT HOLD. Our parents have conditioned us to be led by the hand. Your first word as a toddler was "No." And, you use that word in defiance to your mother's request to "Come here!" In response, your mother grabbed your arm and pulled you to her. When the Threat (who is usually intoxicated) refuses to obey your order to step outside, the Threat is demonstrating two-year-old defiance. And, as a result of parental conditioning, the Threat expects you to grab his or her arm.

If people have been conditioned from childhood to be escorted by the arm, we should take advantage of that behavioral imprinting. The Escort Hold capitalizes on this conditioned expectation: it places you in a position of advantage, places the Threat in a position of disadvantage, and is not offensive to the Threat or the observing members of the public.

Sometimes called the "Position of Advantage" by defensive tactics instructors, the Escort Hold is the starting place for the application of joint manipulation techniques. If the Threat will not allow you to apply an Escort Hold, more likely than not, you will be unable to apply a joint manipulation technique to the Threat's wrist, arm, or shoulder.

The main source of my frustration over the years as a defensive tactics instructor has been the telephone call from a former student who says: "Hey, Webb, you know the wristlock you taught me. Well, it didn't work." After a little deeper investigative conversation, I always discover that it was not a technique failure; it was an application failure.

To give you a little background regarding my defensive tactics training, I hold a sixth degree black belt in Okinawa Kenpo Karate and Kobudo. I was the second black belt instructor licensed to teach by the Okinawa Kenpo Karate and Kobudo Association in the United States. The OKKKA was the late Okinawan karate and kobudo master Seikichi Odo's original organization. When I combined my martial arts background with being a criminal justice officer, I learned three very important things about the application of joint manipulation techniques:

- Even with all my martial arts training, I could not effectively apply a joint manipulation technique to an average size, actively resisting male Threat.
- If with my martial arts background I could not effectively apply joint manipulation techniques to a resisting Threat; then, the average police or corrections officer surely could not.
- The only way I could effectively apply a joint manipulation technique to an unsuspecting inmate or suspect was through deception, verbal distraction, subtlety, and by first applying an Escort Hold. If the inmate or suspect tensed his arm or pull it away, I could not through brute force apply the control technique. After having made that tactical discovery, I started teaching the application of joint manipulation techniques only from an Escort Hold. And, during every training session, I explained to all my defensive tactics students why we start the technique from an Escort Hold. So, now you know why I find those whiny phones calls frustrating.

Teaching defensive tactics to cops is sometimes like the Far Side cartoon, "What Dog's Hear?" Joint manipulation techniques can only be successfully applied from an Escort Hold. If the inmate or suspect tenses his or her arm, you cannot effectively apply the hold. It takes deception and subtlety on your part to get the technique locked on. You cannot forcefully apply the lock," this is what the instructor says. This is what the cops hear, "blah, blah,

blah, break, blah, blah, blah, lunch. blah, blah, blah, we are finished for the day."

Level Four–PHYSICAL CONTROL

The physical control category includes mechanical restraints, the application of direct physical pressure to gain compliance through graduated pain, and the localized application of pain administered through chemical or electronic means to gain compliance. The following is an explanation of the methods of force contained in this category:

MECHANICAL RESTRAINTS. The use of a mechanical restraint is considered the lowest level of physical control. Mechanical restraints have a very high potential for control and a low potential for injury, when the restraint is applied properly. The mechanical restraint category includes handcuffs and leg-irons, nylon restraints and flex-cuffs, restraint boards, restraint chairs, and restraint wraps.

When the handcuffs are applied to the proper location on the wrists, adjusted to the proper tightness, and the double-locking mechanism is engaged; the restraints will not cause permanent injury to the nerves of the wrist or forearm. Handcuffs are round. The wrist is flat. By their design, handcuffs create a space between the handcuff bar and the radial nerve on the top of the wrist and the ulnar nerve on the bottom of the wrist. As a result, the only way a person can be injured by a properly applied handcuff is if that person struggles against the handcuffs.

God gave you a place to apply handcuffs (He is a big supporter of law enforcement): the ulnar/radial notch. This notch creates the indention where the wrist attaches to the hand. The major nerves in the wrist pass through the carpal tunnel there. The tunnel provides a natural protection against the handcuffs.

Properly checking the handcuff for the proper tightness occurs in two phases: First, ask the person if the handcuffs are too tight. It has been my experience that most people will tell the truth about the tightness of their handcuffs. Asking about the tightness of the handcuffs does two things: It helps assess how tight the cuffs are. It gives the jury the impression that you care about the plaintiff's well-being. Perception management is the key to properly managing the use of force incident. Second, physically check the handcuff. To physically check the handcuff for the proper tightness, attempt to slip your index finger between the handcuff bar and the top or bottom of the wrist. If you can slip one-half of your fingernail under the handcuff, it is the proper tightness.

Always document that you asked the person if the handcuffs were too tight, the person's response, that you physically checked the handcuffs for the proper tightness, and you engaged the double lock to protect the person from injury in your written report. This documentation is the first proactive step in winning a lawsuit alleging the misapplication of the handcuffs.

When a person complains of pain from the handcuffs, do not give the standard law enforcement response: "Their not designed for comfort. Shut up." If a handcuffed person complains about the pain caused from the cuffs, check the location of the handcuffs on the wrists. Then, recheck the handcuffs for the proper tightness. Document the person's complaint and that you checked the restraints for the proper tightness in your report.

Of the hundreds of lawsuits that I have reviewed, there has only been one where the suspect was permanently injured from the handcuffs.

The suspect had come to the mountains to camp in the forest and trade magic mushrooms for marijuana with the local dopers. A forest service officer observed what he suspected was drug dealing in a campground. The suspect was detained, handcuffed (with his hands behind his back), and placed in a forest service patrol vehicle. He was secured in the patrol vehicle for two and one half-hours while the officer and two deputies searched his vehicle and campsite.

At approximately thirty minutes into the detention, the suspect called out to the officer. When the officer contacted the suspect, he told the officer that his handcuffs were too tight. The handcuffs had not been checked for the proper tightness or double-locked. "They're not designed for comfort. Shut up and sit back in your seat," the officer relied. When the suspect sat back in the seat, the handcuffs tightened further. When the suspect was taken to jail, the officer discovered the skin and flesh of his hands and forearms had swollen over the handcuffs. He was taken to the hospital to have the handcuffs surgically removed. According to his neurologist, the improperly applied handcuffs had permanently damaged the nerves in his wrist. The lawsuit was settled out of court.

If a suspect complains of wrist pain, visually check the suspect's wrists. A properly applied pair of handcuffs will cause red marks and indentions on the sides of the suspect's wrists. If you observe a red indented ring around the wrists of a suspect who has been properly handcuffed, the red ring is an indication the suspect has been rotating his wrists in the handcuffs and/or pulling against the handcuffs—causing self-inflicted injuries to his wrists. The red ring and any other abnormal marks and cuts should be photographed and noted in your report.

Additional litigation involving the use of restraints results from the application of the total appendage restraint procedure and the restraint chair.

The total appendage restraint procedure (TARP) is commonly referred to as the maximum restraint position or as the "hog-tie." The latter is "street" vernacular and should not be used.

When a suspect is maximum restrained, the hands are restrained (with handcuffs or flex-cuffs) and the feet/legs are restrained with some form of tether (hobble or nylon strap). There are three basic methods of TARP:

The Hobble is connected to the handcuffs:

- The suspect is handcuffed with the hands behind the back in a face-down prone position.
- The suspect's feet are restrained with a cord or nylon strap.
- The suspect's feet are drawn back toward the buttocks and the hobble is connected to the handcuffs.

A hobble attached to the suspect's handcuffs creates a greater potential for a handcuff-related injury. The tension and weight of the suspect's legs can apply increased pressure to the wrists through the handcuffs. Further, this application presents an increased risk of a positional asphyxia death–due to the impairment of the respiratory system created by the outward bowing of the torso.

The hobble is attached to the suspect's waist:

- The suspect is handcuffed with the hands behind the back in a face-down prone position.
- The suspect's feet are restrained with a cord or nylon strap.
- The suspect's feet are drawn back toward the buttocks and the hobble is attached to the suspect's waist (wrapped around the waist or tied off to the belt).

When the hobble is attached to the suspect's waist, there is no additional force applied to the handcuffs; therefore, no increase in the possibility of a handcuff injury. Furthermore, because attaching the hobble to the suspect's waist does not stress the torso, the potential for an in-custody death is reduced.

The legs are pulled forward and attached to the waist:

- The suspect is handcuffed with the hands behind the back in a face-down prone position.
- The suspect's feet are restrained with a hobble.
- The suspect is placed on his or her side.

- The suspect's feet are drawn forward toward the chest and the hobble is wrapped around the waist and secured.

This method was developed as a response to the recent increase in law enforcement in-custody, positional asphyxia, deaths. The advantages of this method are as follows:

- No increase in the risk of a handcuff wrist injury.
- No additional stress to the torso.
- The forward position of the legs assists in keeping the suspect on his or her side; therefore, minimizing respiratory distress.
- This position promotes the transportation of the suspect in a seated position or on his or her side.

As previously mentioned, TARP is associated with positional asphyxia. Positional asphyxia occurs when a person is placed in a position that limits his or her ability to breathe. The positional restriction can be environmental (lying across a raised area), personal (the suspect's body weight impairs the ability to breathe), by an officer kneeling on the suspect's back, or a combination of any or all of the above.

There are three common elements of a law enforcement in-custody, positional asphyxia, death:

- The suspect has an altered mental state: cocaine/meth-induced bizarre or frenzied behavior, drug or acute alcohol intoxication, neuoleptic malignant syndrome—a sudden and unexpected death (generally occurs in psychiatric patients who are taking antipsychotic medication).
- There is a struggle with a law enforcement officer(s).
- The suspect is placed in a position that impairs his/her ability to breathe.

Although it is impossible to completely eliminate the possibility of an in-custody death, the following guidelines will minimize the potential for an in-custody death and limit department and officer liability:

- Determine if the suspect is under the influence of drugs or alcohol, or if the suspect has a history of mental illness.
- Restrain the suspect in a manner that does not impede the suspect's ability to breathe.
- Place and transport the suspect on his/her side or in a seated position.
- Do not place your body weight on the suspect after he or she has been handcuffed and is under control.

- Monitor the suspect's condition and vital signs until released to another officer or medical personnel.
- Document that you followed these procedures in your use of force report.

There are companies that produce body restraint systems that are designed to minimize the risk of a positional asphyxia. Although the designs vary, the concept is universal: the person is wrapped in sheath and secured with nylon straps/harness. These restraint systems are effective in safely securing combative inmates and suspects. Their only shortcoming is price. However, for the fraction of the cost of an in-custody death lawsuit, a department could purchase a restraint system for each patrol car. Food for thought.

There have been a number of lawsuits involving the use of the restraint chair by corrections deputies and officers. Restrain chair liability occurs in three ways:

The chair is not properly secured or fastened to a stable base. Because the chair is not bolted to a stable framework, the inmate is able to flip the chair over, causing injury to the inmate. I reviewed one lawsuit where the inmate, while secured in the chair, was placed on his back (facing up) to prevent him from tipping over the chair. To complicate this application of the restraint chair, the deputy pepper sprayed the inmate to stop him from rocking the chair from side-to-side. It should be needless to say, but the proper mounting of the restraint chair prevents this type of lawsuit.

Alleged excessive force is applied to the restrained inmate. The inmate was punched, slapped, pepper sprayed, neck restrained, and/or Taser shocked while handcuffed, shackled, and restrained in the chair. There have been a number of lawsuits filed alleging the use of excessive force as the inmate resisted being placed in the chair. The application of joint manipulation techniques, pressure points, and the Taser Drive Stun to the inmate's limbs are the more appropriate control methods to use against a rigid, mechanically restrained, inmate who will not sit in a restraint chair.

The inmate was left too long in the restraint chair or the inmate was not checked and evaluated on an established time schedule. You create a proactive defense against lawsuits of this nature by establishing guidelines for checking an inmate who is secured in a restraint chair and maintaining a log that documents when the inmate was checked and the inmate's condition was evaluated. Also, the development of protocols for releasing one limb at a time to increase blood circulation will aid in the prevention of injury and positively manage the jury's perception of your use of the restraint chair.

Pain Compliance

From this point forward in the force continuum, the methods of force rely on the concept of pain compliance for Threat control. Pain compliance is the application of a negative reinforcement through chemical, electronic, or physical means to encourage the Threat to comply with your verbal commands. Behavior can be encouraged and modified in three ways: negative reinforcement, positive reinforcement, and punishment.

Negative Reinforcement is a negative stimulus applied during the action and then removed after compliance is obtained to encourage a specific behavior. For example: You order the Threat to get down on the ground; he refuses. You strike Threat with a baton and order him to get down on the ground. You repeat this process until he complies. When the Threat complies with your commands, you remove the negative stimulus (baton strikes).

Positive Reinforcement is a positive stimulus applied after compliance is obtained to encourage a specific behavior. Positive reinforcement has no applicability as a criminal justice compliance method. To use this method, you are required to carry a bag of M&Ms in your pocket and give the Threat a treat every time he or she complies with your verbal command. Not only will a candy treat not encourage the Threat to comply, but most cops will not willingly share their M&Ms.

Punishment is a negative stimulus applied after the action to discourage a specific behavior. In the criminal justice system, the courts punish criminals—officers enforce the rules and make arrests. Any time an officer applies force to punish the act violates the person's constitutional rights.

PRESSURE POINTS. Pressure point control is the graduated pressure applied to nerve points for pain compliance. Pressure points have a low potential for injury and provide a low potential for control of a determined, emotionally disturbed, intoxicated, or mentally ill Threat: people with altered mental states have higher pain tolerances. The most commonly used nerve points are the mandibular angle (below the earlobe), the infra orbital (center of the upper lip), the ulna nerve (back of the upper arm), the radial nerve (top of the forearm), and hair control (nerves in the nape of the neck).

JOINT MANIPULATION. The joint manipulation category is divided into two levels: come-alongs and takedowns. The use of a come-along technique is considered less force than a takedown. With a come-along, the force is applied with graduated pressure and the person is not subjected to a forceful impact with a hard surface (car hood, counter, floor, wall).

Contrary to common belief, one joint manipulation technique is no more injurious than another. Whenever pressure is applied to a joint there is a possibility of injury. Accordingly, the degree of injury will depend on the physical condition of the person and the amount of the force that is applied to the joint. With that said, there is an exception, the application of finger and thumb locks (digital control) is a higher level of force due to the increased risk of injury–fingers are injured more easily than wrists, elbows, and shoulders. Joint manipulation techniques are divided into four types: wrist locks and twists, elbow locks, shoulder locks, and digital locks.

Bent Wrist Lock: This joint manipulation technique is the simplest and the most widely used law enforcement pain compliance technique. It is commonly referred to as a "Goose Neck" in some defensive tactics circles. To properly apply the Bent Wrist lock:

- Assume an Escort Hold.
- Bring the Threat's forearm vertical to the floor, and bend the wrist at a 90-degree angle.
- With your inside arm, reach under and around the Threat's arm and apply pressure on back of the Threat's wrist, with all four of your fingers.
- With your outside hand, curl the Threat's fingers inward.

Twist Wrist Lock (San Kyo): This is a popular Aikido wrist lock used by law enforcement officers. It requires greater upper body strength to make it effective and more training time to perfect than the Bent Wrist lock. To properly apply the San Kyo:

- Assume an Escort Hold.
- With your outside hand, rotate the Threat's hand (inward) to a palm-out position.
- As the Threat's hand is rotating, raise the arm to a vertical position, forming a right angle to with the floor. In this position, the Threat's fingers are pointing down and the elbow is pointed up.
- With your inside hand's palm on the back of the Threat's hand, fold your fingers over the blade of the Threat's hand and into his palm.
- Reposition the outside hand into a "handshake-grasp" of all the fingers of the controlled hand.
- Lay the Threat's forearm back on your inside shoulder and rotate the Threat's hand inward for control.

Digital (finger) Control: Commonly called finger control, this is the most effective control technique in the mechanical pain compliance category. Moreover, it is the only joint manipulation technique that is truly effective for smaller officers. To properly apply Digital Control:

- Assume an Escort Hold.
- With your outside hand, rotate the Threat's hand (inward) to a palm-out position.
- As the Threat's hand is rotating, raise the arm to a vertical position, forming a right angle to the floor. In this position, the Threat's fingers are pointing down and the elbow is pointed up.
- Slide your inside hand down the outside of the Threat's arm and encircle the wrist with your thumb and index finger.
- With your inside hand's palm on the back of the Threat's hand, fold your fingers over the blade of the Threat's hand and into his palm.
- Reposition the outside hand into a "handshake," grasping only the index and middle fingers (only the index finger if the Threat is extremely large) of the controlled hand. With this grasp, the thumb of your outside hand rests against base of the Threat's fingers.
- Move your inside hand to the back of the Threat's elbow and apply downward pressure.
- Threat control is accomplished by bending the fingers backward and applying downward pressure on the elbow.

Shoulder Lock (Come-along): This pain compliance hold is a leverage control technique that stresses the tendons and muscles in the front of the shoulder. By using the arm as a lever, the ball joint of the arm is rotated out of its socket, therefore, causing pain for compliance. It is mistakenly believed that this technique will dislocate the Threat's shoulder. A dislocation is highly unlikely. In fact, it is more likely that the humorous (bone between the biceps and triceps) will snap from the pressure before the shoulder dislocates. To apply the Shoulder Lock Come-along:

- Assume an Escort Hold.
- With your outside hand, bring the Threat's arm behind his/her back.
- With your inside hand, reach under and up, through the gap between the Threat's forearm and biceps, and apply downward pressure (with your palm) on the back of the Threat's elbow.
- With the Threat's arm trapped between your forearm and biceps (apex of your elbow), increase the pressure to the shoulder by lifting your elbow and pointing your fingers to the floor.
- Grab the Threat's opposite shoulder, clothing, or the hair on the nape of the Threat's neck and pull the Threat back to you, to unbalance him.
- Order the Threat to place the free hand behind his head. With your free hand, grasp the back of the Threat's wrist (behind his/her head) and pull backward for control.

Electronic Control Device: Drive Stun. An electronic control device (ECD) is placed in the force continuum according to its potential for injury. Deploying an ECD in touch or "Drive Stun" mode is considered a less intrusive use of force than a projectile deployment. Therefore, the use of the ECD in Drive Stun mode is placed in the Physical Control category and the probe deployment is placed in the Serious Physical Control category.

The proper use of an ECD in Drive Stun mode has a lower potential for injury than pepper spray. However, the ECD is placed above joint manipulation because the pain applied by a joint lock can be gradually increased until compliance is gained. With an ECD the pain administered is all or nothing.

The electronic control devices that deploy with the touch or Drive Stun modes are the Taser stun gun, Nova stun shield, and Nova stun belt. ECDs produce between 50,000 and 90,000 volts of electricity. However, the voltage that the body receives is much less. For example, the Taser X26 produces 50,000 volts of electricity, but only 1,200 volts pass into the body.

An ECD deployed in Drive Stun mode will not cause neuromuscular incapacitation. Consequently, the Drive Stun utilizes pain compliance as its control mechanism. Because the Drive Stun causes a painful burning sensation and not incapacitation, multiple drive stuns may be required to convince the Threat to submit. Further, because of the intense, localized pain, a Drive Stun may cause an increase in the intensity of the Threat's resistance.

In *Brooks v. City of Seattle,* the Ninth Circuit Court of Appeals ruled that the use of an ECD in touch mode can be lawfully used on a Threat that is demonstrating Static Resistance. To minimize the potential for jury when applying a Drive Stun:

- Apply the shock to the abdomen, arms, buttocks, rear torso, shoulders, or legs.
- Do not intentionally shock the head, neck, chest area, or genital area.

OLEORESIN CAPSICUM (OC). Commonly known as pepper spray, OC is an inflammatory agent that causes the eyelids to spasm, mucus membranes to swell, and an intense burning sensation of the skin. Pepper spray is placed above the use of pain compliance come-alongs because you cannot graduate its application; therefore, you cannot graduate its painful effects.

Although the risk of serious injury is very low, inmates, suspects, and officers have received severe chemical burns to their skin and injuries to their eyes from an OC exposure. In addition, there have been several in-custody deaths after inmates and suspects were sprayed with an OC spray. The specific cause of death in these incidents has been contributed to positional asphyxia, drug abuse, psychosis, and bronchial spasm. However, the medical experts I consulted believe that because OC restricts the airway serious injury or death is possible. Further, at least one manufacturer of pepper spray believes that OC could be fatal.

A quote from the president of a major manufacturer of pepper-spray devices says it all: "You have people who die after they have been sprayed," the president acknowledged. "Does pepper spray have a role in some of these deaths? I will say yes. It is going to have an effect. These are weapons. . . . Clearly, this is not a breath freshener or an underarm deodorant."

Further, because OC causes blindness and respiratory impairment for up to 45 minutes, it should not be used for crowd control. A person exposed to OC must be given post-exposure care and observed until its effects subside for the person's safety.

Most injuries that occur from the use of pepper spray are caused from the subsequent takedown and not as a result of the pepper spray exposure. When spraying a Threat with pepper spray, keep in mind that people are not born with the innate knowledge that when they are sprayed they are required to lay on the ground. Consequently, the verbal command to "Get on the Ground" is very important after spraying a person.

Another liability issue with the use of pepper spray is the area of the body sprayed. The standard target areas for pepper spray are the face, eyes, nose, and mouth. You may notice I did not list the genital area.

In a previous chapter, I discussed the following lawsuit. Because it illustrates the importance of spraying the proper target areas, we are going to revisit the facts of the lawsuit.

The city had started the removal of several trees to build a new parking lot. When the environmentalists got wind of this sacrilege, protesters took up residence in the trees. The city's police department had previous experience with "tree huggers." Based on that experience, the police department devised an innovative plan: They would use a bucket truck to reach up into the trees, place a strap around the protester, pull him or her off the tree, and lower the protester to the ground where officers would make the arrest. On paper, the plan appeared flawless. And, it was for the first protester.

However, eco-protesters are a resourceful lot. When they observed the officers pluck the first of their brethren out of the tree, they took off their hemp belts and belted themselves to the tree trunks.

When the officers in the bucket were lifted to the second protester, the officers realized the protester had strapped himself to the tree trunk. After a brief discussion, the decision was made to cut the protestor's hemp belt. When the belt was cut, the protester's pants fell to his ankles. Apparently skinny, vegetarian, protesters don't have the hips to hold up their loose fitting Patagonia cargo pants. Further the officers discovered, environmental protesters are into all things natural–like not wearing underwear. Unaffected by his exposure, the protester clung firmly to the tree trunk with his pants down around his feet.

The protester's manliness dangled right at the officers' eye level. It was at that point that the plan started to unravel. An officer pulled his pepper spray canister and sprayed the protester's genitalia. The protester climbed down the tree howling like a frightened spider monkey. The remaining protesters were removed from the trees without having their private parts pepper sprayed.

As a result of the genitalia pepper spraying, the protester sued the officers and their department. The City Attorney's primary concern was that the officers pepper sprayed a nontarget area. The department's pepper spray training manual only listed the face, eyes, mouth, and nose as approved target areas. The lawsuit was settled out of court. The department discontinued the use of the bucket truck as a protester removal option.

Takedowns

A Threat that is taken to the ground has less mobility, restricted limb movement, reduced punching power, disrupted balance, and minimal body leverage. For these reasons, a Threat taken to the ground is more easily controlled and handcuffed. As equally important, a prone Threat has limited access to concealed and environmental weapons. Consequently, placing the Threat in a prone position is safer for both the Threat and the officer.

Takedowns use joint locks or a hair hold combined with leverage, movement, pain, and the act of unbalancing the Threat to forcefully take him or her to a hard surface (counter, ground, table, vehicle, wall) for control. Leverage takedowns utilize trips, throws, or body mass to take the Threat to the ground. Takedowns are a higher level of force than come-along techniques because of the increased potential for injury due to the greater force applied to the joint and/or the impact with the floor or another object. The two most often applied joint manipulation takedown techniques are the arm bar and the shoulder lock.

ARM BAR TAKEDOWN. This joint lock is a leverage control technique that stresses the elbow joint by applying a pull/push counter-pressure against the elbow joint. To properly apply an Arm Bar Takedown:

- With your outside hand, grasp the back of the Threat's forearm–near the wrist.
- With your inside hand (thumb down), grasp just above the Threat's elbow.

- With your outside hand, rotate the Threat's hand to a palm-up position and raise it to straighten the elbow.
- With your inside hand, push down–locking the elbow.
- With your outside foot, step forward at a 45-degree angle to force the Threat to the floor–face down.
- Maintain downward pressure against the elbow and place the Threat into the prone handcuffing position.

SHOULDER LOCK TAKEDOWN. This is the takedown application of the Shoulder Lock Comealong. To properly apply the Shoulder Lock Takedown:

- Assume an Escort Hold.
- With your outside hand, bring the Threat's arm behind his/her back.
- With your inside hand, reach under and up, through the gap between the Threat's forearm and biceps, and apply downward pressure (with your palm) on the back of the Threat's elbow.
- With the Threat's arm trapped between your forearm and biceps (apex of your elbow), increase the pressure to the shoulder by lifting your elbow and pointing your fingers to the floor.
- With your outside hand, grasp the top of your inside arm's wrist and apply double pressure to the Threat's shoulder.
- With your outside foot, step forward at a 45-degree angle to force the Threat to the floor–face down.
- Lift up and forward on the Threat's trapped arm to maintain control and handcuff in the prone position.

HAIR TAKEDOWN. Primarily used by officers in the northwest, the Hair Takedown is the most effective pain compliance takedown technique in use by criminal justice officers. A hair takedown is effective for the following reasons:

- A hair takedown is the only pain compliance takedown that can be effectively applied to an actively resisting Threat, because it does not require the manipulation of the limbs (joints) for control.
- A hair takedown causes extreme pain, more quickly, with less effort, than other takedown techniques.
- Because the head is controlled, a hair takedown provides psychological control of the Threat, in addition to physical control.

However, the Threat must have hair long enough to grab to apply the technique. If the suspect has short hair or no hair, a hair control hold cannot be applied.

The Hair Takedown is placed at the top of the Physical Control category for three reasons:

- The force applied to the hair during the takedown cannot be graduated. Consequently, the level of pain applied to the Threat can't be regulated.
- Pressure is applied to the neck when the hair is pulled, increasing the risk of a neck injury. Even though it is safer to pull the head backward than to drive it forward, there is a possibility that the Threat's neck could be injured.
- The Threat is taken to the ground headfirst; consequently, the risk of injury to the head and face is increased. When the Threat's head is pulled forward and down, it is a Threat's natural reaction to straighten the arms downward to cushion the fall and protect his or her face. However, if for some reason the Threat fails to protect his face during the takedown, the face could make contact with the ground.

To properly apply the Hair Takedown:

- With your inside hand, slide up the nape of the Threat's neck and grab a fist-full of hair.
- With your outside hand, slide up the side of the Threat's head and grab a fist-full of hair.
- Pull the Threat's head forward, downward, and toward you to unbalance him or her.
- Step forward at a 45-degree angle with your outside leg and take the Threat to the ground, face down. Attempt to prevent the Threat's face from impacting the ground by pulling the Threat's head back. You may have limited success in preventing the Threat's face from impacting the ground if the Threat is larger than you.
- Maintain control of the Threat's hair, kneel down on the Threat's back, and pull the head backward.
- Maintain control of the Threat's hair with your inside hand. With your outside hand, sweep the Threat's closest arm to the inside and behind his back.
- Trap and control the Threat's arm and handcuff in the prone position.

As you may have noticed, in the described takedown techniques, the Threat is taken forward and down at a 45-degree angle. In most defensive tactics training and martial arts systems, takedown techniques are taught and practiced as circular motions. I was originally taught the circular applications as a defensive tactics and martial arts student. There are technical reasons why takedowns are performed in circular motions. But, the primary reason is that they are practiced in large open rooms on training mats.

When I became a police officer, it became apparent to me that I would never arrest a person in a large open room on training mats. However, I did encounter resisting people who were sitting on sofas, chairs, in vehicles, or standing against counters and walls. Because of the environmental barriers, it was impossible to perform a circular takedown. However, I discovered I could perform the takedown technique at a forward 45-degree angle by myself or with another officer. As a result, I incorporated this modification into my defensive tactics program and in my martial arts classes.

Level Five–SERIOUS PHYSICAL CONTROL

This level of force consists of the force options that the federal courts refer to as "intermediate force." Intermediate force has a greater potential to cause serious physical injury and/or inflicts severe pain.

NON-OC CHEMICAL AEROSOL RESTRAINTS. Non-OC aerosol restraints use the chemical irritants chloroacetaphenone (CN), and Ortho Chlorobenz-alnalonitrate (CS) as control agents. Commonly known as MACE, the powder chemicals irritate the eyes, skin, and respiratory system. Because CS and CN are powders, they exit an aerosol canister with more force than pepper spray (OC is a resin). Consequently, injuries to the eyes have occurred from being sprayed with aerosol irritants at close range. Furthermore, chemical irritants also use aerial burst or pyrotechnic deployment methods. Both of which increase the risk of injury to the persons targeted. Because CN and CS are airborne irritants and not inflammatory agents, they are primarily used for crowd control or to force the exit of a barricaded suspect.

TASER PROBE DEPLOYMENT. Due to the serious injuries and deaths that have occurred from the probe deployment of the Taser, the projectile mode is considered a higher level of force than a Drive Stun. Serious injury can occur from a dart hitting the eye. Death and serious injury can occur through head and face trauma from the neuromuscular incapacitation induced free fall. The use of the electronic control device in probe mode has come under scrutiny by the courts and the public. The following recommendations will minimize the liability associated with an ECD probe deployment:

- If reasonable, give the Threat a verbal warning before deploying the ECD.
- Do not use the ECD to control Threats who are demonstrating "Static Resistance."

- Do not use the ECD on juveniles under 14 years of age, unless deadly force is justified.
- Do not use the ECD on a visually pregnant woman, unless deadly force is justified.
- Do not use the ECD on physically disabled people or the elderly, unless deadly force is justified.
- Do not use the ECD on a driver of a running vehicle or on someone who is operating dangerous equipment.
- Do not use an ECD on a Threat in a situation where the location or the environment could seriously injure him or her from the "free fall," unless deadly force is justified.
- Do not intentionally deploy the ECD to the head, neck, chest, or genital area.
- After multiple cycles of the ECD have proven ineffective in controlling the Threat, transition to another less-lethal force option(s), if reasonable, before escalating to the use of deadly force.
- Officers who carry an ECD should have valid CPR certifications.
- Carry the ECD in a holster on the nonhandgun side of the body.

FOCUSED BLOWS (PERSONAL WEAPONS). Personal weapons are the natural weapons of the body. In an emergency, any part of your body can be used as a weapon. However, the most common personal weapons used by criminal justice officers are the palms, elbows, fists, fingers, feet, and knees. Focused blows play an important and varied role in an officer's application of force. Because focused blows can be applied in a variety of situations, they are divided into four levels:

LEVEL ONE: Low intensity techniques that distract the Threat: crossface with the palm; open-hand slap to the body; finger thrust to the armpit, ribs, or sternal notch; shin rake; etc. Level One focused blows are used as a distraction for the application of joint manipulation techniques to an actively resisting Threat.

LEVEL TWO: Focused blows that cause a limb dysfunction. Strikes to the ulnar nerve (triceps), radial nerve (top of the forearm), femoral nerve (front of the thigh), lateral cutaneous nerve (side of the thigh), and peroneal nerve (back of the thigh). Level Two focused blows can be used as a more aggressive distraction to apply a control hold to a physically stronger Threat or to effect a takedown.

LEVEL THREE: Focused blows that stun the Threat. Controlled hand and forearm strikes to the brachial plexus (sides of the neck) and head will daze and disorient the Threat. Controlled elbow and knee strikes and kicks to abdomen and rib cage will momentarily stun the Threat and rob him of his ability to fully resist.

LEVEL FOUR: Focused blows that cause an immediate incapacitation. There are three ways to incapacitate the Threat:

Shock the Nervous System: A focused blow(s) to the head transfers the energy through the skull into the brain causing a concussion, disorientation, and/or unconsciousness.

Organ Trauma: A focused blow(s) to the torso causes trauma to the internal organs. Internal organ trauma causes incapacitating pain and limits the ability to breathe, i.e., trauma to the diaphragm. Trauma to the external organs (eyes, ears, and nose) will cause incapacitating pain and impaired sensory perception.

Structural Damage: A focused blow(s) to the skeletal structure limits or eliminates mobility and other bodily functions. Examples: dislocated joints, fractures to the limbs, rib cage, and pelvic area limit mobility; fractures to the bones of the skull, nose, face, and throat will cause extreme pain, disorientation, and may limit the ability to breathe; fractures to the spine will cause immediate incapacitation and paralysis.

It is always preferred to implement an aerosol restraint, electronic control device, or impact weapon over the use of Level Four focused blows. However, if you are assaulted and the less-than-lethal device is not in your hand, you cannot safely remove the device from your duty-belt, deploy it, and protect yourself from the blows being delivered by the Threat. In an assault situation, the use of Level Four focused blows is the safest and most effective response you can deploy to defend yourself.

IMPACT WEAPONS. The term impact weapon is used generically to describe any object you deploy that uses blunt force, generated through muscular power, to control the Threat or defend yourself. Impact weapons include, but are not limited to: batons, flashlights, firearms, ax handles, folding chairs, etc. Impact Weapons are considered a higher level of force than personal weapons because a blow from an impact weapon will cause more injury than a focused blow delivered to the same target. An impact weapon should only be used to control a physically resisting, menacing and/or combative Threat when lesser force is ineffective or inappropriate for the circumstances.

Because it is impossible to foresee every possible situation that may require a police officer to use an impact weapon, the mandating of specific baton target areas is ineffective and potentially dangerous to the officer. It is for these reasons that target options and not absolutes are recommended. You must choose which target to strike based on the totality of the circumstances: target availability, level of threat, failure of lesser force options, etc. The following are the recommended target options for the use of an impact weapon:

LARGE BONES and HEAVY MUSCLE (striking between the joints): These areas are least likely to cause serious injury; however, they are less likely to control a large, intoxicated, and/or determined Threat.

BONY SURFACES and JOINTS: These areas cause extreme pain, structural damage, and limb incapacitation. Consequently, strikes to these areas are more effective in controlling large, intoxicated, and/or determined Threats.

TORSO (Excluding the head, spine, solar Plexus, and groin): The torso has a greater propensity for serious injury due to the close proximity of internal organs and/or major nerves.

HEAD, SPINE, GROIN, or SOLAR PLEXUS: These targets are readily capable of causing serious physical injury or death. They should only be intentionally struck when the use of deadly force is justified.

When deploying an impact weapon to control a Threat under normal circumstances, it is not the officer's goal to intentionally break the bones of the legs or arms. However, under extreme circumstances, it may be more desirable to use the baton to disable an unarmed Threat when other less-than-lethal force options have failed than to escalate to deadly force.

POLICE K-9 AS A WEAPON (BITE). The implementation of the police dog as a weapon (bite) is placed above the impact weapon for the following reasons:

- The potential for severe soft tissue damage and the high risk of infection.
- Temperaments vary, making police dogs' behavior unpredictable as a use of force option.
- A police K-9 cannot distinguish between a suspect, victim, witness, an innocent citizen, or a police officer. There have been a number of lawsuits filed where the K9 attacked the victim, a witness, or bystander. For example: Officers responded to a robbery of a restaurant. The officers decided they needed a canine unit to determine whether the armed suspects were hiding in a trash bin area behind the restaurant. The handler released the dog from its leash. The dog left the trash area, ran past two handcuffed suspects, and bit one of the robbery victims. The victim sued. The city settled the lawsuit for $250,000.00.
- The high police liability associated with the use of a police K-9 as a suspect apprehension tool. Police defense attorneys are very concerned that a horrific police dog bite case will make it to the appellate courts and establish the use of the K9 as deadly force.

LESS-LETHAL TECHNOLOGY. Beanbag projectiles, plastic ball projectiles, rubber bullets and batons, and flash/percussion grenades have the potential to cause serious physical injury or death–depending on the shot placement and/or distance from the Threat when they are deployed. However, they are excellent force options to use as an alternative to deadly force or in lieu of placing yourself in a situation where you may be forced to use deadly force.

Beanbag projectiles, rubber bullets, and rubber batons are termed "Extended Range Impact Weapons" by the manufacturers of these weapons. It is important to keep in mind these projectiles are "less-lethal" not "less-than-lethal." There have been several serious physical injuries and suspect deaths resulting from the use of these weapons.

In *Deorle v. Rutherford,* the Ninth Circuit Court of Appeals ruled that the use of impact munitions is a greater level of force than a police dog bite. Further, the court ruled that when reasonable an officer must issue a verbal warning before deploying the less-lethal weapon. In disregard of this ruling, some officers still continue to use impact munitions on nonviolent suspects and cost their cities and counties thousands of dollars in jury verdicts and out of court settlements. As an example, officers shot a man several times with beanbag projectiles when he refused to drop his hand-held video camera as he recorded the officers searching his neighbor's yard. A jury concluded the officer used excessive force. An officer from the same department shot a fourteen year-old girl with a beanbag projectile after a male officer had taken her to the ground. The shooting was recorded on a surveillance video camera. The news media had a field day with the video. The city settled the lawsuit.

However, when properly deployed, an extended range impact weapon is a valuable tool in positively influencing the jury's perception of a police shooting. Jurors are much more likely to find a police shooting justified when they learn that the officer(s) used impact munitions prior to using deadly force. Shooting a suspect with beanbag rounds prior to deploying deadly force gives jurors the impression you exhausted all lesser force options before deploying deadly force.

VASCULAR NECK RESTRAIN. The neck restraint has been commonly referred to as the "carotid restraint" or "sleeper hold." It was termed the carotid restraint because it was believed blood was prevented from entering the brain by restricting the blood flow through the carotid arteries only. However, research has shown that compressing the carotid arteries and the veins that carry the blood away from the brain is what causes unconsciousness. This compression of the veins creates back-pressure that prevents oxygenated blood from entering the brain. Studies have shown a reduction of blood flow into the brain by approximately 85 percent within ten seconds of the application of the neck restraint is possible. I have had officers in training pass out from very light pressure applied to their necks while demonstrating the proper application of the neck restraint.

The neck restraint is used as a submission hold in mixed martial arts competitions. It is common for a combatant to be rendered unconscious by a "choke hold" in the octagon without sustaining injury. There is a reason for this: Professional mixed martial artists are well-conditioned athletes. They are not unhealthy drug users under the influence of alcohol, cocaine, crank, or heroin, nor are they middle-aged, drunk, smokers.

Consequently, applying pressure to the sides of the neck can have serious health risks: Trauma to the vagus nerve (this nerve regulates heart rate) or stroke (the pressure to neck can cause plaque accumulated in the arteries to break free). At the Oregon Academy, I have had two older students suffer strokes from practicing the neck restraint in supervised defensive tactics training. Because of its potential for serious jury, the neck restraint is placed at the top of the Serious Physical Control category.

To minimize the civil liability associated with the use of the neck restraint, it is necessary to provide the Threat with proper post-neck restraint care after its application–whether the Threat is rendered unconscious or not. The following are guidelines for providing proper post-neck restraint care.

After the Threat has been handcuffed and (if necessary) Maximum Restrained, place the Threat in a seated position. Gravity assists in restoring blood flow to the brain.

The Threat should have constant surveillance of his vital signs and physical condition until released to a medical technician or another police or corrections officer. To monitor the Threat's condition:

- Check the pulse.
- Check the breathing.
- Check for a history of mental illness.
- Check for drug or alcohol impairment.
- Check for evidence of physical injury.
- Check for the equal dilation of the pupils. The unequal dilation of the pupils indicates a head injury or stroke.
- Check for physical distress due to the struggle or position.
- Be prepared to give CPR.

Level Six–DEADLY PHYSICAL FORCE

Deadly force is any force under the circumstances in which it is used that is readily capable of causing death or serious physical injury.

In law enforcement, the firearm is most often associated with the officer's use of deadly force. Some officers have a misunderstanding regarding the potential civil liability associated with using a firearm that they are not "qualified with." An officer incurs no greater liability in shooting a suspect with a nonagency-approved firearm. The question in a wrongful death lawsuit is whether the officer's use of deadly force was justified, not which gun the officer used.

For example, during a domestic violence investigation, you are disarmed and taken hostage. At some point during your captivity, you are able to obtain one of the suspect's guns and shoot him. Does the fact that you are not qualified with the suspect's handgun make your use of deadly force less justified? Of course not. The reason we qualify with our firearms is not to minimize the civil liability in shooting the right person. We qualify to minimize department liability when, in those rare incidents, we miss our intended target and shoot an innocent person. Demonstrating proficiency with your firearm creates a defense against the (sure to follow) negligence lawsuit.

In this chapter, we discussed the importance of a force continuum from both a training perspective and an officer's application. Moreover, I explained the hierarchy of force and the rationale behind the placement of each force option. Now, its time to take the next step in managing the use of force incident. In the next chapter, we will discuss how to properly document your use of force.

Chapter 6

DOCUMENTING THE USE
OF FORCE INCIDENT

To properly document the use of force incident, it is critical that you make the paradigm shift from being an objective reporter of the facts to a proactive defendant in a potential lawsuit. Properly documenting the use of force incident is crucial to building an effective defense against allegations of excessive force. Documenting your use of force occurs in four stages of the incident:

Stage One: As the action is unfolding, create a proactive defense by recording the Threat's behavior and your use of force with your patrol car's video camera or create an audio recording of your verbal commands and the Threat's volatile rants via your police radio.

Stage Two: After the scene is secure, document the physical evidence by properly photographing the crime scene, damaged property, and your injuries and the Threat's injuries.

Stage Three: After the evidence has been photographed, properly collect and package the physical evidence.

Stage Four: Create a written record of the incident in a properly prepared use of force report.

There is a difference between documenting the use of force incident and reporting the arrest of a cooperative suspect or recording the findings of a criminal investigation. In documenting the use of force incident, you are creating a foundational defense against a lawsuit that may not go to trial for up to five years. I know you are saying to yourself, "I know how to conduct a criminal investigation." I am quite sure you do. However, as you are aware, specific circumstances require special investigative knowledge. Accordingly, in this chapter, I will explain the specific documentation strategies, forensic techniques, and report-writing guidelines that are required to effectively memorialize the use of force incident.

Using the Car Video to Enhance Your Defense

If a picture is worth a thousand words, a video recording is equivalent to the Harry Potter series. Most jurors are visual learners, and they are in court to learn what happened in your use of force incident. Consequently, a video documentary of the incident can greatly bolster your defense. On the witness stand, you can describe the Threat's appearance, bizarre behavior, profanity, and menacing actions, but your testimony will not have one-tenth of the impact that a video has on the jury. However, a video recording can be a double-edged sword. When you properly perform on the video, you are almost guaranteed a defense verdict. However, even if your use of force is justified, if you pander to the camera, overreact, have an emotional outburst, or appear insensitive, the video may damage your defense beyond rehabilitation.

Here are guidelines for making an effective video documentary of the use of force incident with your patrol car video camera.

KEEP YOUR VERBALIZATION DIRECT, CONTROLLED, AND PROFESSIONAL. The more you say on video the more ammunition you give the plaintiff's attorney to shoot holes in your credibility. Stick to the script: give clear commands, present the Threat with his or her options, explain the consequences of not complying, and get a confirmation that the Threat will not cooperate: "Is there anything I can do or say to get you to comply?" When video recording a use of force incident, keep in mind that your verbalization provides the proper context for the visual images of the use of force.

The lack of audio on the Rodney King video damaged the officers' defense. If the video camera had recorded Rodney King making threats and the officers using proper verbal commands with each strike of the baton, the outcome of their criminal trial may have been different.

DO NOT ANTAGONIZE, DEMEAN, OR DISRESPECT THE THREAT. Generally, jurors are not sympathetic to criminals, so don't say anything that makes you sound like a vindictive ass and the Threat appear as a victim of your dysfunctional personality. In a shooting of an unarmed drunk driver, the plaintiff sued for $1,000,000.00. After viewing the patrol car's video of the incident, the jury awarded the plaintiff $3,000,000.00. When the defense attorney polled the jury, the jurors stated that the award was increased because the officer antagonized and demeaned the plaintiff during the arrest. As a result, the jurors felt it was necessary to punish the officer.

SOFTEN YOUR PERFORMANCE—APPEAR COMPASSIONATE AND CONCERNED. Cops have a reputation as being cold and arrogant. When your actions are being video recorded, you do not want to be perceived as Robo Cop. To soften a jury's perception of you, immediately call for medical assistance and tell the Threat medical is coming, attempt to calm the Threat down by using a compassionate tone, check the Threat for injuries, and ask the him or her if the handcuffs are too tight. The more caring you appear, the less likely a jury is to conclude that your force was excessive.

DO NOT PANDER TO THE CAMERA. The difference between a good performance and a bad performance by an actor is that a bad performance looks like acting–the dialogue and the actions appear contrived. When you pander to the video, you insult the jurors' intelligence. Further, they are offended by your blatant attempt to manipulate them. In a fatal drunk driver arrest, the officer is heard and seen pandering to the video camera. The officer knelt next to the handcuffed suspect and said, "Gee, Bob, if you had not resisted arrest, you would not of hurt your back. If your back hurts whose fault is that? All you had to do is turn around and put you hands behind your back, and you would not have gotten hurt." It was this and other poorly managed perceptions caught on video that led to a multi-million dollar out-of-court settlement.

Using Dispatch Audio to Enhance Your Defense

If your patrol car is not equipped with a video camera, you can create an audio recording of the incident with your portable radio. By keying your microphone, your verbal commands and the suspect's threats will be recorded on the dispatch center's communication recording system. An audio recording of the use of force incident can have a more powerful impact on a jury than viewing a video. With an audio recording, the jury uses their imagination to create mental images of what is occurring. What we imagine is often much more dramatic than what actually happens in real life. Consequently, an audio recording of the use of force incident can play a key role in your defense. The following are guidelines for properly using your portable radio or car radio to audio record the use of force incident.

Record the suspect's threats and rants: Hearing the anger, hostility, intensity, and volume of the suspect's threatening verbalization gives the jurors a clear representation of the mind set of the Threat and the dangerousness of the situation.

RECORD YOUR VERBAL COMMANDS. Hearing the emotion, fear, and stress in your voice allows the jury to emphasize with the concern you have for your safety.Your pleas for cooperation demonstrate to the jurors that you gave the suspect reasonable opportunity to comply before using force. In the shooting of an armed suspect at a rural mini-mart, the deputy did an outstanding job managing the perceptions of the use of force incident. While using his patrol car as cover, the deputy used his portable radio to record the suspect's verbal threats and his verbal commands. "Sir, drop the gun. Please don't make me shoot you. Drop the gun. Please don't make me shoot you," the deputy can be heard repeatedly saying on the recorded radio transmission. After several pleas to drop the gun, the deputy's three gunshots can be heard on the audio recording. The audio recording was so effective in positively managing the perception of the deputy's use of force that after the plaintiff's attorney received a copy of the recording the plaintiff's family withdrew the lawsuit.

KEEP YOUR VERBALIZATION DIRECT, CONTROLLED, AND VOID OF PROFANITY. At this point in our discussion of how to properly manage the use of force incident, I have bludgeoned you with the importance of proper verbalization. Therefore, as an act of compassion, I will only offer a rhetorical question regarding this guideline: In the example above, would the outcome have been the same if the deputy had said, "Drop the f . . king gun!"

Properly Photographing Injuries

Do not photograph the Threat's wound(s) until hospital personnel have treated him or her. From the perspective of managing the use of force incident, there is a substantial difference between a photograph of a bloody, gaping wound and a clean, stitched cut. You do not want photos of a blood-covered shirt, a bloody face, and an unstitched wound shown to the jury. Photographing the Threat's injury at the hospital takes no more effort or time. You have to transport the Threat to the hospital and provide security while he or she is receiving medical treatment, anyhow. So, the only change in protocol is in what order you photograph the injury. A protocol change that will pay dividends in properly managing the jurors' perception of your use of force incident.

If paramedics at the scene treat the Threat, photograph the areas of the body that were struck by personal weapons or baton blows. Additionally, photograph the areas that were shocked by a Taser Drive Stun or a probe deployment. Fresh marks left on the body from ECD shocks, focused blows, and baton strikes appear as a light discoloration of the skin or as light red spots and streaks. Strategically, you want to produce at trial photographs of these fresh marks. The marks become more pronounced and distinct a day or two after the incident. Consequently, the plaintiff will take photographs of the marks when they look their worst. If you have not proactively photographed the marks at the scene, your attorney cannot offer the counter-theory that you did not inflict the injuries represented in the plaintiff's photographs.

The opposite is true for photographing an officer's injury(s). Photograph an officer's injuries before he or she receives medical treatment. The jury's sympathy for the officer can be enhanced through the viewing of the disturbing photographs of the officer's untreated injuries.

Taser Evidence Collection

The forensic evidence of a Taser deployment is very important in an excessive force lawsuit. From the location of the blast doors, AFIDs, probes, and wires, a forensic expert can determine your location and distance from the Threat when the Taser was deployed. The condition of the probe leads (wires) can be used to collaborate your stated distance from the Threat. Listed below is the forensic evidence your attorney will want photographed, collected, and preserved:

- Photograph the areas where the electrodes or probes contacted the body, whether there are or are not visible marks. In most lawsuits involving the Taser, the plaintiff claims he or she was shocked more times than you have stated in your report.
- Photograph the spent cartridges, blast doors, and AFID tags in the location where they were found. Often, your version of the incident is different from that of the plaintiff's account. With photographs of the various Taser parts and the location where they were found, a forensic expert can establish the location from where the Taser was fired.
- Photograph the probe wires in the condition and location where they were found. Taser wires are folded into the cartridge and unfold when the cartridge is fired. Straightened wires indicate a deployment at the maximum effective range, the dart missed its target, or the suspect continued to run away. Wavy wires indicate a close to mid-range deployment, depending on the amount of bend left in the wires.
- Collect the probe leads. Do not coil the wires around the cartridge—fold the wires into eight to ten-inch lengths. Wrapping the wires around the cartridge destroys the fold pattern of the wire.
- Collect the probes. The forensic evidence left on the probe can determine whether the probe hit the body or missed. Probe darts are not uniform—probes are slightly unique to each cartridge. A dart detached from its wire can be matched to the other probe in the cartridge.
- The basic rules of evidence for a Taser deployment: With every probe deployment, collect the probes, wires, AFID tags, blast doors, and the cartridge as evidence. With every Drive Stun or probe deployment, photograph the areas of the body that were Drive Stunned or darted, regardless whether or not there are visible marks.

With lawsuits involving the use of the Taser, the plaintiff's attorney views the Taser's internal record as the smoking gun of excessive force. The internal record only documents the activation's date, time, and the length of the cycle. There is no designation to identify whether it was a spark test, an officer playing around, or a deployment. Also, if the Taser is shared, the internal record will not indicate which officer activated the Taser. The following recommendations are offered to correct the areas that the plaintiff attorneys have successfully challenged regarding an officer's Taser usage documentation:

- Every time the Taser is used in a use of force incident, whether activated or not, a copy of the Taser activation record should be submitted with the use of force report.
- Synchronize the Taser's internal record program with the download computer's date and time.
- If Tasers are assigned by shift and not to specific officers, each officer should document the Taser carried at the start of each shift: paper log, notebook, CAD.
- Each time the Taser is activated the activation should be documented in a report, notebook, or CAD entry.
- Establish a Taser Download Schedule–the length of time between downloads is dependent on the frequency of use.
- Maintain a record for each Taser's activation log.
- Create policies governing the reporting of Taser activation and provide training in those policies.
- Frequently check the officers' adherence to the Taser activation reporting policy.

In a lawsuit where the officer Drive Stunned and darted the suspect with the Taser, the absence of the Taser's activation documentation became the focus of the plaintiff's attorney's questioning during the officer's deposition. The officer being deposed is a member of the department's command staff, the department's Taser instructor, and a use of force instructor. Here is an excerpt of the deposition:

Question: What verification do you have of the use and deployment of Tasers?

Answer: We have our own account (with Taser International). And the conversation that I had with the Chief was that if something major happened, that we would try to get the data downloaded.

Question: How would you have done that?

Answer: We would have sent it to Taser International.

Question: And did you do that after this incident?

Answer: No.

Question: Why?

Answer: Because we lost track of the Tasers and we don't—we didn't even see this as a huge event. It was a disorderly conduct case at that time.

Question: Are you aware that a Taser was removed from its holster on Friday night at the fair grounds as well?

Answer: I don't know.

Question: Who would have had possession of the Taser on Friday night?

Answer: I don't know.

Question: Was it you?

Answer: I don't know.

Question: What kind of records would show who was—who had custody of the Taser on Friday night?

Answer: There wouldn't have been.

Question: There are no records of who is issued the Taser on any given night?

Answer: No, there wasn't.

This example illustrates how important proactively documenting Taser usage is to a lawsuit. Documenting and/or reporting every activation, application, and deployment creates a foundation for countering accusations of excessive force. An *activation* is defined as a nonuse of force discharge of electricity. An *application* is defined as placing the laser sight on the Threat, placing the electrodes on the Threat's body without delivering a shock, or displaying an electrical arc as intimidation. A *deployment* is defined as the delivery of an electric shock to the Threat through probe or Drive Stun modes. Here are the benefits of documenting every Taser usage:

- Documentation assists in distinguishing between a test activation and the shocking of a Threat on the internal Taser record.
- Documentation assists in establishing a defense against the allegation of misuse or excessive force.
- Requiring officers to document their Taser usage discourages questionable Taser usage or the improper application of the Taser.

Writing an Effective Use of Force Report

Although there are similarities between an incident report and a use of force report, a properly written use of force report contains specific justification information and much greater detail. Regardless of which format your department uses, all written incident reports contain the same basic information: who, what, where, when, and how. Generally, officers are discouraged from speculating as to why in their incident report. And stating emotions are taboo. However, in a use of force report, the question "why" and the emotion of fear are foundational elements.

In a use of force report, "why" is the essential question to answer. It is the answer to "why" that justifies your use of force: Why did you choose that force option? Why did you shoot the Threat? Why did you apply the force option so many times? Why did you escalate your level of force? Why didn't you deescalate your level of force? Why didn't you wait for back-up? Why didn't you retreat? Why did you handcuff the Threat? As you can see, "why" is the existential question that justifies your force.

The second most important element is the explanation of your fear. Fear justifies your initial use of force. Fear justifies the escalation of your force. A fear of injury or death defines a person as an immediate threat. The fear of death or serious physical injury justifies the use of deadly force. A fear for the community's safety is required to lawfully shoot a fleeing suspect. An admittance of being afraid is a fundamental element in the justification of force, and it is an emotional state that many officers are reluctant to admit experiencing.

In addition, an effective use of force report documents the following factors if they apply to the use of force incident:

THE WEATHER AND/OR LIGHTING CONDITIONS. Fog and rain can impair your ability to visually detect a weapon. Snow and ice make physically struggling with a Threat more dangerous from a slip and fall. All four conditions can impair your ability to apply physical control techniques. Street and porchlights will backlight your approach. Limited light situations make it difficult to see danger cues, suspects, and weapons. Going from a brightly-lit environment to a dimly lighted room or vice versa will temporarily impair your vision. All these adverse weather and lighting conditions increase the danger to you.

PEDESTRIAN AND/OR VEHICULAR TRAFFIC CONGESTION OR FLOW. When dealing with a dangerous situation, moderate to heavy pedestrian traffic justifies an escalated level of force to protect the pedestrians from harm. The more quickly you gain control of a dangerous situation or Threat the less likely it is that a pedestrian will be injured.

When attempting to control a resisting Threat on or near a roadway, moderate to heavy vehicle traffic justifies the use of a higher level of force to quickly control the situation for your and the Threat's safety. The heavier the traffic, the greater the risk that you or the Threat will be struck by a vehicle as you struggle. Further, moderate to heavy traffic increases the risk that the Threat will be struck by a vehicle while fleeing.

AVAILABILITY OF BACK-UP OFFICERS. At trial, the plaintiff's attorney will make the argument that if you had waited for back-up officers you could have used lesser force to control his client. Under certain circumstances, this argument can appear plausible to a jury. You can proactively take the sting out of this argument if you explain the relationship between the immediate need to use force and the availability of back-up in your report.

There are times when an officer must act immediately to protect himself or herself, another person at the scene, or the community from a dangerous person. In these situations, even waiting seconds (much less minutes) for back-up officers to arrive could mean the difference between life and serious injury, death, or a hostage situation.

YOUR DISTANCE FROM THE THREAT. The closer the Threat, the greater the danger. Distance equals time, which equals options. The closer the Threat is to you the less time you have to react. So, we agree that the distance between you and the Threat can be justification for an escalation of force. So, how many times have you been threatened by a suspect in a confined space and wrote in your report: " I contacted Mr. Smith in the master bedroom. I told Mr. Smith he was under arrest. At that time, he threatened me. In response, I shot him with my Taser." Why didn't you state in your narrative that you were six feet away from Mr. Smith when he threatened you? Was the distance between you and Mr. Smith a factor in your decision to deploy the Taser?

Or, how many times have you gone into a cell to remove a inmate who was sitting on the bunk and you wrote in your use of force report: "Inmate Jones refused to turn around, kneel down, and place his hands behind his back. I entered his cell and physically extracted him from the cell." Did the fact that the cell configuration only allowed a reactionary gap of four feet between you and the inmate when you enter the cell influence what level of force you used for the cell extraction?

In either example, if the distance from the Threat was a factor in determining in what level of force to use, why didn't you put it in your report?

In addition to the previously identified factors, an effective use of force report contains the following informational components:

DESCRIBE HOW YOU APPLIED THE TECHNIQUE OR FORCE OPTION. An effectively written use of force report states not only what technique or force option you deployed, but the report describes how you applied it. A lawsuit can take between two to five years to go to trial. Will you remember how you applied a force option five years after the arrest or cell extraction? Most officers don't. Stating that you don't remember in a deposition or the witness stand is not an effective defense against an allegation of excessive force. Effective use of force reports describe how the technique was applied in a step-by-step fashion. Here is an example:

> I placed Mr. Smith in an Escort Hold by grasping the fingers of his right hand with my right hand and placing my left hand on his elbow. The Escort Hold was ineffective in removing Mr. Smith from the bar. Consequently, I applied a Bent Wrist lock. I applied the wrist lock by bringing Mr. Smith's right arm up to a vertical position and bending his wrist and fingers downward at a right angle with my right hand. With my left hand, I reached under Mr. Smith's right arm and trapped his arm between my left elbow and my left hand. I gradually applied downward pressure against the back of Mr. Smith's right hand with the palm of my left hand until he complied with my verbal commands to exit the bar.

By describing how you applied the techniques in your report, you will remember how they were applied two years later during your deposition and three years later at trial. Further, your supervisor, defense attorney, and the plaintiff's attorney will understand how you applied the force.

EXPLAIN WHY YOU USED THAT METHOD, TECHNIQUE, OR LEVEL OF FORCE. Not what, but why? Included with the explanation of how you applied the force option, you should explain why you chose that particular level of force. Just to refresh your memory, the use of force starts with your presence and escalates to deadly force. Accordingly, two situations justify the escalation of force: A particular level of force is inappropriate to use given the immediate level of threat. A lesser force option has proven ineffective in accomplishing your goal, which is to control the Threat.

In my previous example I not only described how I applied the physical control techniques, I explained why I escalated my force: "The Escort Hold was ineffective in removing Mr. Smith from the bar. Consequently, I applied a Bent Wrist lock." I escalated my force because the lesser force option had proven ineffective in accomplishing my goal, which was to remove Mr. Smith from the bar.

In the following example, I use the force justification that the deployment of a lesser force option is inappropriate given the immediate level of threat:

> After speaking with the bartender, I contacted Mr. Jones. He was sitting alone at a table in the northeast corner of the bar. When I approached Mr. Jones, I noticed he was holding a large glass beer mug in his right hand. I asked Mr. Jones to put the beer mug on the table. He refused. To impair his ability to strike me with the mug, I kept the table

between us as a barrier. I told Mr. Jones that the bartender wanted him to leave the bar. Also, I asked Mr. Jones to step outside with me. He refused to leave the bar. I told Mr. Jones that if he did not leave the bar he would be arrested for trespass. Mr. Jones told me he wasn't going to leave the bar, no matter what I said. Because of his refusal to leave, I told Mr. Jones that he was under arrest, and I ordered him to drop the mug. He glared at me and said, "If you want the mug, come get it."

I moved to Mr. Jones' left side, unholstered my X26 Taser, and placed the laser sight's red dot on his lower left rib cage. At the same time, I told Mr. Jones that if he did not drop the mug and place his hands behind his back I would shock him with the darts of the Taser. He refused to comply with my verbal commands, and he was not intimidated by the display of my Taser. As a result, I deployed my Taser in probe mode to Mr. Jones' lower left side. When the Taser cycled, he fell off his chair and onto the floor. Mr. Jones was incapacitated with one Taser cycle; he was handcuffed without further resistance. I deployed the Taser in probe mode for the following reasons:

- My presence in uniform, display of the Taser, the use of verbal persuasion, and my verbal commands were ineffective in convincing Mr. Jones to put down the glass mug and submit to being handcuffed.
- When I interviewed the bartender, he told me that Mr. Jones was highly intoxicated, and he was angry over being cut off from buying more beer. Knowing that an intoxicated and angry person has a higher pain tolerance, I was afraid that if I applied a lesser force option, it would be ineffective in controlling Mr. Jones and he would hit me with the glass mug.
- Mr. Jones is six feet and three inches tall and weights 230 pounds. I am five feet and nine inches tall and weigh 165 pounds. Based on our size and strength difference, I was afraid that if I went "hands-on" with Mr. Jones he would overpower me, disarm me of my handgun or Taser, and seriously injure or kill me.

As you can see, it is as equally important to explain why you escalated your force as it is to describe how you deployed the force option. Also, in my example, I used the Particularized Narrative Format to clearly explain my use of force justification. The benefits of using this format are explained later in this chapter.

AVOID GENERAL TERMS: AGGRESSIVE, THREATENED, RESISTED, STRUGGLED, ETC. Instead, describe in detail the Threat's behavior or actions which necessitated the force. There is a wide range of aggressive behaviors, many of which do not justify the escalation of force. The same is true of threatening behavior. I can threaten to tell your mother or to stomp you to death; the two threats are not equal in potential harm. Further, the act of resisting arrest occurs in a number of ways: become deadweight, pull away, or an assault. Each act of resisting justifies a different level of force. The term *struggled* defines what, not how. To effectively justify your use of force in a written report, you must describe specific actions. Here is an example:

> When I attempted to apply the arm bar takedown to Mr. Carlson, he tensed the muscles in his arm, violently pulled his arm away from me, and spun to his right. To prevent Mr. Carlson's escape, I grabbed the back of his jacket collar. When I did, he bent forward, spun back toward me, placed both his hands on my chest, and forcefully pushed me backward. Then, he front kicked me in the stomach.

As my narrative illustrates, Mr. Carlson did more than just "resist" or "struggle." His actions were violent and combative.

DESCRIBE THE THREAT'S PHYSICAL SIZE AND APPEARANCE. Include facial expressions, threatening gestures, and pre-existing injuries. Descriptive details create powerful mental images. If I write in my report I made contact with John Smith, what mental picture of him did you form? An average guy. But, if I state Mr. Smith is six feet and five inches tall, weighs two hundred and twenty five pounds, and has a body builder's physique, what mental image do you have of him? Conan the Barbarian. Furthermore, describe the pre-existing injuries the Threat had before your use of force. Often, Threats receive injuries from falls, fights, and vehicle accidents before you arrive at the scene. If you don't document his pre-existing injuries in your use of force report, the plaintiff's attorney will claim that your use of force inflicted all the Threat's injuries.

DESCRIBE THE SCENE OF THE INCIDENT IN DETAIL. Include environmental weapons, physical barriers, and specific locations. We are conditioned to only think of conventional weapons as dangerous objects: car, club, gun, and knife. However, almost any item, tool, substance, or utensil can cause serious physical injury or death: pencil, glass bottle/mug, steam iron, screwdriver, crescent wrench, hammer, shovel, blood, cleaning solution, fork, or frying pan—the list is endless. The close proximity of environmental weapons to the Threat is justification for the escalation of force.

Placing a physical barrier between you and the Threat has two benefits: First, placing a barrier between you and the Threat minimizes the need to use force. More often than not, a Threat will not attack unless he is 100 percent certain the attack will succeed. Placing a physical barrier between you and the Threat creates an element of doubt. Second, if the Threat comes around or over the barrier to attack you, he has demonstrated his intent to harm you; consequently, his demonstrated intent justifies an escalation of force.

Lastly, specific locations in a building or residence create greater risk to you. People keep firearms in their bedrooms. A kitchen has dangerous utensils. A bathroom has corrosive cleaning solutions, razors, and scissors. Tools are stored in a garage or outbuilding. You are intuitively aware of these dangers. That awareness is justification for the escalation of force. Document these force justification circumstances or factors in your report.

IDENTIFY THE OFFICER VERSUS THREAT FACTORS AND INFLUENTIAL CIRCUMSTANCES THAT NECESSITATED THE FORCE. If you do not identify and document the officer versus threat factors and influential circumstances in your use of force report, but you use them in your justification in your deposition or at trial; the plaintiff's attorney will claim that they were not considerations when you used force on his or her client. Further, the plaintiff's attorney will opine to the jury that you identified these factors or circumstances as, after the fact, fabrications to justify your use of force. As the old law enforcement adage goes: If it is not written down, it didn't happen.

DESCRIBE THE FIRST AID/POST-FORCE CARE GIVEN. If I have stated it once in this book, I have stated a hundred times: properly managing the use of force incident is all about positively managing the jury's perception of you. Providing post-force care to the Threat creates the impression that you care about the Threat's comfort and well-being. The better care you provide the kinder and gentler you appear to the jury. A common jury perception is that kinder and gentler officers do not use excessive force. For example: Wiping pepper spray off the Threat's face with moist towelettes makes you appear compassionate. Performing a cursory search of the Threat for injuries makes you look like a caregiver and not a butt-kicker. Inquiring about the Threat's pre-existing injuries, mental health, and medical history demonstrates that you are concerned about the Threat's physical and mental well-being. I know you are rolling your eyes at these suggestions, but there is a reason why people love firefighters and paramedics–the perception is that they care.

ECD Reporting Guidelines

The use of an electronic control device requires a specific set of report writing guidelines to properly manage the use of force incident. At trial, the plaintiff's attorney will challenge any statement that you make regarding the deployment of an ECD during an internal affairs interview or in a deposition that is not in your report. Most ECD use of force reports read like this: I came. I saw. I shocked. That may be what happened, but it is not a defense in an excessive force lawsuit.

Every time a Threat is intimidated, threatened, touched, or shocked with the ECD a report should be written. Your report should state:

- Whether you used a probe deployment, Drive Stun, electrode touch, or laser dot and why you chose that method of deployment.
- The location(s) of the probe punctures or the area(s) on the body Drive Stunned, or touched.
- How many times the Threat was shocked and why?
- What other types of force were used prior to the ECD.
- The composition of the surface the Threat hit after the free-fall and objects impacted.
- If medical was called, the names of the medical personnel.
- The area shocked should be photographed, regardless of whether or not the Threat has observable burn marks or punctures wounds on his skin. Copies of these photographs should accompany your report.
- A copy of your Taser activation log with the incident's activation date and time highlighted should be filed with your use of force report.

A Specific Use of Force Report

Litigation has shown that using two types of reports to document the same use of force incident creates more problems than any imagined benefit. I know this statement goes against conventional wisdom, but it has been my experience that most conventional wisdom is not based on fact. A use of force report form that contains "check the box" explanations and a diagram of a gender-neutral body has only limited space to write the narrative. Consequently, you are forced to write your detailed use of force narrative and justification in an additional report. This two-report methodology has caused the following problems for officers and their attorneys:

ONE OF THE REPORTS IS LOST. If your department requires you to complete two reports on the same use of force incident, the plaintiff's attorney expects to receive copies of two reports. If the plaintiff's attorney doesn't, he or she will claim at trial that your department intentionally destroyed the one report because it contained information that would damage your defense. Even worse, when a department lost one the reports, the supervisor had the officer complete another report (off memory) months later. Then, after the officer's reports were given to the plaintiff's attorney, the original report surfaced. Of course, the information in the original report differed from the report written months later.

THE INFORMATION CONTAINED IN THE "USE OF FORCE REPORT" CON-FLICTS WITH THE INFORMATION IN THE NARRATIVE REPORT. This is a common problem. A standardized form cannot identify all the elements of a use of force incident. Therefore, your narrative report will contain more specific information than a "check the box" report. As a result, the information contained in the narrative report may appear to conflict with the other report. Further, most "Use of Force Reports" have a small lined section that requires a narrative. Because you write narratives in two different reports, often your two narratives contain conflicting information.

These may not appear as important issues to you, but to the plaintiff's attorney they set off red flags. What you must understand is that most plaintiff's attorneys believe that the government killed JFK, the military is hiding aliens in Area 51, George W. Bush caused the Katrina hurricane, and the use of force by police is fraught with corruption and cover-up. Therefore, conflicting information in your reports or the loss of evidence is viewed as proof that your department is trying to sanitize your use of excessive force.

As I have said, I do not recommend you use a standardized use of force report form. However, if you or your department are determined to use such a form, I recommend that you use it only for gathering statistical information, that the form does not have a narrative section, and you title it as a "Use of Force Statistical Analysis Form." In titling it as a statistical analysis form, the title supports your assertion that the form is only used for tracking the number and types of force used by your officers.

You will get a feel for how a plaintiff's attorney views a discrepancy between an officer's "Check the Box" use of force report and his narrative report from the following excerpt of the officer's deposition:

> *Question:* Now, this document (Use of Force Report) does not indicate the number of times that you sprayed–there is a section on this report called defensive spray and it says a number of times the type of spray that was used, the brand, nozzle, the distance from the suspect, the duration of the spray, was it effective? If no, the reason why. And, then there is a drawing of a body, and you are supposed to shade the areas where it's sprayed. That information is not contained in your incident report, is that correct?
>
> *Answer:* That's correct.
>
> *Question:* But it's additional information, very specific information about that use of force, correct?
>
> *Answer:* Yes.

The attorney makes a valid point. This is important information, so why is it not in the officer's narrative use of force report? Unfortunately for the officer, the attorney received copies of his Use of Force Report and his narrative report during the discovery process. Now, she is using the reports as a weapon against him during his deposition.

Use of Force Report Writing Format

A good narrative use of force report is hard to write, and it is even harder to read and quickly access specific information buried in the body of the narrative. It is for these reasons, I developed a format of report writing I call the Particularized Narrative Format. Like you, I wrote my incident and use of force reports as a narrative in large, rambling, blocked paragraphs. Then, I accepted a training position at the Oregon Police Academy. At the Oregon academy, I spent eleven years writing instructor development and training manuals. If you are a trainer you know training manuals are written in a step-by-step format. Training manuals are written this way so you can effectively teach the skill or curriculum in a progressive building-block fashion. Further, breaking the skill or curriculum down into a progressive list of steps makes the manual much easier to read and comprehend. Moreover, by bulleting the elements in progressive steps, emphasis is placed on key points.

Naturally, when I left the academy and went back on patrol, I wrote my incident and use of force reports as I wrote training manuals—in an itemized step-by-step format. In using this format, I found it easier to organize the report and explain what happened in chronological order. In addition, by listing what I observed and/or did as separate elemental blocks, I discovered my reports contained more detail and flowed in a more logical sequence. I received tremendously positive feedback on my format from those who reviewed my reports. My supervisors found the format easy to read. Detectives found the step by step explanation of what I had done beneficial during follow-up investigations. Prosecutors commented that the particularized format effectively identified the elements of the crime and it increased their efficiency in court.

Although, you can use this format in any form of narrative report I am only going to explain the use of the Particularized Narrative Format in writing a use of force report. Here are the benefits of using this format:

- It provides a more complete and descriptive explanation of what happened.
- It gives your use of force report a more professional appearance.
- It assists in describing the incident in chronicle order.
- It makes your report easier to read and comprehend.
- It clearly explains your use of force justification.
- It clearly describes your application of force.

The use of enumerated particularized informational elements to describe your observations, your actions, and your force justification is what distinguishes the Particularized Format from the traditional, block narrative, report writing method.

The particularized format consists of three structural parts: Contextual Paragraph, Preparatory Statement, and Particularized Elements.

The Contextual Paragraph is a block paragraph that describes the context of the incident. Additionally, it provides the background information necessary to smoothly transition into the Preparatory Statement.

The following Contextual Paragraph describes the context of the incident and provides the background information required to smoothly transition into the Preparatory Statement:

> On March 15, 2010, at about 2300 hours, I responded to a report of a domestic disturbance at 1902 Linda Vista Avenue. I arrived at the scene at 2310 hours. I parked three houses east of and on the same side of the street as 1902 Linda Vista Avenue to wait for the other responding officers. As I waited for the cover officers to arrive, I rolled down my driver's door window to listen for sounds of distress or violence that may come from the target residence. From my patrol car, I could hear a male voice yelling obscenities from the direction of 1902. At 2312 hours, the cover officers arrived at my location. At that time, Officer Burright, Officer Dague, and I exited our patrol cars and approached 1902 Linda Vista Avenue.

A Preparatory Statement precedes each series of Particularized Elements. The Preparatory Statement establishes the foundation for the actions, justifications, or observations listed in the Particularized Elements.

The following Preparatory Statement establishes the foundation for the Particularized Elements:

> *When we were within thirty feet of the front yard of 1902 Linda Vista Avenue, I observed the following:*

The following Particularized Elements list the officer's observations when he arrived at the scene:

> 1. *An older man standing in the middle of the front yard swinging a baseball bat at two younger men. The young men had no visible weapons.*
> 2. *The younger men backing away from the older man.*
> 3. *A woman standing in the open front door of the residence. She had no visible weapons.*

The following Contextual Paragraph provides the background information to smoothly transition into the following Preparatory Statement:

I took cover behind a tree that was approximately twenty feet south of the men in the front yard, unholstered my handgun, and verbally challenged the men.

The following Preparatory Statement establishes the foundation for the Particularized Elements:

I took control of the suspects through the following actions:

The following Particularized Elements list the actions the officer took to take control of the suspects:

1. *I illuminated the suspects with my flashlight and identified myself as a police officer.*
2. *I ordered the suspect with the baseball bat to drop the weapon. He complied.*
3. *I ordered all three suspects to lay face down on the ground with their arms out to their sides, palms up, and legs crossed. The suspects complied.*
4. *Officers Burright and Dague handcuffed and searched each suspect while I provided cover.*
5. *While I stayed with the handcuffed suspects in the front yard, Officers Burright and Dague retrieved their patrol cars. The two unarmed suspects were placed in Officer Dague's vehicle. The armed suspect was placed in Officer Burright's vehicle.*

In the previous example, I demonstrated how to list your observations and actions as particularized elements. In the following example, I demonstrate how to list the Threat's behaviors, your deployment of force, and your force justification as particularized elements:

Preparatory Statement:

I told Markus that he was under arrest for domestic assault. I told him to face away from me, interlock his fingers behind his back, and not to move. Markus refused to follow my verbal commands by doing the following:

Particularized Elements:

1. *Instead of turning around, he stepped back with his right foot into a bladed stance.*

2. *Markus' face turned bright red and his lips started to quiver.*
3. *Markus balled his hands into fists and tensed his arms at his sides.*
4. *In a loud and threatening voice, he told me "F . . k you! I am not going to jail!"*

Preparatory Statement:

I moved to the north side of the living room and placed the sofa between us as a physical and psychological barrier. At this point, Markus and I were approximately six feet apart. From behind the sofa, I did the following:

Particularized Elements:

1. *I pulled my Taser and placed the laser dot/sight on Markus' lower abdomen.*
2. *I ordered him to "Get down on the ground!" Markus yelled, "I will kick your ass!" (as he moved around the sofa toward me).*
3. *I fired my Taser—both darts hit him in the lower torso. He fell to the floor face down.*

Preparatory Statement:

I chose to deploy my Taser for the following reasons:

Particularized Elements:

1. *Markus had previously assaulted his live-in girlfriend (Sara Williams). I was afraid that if I attempted to control him with a come-along technique or a similar lesser use of force option he would assault me.*
2. *Sara Williams told me that Markus was a black belt in jiu-jitsu. I have only received eight hours of police ground defense training, and I was afraid if I grappled with Markus he would take me to the ground, choke me unconscious, disarm me, and kill me and Sara Williams with my handgun.*

Preparatory Statement:

After Markus was stunned with the Taser, I did the following:

Particularized Elements:

1. *I ordered him to "Place your hands behind your back! Don't move!" He complied.*

2. *I removed the spent Taser cartridge, reloaded a new one, and holstered my Taser.*
3. *I pulled my handcuffs from my belt and told him to "Raise your right hand!" He complied.*
4. *I moved to Markus' right side and grabbed his right hand with my right hand (palm to palm).*
5. *With my left hand, I placed the handcuff on his right wrist.*
6. *I pinned him to the ground by placing my right knee on the back of his neck and my left knee on his back—I straddled his handcuffed arm.*
7. *I applied the handcuff to his left wrist, cursory searched his waistband and pockets for weapons (I found no weapons), checked the handcuffs for the proper tightness, and double-locked the handcuffs.*
8. *I stepped off Markus, rolled him to his left side, and intrusively searched his clothing for weapons—I found no concealed weapons.*

As you discovered by reading through the examples, this report format is easier to read than a monolithic, block paragraph report. It creates a smooth transition from one event to another in chronological order. And, because the writer focuses on one element at a time, it naturally facilitates the inclusion of important details into the report.

As an expert witness and use of force instructor, I have been asked to review and evaluate hundreds of use of force incidents. The main source of the information that I use to evaluate a use of force incident comes from the officers' use of force report. Often the officer's report is grammatically correct, but the way it is written makes it very difficult to determine which person did what action. As I have stated previously, a use of force report is different than a standard incident report. The main difference between the two reports is that there is no jeopardy to you personally with a poorly written incident report. However, a poorly written use of force report can hurt your defense in both a civil lawsuit and your criminal prosecution. To help you get the most out of your use of force report, here are a few basic rules you can use to make your use of force more reader friendly:

Rule One: **Do not use two personal pronouns to identify a person in the same sentence. Instead, use a proper noun and then a personal pronoun.**

The most commonly used personal pronouns in use of force reports are he, she, him, her, they, and we. Using a personal pronoun to identify a person more than once in a sentence makes it very difficult to track which person performed what action when the incident involves multiple people. Here are a few examples:

- I contacted John Smith in the kitchen, and he gave me the following statement: (Clear)
- I contacted him in the living room, and he gave me the following statement: (Unclear)
- Mary Jones stated she had been hit with a closed fist. (Clear)
- She stated she had been hit with a closed fist. (Unclear)

When using all pronouns with multiple people involved, it becomes nearly impossible to keep straight what each person did or said.

The following is an example of a narrative written with multiple pronouns:

> On this date and time, I made contact with Sara Rogers at her residence, 226 Brooks Street. She told me that her boyfriend, Jim Johnson, had assaulted her. Further, she told me that three of her friends Sally Davis, Justin Simms, and Daryl Thompson witnessed the assault. They were at her residence when I arrived. Johnson had left the residence before I arrived. I interviewed all four people at the scene.
>
> She told me that they were having a party at her house. They all had been drinking, but only Johnson was intoxicated. She and he had an argument over letting him drive to the store to buy more beer. When she took the car keys from him, he pushed her down. Simms stepped between her and him. He grabbed the keys and threw them across the room, accidentally hitting Davis. She got in his face and asked him, "What is your f . . king problem?" He told her that he was trying to prevent him from driving. Then, he pushed him down and took the keys from her. Then, he stepped outside onto the front porch.
>
> Thompson and Simms went out onto the porch to talk to him. As they spoke with him, he threw a punch at Simms. The punch missed him and mistakenly hit Thompson in the face. They all wrestled on the ground for several minutes. He broke free, grabbed the car keys, and he ran down the street.

Can you easily determine who did what in that narrative? When I read a report written in that fashion, I have to keep a separate sheet of notes outlining which person did what to who.

The following is the same narrative written with a proper noun and a subsequent pronoun for each person:

> On this date and time, I made contact with Sara Rogers at her residence, 226 Brooks Street. Sara Rogers told me that her boyfriend, Jim Johnson, had assaulted her. Further, Sara Rogers told me that three of her

friends Sally Davis, Justin Simms, and Daryl Thompson witnessed the assault. Davis, Simms, and Thompson were at Sara Roger's residence when I arrived. Jim Johnson had left the residence before I arrived. I interviewed all four people at the scene.

Sara Rogers told me that Jim Johnson, Sally Davis, Justin Simms, and Daryl Thompson were having a party at Sara Roger's house. They all had been drinking, but only Jim Johnson was intoxicated. Sara Rogers and Jim Johnson had an argument over letting him drive to the store to buy more beer. When Sara Rogers took the car keys from Jim Johnson, he pushed her down. Justin Simms stepped between Rogers and Thompson. Justin Simms grabbed the keys and threw them across the room, accidentally hitting Sally Davis. Davis got in Justin Simms' face and asked him, "What is your f . . king problem?" Simms told Sally Davis that he was trying to prevent Jim Johnson from driving. Then, Johnson pushed Justin Simms down and took the keys from Sally Davis. Then, Johnson stepped outside onto the front porch.

Daryl Thompson and Justin Simms went out onto the porch to talk to Johnson. As they spoke with him, Jim Johnson threw a punch at Justin Simms. The punch missed Simms and mistakenly hit Daryl Thompson in the face. Simms, Thompson, and Johnson wrestled on the ground for several minutes. Johnson broke free, grabbed the car keys, and he ran down the street.

I realize it requires more effort to write out the people's names, but it provides a much clearer narrative of incident.

Rule Two: *Use parentheses to more clearly define the person's identity or role in the incident.*

In a complicated use of force incident, it is easy for the reader to lose track of important distinctions or become confused about a person's role in the incident. The use of parentheses to state a person's identity or role in the incident allows the reader to focus on the important elements and not waste the reader's time researching the person's connection to the incident.

The following are examples of the use of parentheses to clearly define identities and roles:

When I forced open the front door, I observed the following:

- A woman (later identified as Mary Smith) sitting on the couch crying.
- A man (the suspect) standing in the middle of the room holding a knife in his right hand.

- A small female child (the woman's five-year-old daughter, Kimberly Smith) curled in a fetal position in the northwest corner of the living room.

The use of parenthetical information prevents the reader from having to switch back and forth between the body of the report and the cover sheet to identify the role of the person being referred to in the narrative.

In this chapter, I explained the elements of a properly written use of force report, the benefits of using a Particularized Narrative Format, and the rules for writing a more reader-friendly use of force document. It is one thing to understand each individual component of a particularized narrated use of force report. It is a far more difficult task to combine the elements into a cohesive narrative of the use of force incident. Aware of this challenge, I have provided you with the following example to use as a model to illustrate how all the elements come together to create a clear narrative of the use of force incident.

Particularized Narrative Use of Force Report

On above listed date and time, I responded to a report of a domestic disturbance at 396 Martin Way. The next door neighbor had reported hearing loud male and female voices arguing and glass breaking. When I was dispatched to the call, the Com Center gave me the name of the reporting person (Julie Hanson) and her telephone number.

At 2112 hours, I parked my patrol vehicle three houses east and on the same side of the street of 396 Martin Way. At that time, Officers Watson and Turner informed me that they had an estimated time of arrival to my location of seven minutes. As I waited for the cover officers, I made telephone contact with Julie Hanson (reporting person) to gather intelligence regarding the disturbance. During our conversation, Ms. Hanson gave me the following information:

1. The residents of 396 Martin Way are John and Martha Simpson. The Simpson's have two minor children living in the residence: John Jr. who is eight years old and Susan who is six years old.
2. She is aware that the Simpson's have a history of domestic violence. Approximately six months ago, Martha Simpson (wife) went to her (Julie Hanson) residence after being assaulted by John Simpson (husband). At that time, she (Julie Hanson) did not report the incident.
3. Prior to calling 911, she heard a male voice yell threats and use abusive language (she can't remember the exact verbiage) and a woman's voice yell, "Don't you hit me again." Then, she heard glass breaking.

As I waited for Officers Watson's and Turner's arrival, I rolled my patrol car window down to listen for indications of violence being emitted from the Simpson residence. From my location, I could hear faint male and female voices arguing. But, no threats or screams or other indications of violence that would require my immediate intervention.

At 2118 hours, Officer Watson and Turner arrived at my location. I briefed the officers on the information that I had received from Julie Hanson. During the briefing, it was decided that Officer Watson would interview Martha Simpson, and Officer Turner and I would interview John Simpson.

As we approached the Simpson residence, I heard and observed the following:

1. The residence's front windows and blinds were open. The front door was open, but the screen door was closed. Through the open front windows, I could see a man and a woman standing in the front room.
2. I could hear a male voice yelling obscenities and a female crying.

We made a tactical approach to the residence's front door. After arriving at the front porch, I stood to the right of the front door, while Officers Watson and Turner stood off the porch at right angles to me. After listening at the door for several seconds to gather intelligence, I knocked on the screen door and announced: "Police department. Please come to the door." Within a few moments, a woman (Martha Simpson) came to the door. When she opened the screen door, I made the following observations:

1. She had red, teary, and swollen eyes.
2. She was missing a patch of hair from the left side of her head.
3. She had a red spot and a raised bump near her left eye.

I asked Martha Simpson to step outside and talk to Officer Watson. When she stepped onto the front porch, Officer Turner and I entered the residence. When I stepped through the front door, I made the following observations:

1. A man (later identified as John Simpson) was standing near a broken television set near the north wall of the living room.
2. An armchair was tipped over in the middle of the living room.
3. There were multiple pieces of broken dishes on the floor of the adjoining dining room.

I introduced Officer Turner and myself to Mr. Simpson and told him I needed to speak with him. Mr. Simpson told me that I had no reason to enter his house, and he ordered me to leave. I explained to Mr. Simpson that we had received a report of a domestic disturbance at his residence, and we needed to investigate the incident. In response, Mr. Simpson yelled, "I am not talking with you, now get the f . . k out of my house." As he yelled, I observed the following indications of potentially violent behavior:

1. His body tensed, the veins bulged in his neck, and his body started to shake.
2. Mr. Simpson clenched his fists and paced side-to-side in the middle of the living room as he glared at me.
3. While he paced, he would call Martha Simpson derogatory names and yell "Martha, don't you f . . king say anything to the cops–do you hear!"

I told Mr. Simpson that Officer Turner and I were not going to leave until we had finished our investigation. Further, I told Mr. Simpson that the more cooperative he was the sooner we would leave. "F . . k you. Get the hell out of my house," was his response. Shortly after that response, Officer Watson informed me, from the front doorway, that probable cause existed to arrest Mr. Simpson for assault. As Officer Watson kept Mrs. Simpson outside on the porch, I told Mr. Simpson he was under arrest for domestic assault. When I placed Mr. Simpson under arrest, he did the following:

1. He stepped back into a fighting stance with his body bladed.
2. He slapped the sides of his thighs with the palms of his hands, clenched his fists, and raised his hands like a boxer.
3. "Come on. Let's do this," he yelled as he took a step toward me.

In response to Mr. Simpson's aggressive behavior, I performed the following defensive actions:

1. I pulled my Taser and placed the laser dot/sight on his lower abdomen as I retreated away from Mr. Simpson.
2. I ordered Mr. Simpson to "Get down on the ground!" I gave this order four times.
3. "I will shock you with the Taser if you don't get on the ground," I warned Mr. Simpson.
4. After my fourth order and second warning, I deployed my Taser. Mr. Simpson and I were approximately ten feet apart. The Taser's probes hit Mr. Simpson in the lower abdomen. As a result, Mr. Simpson fell forward to the ground, incapacitated by the Taser shock.

5. After the Taser had stopped cycling, I told Officer Turner to handcuff Mr. Simpson. He was handcuffed without further aggression or resistance.
6. I removed the spent Taser cartridge from my Taser and placed it on the ground. Then, I reloaded my Taser with a new probe cartridge.
7. I removed the Taser Probes from Mr. Simpson's abdomen and swabbed his puncture wounds with an alcohol towelette.

I deployed my Taser in probe mode for the following reasons:

1. Mr. Simpson had an altered mental state. I could tell by his actions, body language, demeanor, and verbalization that he was extremely angry. I know that a person with an altered mental state has a higher tolerance to pain. Therefore, I feared that if Officer Turner and I attempted to apply a lesser control option it would be ineffective and Mr. Simpson would assault us.
2. Mr. Simpson had committed a violent crime–domestic assault. Further, I had received information from Julie Hanson that he had a history of violent behavior. Consequently, I was afraid that if Officer Turner and I attempted to apply physical control holds to Mr. Simpson's limbs–based on his history of violent behavior–Mr. Simpson would assault us and disarm Officer Turner, or me of our handguns and kill Martha Simpson and/or Officer Turner or me. I am personally aware of an incident where one officer was disarmed and killed with his own handgun and his cover officer seriously wounded, while attempting to take an unarmed domestic violence suspect into custody.
3. Mr. Simpson is six feet and two inches tall, weighs two hundred and fifteen pounds, and has an athletic build. I am five feet and nine inches tall and weigh one hundred and seventy-five pounds. Officers Turner and Watson are two female officers who are both under five feet and five inches tall and weigh less than one hundred and thirty pounds each. I know from my personal experience in attempting to control larger and stronger Threats that we (Turner, Watson, and me) could not control Mr. Simpson through the physical control tactics. Because of our size and strength inferiority, I was afraid Mr. Simpson would seriously injure me or one or both of the other officers if we grappled with him.

While I stayed with Mr. Simpson, Officer Turner left the residence to get her patrol car and a camera. When Officer Turner returned with the camera, I took the following photographs:

1. Two Taser puncture wounds to Mr. Simpson's abdomen (two photos).
2. The location where Mr. Simpson landed on the floor from the Taser shock (one photo).
3. The Taser probes (two photos)
4. The probe wires (two photos).
5. The cartridge blast doors in the locations where they were found (two photos).
6. The AFIDs in the locations where they were found (four photos).
7. The living room–from a north to south view (two photos).
8. The dining room–from an west to east view (two photos)
9. The left side of Martha Simpson's face (two photos).

After I had photographed the scene, the injuries, and the evidence, I collected the Physical Evidence:

1. The two Taser probes, two wires, and the cartridge. I folded the wires into eight-inch sections and placed all the items in evidence bag #1.
2. The two cartridge blast doors were placed in evidence bag #2.
3. Twelve AFIDs were collected (as a sampling) and placed in evidence bag #3.

While I was photographing and collecting the evidence, Officer Turner transported Mr. Simpson to the county jail and lodged him on domestic assault and resisting arrest charges.

On this date at 2354 hours, Sgt. Johnson downloaded my Taser activation information (Taser number 31) and provided me with a copy of the Taser activation log printout that documents the use of my Taser during this incident. The copy of that printout is submitted with this report.

As you can see, the Particularized Narrative Format lays out the incident in an easy to follow chronological order, creates a more detailed reporting of the facts, and facilitates a comprehensive documentation and justification of the officer's use of force.

In this chapter, we discussed the guidelines and strategies for properly documenting the use of force incident. Furthermore, I explained the difference between writing an incident report and an effective use of force report. In doing so, I outlined the pitfalls of using a "check the box" use of force report, and I introduced you to an innovative report writing format.

In the next chapter, we move beyond viewing the use of force incident in the past tense and discuss recommendations for proactively managing the use of force incident at the scene as the officer that deployed the force.

Part III

MANAGING THE USE OF FORCE INCIDENT

Chapter 7

MANAGING THE USE OF FORCE INCIDENT FOR THE OFFICER

Nothing is more costly to a law enforcement agency in public trust and treasure than a poorly managed use of force incident.

The officer was called to the witness stand. He moved forward, stopped in front of the court clerk, raised his right hand, and swore to tell the whole truth and nothing but the truth. With the judge's permission, he took the witness stand. The officer sat down and looked at the expressionless faces of the jury. The officer looked for a comforting smile, but all he could find were blank stares. The officer was the first witness called to testify in his civil rights lawsuit. He was dressed in a conservative suit and armed with his three-page use of force report.

The officer had testified in criminal court, traffic court, and grand juries more times than he could remember. But those court appearances were different than today. When he testified in the past, he wore a uniform and testified as the accuser. This day he was on trial; he was the accused; accused of violating the civil rights of a man he had arrested three years earlier. That man, the plaintiff, now sat next to his attorney at a table across the aisle. That man looks much different than he did the night he was arrested. He has cut his long shaggy hair, shaved off the scruffy beard, and covered his tattoos with a coat and tie. He looks more like a stockbroker than a wife-beating drunk.

The officer was called as the plaintiff's first witness. By being called as a witness for the plaintiff, the plaintiff's attorney gained the strategic advantage of directly examining the officer. The officer's attorney will have to try to repair any damage done with a cross-examination. The officer is on his own; all his attorney can do is object to the form of the plaintiff's attorney's question. The officer's testimony will make or break his defense, and he feels the suffocating pressure of being on trial.

It has been three years, twelve months of graveyards, and hundreds of calls for service since he had used force on the plaintiff. As he reviewed his three-page report, the officer began to wish he had put a little more effort into his use of force report. Before this trial is over, the officer will wish he had written a report with the detail of a NASA training manual and taken a lot more photographs.

The plaintiff's attorney's direct and redirect examinations were probing, relentless, and layered with questions that were limited to "yes" or "no" answers. When the officer attempted to give a more detailed explanation, the judge would tell him to only answer the question the attorney asked. However, the questions that the officer was most uncomfortable with were the ones he could not answer. He learned very quickly, from the expressions on the jurors' faces, that the answer "I don't remember" was not the answer they wanted to hear.

Then, there were the questions he did not want to answer. Questions like: Why didn't his report contain details of how the plaintiff resisted? Why didn't his report explain his use of force justification? If he received a bloody nose and a scrape on his face from the plaintiff's punch, why weren't his injuries photographed and his bloody uniform collected as evidence? The only answer he could give was "I didn't think it was necessary."

Why didn't he include this information in his report or collect his uniform as evidence? Because he did not think that the arrest would end with him being a defendant in federal civil rights lawsuit.

This scenario is played out every day in federal courts across the United States. Officers who have responded to the calls to protect and serve and then find themselves as defendants in civil rights lawsuits. Officers, who after taking the witness stand, learn a hard lesson on the importance of properly managing the use of force incident.

You don't have to be one of those ill-prepared officers. By following the twelve litigation proven rules for managing the use of force incident listed below, you will proactively lay the groundwork for your defense. As a result, your credibility will be unimpeachable, and a defense verdict a predictable outcome.

Rule One: Determine if the action is worth the risk of injury to yourself or the Threat.

There are times when you must make a split-second decision regarding how much force to use. However, those incidents are far and few between. In the majority of use of force incidents, you are afforded the time to make a reasoned use of force decision. As part of the decision-making process, you should weigh the potential for injury against the need to act. When using force, there are two categories of injury that you or the Threat can sustain: physical and financial. To determine whether the contemplated action is worth the risk of injury, you should ask yourself these four questions:

Is my forthcoming response motivated by anger? If your answer is yes, you need to take a step back and reassess the situation. Remember, when you're in a state of emotional stress, your ability to choose the best course of action is impaired. The law may allow you to remain on a person's property, make a custody arrest, or tow a vehicle but how will a jury view your emotionally highjacked decision? They won't like it. When you're angry, if you are not legally required to take action, don't. However, your anger does not absolve you of the responsibility to make a lawful, necessary arrest. If the jury is presented with evidence that you were angry when you made the arrest, admit it. Then, explain you took a step back and evaluated the necessity for the arrest and made a public safety decision to arrest the suspect, not an emotional one.

Is the decision to place myself in harms way based on a calculated risk? If your answer is no, do not rush in. As a police officer at the scene, you are the stable element in a volatile mix of emotions. By rushing in without a tactical plan, you may inadvertently cause the situation to escalate. Further, if you recklessly respond to a dangerous situation and you are killed or seriously injured; you cannot control the situation, render aid to the injured, or protect others from harm.

What is the probability that I will be administratively disciplined, civilly sued, or criminally prosecuted? If the probability is more likely than not, you need to consider another plan of action. The small amount of personal satisfaction you may receive from using force does not offset the emotional, mental, and financial stresses of having your employment terminated, being criminally prosecuted, and/or civilly sued.

Does the level of the offense or the person's behavior justify the risk of seriously injuring the person? As you know, *Graham v. Connor* requires you to consider the immediate threat and the severity of the crime before you make a use of force decision. When making this decision, keep in mind: Not all offenses are equal under the law. Not all types of threatening behavior are equally ominous. Not all types of resistance are equally violent. Not all ages, genders, or sizes are equally dangerous. Not all force options are equally injurious.

Rule Two: Use the least amount of force necessary to accomplish the legitimate corrections or law enforcement objective.

In *Graham v. Conner,* the Supreme Court stated that your force must be objectively reasonable. The Supreme Court established this vague standard because the justices did not want to dictate when officers could use specific force options. As a result, when discussing the use of force, we always circle back to the question: What makes a specific force option objectively reasonable? There is no definitive answer. Only a conceptual one: reasonableness is based on the totality of the circumstances. As a result, without a definitive answer, the lower courts are forced to reactively determine when a force option is excessive under certain circumstances i.e., the Ninth Circuit's Taser rulings. So, what is the solution? Use the least amount of force necessary to control the situation or Threat. When you use the least amount of force necessary, it is always objectively reasonable. This recommendation is not based on a legal requirement; it is based on a common sense defensive strategy.

Rule Three: When using force give the appropriate verbal commands.

When managing the perceptions of witnesses and jurors, no other action is more important than the use of appropriate verbal commands. Witnesses (both civilian and criminal justice) often do not see the actual use of force, but they hear the officer's verbal commands. As we previously discussed, independent witnesses have tremendous credibility with jurors. There is nothing better for your defense than to have an independent witness tell the jury how professional you were when confronted with a dangerous and volatile situation.

In an incident involving the shooting of a homeless man with a knife, the only witness to the shooting (a college professor) told the investigators: "The officer told him to drop the knife four times. The man responded by telling the officer to drop his gun. The man started really cussing and swearing. The officer gave a fifth order to drop the knife and a warning not to come any closer. Then, the officer fired five quick shots." These are good witness statements, but the witness went on to say, "I was struck at the time how controlled and polite he (the officer) was as he faced the man with the knife." That is a multi-million dollar witness statement. Those priceless statements did not happen by accident, coincidence or as a gift from the gods. They are the direct result of the officer's deliberate use of the proper verbal commands.

In the shooting of a fleeing shoplifter who turned on the officer with a knife, the only witness did not see anything–but from inside her residence she did hear the officer's verbal commands: "Get on the ground! Get on the ground! Drop the knife! Drop the knife!" "The commands were followed by gun shots," she added.

In both shooting, because of the witnesses' statements, the suspects' families chose not to pursue wrongful death lawsuits. This is what happens when officers properly manage the use of force incident: they prevent lawsuits by proactively influencing witness perceptions.

In a lawsuit involving the shooting of an allegedly armed man, five officers followed the suspect one hundred yards down the street, guns drawn, yelling verbal commands. The street was lined with two-story apartment buildings. After the shooting, investigators found twelve witnesses who heard the officers' verbal commands, but only one witness who saw the shooting.

All twelve witnesses gave the same account. They were sitting in their living rooms watching television when they heard: "Get on the ground! Let me see your hands! Get on the ground! Let me see your hands! Then a shot rang out." They could not see the officers or the suspect because trees blocked their view. However, one witness heard and saw the shooting. She was sitting in the living room with her husband when the officers' verbal commands caught their attention. They moved to the living room window and saw a man in a trench coat walking away from the officers with his hands in his coat pockets. The officers followed with their guns drawn. Suddenly, the man turned toward an officer. "I turned to my husband and said–Oh, no, he is going to shoot the officer," the witness told the jury.

When the officers handcuffed and searched the suspect, they failed to find a handgun. Officers canvassed the area, but no gun was found. The suspect sued the police officer for excessive force. Based on the witnesses' statements, the jury found the shooting justified.

It is no accident that the three shootings ended favorably for the officers. The officers properly managed the witnesses' and the jurors' perceptions of the shootings through their use of appropriate, professional verbal commands.

Rule Four: When using force, avoid using profanity, sarcasm, and bravado.

We have previously discussed at length the negative impact profanity, sarcasm, and bravado has on a jury's perception of you and your use of force. So, enough has been said regarding this perception problem. However, in the hundreds of use of force incidents that I have reviewed, there is only one incident where the use of profanity helped the officer's defense.

While investigating a domestic violence complaint, three officers confronted the suspect in a hallway of an apartment building. The suspect was told he was under arrest and a struggled ensued. Two of the officers took the suspect to the ground. The suspect continued to forcefully resist. Because the two officers were unable to control the suspect, the third officer decided to deploy the Taser in probe mode. Because the third officer was experiencing the cognitive effects of stress, the officer mistakenly pulled her handgun and not the Taser. Believing she had pulled her Taser, the officer fired one round into the struggling suspect. When the handgun fired, the startled officer yelled, "Oh, F . . k!" At that moment, the officer realized she had mistakenly pulled her handgun.

During the internal affairs investigation, the detectives interviewed the other occupants of the apartment building. None of the occupants witnessed the shooting, but they all gave the same account of what they heard: "Stop resisting! Give me your hand! Stop Resisting! Give me your hand! Then, I heard a gun shot and someone yell: Oh, f . . k!" The independent witnesses' statements supported the officer's claim that the shooting was accidental.

Rule Five: Inquire about injuries the suspect may have received before you arrived at the scene.

Often before you arrive at the scene, the suspects have been fighting. I cannot emphasize enough the importance of asking the suspect if he had received any injuries from the previous struggle. Sometimes the suspect will admit that he suffered an injury during the prior fight. Other times, he will tell you to go pound sand. Either way it is a "win/win" for you. If he tells you the injury happened during the fight with the other suspect, you have an admission that the injury was not caused by you. If he tells you to go pound sand, the fact that you inquired about his injuries makes you appear caring to the jury.

If you don't inquire about injuries, you have no defense against his claim that your use of force caused all his injuries. This happened in a lawsuit involving the arrest of a suspect for assault on a police officer.

The officer responded to a fight in a third-story apartment. When the officer entered, he observed a woman standing against the living room wall and two men wrestling on the floor. One man was the woman's boyfriend and the other was her ex-husband. The officer yelled, "Break it up!" The men separated. The boyfriend stood next to the woman. The ex-husband confronted the officer in the middle of the living room. Just as a cover officer walked through the front door, the ex-husband sucker-punched the first officer. The officers took the suspect to the ground. After the officers struggled with the suspect for several minutes, he was pepper sprayed and handcuffed.

The officers asked the suspect to stand up and walk to the patrol car, but he refused. The officers lifted the suspect by his arms and dragged him down three flights of cement stairs. When the suspect was placed in the patrol car, he started kicking the rear passenger window. Fearing the suspect would break out the window, the officers removed him and restrained his feet to his handcuffs with a nylon cord. When the officers picked up the maximum restrained suspect, he struggled–causing the officers to drop him on the asphalt driveway.

The suspect was transported to jail. At the jail, a nurse evaluated his injuries. The suspect was transported to the hospital for further evaluation. He was diagnosed as having a broken foot, cracked ribs, and facial bruising and cuts.

In the suspect's civil rights compliant, he alleged that all his injuries were caused by the officers' use of excessive force. Unfortunately for the officers, their defense was weakened by not asking the suspect if he had been injured in the fight with his ex-wife's boyfriend and by not checking for injuries after he was handcuffed. The city settled the lawsuit.

Rule Six: Photograph all officer and suspect injuries.

All jurors know, from watching television, that it is standard police procedure to photograph evidence. If you fail to follow standard investigative procedure when documenting your use of force incident, the plaintiff's attorney will accuse you of not taking photographs to cover up your use of excessive force. And that is exactly what the plaintiff's attorney did during the civil rights trial of an arrested drunk driver.

During the redirect examination, the plaintiff's attorney asked the officer to explain the process for investigating an assault. The officer explained that the witnesses, the victim, and the suspect are interviewed. The victim and the suspect are checked for injuries. The victim's and the suspect's injuries are photographed, and any physical evidence is collected.

When the officer was finished explaining the investigative process, the plaintiff's attorney asked if he had interviewed the passengers in the suspect's vehicle. He had not. The plaintiff's attorney asked if he had checked the suspect for injuries. "No," the officer replied. "Did you photograph my client's injuries?" The plaintiff's attorney queried. "No. I didn't," the officer answered. "You testified that my client punched you in the face, causing your nose to bleed and a cut on your cheek, did you take photographs of your injuries?" The attorney probed. "No," the officer admitted. "Why not?"

The plaintiff's attorney delivered the fatal blow to the officer's credibility. Because the officer had failed to follow proper investigative procedure, the jury was skillfully led to believe that the officer was being dishonest about the assault to justify his use of excessive force on a belligerent drunk driver.

Rule Seven: Charge the suspect with the appropriate crimes.

As is often the case when arresting a drunk driver, the suspect was cooperative until the officer applied the first handcuff. When the first cuff went on, his oxygen-deprived brain realized he was going to jail. The suspect jerked his handcuffed arm away and ran down the street. The officer regained his balance, gave chase, and football-tackled the fleeing drunk driver–pile driving him face-first onto asphalt. From the tackle, the suspect received cuts to his face and forehead and an injured shoulder. Medical was called to the scene, and the suspect was transported to the hospital. The officer followed the ambulance to the hospital and issued the suspect a citation for drunk driving.

Does this seem familiar? In your incident, why didn't you charge the suspect with resisting arrest and attempted escape? I know, I know, if you charge the driver with resisting arrest and attempted escape, it adds pages to an already lengthy DWI report. And experience has taught you that the prosecutor will dismiss the resisting and escape charges if the suspect pleads guilty to drunk driving. Moreover, the driver already has paid a price for resisting and trying to escape with a bruised face and an injured shoulder. So, what's the point? The point is that if you don't charge the suspect with resisting arrest and attempted escape, it undermines your credibility with the jury during the civil rights lawsuit.

Your reason for using force is that the suspect resisted your arrest and tried to escape. In a civil rights lawsuit, it is the plaintiff's attorney's strategy to convince the jury that you are not being truthful. As part of the attack on your credibility, the plaintiff's attorney will raise the question (and the jury will wonder why?) that, if in fact, the suspect did resist arrest and try to escape, why didn't you charge him with those crimes?

Charging the suspect with the appropriate crimes is especially important when there are no witnesses. In that situation, it is your version of what happened against the suspect's version. By not charging the suspect with the appropriate crimes, you open yourself up to the plaintiff's attorney's theory that you fabricated the resisting and escape story to justify your use of excessive force.

Rule Eight: If injured (even slightly) seek medical attention.

The only other professionals who have as much credibility with a jury as criminal justice officers are paramedics, doctors, and nurses. In almost every use of force incident where the suspect is injured, an emergency room physician examines him or her. As part of that examination, the physician will inquire about the cause of the injury. In all use of force incidents, the patient tells the doctor that the injuries were caused by police excessive force. It is not the doctor's responsibility to evaluate the veracity of the patient's explanation. The doctor simply documents what he is told in the examination notes.

As a result, often the physician is called to testify by the plaintiff's attorney. At trial, the physician will have no recollection of suspect's examination.

Consequently, the doctor recites what is written in his treatment notes. The following are the actual doctor's notes from an examination of a plaintiff who was injured in a use of force incident. The doctor testified at trial from these notes:

Office Examination

Chief Complaint: Left Wrist

Ms . . . . is a 28-year-old woman seen in the office today having been referred from the Medical Center Emergency Room where she presented on the 11th complaining of left (nondominant) wrist pain. When asked the mechanism of injury, Ms . . . .'s response was that it was due to "police excessive force." Evidently, her wrists were twisted behind her back.

The physician's testimony is nonjudgmental regarding the officer's use of force, but it is still problematic for the officer's defense. The jury has heard from a credible source the phrase "police excessive force" associated with the plaintiff's injury. In this particular incident, after hearing all the evidence, the jury found the officer had used excessive force.

You can strengthen your defense with the same tactic. If you are injured (even slightly), document your injury through a medical examination. In doing so, your testimony about being injured during the struggle with the plaintiff will have more credibility if an emergency room physician substantiates your injury. Further, your medical examination is covered through workman's compensation, so what is there to stop you?

Rule Nine: Collect your damaged or soiled uniform as evidence.

How many times have you been involved in an altercation with an inmate or suspect and your uniform was torn, bloodied, and/or soiled with dirt and mud? When that happened, what did you do with your uniform? Did you package it as evidence of the suspect's resistance or assault? Probably not. More than likely, you repaired and laundered it because uniforms are expensive. Uniforms are costly, but not as expensive as losing a civil rights lawsuit.

Jurors like physical evidence. You can show jurors photographs of your damaged uniform to support your testimony that the suspect ripped the badge from your shirt, bloodied your nose, and wrestled with you on the shoulder of the road. But, photographs do not have near the impact as your actual torn, bloody, and soiled uniform. The presentation of your actual uniform to the jury brings a three-dimensional reality to the level of intensity of the physical altercation.

In a lawsuit involving the use of force on a husband who interfered with his wife's arrest, the deputy's badly torn uniform was a key piece of evidence in the jury determining his use of force was reasonable. However, the incident involved two deputies; the other deputy was not so fortunate. When the deputies attempted to arrest the woman on an outstanding warrant, the husband stepped between the deputies and his wife. A hellish fight ensued.

The deputies' uniforms were shredded during the melee. One deputy placed his torn uniform into evidence. The other did not. The jury found the deputy who had not placed his uniform into evidence guilty of using excessive force. The importance of collecting your damaged and/or soiled uniform as evidence cannot be overstated.

Rule Ten: Explain the necessity for the force to onlookers and potential witnesses.

Onlookers and potential witnesses process what they observe and hear through a filter of their past experiences with law enforcement officers. That filter can have a positive, negative, or neutral influence on the witnesses' impressions of your use of force. Inasmuch, witnesses' perceptions are formed through their limited knowledge of the incident and influenced by what they personally experience, hear, or observe at the scene. The witnesses' perceptions of Officer Jerry Walton's use of force incidents are classic examples of this.

Aware of these influences, a plaintiff's attorney will send out a private investigator to canvas the area in search of witnesses who share their opinion of the incident. Some plaintiff's attorneys go so far as placing advertisements in the newspaper asking for witnesses to contact his or her law firm. To thwart the plaintiff's attorney's search for sympathetic witnesses, you should explain the background of the incident and the necessity for the force to onlookers and potential witnesses. In doing so, you proactively build your defense against a potential citizen complaint or excessive force lawsuit.

I first recognized the benefit of explaining the background and justification for the use of force to witnesses when I consulted on a Washington State excessive force lawsuit. It was the most diverse and interesting incident that I have ever reviewed. The facts of the lawsuit are as follows:

While patrolling in a tough residential neighborhood, two officers witnessed a car make a wide turn and run into a fence. The officers stopped the car and contacted two young women, ages fourteen and fifteen. Neither had a driver's license. While the officers were talking with the young women, their five-year-old brother looked at the living room window and saw his sisters stopped by the police. The brother informed his parents, and shortly afterward, a very irate father contacted the officers and cut loose with a tirade. The mother tried to pull her husband away from the officers. As a result, a fight broke out between the parents. The parents' yelling and swearing brought support from the rougher elements in the neighborhood. Within minutes, the officers were in the center of a neighborhood riot. By the witnesses' estimates, the officers were being mobbed by over twenty-five combatants. Even the two daughters joined in on the assault. And, in the chaos, the five-year-old brother stabbed an officer in the leg with a steak knife.

The 911 Communications Center received over twenty calls from neighbors frantically reporting the mob was trying to kill the officers. In response, over a dozen cover officers responded to the scene. When the mob heard the sirens of the responding officers, they melted back into the neighborhood. When the cover officers arrived, the entire family was taken into custody.

A neighbor from across the street saw the family being handcuffed and placed in patrol cars. She knew the family and was aware that an infant was left unattended in the suspects' residence. The neighbor came out onto her front porch to report the situation to a nearby officer. As she called out to the officer, he yelled "Get the f . . k back into your house." The officer gave this command four or five times as she tried to tell the officer about the abandoned infant. Unable to convey the information, she entered her house, exited through the back door, walked around the block to the back of the suspect's residence, and rescued the infant. Unfortunately for the officers' defense, the neighbor/witness was not a drug addict or a felon. She was a registered nurse with a distinguished career at a local hospital.

The next morning, when the family was released from jail, they contacted a civil rights lawyer. The following day their attorney sent a private investigator to the neighborhood in an effort to find credible sympathetic witnesses. The investigator found several good witnesses. But the best witness was a registered nurse who had witnessed the entire incident from across the street and rescued the abandoned infant. Her perceptions of the officers' use of force were formed from her limited understanding of the incident and her negative experience with the indifferent and profane officer. Her potentially damaging testimony was a major reason why the city settled the lawsuit.

However, the outcome of the lawsuit could have been different. If at the conclusion of the incident, an officer had gone door-to-door contacting witnesses and giving them a full accounting of what had happened, the witnesses may have formed a more favorable perspective of the use of force incident. If an officer had contacted the nurse and explained to her that the police department had received dozens of 911 calls reporting that the mob was killing the officers and one officer had been stabbed, her perspective of the incident may have been more police friendly. Further, if the officer had apologized for the officer's indifference and use of profanity and explained to her the reason for the officer's overreaction (the officer was concerned for her safety and under a great deal of stress) she may have been transformed into a positive defense witness.

In over twenty years of teaching the importance of explaining the necessity and justification for using force to witnesses, I have encountered more than a few officers who have told me: "I don't have time to canvas the neighborhood looking for potential witnesses and explaining to them what happened and why." My response is always the same: "You can't afford not to find the time. How long could it take—an hour? By properly managing the use of force incident, you are potentially saving your city a hundred thousand dollars or more. That pays for a lot of overtime and training."

Rule Eleven: Do not make any statements without your attorney present.

I was at home when I received a telephone call from an officer who had been involved in a shooting earlier in the week. He called to discuss his shooting and vent about his treatment by the investigators. "The detectives are treating me like a homicide suspect," the officer lamented. "They're accusing me of lying," he said with a tremble in his voice. "Did you give them a statement without legal representation?" I asked. "Yeah," he replied with a sigh of regret. "I told you in class never consent to speak with the detectives without an attorney present," I scolded. "I know, but I didn't think I needed an attorney—I didn't do anything wrong," he replied.

The officer went on to explain that he met with the detectives a few hours after the shooting and voluntarily answered their questions. As the hours and days passed, his recollection of the details became clearer and the sequence of the events more coherent. At mid-week, he was interviewed again by the same detectives. This meeting included a walk-through at the scene. Prior to calling me, he had met a third time with the investigators. However, this meeting was not about fact-finding; it was a criminal interrogation. The detectives accused him of not being truthful; they had found conflicts and inconsistencies between the statements he made during the first and second interviews. The officer was livid that the detectives inferred he was lying.

To put the interrogation in perspective for him, I asked him: "You're a cop—what do you think when a suspect changes his story over a series of interviews?" "I think he is lying," he admitted. Then, I explained that most detectives do not receive training in how to properly investigate a police shooting.

An important aspect of that training, I told him, is an explanation of the negative effects that stress has on perception, memory, and comprehension. Because the detectives were unaware that officers under extreme stress experience time and distance distortion, memory lapses, event confusion, and over time can more accurately recall the sequence the events, and of course, the detectives believe you are being dishonest when you remember more details as time passes, I added. When we finished our conversation, the officer had a better understanding of the detectives' suspicions and he learned a valuable lesson: request legal counsel before giving any statements.

Unfortunately, this scenario is the norm and not the exception. In the best case scenario, the investigators are there to document what happened in your own words. In the worst case scenario, they are there to find fault with your use of force. The latter happens more often than may you think. As much as we do not want to believe it happens, public outrage and political motivations can influence investigations of high profile use of force incidents.

From a lawsuit's perspective, your attorney's most needlessly challenging hurdle to overcome is your post-use of force interview(s) with internal affairs (IA). As my previous example illustrates, your statements given right after your use of force incident may conflict with those made in follow-up interviews. To make matters worse, your interviews are audio and video recorded as evidence. As a result, the plaintiff's attorney will play your conflicting statements to the jury in an attempt to discredit your trial testimony. To explain your inconsistencies and factual errors, your attorney will call an expert to explain the effects of stress on your perception, comprehension, and recollection of the incident.

This defensive move is usually effective in neutralizing the damage done by your internal affairs statements. However, a proactive defense is always more effective than a reactive one. If you have legal representation at your internal affairs interviews, your attorney will ensure your statements are appropriate, consistent, and defensible.

The importance of having legal counsel during your internal affairs interviews cannot be stressed enough. In fact, it is so important that the Northland Insurance Company requested that the officers who attended the Oregon Academy and the academy sponsored instructor development courses be informed that if they were involved in a police shooting Northland would provide them with free legal counsel.

Rule Twelve: The Garrity Rule does not apply to civil lawsuits.

The Garrity Rule originates from the United States Supreme Court ruling of *Garrity v. New Jersey*, 385 U.S. 493 (1967). The case involved the criminal prosecution of officers for fixing traffic tickets. The officers were told that they had to answer questions or forfeit their employment under a New Jersey statute. Under duress, the officers confessed. The officers filed an appeal, and the U.S. Supreme Court overturned their convictions based on the Fifth Amendment's protection against self-incrimination.

In Garrity, the Supreme Court stated a law enforcement officer has the right to be free from compulsory self-incrimination. Under Garrity, your department can compel you to give statements under the threat of discipline or discharge; however, your statements may not be used in your criminal prosecution. Representing the majority, Justice Douglas wrote: "We conclude that policemen, like teachers and lawyers, are not relegated to a watered-down version of constitutional rights."

Under Garrity before you can be disciplined for refusing to answer questions related to your use of force incident, your administration must do the following:

- Order you to answer the questions under the threat of disciplinary action. The order can be oral, written or implied.
- Ask only questions that are specifically, directly and narrowly related to your official duties or your fitness for duty.
- Advise you that your answers will not be used against you in subsequent criminal proceedings.

If after being given the Garrity Warning you refuse to answer questions, you may be disciplined for insubordination.

The Garrity Rule only shields you from self-incrimination during a criminal prosecution. Your compelled statements can be used in a lawsuit against you or your department. Consequently, to proactively diminish the negative impact that your contradictory statements may have on a civil rights lawsuit, you should qualify your statements with the following disclaimer:

"I have just experienced a traumatic incident; consequently, my recollections of what happened in this incident may not be accurate."

This disclaimer preemptively explains the reason for any mistakes or contradictory information given during your preliminary and follow-up internal affairs interviews.

Then, at the civil trial when the plaintiff's attorney confronts you with the conflicting statements, you counter by explaining that during the IA interviews you warned the investigators that you had just experienced a traumatic incident and because of the effects of stress your recollections of the incident may not be accurate.

In this chapter, I gave you a blueprint for properly managing the use of force incident as an officer at the scene. In the next chapter, we will discuss the detective's role in properly managing the use of force incident, not from the perspective of a detective who has used force in performance of his duties; the rules for managing a use of force incident are the same regardless of the officer's position in the department. In the following chapter, I will provide insights in the training and information required for a detective to conduct a proper investigation into an officer's use of force.

Chapter 8

MANAGING THE USE OF FORCE
INCIDENT FOR DETECTIVES

In the new millennium, all officer-involved shootings and misconduct complaints are investigated. Large criminal justice organizations have specific investigative units that specialize in conducting officer misconduct investigations. These units are referred to as the Department of Internal Affairs or the Division of Professional Standards. Large is a relative term. In southern California, a two hundred-officer department is considered a medium size law enforcement agency. In Montana, it is the largest in the state. Regardless of the size of your department, if you are involved in a shooting or other high profile use of force incident, you will be the focus of an IA investigation.

Unless you work for a very large department, a criminal investigator from within your agency will investigate your incident. In rare cases, the investigation will be conducted by an outside agency. Since the majority of law enforcement agencies in the United States have fewer than fifty sworn officers, for some of you, a member of your command staff will conduct the investigation. Regardless of who performs the investigation, it will be conducted as a criminal investigation with little, if any, consideration given to the subsequent civil rights lawsuit.

This is often a source of contention between your city or county liability management division and your agency's administration. All administrators start their careers as cops, so their orientation is law enforcement and not liability management. It is this cop orientation that gives risk managers gastrointestinal problems and civil defense attorneys insomnia.

The main source of the contention between these two symbiotic groups is not interpersonal; it is philosophical. Traditionally, the risk management people tell the cops: "You are killing us with these lawsuits." The cops counter with: "You don't understand our tactics and when you put the numbers in perspective we don't see a problem." An article in a major newspaper illustrates this tension. The headline: "City has spent nearly $6.2 million to settle suits against police." According to the article, the average excessive force settlement was approximately $97,000.00. This information was part of a report that the city attorney gave to the city council. The police chief's response? "Excessive force incidents are isolated and need to be put in context, considering our police officers make more than 400,000 public contacts a year. The statistics show we have a well-behaved, well-controlled police force," the chief told the city council.

I've conducted training at this police department. The department's officers that I have worked with were exceptional. However, the settlement dollars tell the tale: The department has a problem with managing its use of force incidents.

Although there are similarities between a civilian criminal investigation and an internal affairs investigation, the internal affairs investigation requires the detective to think outside of the box to properly manage the use of force incident. When conducting an internal affairs investigation, the detective must consider the following: Law enforcement officers are given special enforcement, operational, and investigative powers. Officers have broad authority to use force in the performance of their duties. And officers are provided training in specialized procedures, tactics and techniques.

When it comes to properly managing the use of force incident, there are pros and cons to having an outside agency perform the internal affairs investigation. The benefit is in positive public relations. Having an outside agency conduct the IA investigation prevents the anti-police critics in your community from accusing the department of covering up incidents of excessive force and protecting your own. Further, the officer involved will hopefully receive an objective investigation free from political and public pressure.

The downside is that the investigator will not be familiar with your department's policies, use of force training, and patrol procedures and tactics. As a result, the investigator may overlook valuable information that your administrator requires to make a fair and defensible decision.

However, the same problem can occur with a detective from within your own department. When there is a problem with an internal affairs investigation, it is not because the detectives lack experience in conducting criminal investigations. The fumble comes from the detectives' failure to scratch below the surface of the incident.

In a civilian criminal investigation, the detectives consider the evidence, motivation, means, and opportunity. In an officer-involved use of force incident, there is one more critical element to consider–the officer's training. When it is all said and done, the important question is did the officer perform the way he or she was trained? When investigating an officer's use of force, you must keep in mind the Golden Rule of Internal Affairs Investigations: If the officer followed department or academy training, then the officer is absolved of any wrongdoing.

In the following example, the detectives failed to follow the IA Golden Rule. As a result, the officer was subjected to the burden of disciplinary action and the department suffered the public humiliation of losing the labor relations arbitration.

Officer Scott McCollister was given the longest unpaid disciplinary suspension in the history of the Portland Police Bureau for the Kendra James' use of force incident. Kendra was a passenger in a car that was stopped by Officer McCollister and two other officers. The officers were aware that Kendra had a warrant for her arrest. After the driver and another passenger were removed without resistance, Kendra jumped from the back seat into the driver's seat and started the car.

As Officer McCollister tried to extract Kendra, she pulled away–forcing Officer McCollister to partially enter the car. Kendra put the car in motion, and it accelerated with Officer McCollister hanging halfway out of the open driver's door. Fearing he would fall and be run over, Officer McCollister fatally shot Kendra.

Although his department and a federal jury determined the shooting was justified, the administration concluded that Officer McCollister's decision to pull Kendra from the car was tactically unsound and therefore violated department policy. As a result, Officer McCollister was given a one hundred and sixty-five day unpaid suspension. I consulted on the lawsuit and testified on his behalf at the labor relations hearing. At the conclusion of the hearing, the arbitrator reversed the suspension, ruling that the department never conducted a full investigation into the shooting.

"My finding is based on my conclusions that the failure to conduct a thorough IAD [Internal Affairs] investigation led to a fatal gap in the information available to the Chief on which to base his decision," wrote the arbitrator in his 44-page opinion.

The arbitrator's ruling illustrates the important role that investigators play in properly managing the use of force incident. To properly investigate an officer-involved shooting or an excessive force complaint, a detective is required to possess a thorough knowledge and understanding of the contemporary practices and standards of law enforcement or corrections.

More than 95 percent of excessive force complaints involve corrections and/or patrol officers. A detective's responsibilities are different than those of the street officer. Consequently, a detective's knowledge of contemporary patrol practices and officer safety tactics diminishes over time. Moreover, in an incident involving a corrections deputy/officer, the investigator may not have the correctional background required to effectively investigate an allegation of excessive force in the correctional facility.

It is for these reasons, before interviewing the officer; the investigator should familiarize him or herself of the following: *Tennessee v. Garner, Graham v. Connor, Whitney v. Albers,* the Americans with Disabilities Act, and the applicable appellate court rulings for his or her district.

The listed Supreme Court rulings and the ADA standards are explained in Chapter 3. To establish whether or not the officer's use of force was congruent with constitutional standards, I recommend you prepare a list questions to use during your officer interview. The following are example lists of prepared questions:

Tennessee v. Garner (Deadly Force–Police)

- What did the suspect do or say that made you fear that you (or another) would be seriously injured or killed?
- What other specific circumstances or factors made you fearful of being seriously injured or killed?
- Did you have specific knowledge that the suspect had committed a crime involving the use or threatened use of serious physical harm? How did you gain that knowledge?
- Did you issue a verbal challenge to the suspect before using deadly force? If not, why?
- What is your justification for shooting the fleeing suspect?

Graham v. Connor (Nondeadly Force–Police and Corrections)

- What were the actions and/or behaviors that you heard or observed that led you to believe the suspect was an immediate threat to you or another person?
- What specific knowledge did you have regarding the suspect or the incident that led you to believe the suspect was an immediate threat to you or another? Why was this information important?
- Was the severity of the crime that the suspect committed or allegedly committed a factor in determining what level of force to use? If, so, Why?
- Did the suspect resist arrest? If he or she did resist, how did that level of resistance influence your use of force decision?
- Did the suspect attempt to escape from your custody? If so, how? Why was this an important factor in your decision on how much force to use?

Whitney v. Albers (Corrections Deadly and Nondeadly Force)

- What were the actions and/or behaviors that you heard or observed that led you to believe the inmate was an immediate threat to you, another person, or himself/herself?
- What knowledge did you have regarding the inmate or the incident that led you to believe the inmate was an immediate threat to you or another? Why was this information important?
- What are the legitimate correctional objectives that justify your use of force? How did these objectives influence your use of force decision?
- What makes you believe your force was reasonable and not applied sadistically or maliciously?

Americans With Disabilities Act (Reasonable Accommodation)

- Were you aware the suspect/inmate had a physical disability? If so, how did you become aware of it?
- Did you ask the suspect/inmate if he or she had a disability or limitation that may cause an injury to the suspect if handcuffed behind the back?
- Did you physically and/or visually check the suspect/inmate for indications of a physical disability or limitation? If so, how?
- What actions or behaviors made it unreasonable to modify your tactics to accommodate the suspect/inmate's disability?
- Did you modify your normal tactic or procedure to make a reasonable accommodation for the suspect/inmate's disability? If so, how?
- What reasonable accommodation(s) did you make, if any? If you did, what were they?

Bryan v. McPherson (Taser Probe Deployment)

- What offense had the suspect/inmate committed when you deployed the Taser? Was this offense a traffic violation or nonviolent misdemeanor?
- What made you believe that level of offense justified the use of the Taser in probe mode?
- Was the suspect/inmate demonstrating passive resistance when you deployed the Taser? If not, how was the suspect/inmate actively resisting?
- Did you consider other tactics to resolve the situation prior to deploying the Taser? If not, why? If you did, which tactics, and why weren't they deployed?

- Did you warn the suspect/inmate the Taser would be deployed? If not, what were the circumstances that caused the warning to be unreasonable?

Brooks v. City of Seattle (Taser Drive Stun)

- When you Drive Stunned the suspect/inmate, did you follow department policy on the use of the Taser? If yes, what does that policy allow you to do?
- Did you verbally warn the suspect/inmate that he or she would be Drive Stunned? If so, how many times?
- Did you display the Taser arc to the suspect/inmate before delivering the Drive Stun?
- Did you attempt to control the suspect/inmate with lesser control tactics before Drive Stunning the suspect/inmate? If so, which control techniques? What was their effect?
- Did you consider the suspect/inmate's physical condition when choosing which location on the suspect/inmate's body to Drive Stun? If so, why?

Not only will having a list of questions based on the constitutional standards give your interview more continuity, it will prevent you from making mistakes that hurt your credibility with the officer. In a use of force incident where an officer tasered an intoxicated combative minor at a party, the boy's father filed an excessive force complaint with the city council.

Because the incident was controversial, the city council asked an outside agency to conduct the internal affairs investigation. During the officer's interview, the detective referred to *Tennessee v. Garner* as the standard for using nondeadly force. The officer, a use of force instructor, correctly pointed out that *Graham v. Conner* was the ruling that established the standards for using nondeadly force. The detective stubbornly insisted the the ruling was *Garner*. The officer left the interview, retrieved his use of force training manual, and proved to the detective that *Graham* was the correct standard. From that exchange, the detective lost all credibility with the officer, and as a result, his ability to effectively conduct the interview.

In addition to reviewing the legal standards that regulate the use of an officer's force, you should review the following:

The Officer versus the Threat Factors and Influential Circumstances that justify the escalation of force.

These factors and circumstances are discussed in Chapter 4. As with the legal standards, I recommend creating a list of questions based on these factors and circumstances to use during your interview. By asking the officer if the factor or circumstance was a consideration in his use of force decision, you establish the officer's justification for the use of force, or the lack thereof.

The following are example interview questions regarding the Officer versus Threat Factors and Influential Circumstances:

Officer versus Threat Factors

- Did you have previous knowledge of the suspect/inmate's combat skill level or fighting ability? If so, why was that important?
- Did your age or the suspect/inmate's age influence your use of force decision? If so, why?
- Did your gender or the suspect/inmate's gender influence your use of force decision? Please explain why? Or why not?
- Did the suspect/inmate's mental or emotional state influence your decision on how much force to use? If so, why?
- Did the size and strength difference between you and the suspect/inmate play an important role in your use of force decision? If so, why?
- Did having to control multiple suspect/inmates or other people at the scene influence your use of force decision? If so, how?

Influential Circumstances

- Did the confined space in which you confronted the suspect/inmate influence your use of force decision? If so, how?
- Did the inability to safely disengage from the suspect/inmate or the situation influence your use of force decision? If so, how?
- Was the suspect/inmate in close proximity to a weapon? If so, what was the weapon? How did the presence of a weapon influence your use of force decision?
- Were you injured or become exhausted during the struggle with the suspect/inmate? Did that influence your use of force decision? If so, why?
- Did the terrain or environment at the scene influence your use of force decision? If so, how?
- Did your previous experiences in dealing with similar suspect/inmates or situations influence your use of force decision? If so, why?

- Did you have any special knowledge regarding the suspect/inmate that influenced your use of force decision? If so, what was it?
- Did you have any special knowledge regarding the handling of this specific type of call/incident that influenced your use of force decision? If so, please explain.
- Do you have any physical disabilities or limitations that influenced your use of force decision? If so, what are they? Why were they important?
- Did the suspect/inmate's sudden attack have an impact on your use of force options? If so, why?
- Did the distance from the suspect/inmate influence your choice in which use of force option to deploy? If it did, why?

The Department's Use of Force Training Program.

It is vitally important that you review the department's use of force training program in preparation for an investigation into an officer's alleged use of excessive force or misconduct. To prepare for your investigation, you need to review the relevant lesson plans, training manuals, training videos, and PowerPoint presentations. Further, I recommend you interview the department's use of force or defensive tactics instructor. This is crucial to conducting a fair and informed internal affairs investigation. A police captain, investigating an excessive force complaint, discovered the importance of this research the hard way.

The captain's department had received a complaint involving an officer's use of pepper spray. The incident started as a traffic stop for speeding. The driver had just been married and was en route to the wedding reception with his new bride, best man, and maid of honor in the car. All the occupants were dressed in formal wedding attire.

When the officer ran the driver's status, he discovered the driver had a misdemeanor warrant. When the officer told the driver he was under arrest, the driver–a very large man–told the officer that if he was going to jail on his wedding day he was not going to go easy. With that warning, the officer pepper sprayed the driver. Unfortunately, the bride, best man, and maid of honor were accidentally pepper sprayed, too.

The captain called me and asked for an overview of the academy's pepper spray training. I told the captain that our program consisted of a four-hour use of force lecture and an hour exposure exercise. The captain explained that his department's program consisted of a thirty-minute use of force overview and a two-hour application and exposure segment. He inquired why the academy spent so many hours on the use of force? "Officers don't get sued for using pepper spray–they get sued for making bad use of force decisions," I replied. As we discussed pepper spray training, I mentioned that a local police department had created a pepper spray training video that several departments had integrated into their training.

In that video, the instructor tells officers that it is no longer necessary to go "hands-on" with suspects. The instructor even used the phrase "spray them, don't touch them." There was a long silence on the other end of the telephone. Then, the captain lamented: "We use that video in our training. I had no idea it said that. I have an officer on disciplinary suspension for doing what we trained him to do." Ouch! The administration lost the officer's arbitration hearing. The city quietly settled the nuptial lawsuit.

The effects of stress on an officer's judgement and ability to accurately recall the facts of the incident.

Our physiological reactions to stress originate from a time when human beings were on the lower end of the food chain. When we wore animal skins and killed our food and defended ourselves with stones and flint-tipped spears, our natural reactions to stress ensured our survival as a species. Primitive man, as we still do today, experienced tunnel vision and auditory blocking when his heart rate reached one hundred and forty-five beats per minute. The natural narrowing of his vision was an important focal change when trying to stab an attacking short-faced bear with a spear. Or, when a group of hunters came face-to-face with an animal that viewed them as lunchables, their bodies naturally buffered their hearing so not to be distracted from the task at hand–surviving the encounter.

Cops may not wear fur (that's not PC) or defend themselves with obsidian-tipped spears, but they still experience the physiological effects of stress when faced with life-threatening situations.

When I spoke with a deputy a day after his shooting, he suffered from memory lapses. He had distinct recollections of making the traffic stop, seeing a bulge under the driver's jacket as he exited the Bronco and walked toward him, and seeing the back of his shoulder rise–as he reached for the gun in his shoulder holster. The next thing he remembered was looking down the barrel of a 44-magnum revolver.

He saw nothing else, but that great big hole in the end of the barrel. And that hole looked like it was a foot in front of his face. The deputy didn't remember bringing his handgun up that he had concealed behind his back. He didn't remember firing his weapon. The deputy didn't even hear the gunshots. All he remembered about the shooting was seeing the gun fly from the suspect's hand in slow motion and the suspect fall backward in an even slower motion. The deputy had no memory of pointing his gun or pulling the trigger. Did this mean the deputy was covering up a mistake? Of course not. He experienced what most cops do when involved in a shooting: tunnel vision, time and space distortion, auditory blocking, and memory lapses.

Another negative side effect of stress is impaired judgement. When I was working as a deputy sheriff, another deputy and a sergeant were taken hostage while making an arrest for domestic violence. During the struggle, the suspect pulled the deputy's handgun from his holster and then disarmed the sergeant. As the sergeant distracted the suspect, the deputy escaped out the front door. The suspect told the sergeant that he was going to walk him out to his patrol car, execute him, and steal his car. As they walked to the front door, the sergeant believed that when he opened the door the deputy would yell: "drop," he will fall to the ground, and the deputy would kill the suspect. In short, a tragic beginning would have a happy ending.

Unfortunately, the sergeant did not know that the suspect had the deputy's gun; he thought the suspect had accessed a gun hidden in the chair. It was not until he opened the front door and saw the unarmed deputy that he realized the suspect had the deputy's gun. The sergeant also remembered that neither he nor the deputy placed a shotgun or rifle in their cars at the beginning of the shift. At that point, it became crystal clear to the sergeant that the bad guy had all the guns, and he was about to be executed.

A next door neighbor looked out his front window and saw the unarmed deputy take cover behind his patrol car. Further, the neighbor observed the unarmed sergeant being held at gunpoint. Being a law enforcement supporter, he went to his gun cabinet and loaded a scoped .270 caliber hunting rifle and armed the deputy.

Gunshots were exchanged between the deputy and the suspect. During the gunfight the sergeant took cover behind a tree. The neighbor handed the sergeant a loaded 12-gauge shotgun. The sergeant looked at the shotgun, handed it back to the neighbor, and said: "I don't want this. I want one of those." As he pointed at the deputy's scoped rifle. The neighbor, shrugged, went back into his house and exchanged the shotgun for a rifle.

During the sergeant's debriefing he was asked, "Even if you wanted a rifle, why didn't you keep the shotgun until you got a rifle?" He looked down, in deep thought, and replied, "I don't know." The reason: The sergeant's judgment was impaired by the extreme level of stress he was experiencing. He was reacting, not thinking.

The deputy's judgement was impaired by stress as well. At some point during the gunfight, the deputy sought cover behind an aluminum gate. The suspect had taken cover behind a building and he would randomly pop out and shoot from around the corner. From behind the gate, the deputy prepared to shoot. However, because he was suffering from tunnel vision and an impaired mental process, he did not realize the scope sat on top of the rifle's receiver.

Consequently, when he looked at the corner of the building through the scope, the top rail of the gate blocked the muzzle of the barrel. The moment the suspect popped out, the deputy pulled the trigger and blasted a large hole in the aluminum gate. Shortly afterward, the suspect ran out of ammunition and surrendered.

As the previous examples illustrate, when investigating a use of force incident, you must take into account the influence that stress has on the officer's tactics, judgement, and ability to remember details and events.

The department's patrol procedures and tactics.

In Officer McCollister's investigation, the detectives were apparently unaware of the Golden Rule of Internal Affairs investigations. In most law enforcement agencies, the chief, sheriff, or administrator is unaware of the specific patrol procedures and/or tactics their officers are taught during inservice training or at the academy. Consequently, the Boss will rely on your investigation to provide him or her with the pertinent information necessary to make an informed decision regarding the appropriateness of the officer's actions. There are two key questions that every administrator needs answered to make a defensible decision.

1. What are the department's authorized procedures and/or tactics for handling the use of force incident in question.
2. Did the officer follow the approved procedures and/or tactics?

During Officer McCollister's arbitration hearing, the department's patrol tactics and use of force instructor testified that Portland officers are trained in tactics for physically removing resistive suspects from vehicles. Further, the instructor testified that Officer McCollister used the tactics he was taught when he attempted to extract Kendra James from the vehicle. Apparently, these were two critical pieces of information were left out of the Internal Affairs investigator's report. They were main reasons for the arbitrator's reversal of the officer's disciplinary suspension.

The patrol procedures and defensive tactics that are taught at the academy.

Your state's Peace Officer Standards and Training Board/Council approves the police and corrections curriculums taught at the academies in your state. In doing so, the operational procedures and tactics taught at the academy establish baseline standards for an officer's performance in a use of force incident.

The second mistake the detectives made in Officer McCollister's investigation is they did not review the arrest and vehicle stop tactics that officers are taught at the Oregon Academy. If the detectives had reviewed the academy's curriculum, they would have discovered that Officer McCollister actions were in accordance with academy training.

Knowing that an officer who follows his academy training is always in good legal standing, Officer McCollister's attorney called upon me to explain the patrol procedures and defensive tactics taught at the Oregon Academy. Further, I testified that Officer McCollister's actions and tactics were in accordance with academy training.

When conducting an IA investigation into the appropriateness of an officer's use of force or tactics, keep in mind that academy training is the standard by which an arbitrator, a judge, or a jury evaluates the officer's actions.

Furthermore, I recommend investigators stay updated on evidence-processing procedures for new force options. This information can be obtained from forensic experts who specialize in police use of force lawsuits. For example, it is common practice for investigators to wrap the Taser wires around the spent cartridge when collecting the barbs and wires as evidence. Wrapping the wires around the cartridge destroys the fold pattern of the wire.

By examining the sharpness of the folds, a forensic expert can determine the distance between the officer and the suspect when the Taser was deployed. The straighter the wire the further the distance. Further, straightened Taser leads indicate the probe missed, the suspect was running away, or the shock did not incapacitate the suspect.

When the Taser is deployed in probe mode, AFIDS (small circular confetti) are ejected with the probes. From the location of the AFIDS, a forensic expert can determine the officer's location when he fired the Taser. Furthermore, if the Taser is fired at close range, the suspect will have AFIDS in his hair and clothing. This is important evidence if the suspect claims he was shocked with the probes at close range, but the officer denies deploying the Taser.

When investigating an incident involving the use of kinetic energy weapons, knowing the injury potential and effectiveness of a police baton, beanbag projectile, plastic ball projectile, or Arwen baton can be critical information. In a lawsuit involving the fatal shooting of an unarmed suspect, the officers deployed the Taser and beanbag projectiles before using deadly force.

During the trial, the plaintiff's attorney theorized that had the officers used their police batons to disable the suspect the use of deadly force would not have been necessary. And he called a use of force expert that testified that a baton blow would have disabled the suspect. The officer countered by stating a baton blow is no more effective in disabling a suspect than a beanbag projectile.

During the expert's cross-examination, the officer's attorney asked the expert if the beanbag round developed more force than a baton blow? The question was actually delivered more as a statement. The expert testified that the expandable baton, with its small diameter metal shaft, wielded by a two hundred-pound male officer would deliver a more effective blow than a beanbag round. Additionally, the expert explained that the lead shot-filled cloth bag would flex on impact, distributing its energy over a wider area. In contrast, baton's metal shaft would not give, transferring all its energy to a small focal point. Further, the expert stated that a baton swing has follow-through that enhances the force of the blow. At the end of the expert's explanation, the defense council wished he had not asked the question.

If the IA investigators had consulted with the medical examiner or a forensic pathologist on the impact differential between a beanbag projectile and a steel baton, they could have used that information to evaluate the validity of the officer's justification for not deploying his baton in lieu of using deadly force. And had that information been included in the investigator's report, the officer's attorney would not have been blind-sided by the expert's explanation.

As criminal investigators, detectives often do not see the bigger picture regarding an officer's use of force incident. This investigative tunnel vision occurs because detectives spend 99.9 percent of their time investigating civilian suspects. Further, because a civilian suspect rarely gets civilly sued after being exonerated of any wrongdoing, the detectives do not see the impact that their investigations have on civil liability. As a result, an improperly conducted IA investigation can severely damage the officer's defense in an excessive force lawsuit.

The most damaging mistake an IA investigator can make is to ask another department's defensive tactics instructor to evaluate the officer's use of force. A defensive tactics/use of force instructor's report that criticizes the officer's use of force contributes very little to the investigation, but inflicts a major amount of damage to the officer's lawsuit defense.

In an excessive force lawsuit involving the death of a drunk driver, the incident was captured on the arresting officer's patrol car video camera. The suspect physically resisted arrest. In response, the officer took the driver to the ground and kneeled on his back, as he was trained to do. Unknown to the officer, the pressure from kneeling on the suspect's back ruptured an internal organ. The driver bled to death internally. The arresting officer's department asked an outside law enforcement agency to conduct the IA investigation.

When the patrol car video is viewed in real time, the officer appears to kneel on the suspect. However, the detective had the video copied in slow motion. This was the detective's first mistake. When the video is played in slow motion, the officer appears to deliver a knee strike to the driver. The altered speed of the video does not accurately represent the officer's use of force. To make matters worse, the detective asked his department's defensive tactics instructor to review the slow motion video, evaluate the officer's use of force, and submit a report with his conclusions.

This was the detective's most damaging mistake. In his report, the instructor stated that the officer did not kneel down on the suspect as the officer claimed. But, in actuality, the officer knee struck the driver in the back. Further, the instructor stated that the officer's force was clearly excessive.

A grand jury cleared the officer of any criminal wrongdoing. I was asked by the city's insurance company to review the use of force incident. It was my opinion that the officer's use of force was reasonable. Also, I stated that the defensive tactics instructor had erred when he used the slow motion video to form his opinion. However, because of the troubled IA investigation, the insurance company agreed to a million-dollar settlement.

I would like to take a moment to reiterate that this chapter was written for detectives and investigators who conduct investigations into officers' use of force incidents. Consequently, the information contained in this chapter was presented with a liability management bias in an effort to provide a proactive defense to the subsequent lawsuit that is likely to be filed against the officer.

The recommendations and guidelines contained in this chapter were written with an assumption that the officer involved in the use of force incident lawfully applied deadly or nondeadly force. With this disclaimer stated, I would like to give you a few of my thoughts to ponder regarding the interview of an officer who has been involved in a use of force incident.

From the managing the use of force incident perspective, there are three categories of internal affairs investigations: officer-involved shooting, excessive force, and officer misconduct. Any one of those categories can end with the officer being criminally prosecuted. All of them will probably end with the officer being sued, whether the officer is exonerated or found at fault.

In most use of force incidents, there are independent witnesses. Therefore, you will have interviewed the witnesses before you interview the officer(s). As a result, you will have formed an opinion as to whether the officer used excessive force. If you believe the officer's force was lawful (and you have a shred of humanity), you will *order* the officer under *Garrity* to give a statement to protect him or her from an idiot prosecutor who has not the faintest understanding of police use of force.

To make my point, I want to take you back to my experience at the Oregon Public Safety Academy. As you remember, I was a retread officer in a use of force class taught by a county deputy district attorney. When he gave the class a hypothetical shooting scenario, I told him I would shoot the unarmed suspect as allowed by *Tennessee v. Garner*. Even though, as a police officer, I could constitutionally shoot the dangerous fleeing suspect, the prosecutor warned that he would prosecute me if I were an officer in his county. So, you can see why the Garrity Rule has personal meaning to me.

As you know, the Garrity Rule protects officers from self-incrimination. By ordering the officer to answer your questions or be disciplined, the officer's statements cannot be used against him or her in a criminal prosecution. As part of your investigative procedure, I recommend you provide the officer with a formal Garrity Warning. The following is an example of a standardized Garrity Warning form:

> I, _____, am being questioned as part of an investigation by this agency into potential violations of department rules and regulations, or for my fitness for duty. This investigation concerns: (List the incident and case number)
>
> I have invoked my Miranda rights on the grounds that I might incriminate myself in a criminal matter.
>
> I have been ordered by my agency to answer all questions under the threat of discipline. If I refuse to answer, I may be subject to discipline for that refusal which can result in my dismissal from this agency. No answer given by me, nor evidence derived from the answer, may be used against me in any criminal proceeding, except for perjury or false swearing.
>
> I understand that I must now answer questions specifically, directly and narrowly related to the performance of my official duties or my fitness for service.
>
> Anything I say may be used against me in any subsequent department discipline or a civil lawsuit.
>
> I have the right to consult with an attorney, a representative of my collective bargaining unit, or another representative of my choice, and have him or her present during the interview.
>
> Deputy/Officer/Troop's Signature:
> Department Representative's Signature:
> Date:
> Time:

In closing, I have one last thought on interviewing an officer that has been involved in a shooting. Previously, I have explained the effect that stress has on an officer's cognitive abilities. By now you have learned that if you interview an officer within twenty-four hours of his or her shooting, the information that the officer provides is going to be unreliable, distorted, and incomplete. Further, in most shooting, there are civilian and officer witnesses that can provide you with the general details of the incident—certainly enough information for a press release. Therefore, managing the use of force incident aside, there are no valid reasons for not allowing the officer to decompress, receive peer and professional counseling, and let him process the incident before he is interviewed. I am not saying you should give the officer a three-week vacation before you conduct the interview. But give the officer a few days to put the incident all together. The officer may be a homicide suspect, but he or she is still is one of the good guys.

In this chapter, we discussed the critical differences between conducting a civilian criminal investigation and a police internal affairs investigation. Although, 90 percent of the investigative techniques in a detective's skill set are pertinent to an IA investigation, a working knowledge of the other specialized 10 percent is critical to properly managing the use of force incident.

In the next chapter, we will explore the first-line supervisor's role in properly managing the use of force incident. Rather than delve into the traditional supervisory role in monitoring an officer's performance, we will explore the supervisor's role as a mentor in managing the use of force incident.

Chapter 9

MANAGING THE USE OF FORCE
INCIDENT FOR SUPERVISORS

As a supervisor, if I were to ask you: What proactive role do you play in minimizing liability for your department? What would you say? I don't know what answer you would give. But I know what answer you should give: I play the role of diplomat, mentor, performance coach, and use of force instructor. As a first-line supervisor, those are the roles you should play to proactively minimize complaints of excessive force and win lawsuits. Put another way, you must lead your troops by example to proactively manage the use of force incident. Supervisor may be your title, but leadership is what effective supervisors provide their officers in properly managing the use of force incident.

The Power of an Apology

As a supervisor, you play an important role in positively influencing perceptions at the scene of a use of force incident. As the on-scene supervisor, you are in a position to prevent potential complaints and lawsuits. Many potential use of force complaints can be circumvented at the scene by a supervisor skilled in managing the use of force incident. Unfortunately, as is often the case, supervisors—believing they are supporting their troops—miss an opportunity to prevent a lawsuit by simply offering an apology. The phrase "I don't apologize when my officers are right" has been the catalyst for more than a few lawsuits.

For example, in a lawsuit involving the investigative detention of a husband and wife, an apology by the supervisor would have prevented the lawsuit. The plaintiffs, who were building a decorative block patio, had made arrangements with the manager of a home improvement store to pick up several dozen-cement blocks after the store had closed. The blocks were left outside the security fence on a wooden palette. The plaintiffs, the husband a realtor and his wife a legal assistant, were loading the blocks into the back of a late model truck when the manager of a variety store drove by and observed the suspicious activity. The manager drove to the police department and reported the possible burglary in progress.

Several officers and a sergeant responded to the home improvement store. After watching the plaintiffs load cement blocks for approximately fifteen minutes, the officers moved in and high-risk handcuffed the couple at gunpoint.

As the officers ordered the couple to prone out on the ground, both the husband and wife told the officers that they had purchased the blocks and that there was a payment invoice on the truck's seat. It is important to note that the husband was wearing dress slacks and a dress shirt and the wife was wearing designer jeans and a conservative blouse. Not your standard burglar attire. Not to say they could not have been burglars, but the suspects did not fit the criminal profile. The couple was handcuffed, searched, and placed in patrol cars.

After the plaintiffs were detained, an officer retrieved the sales receipt that verified the plaintiffs had purchased the blocks. The couple was released without an explanation for their detention. The unhappy wife confronted the sergeant and asked for an apology for the inconvenience of being handcuffed and the embarrassment of being searched by a male officer. "I don't apologize when I am right," the sergeant quipped. Then, the sergeant and the officers drove away. Feeling wronged by the officers, the homeowners filed an excessive force lawsuit.

All the homeowners wanted was an apology. An apology is not an admission of wrongdoing. It is an acknowledgement that the homeowners are entitled to be upset at being treated like burglary suspects. An apology does not cost your department a dime, but civil rights litigation can cost thousands, if not hundreds of thousands of dollars.

As one enlightened police supervisor told me, "I apologize to upset citizens all the time. I don't apologize for our tactics. I apologize for the inconvenience and the discomfort that we may have caused them. Most of the time, all they want is for me to acknowledge that we (cops) understand how they feel." Furthermore, an apology by a supervisor should be accompanied with the background information regarding the incident, the justification for the use of force, and/or an explanation of the tactics.

In the incident with the homeowners, the officers did not do anything wrong, but neither did the homeowners. They were just victims of circumstance. When the officers discovered that the plaintiffs had purchased the blocks, the sergeant should have apologized for taking them down at gunpoint, handcuffing them, and searching her. Then, the sergeant should have explained to the homeowners that the police department received a report of a burglary in progress, burglars are often armed, and 20 percent of officers killed investigating burglaries in progress are faked out by the suspect. Do you think an apology and an explanation would have prevented the homeowners' lawsuit? I know it would have. I spoke with her attorney. That was all she wanted.

Now, if you are one of those supervisors who finds this "warm and fuzzy" approach to circumventing lawsuits offensive to your cop sensibilities, you need to cowboy up and take one for the team. This is not about you, your ego, or your old school attitude. It is about doing what is best for the department and your officers. Still not convinced? This next example may change your mind.

Deputies and police officers performed a high-risk vehicle stop on a van driven by a suspected purse-snatcher. The 911 dispatcher received a report that a person in a red mini-van had stolen a purse from a car parked at a roadside rest area. The witness did not remember the van's license plate number, but she was able to provide the van's direction of travel. The officers caught up with a red min-van near the rest area traveling in the same direction as the reported suspect vehicle and performed a high-risk vehicle stop.

Why conduct a high-risk stop on a purse-snatcher? The officers could not provide a coherent explanation for taking the occupants out of the van at gunpoint. If you haven't identified the obvious reason, go back and review the "Stupidity" section in Chapter 1.

When the van stopped, the driver exited and identified himself as a federal parole officer. As he made this announcement, he displayed his badge and ID. The deputies high-risk handcuffed the parole officer and his wife. Also in the van was the officer's teenage son, who had recently undergone shoulder surgery. When the teenager was ordered out of the van, his father informed the officers of the recent surgery and asked that his son not be handcuffed with his hands behind his back. The deputies ignored the father's warning, forcefully pulled his son's arms behind his back, and re-injured his shoulder. The van was searched and no stolen purse was found. Thereupon, the parole officer and his family were released. Tragically, as a result of the handcuffing, his son had to undergo another surgery to repair his shoulder.

The parole officer met with the Sheriff to discuss the incident. The officer stated that as a law enforcement officer he understood the effect that adrenaline has on officers performing their duties. Further, the officer told the Sheriff that he had warned the deputies about his son's shoulder condition, and the deputies handcuffed his son's arms behind his back anyway–injuring his shoulder. In an attempt to be reasonable about the incident, the parole officer told the Sheriff that he only wanted an apology for the way his deputies treated his wife and son. You know what is coming next, don't you? The Sheriff told the parole officer that he does not apologize when his deputies do the right thing. Dissatisfied with the Sheriff's unapologetic response, the officer contacted an attorney and filed excessive force and ADA lawsuits against the sheriff's office and the police department. The county settled the lawsuit for $450,000.00 and the city settled for $350,000.00. Do I need to say more about the importance of warm and fuzzy apologies? I didn't think so.

A View of Force

After the Rodney King incident sent a quake through the rank and file of the criminal justice community, the Los Angeles County Sheriff's Department Psychological Services Unit published an internal report titled "A View of Force." The document was published to provide first-line supervisors and mid-level commanders with an understanding of the psychological dynamics of police excessive force. The report provided an overview of the causative factors of excessive force, but it offered little in the way of organizational solutions or supervisory remedies for its prevention. However, the report did have one nugget of information that was germane to the first-line supervisor's role in managing the use of force incident. And that information is as pertinent today as it was the day the report was issued.

According to the Unit's research, approximately 15 percent of law enforcement officers will never intentionally behave inappropriately, no matter how much peer pressure is applied. The report refers to these officers as the "Untouchables." These officers are self-regulated by an innate sense of right and wrong. They are the saints of the department. As in all things in the natural world, every action has an equal and opposite reaction. The same is true for a police force. Conversely, their research discovered that 15 percent of law enforcement officers will always do the wrong thing, even when given the opportunity to do the right thing. Further, they will continue their inappropriate behavior despite all supervisory efforts to change them. The report labeled these officers as the "Already Gone." These rogue officers are the unrepentant sinners of the department.

The report identified the middle 70 percent of officers as the group of most concern. This group's behavior can be influenced depending on which 15 percent (saints or sinners) is the dominant force at the scene. The report referred to this swayable majority as "Fence Sitters." The following are litigation examples of the three officer categories:

UNTOUCHABLE. Even your best officers can be sued for allegedly violating a suspect's civil rights, as a decorated officer, with over twenty years of exemplary service, discovered. The officer responded to a report of a man stopping traffic on a busy roadway. When the officer arrived at the scene, he observed a man in his forties standing in the middle of the street blocking traffic. The officer called out to the man. The suspect looked at the officer, grunted, and walked away. Does the suspect's response seem familiar to you?

The officer chased and caught the suspect and a struggle ensued. Due to the suspect's extreme strength, the officer was unable to control him. The suspect broke free and ran toward a group of houses. Fearing the suspect would enter a residence and harm the occupants, the officer tackled the suspect. Unable to gain control of the suspect, the officer pulled his expandable baton and struck the suspect on the arm. The baton blow caused the suspect to submit. It was later discovered that the baton blow broke the suspect's forearm.

Does the officer's use of force appear reasonable to you? I testified in the officer's lawsuit that it was. Here was my justification: The officer attempted to control the suspect with lesser physical control techniques prior to escalating to the baton. Further, it was reasonable for the officer to believe that a suspect who had overpowered him and escaped would enter an occupied residence and attack or take the occupants hostage.

Unfortunately, the officer was unaware that the suspect was severely mentally disabled and that he had walked away from a group home. When the officer yelled to the suspect, it frightened him. The suspect was not trying to escape; he was running back to the safety of his group home. Of course, the officer had no way of knowing this when he used force on the handicapped suspect. Accordingly, the officer's force was objectively reasonable, given the information available to the officer at time. Regardless, the suspect's family filled an excessive force lawsuit against the officer. At the end of the three-day civil rights trial, the jury concluded the officer used reasonable force. The officer's outstanding service record was the determining factor in the jury's defense verdict.

FENCE-SITTERS. A large percent of the use of force incidents that result in out of court settlements involve one or more rogue officers and one or more swayable officers. Rogue officers have strong, aggressive personalities. Consequently, they take charge of the incident, dictate the tactics, and set the tone for the use of force. As a result, the influenceable officers tune into the collective tactical consciousness. The result: a law enforcement version of the *Lord of the Flies* with the suspect or inmate playing the role of the kid who suffers at the hands of the frenzied group. The antidote to this toxic affliction of GroupThink is a counterbalance of strong leadership by the on-scene supervisor. The following lawsuit illustrates the importance of competent supervisory leadership at the scene of a use of force incident.

The officers responded to a "man with a gun" call. Two next-door neighbors had been feuding over the placement of a fence for months. One afternoon, the female neighbor went to the elderly male neighbor's house to complain about his fence. When she knocked on his front door, the elderly neighbor came out of his open garage holding a replica flintlock pistol. The elderly neighbor had been showing a friend his pistol in the garage when he heard the knock on the door.

When the two met in front of the garage, the female neighbor demanded he remove his fence. In response, the elderly neighbor told her to get off his property. The female neighbor refused to leave. Having the legal right to protect his property, he pushed her backward out of his yard. During this heated exchange, the elderly man held the pistol down at his side and at no time did he point the pistol at the woman or threaten her with it.

The unharmed female neighbor returned to her residence and reported to the police department that her neighbor had menaced her with a handgun. As a result, six officers responded to the scene. However, none of the officers contacted the victim to gather intelligence or ascertain what had actually happened. It was not until after the suspect was arrested that an officer interviewed the victim and the witnesses.

The only department member to have any contact with the victim prior to the suspect's arrest was the sergeant. The sergeant arrived late at the scene. As he walked toward the suspect's residence, he observed the reported victim standing near the fence. In the sergeant's deposition he states:

> "Well, when I arrived, I went up to this lady that was standing by her fence and said, he has a gun. So I confirmed now that there was a gun. It was quick. She confirmed what dispatch told me on the air. So, then I just went over to the officers."

When the sergeant arrived at the parameter, the officer who had developed the tactical plan briefed him. The sergeant made telephone contact with the elderly man, told him that the police were outside his residence, and asked him to exit his house. The unarmed elderly man, wearing a thin white T-shirt, white shorts, and socks, came out of his residence.

The officers ordered the suspect to put his hands in the air and walk toward them. The suspect raised his hands as high as he could. He had previously injured his shoulder and had arthritis in both shoulder joints, so he could not straighten his arms. The officers' forced the elderly man to his knees. As he was forced down, the elderly man told the officers that he had previously injured his shoulder and that he could not put his arms behind his back. In response, one officer stepped on his toes and smashed them into the cement driveway. Two other officers applied wristlocks and forced his arms behind his back. A third officer delivered knee strikes to the elderly man's thigh, hip, and rib cage. The sergeant witnessed the use of excessive force, but he did not intervene. The suspect suffered a shoulder injury, bruised ribs, scraped and bloody toes, and developed blood in his kidneys.

The suspect was arrested for assault and threatening a person with a weapon. The district attorney's office dismissed the criminal charges, and the elderly man filed an excessive force lawsuit against the officers. The city settled the lawsuit.

This incident is a classic example of "Fence Sitters" being influenced by "Already Gones." At no time during the development phase of the tactical plan did an officer suggest they contact the victim to determine if probable cause existed for an arrest. In fact, if the officers had contacted the alleged victim, they would have learned that the dispute over the fence had been going on for months, the elderly man never threatened the woman with the gun, and he only pushed her off his property after he had told his neighbor several times to leave and she refused. Moreover, the officers would have learned that the woman embellished the incident to get her neighbor arrested.

Further, this whole tragic incident could have been avoided if the sergeant would have taken an active leadership role at the scene. Providing supervisory leadership is not micromanaging your officers. It is, however, a key element in preventing false arrest and excessive force litigation.

As Colin Powell points out in his book, *The Leadership Secrets of Colin Powell,* a supervisor should always "scratch below the surface." General Powell goes on to explain that a supervisor should never accept information or evaluate a situation on its face value.

As a supervisor at the scene of a use of force incident, you are responsible for the objective evaluation of the known facts, the tactical plan, and the officers' use of force. An objective evaluation can only be obtained by asking questions. As in this incident, the sergeant should have field interviewed the alleged victim, when he spoke with her at the fence. If he had, the sergeant would have learned that the elderly neighbor did not threaten her with a handgun. This one piece of information would have changed the dynamic of the incident.

In addition, if the sergeant had asked the officers if they had interviewed the victim, he would have discovered they did not have probable cause for an arrest. Knowing that older people suffer from hearing loss, arthritis, osteoporosis, and preexisting injuries, the sergeant should have asked the officers if they had an alternative tactical plan to deal with an elderly suspect who may have limitations or disabilities.

Last, but not the least, the sergeant should have intervened in the officers' use of excessive force on the elderly suspect. The Fence Sitter Syndrome may explain why the other officers at the scene did not intervene, but the syndrome does not absolve the officers of their responsibility to protect the suspect from the use of excessive force. As this incident illustrates, officers are not the only Fence Sitters. Supervisors can sit on the fence as well. And when they do, supervisors stop being leaders and become followers.

ALREADY GONE. Rogue officers lead their departments in excessive force complaints, settled lawsuits, and lost civil rights trials. However, because the suspect or inmate is often of questionable character (involved in criminal activity) and there were no credible witnesses or a video recording of the use of force incident, rogue officers are very seldom held accountable for their bad behavior. When they are held accountable, it is because credible independent witnesses observed the incident or their actions are video recorded.

In the following incident, two credible independent witnesses observed the officers' actions. Based on their testimony, the jury concluded the rogue officers used excessive force.

Three African American men had gone downtown to celebrate a holiday. When the bars closed, they returned to a multi-level parking structure where their vehicle was parked. Two of the men entered their vehicle. The third man left to pick up a pizza. When the third man returned to the parking garage, three officers confronted him. The officers told the third man that they were looking for two groups of African American males who had recently been involved in an altercation: one group was clad in white T-shirts and the other in black T-shirts.

The officers followed the third man to his vehicle. When the officers contacted the two other men, they asked for their identification. At that point, the driver of the vehicle informed the officers that he had a concealed weapon permit and that he was armed.

Upon hearing that the driver possessed a conceal weapon, the lead officer yelled, "He's carrying! He's carrying! And, all three officers drew their handguns. To keep the driver's hands away from his concealed handgun, the lead officer cut the driver's seatbelt strap. Then, all three men were pulled from the car and handcuffed. When one of the men asked, "What have we done wrong?" An officer replied, "If you say one more word, I'm going to shoot you." To make the incident even more outrageous the lead officer, without provocation, punched the concealed weapon permit holder three times in the groin.

At the civil rights trial, one of the men told the jury: "I thought that I was one peep away from getting shot." Further, he told the jury that what he found most chilling about the incident was how angry and disappointed the lead officer seemed when the officers' aggressive actions were not met with equally as aggressive resistance from the three men.

The officers told a different story. The officer's claimed they had previously seen two of the men among the troublemakers dressed in white T-shirts. In addition, the officers stated they had contacted the three men sitting in the car previously and told them to leave the garage. And, they became concerned when the men were still sitting in their car twenty minutes later. Further, the officers testified that the three men were angry, belligerent, and argumentative.

However, two credible independent witnesses contradicted the officers' version of the use of force incident. It is worth mentioning that one of the officers involved in this incident was a patrol sergeant. As this lawsuit demonstrates, line officers are not the only group to be plagued by "Aready Gones." The jury awarded the three men $175,000.00.

Don't Let the Little Things Slide

A fundamental element in preventing the use of excessive force is the effective supervision of your officers. However, as you know, supervising cops is a tough job. They are an independent, ego invested, never wrong, union protected group who do not take criticism well. To make the supervision of cops even more challenging, our traditional disciplinary process is modeled after the American justice system. As you know, the basic premise of our justice system is that the wrongdoing must be followed by a punishment. In our quest to blend punishment and rehabilitation with having the discipline fit the policy violation, we have taken the American justice system and superimposed it onto law enforcement's progressive-disciplinary process.

The following are the problems that occur when using the justice system's philosophy of correction as a management strategy to correct misbehavior and poor officer performance:

DISCIPLINE IS OFTEN NOT CONSISTENTLY APPLIED FOR THE SAME POLICY VIOLATION. If two officers inappropriately use the Taser in separate incidents, the supervisor may issue a written reprimand to the officer who has had performance problems in other areas. The other officer, with an otherwise satisfactory performance record, may not even receive verbal counseling.

When disciplinary action is not administered consistently and fairly, you become viewed as a supervisor who has "pets." As a result, officers will interpret your disciplinary action as being unjust and your criticism invalid. Effective supervisors are trusted by their subordinates. Trust is earned through a demonstration of fairness, honesty, and mutual respect.

Another perception dynamic, officers often confuse being treated equally with being treated fairly. Being treated equally means everyone receives the same bounty regardless of his or her individual contribution or performance. Being treated fairly means each officer receives what he or she deserves. The individual treatment can be positive (advancement or recognition) or negative (corrective discipline).

At the Montana Academy, I supervised a cadre of law enforcement and corrections officers who managed training programs, instructed classes, and supervised student officers.

After an exceptionally challenging training segment, I wanted to demonstrate my appreciation to the staff members whose performance was exceptional during the grueling five-month training marathon. Knowing that cops like law enforcement toys, I gave each deserving officer an expensive tactical folding knife. As cops do, the training staff got together and compared gifts.

An officer who did not receive a meritorious gift came to my office. The officer asked if it was an oversight that he did not receive a knife? "No," I replied. "That's not fair," was his rebuttal. "Its not even treatment, but it is fair treatment," I retorted. I went on to explain that I do not treat people evenly; I strive to treat them fairly. Further, I explained that I had coached him on a number of occasions when he dropped the ball during the past five months. I ended my philosophical admonishment by informing him that when his work performance exceeded my expectations he would be recognized for it.

Within thirty days of our conversation, the officer's performance exceeded my expectations. As a result, I proudly rewarded his exceptional performance with an equally expensive tactical folding knife. To be an effective leader, mentor, and supervisor, you must routinely remind your officers that you will not treat them all equally, but they will all be treated fairly.

OVER TIME, TREATING OFFICERS LIKE TRAFFIC VIOLATORS LOSES ITS ABILITY TO CHANGE BEHAVIOR. Officers get desensitized to it, and bargaining units find ways to minimize its impact. Here are two examples: In a department that polices a hypersensitive community, the administration implemented a policy forbidding an officer from accusing a suspect of lying. It hurts the criminal's self-esteem—my rationalization, not the city council's. Needless to say, this policy had become an ongoing joke among the department's officers.

The department's written reprimands are issued on colored paper. Every time an officer is seen holding a piece of colored paper, the officer gets jazzed at briefing for calling a liar a liar. The absurdity of the policy combined with the frequency of which the written warning are issued made a mockery of the disciplinary process.

Furthermore, bargaining units and police unions have negotiated the sting out of issuing written warnings to officers. Many law enforcement labor contracts have a sunset clause for written reprimands. In my conversations with officers throughout the U.S., officers routinely comment about taking a written warning for a policy violation knowing that in six to twelve months it will be removed from their personnel file. Consequently, the threat of disciplinary censures like "I am going to write you up" have lost their intended ability to improve the officers' misbehavior.

Lastly, and the Most Important, Supervisors Often See the Progressive Disciplinary Process as the Start of an Employment Termination and Not the Beginning of a Benevolent Employee Rehabilitation. Stated more plainly, they see the formal disciplinary process as a mechanism to build a case against an officer. Fearing that if they take corrective action the officer will be marked for termination, supervisors often overlook the little misbehaviors. I can tell you from personal experience in supervising law enforcement officers that if you let the little things slide they will grow into bigger problems. This is especially true in managing the use of force incident.

Now, I am not saying that the use of progressive discipline is inappropriate or invalid. When applied properly, it is the most humane method to fix an officer's performance problem and correct misbehavior. However, the point that I want to stress is that to turn a poor performer into an exceptional officer requires a supervisory paradigm shift; from just getting compliance to creating self-directed outstanding performance.

The first proactive supervisory step in minimizing citizen complaints and excessive force lawsuits is not letting the little misbehaviors go uncorrected. I cannot stress the importance of addressing the smallest missteps or misbehaviors as soon as you become aware of them. By addressing the little infractions, you prevent more dramatic misbehaviors from occurring. As a first-line supervisor, you establish what is acceptable and what is not acceptable by what behaviors you address or ignore.

As an example, you observe an officer intentionally apply more force to the wrist of a handcuffed suspect than is necessary as he walks the prisoner to the car. Why did the officer crank on the suspect's wrist? To punish the suspect for being a drunken idiot and the officer believed he could get away with it. By not addressing the officer's misbehavior you unintentionally do four things, (1) you send a message to the officer that it is acceptable to inflict unjustified pain on a suspect; (2) you send the same message to the other observing officers at the scene; (3) you are ensuring that future arrested suspects will be subjected to similar mistreatment because your officers know they can get away with it; and (4) and most importantly, you are creating an environment where more severe levels of unjustified force are likely to be used on suspects.

When you confront an officer for intentionally applying too much pressure to a handcuffed suspect's wrist, you are preventing that officer from tasering a handcuffed suspect or shooting a restrained suspect with a bean-bag projectile in the future. By addressing the minor use of inappropriate force, you send the message that you will not tolerate the use of force that is clearly excessive.

By taking a proactive approach to addressing the least significant use of force issues, you accomplish four things: You protect the members of your community from the use of unnecessary force. You protect your officers from punitive disciplinary action. You protect your department from excessive force lawsuits and the damaging media attention that results from such litigation. And, you protect yourself from disciplinary action for not preventing your officers' use of excessive force. Many first-line supervisors have discovered the hard way that prevention is the best cure for excessive force complaints.

Coaching and Not Criticizing

A coaching session is an organized conversation between you and the officer regarding the need to correct a behavior and/or improve the officer's performance. Further, an effective coaching session has specific objectives and follows a previously developed outline.

The coaching session should address only one behavioral problem at a time. Addressing multiple behavioral issues in one coaching session diminishes the effectiveness and the corrective impact of the session. The coaching process consists of four distinctive phases

1. Pre-counseling preparation
2. Supervisor and officer conversation
3. Agreement documentation
4. Behavioral monitoring.

Precounseling Preparation

In preparing for a coaching session, you should first identify the officer's misconduct or substandard performance and list the performance deficiency as the title in your coaching outline. In managing the use of force incident, an officer's misconduct or substandard performance falls into one of six categories:

TACTICS. Actions that created an unnecessary risk to the officer/Threat or that facilitated the necessity for the use of force: Ignoring or leaving cover, failure to wait for back-up officers, or the failure to maintain a proper reactionary gap.

VERBALIZATION. An exhibition of bravado, antagonism, inappropriate threats, patronizing comments, rudeness, sarcasm, or the use of profanity.

USE OF FORCE. The use of force that is excessive in relationship to the Threat's behavior or insufficient in relationship to the level of resistance or immediate threat.

EVIDENCE COLLECTION. Failure to photograph or improperly photographing the Threat's or the officer's injuries; failure to collect the officer's soiled or damaged uniform as evidence; failure to photograph and properly collect force option evidence (Taser AFIDs, probes, wires, blast doors; impact projectiles and casings); failure to document an officer's injuries through medical examination; failure to identify and/or interview the witnesses.

PERCEPTION MISMANAGEMENT. Failure to seek out and contact onlookers and potential witnesses and explain the background of the incident and the necessity for the use of force.

INCIDENT DOCUMENTATION. Failure to properly identify the Officer versus Threat Factors and/or Influential Circumstances, failure to stipulate the legal standard, and failure to include the "key elements of a use of force report" in the written report.

Once you have identified the misbehavior, you list in your coaching outline the established standard of conduct and the difference between the officer's conduct and the established standard. The established standard of conduct is stated in the policy that regulates officer behavior. The following are examples of officer performance deficiencies couched in terms of required and actual behavior:

Policy: Officers will treat all citizens with respect and conduct themselves in a professional manner at all times.

Behavior: On August 12th, during the arrest of Samuel Jones, I overheard Officer Michael Brown call Mr. Jones a "dumb ass" as he handcuffed Mr. Jones.

Policy: Officers will not deploy the Taser in probe mode to a handcuffed suspect or inmate.

Behavior: On October 3rd, during the DWI arrest of Brad Webber, Officer Mary Johnston tasered Mr. Webber as he laid handcuffed

face down on the pavement. I received a complaint from Mr.
Webber. The tasering was recorded on Officer Johnston's patrol
car video camera.

Policy: Officers will properly collect and store all evidence of a Taser
deployment in probe mode.

Behavior: On November 5th, Officer Bill Williams improperly collected
Taser evidence by wrapping the Taser leads around the spent
cartridge. Officer Williams had deployed the Taser in probe
mode to Henry Beckner.

Policy: Officers may use objectively reasonable nondeadly force on a
person to effect an arrest, restrain a lawfully detained suspect,
and protect the officer or others from the use of nondeadly
force. When using nondeadly force on a person, the officer will
consider the immediate threat to the officer or others, the severity of the crime the person has committed, and whether the person is resisting arrest or attempting to escape.

Behavior: On December 2nd, I observed Officer Dan Steele knee Martin
Davis in the groin. Mr. Davis was handcuffed and passively
resisting being placed in the patrol car.

Policy: Officers will prepare a complete and accurate use of force
report when nondeadly force is used on a person.

Behavior: Officer Todd Evans failed to state in his use of force report,
Incident Number 010-01335, the Officer versus Threat Factors
and Influential Circumstances that justify the use of the Taser in
Drive Stun mode on Mark Teem.

In each of the above listed behavioral examples, there are no stated supervisory judgements and no generalizations of the officer's actions. The behavioral statement simply provides a clear description of the officer's behavior
in contrast to what the policy required.

In addition, your pre-coaching outline should include, if applicable, a
summary of each previous coaching session related to the performance issue
to be addressed. Each summary should include the date and time of the previous coaching session, the established standard of conduct, the difference
between the established standard and officer's conduct, and what the officer
agreed to do to improve his or her performance.

Now, with the misconduct identified, the difference between the officer's
conduct and the established standard stated, and any previous related performance counseling sessions listed in your coaching outline, you are ready
to conduct your coaching session.

Supervisor and Officer Conversation

The coaching session is referred to as a supervisor and officer conversation because the discussion is an informal behavioral intervention and not part of the punitive disciplinary process. The supervisor and officer conversation has four goals:

- To put the officer on notice that his or her conduct does not meet the department's established performance standards. As I previously explained, when you call attention to the small infractions, you proactively prevent more severe policy violations from occurring. When an officer is aware that you are diligent regarding your supervisory responsibilities, the officer will, as a result, become more professional in the performance of his or her duties.
- To eliminate the behavioral problem without having to implement formal punitive disciplinary action. Most formal discipline, no matter how carefully it is administered, has a negative impact on the officer's commitment to the department. Furthermore, the anger, insecurity, stress, and unhappiness the officer experiences from being formally disciplined are passed on to the officer's family. In your conversation with the officer, you need to bring to light these less obvious consequences.
- To gain the officer's agreement that the behavior was inappropriate and the officer will not commit the offense again. An agreement that the officer will correct the behavior is important in two ways: One, if an officer acknowledges that the behavior was inappropriate and agrees to improve, the officer is more likely to live up to the commitment to change. And two, if the misbehavior is repeated, the agreement can be used as leverage in the subsequent coaching session. The subsequent follow-up coaching session should not only address the reoccurring problem, but also, the officer's failure to honor the previous agreement to change his behavior.
- The proactive prevention of citizens' complaints and excessive force lawsuits. By addressing an officer's minor missteps regarding the management of the use of force incident, you safeguard the officer and your department from litigation. Moreover, if the officer continues to demonstrate unacceptable behavior, you have laid the groundwork for defensible and fair progressive disciplinary action.

When initially conducting the coaching session, start by informing the officer that you have a concern that needs to be addressed. Taking this approach, or one similar, establishes an informal tone to your conversation. Keep in mind, the coaching session is supposed to be an intervention and not an inquisition. Expressing your concern over an officer's performance instead of accusing the officer of wrongdoing is less likely to make the officer defensive. Further, by stating your concern and asking for the officer's help in solving the performance problem, the officer becomes invested in the agreed-upon solution. When officers are involved in solving their performance problems, they are more likely to follow through with the agreed-upon corrective action.

Next, before explaining your concern, comment on the positive aspects of the officer's performance. In reality, most officers spend their shift performing their duties professionally, with little or no mistakes. Identifying the good things that the officer has done sets a positive tone for the conversation and will make the officer more receptive to your corrective criticism. In using this approach, the officer will view the coaching session more as a mentoring activity and less as an informal discipline. By taking this more positive approach to corrective counseling, you will make headway in dispelling the old law enforcement adage: "One ah shit, cancels out one-hundred atta boys."

In addition, you should to go into the coaching session with an open mind. Things sometimes are not always as they appear. Before rushing to make a judgement regarding the officer's conduct or performance, ask the officer for an explanation. There may be facts or mitigating circumstances unknown to you that change the assumed dynamic of the situation. More than once, I have entered into a counseling session with a preconceived impression of the subordinate's performance only to discover the situation was not as I initially believed.

After the performance issue has been addressed and the officer has agreed to correct his or her behavior, the details of the coaching session need to be documented.

Agreement Documentation

After the supervisor and officer conversation has concluded, you need to memorialize the details of the conversation. The agreement documentation should consist of a brief summary of the coaching session. This summary should include:

- The officer's name, date and time of the coaching session, and the location where the session was held.
- The misbehavior or performance problem and, if applicable, the policy violated.
- A factual, nonjudgmental, description of the officer's behavior or performance problem.

- A detailed account of what the officer agreed to do to correct the behavioral problem.

The coaching outline and the agreement documentation should be kept in a supervisory file for use in subsequent coaching sessions, if the officer's behavior or performance does not improve.

Behavioral Monitoring

Once you have coached an officer on a performance deficiency and the officer has expressed a commitment to change, you must monitor the officer to determine, if in fact, the officer's behavior has improved. Furthermore, behavioral monitoring involves more than just determining that the officer has corrected that one performance problem. It involves looking for all the things your officer does right and then reinforces those behaviors through your recognition of the officer's positive performance.

In my instructor development courses, I always ask the instructors candidates this question: "When your supervisor calls you into his or her office, how many of you say to yourself: 'Great! I am going get recognized for all the outstanding things I done this week?'" This question is always good for an eruption of hysterical laughter. After the laughter dies down, I follow-up that question with: "How many of you have this as your first thought: What did my supervisor find out about?" This question is always greeted with nods and grins. The students' reactions are a sad commentary on the way we monitor our officers' performance.

If you want to create a positive change in an officer's performance, you do so by pointing out all the things the officer does right, just not the things the officer does wrong. Even your most performance-challenged officer will do something right. As my grandfather used to say: "Even a broken clock is right twice a day." Keep in mind that the brilliance of an officer's performance is relative to the officer's abilities. If you are not finding positive things to complement on, you have either set the performance bar too high for the officer's abilities or you are ignoring the good things the officer is doing. Either way, it is an injustice to the officer and your department.

Officers who are recognized for their positive contributions to the law enforcement mission become committed to doing the right things. As a result, they actively strive to properly manage their use of force incidents, circumvent citizen complaints, and protect their departments from civil litigation and bad press.

I have used this coaching and behavioral monitoring strategy extensively as a supervisor with excellent results. Through the coaching and behavioral monitoring process, I was able to improve the performance of all my civilian and law enforcement employees. By using a minimum of a ten-to-one ratio of positive performance comments to one corrective coaching session, I was able to turn problem employees around, motivate sub-performers to incrementally improve their performance, inspire average performers to be great, and exceptional performers to accomplish more than they believed was possible.

One additional benefit of using the coaching and behavioral monitoring strategy is that it makes an officer's annual performance evaluation a meaningless formality.

As you are aware, at its best, the annual performance evaluation is ineffective in motivating officers to improve their performance. At its worst, it denigrates officer morale and motivation and makes a mockery of a performance evaluation process. Riddle me this Batman: Does being called into your supervisor's office once a year to be rated on a scale from one to five on vague predetermined performance categories motivate you to be the best that you can be? Of course it doesn't. You endure the evaluation process, and you go back to doing what you have always done.

As I previously stated, at its worst, the annual performance evaluation can have a negative impact on an officer's morale and commitment to the organization. During one of my annual performance evaluations, I received two's on all my performance categories. Five was the lowest rating and one was the highest. Believing that I deserved at least a few ones, but knowing how the government employee evaluation process worked, I asked my supervisor what I needed to do to bring my twos up to ones? "You can't," my supervisor answered. "I can't?" I responded incredulously. "No one gets a one rating. If I give you a one, there is no room for improvement," he explained. This was the most screwed-up logic I had ever heard. Not only was I not motivated to improve my performance, my intelligence was insulted. When I walked out of that performance evaluation session, I told myself that when I became an administrator I would implement a meaningful, ongoing, employee evaluation process. The coaching and behavioral monitoring philosophy was the perfect improvement to an antiquated and dysfunctional government employee evaluation system.

By continually providing my staff members with positive feedback on what they were doing well and addressing and correcting their mistakes as they happened, six things occurred: (1) their overall performance continue to improve; (2) they were more motivated and committed to our mission; (3) they made fewer mistakes; (4) it took the fear and anxiety out of their annual performance evaluation—because they knew on a minute by minute basis how their performance was be perceived and rated; (5) they received outstanding annual performance evaluations, because they had months to correct any performance problem; and (6) it made conducting their organizationally mandated performance evaluation effortless to develop: I had spent the previous twelve months incrementally accomplishing what the annual evaluation was theoretically supposed to improve upon.

If you are still skeptical about the benefits of the coaching and behavioral monitoring strategy, you can read the results for yourself. When I was director of the Montana Law Enforcement Academy, I asked my staff to rate my supervisory performance. The following is the actual employees' response:

> "Pursuant to your request, each of the full-time employees at the Montana Law Enforcement Academy were asked what they thought of you as a supervisor and a leader. The following, in no particular order are their responses:
>
> The staff believes you to be open, honest and a direct leader. They find you to be open-minded and fair. They feel as if they can talk to you anytime about anything and you will listen and not judge. They find that you are honest about your feelings and in your dealings with them. They respect the fact that you are direct about what you want them to do but find that you are not degrading or demeaning. You never ask them to do something that you are not willing to do yourself.
>
> They believe that you allow everyone to express their opinions and ideas either individually or in staff meetings and that those opinions and ideas are not summarily discounted or ignored because of their job title or position at the academy. Most often you allow them to act on those ideas, and on the occasions when they are not allowed to act, you give them a reason for your decision. They find that you have confidence in their skills and trust that they know their job tasks and duties better than you do. They indicated that they go to you for help and advice about ways to better their performance or seek ways to enhance their productivity. They feel that you take great effort to understand what each of them does and you try to make their job easier or more productive by providing the tools and equipment necessary.
>
> They indicated that they don't feel smaller or less important to you than any other staff member. They think, that no matter who they are or what job they do, they are part of the "staff." Some have experienced pervious leadership that divided the staff into sections that made them feel as though they were not part of the "A Team." Since you have become the Academy Director, that is not the case and they are grateful for your treatment of them. They feel that there is only one team and that everyone is included. They indicated that there was a growing and learn-

ing period of time, where both the staff and you were assessing each other. But that the team is complete and you are their leader, without exception.

They believe that you have created an environment at the academy that allows them to perform their duties to the fullest of their abilities. They said that other people are envious of this work environment and the leadership you provide. They feel that they are encouraged to think outside the box. They feel that they are capable of more than they have been allowed to do in previous positions or under previous leadership and that you do not hold them back from excelling. They want to do more, work harder and longer, and in some cases sacrifice in other areas of their lives to ensure that they do not disappoint you. They believe that you lead by example and that you expect a great deal of yourself, so they emulate that by expecting more from themselves and each other. You lead them, not manage them. They believe that you manage resources not people.

They have seen you be generous with praise for deeds and jobs well done. For those that have been counseled by you for mistakes made or jobs not completed, they said you were fair and listened to their explanations of any problems they had doing the job or the reasons for the mistakes made. But, what was most important to them was that once counseled about a problem, you did not hold that against them. In the past they had experienced from other managers that mistakes haunted them for years, but they had no fear of that happening with you.

They believe that you are dedicated to your job, the staff, and the students. They believe that you see the students as the most important reason for our existence. They see that you have a progressive and far-sighted perception and grasp of the future of law enforcement. They believe that you have successfully provided cutting-edge, scenario-based training, to several hundred criminal justice professionals, and will continue to improve the training until it is the best in the nation.

They believe that you encourage the students to be the best they can be, both professionally and personally, to survive in a dangerous profession, and to lead others into the future. They have seen you counsel students individually and as a group and believe that you treat them with respect, encouraging them to excel personally and professionally. They have seen you discipline students to the point of expelling them from the Academy. This has, on occasion, resulted in the officer losing his/her job. They have seen you agonize over that decision and take into consideration that impact the decision has on the student, their agency, and most importantly their family. This shows them that you are compassionate and caring but firm. They feel that if you treat students in this manner that they expect and have seen you treat them in the same way."

It is important to note that each academy staff member personally signed this evaluation.

As a supervisor, this staff evaluation was the most meaningful accolade I have ever received and will ever receive. It validated my personal beliefs about leadership and the benefits of coaching.

Coaching your officers has a direct, positive, impact on the way they perform their duties. This positive outcome is not an accidental, trickle-down result. It is a holistic approach to providing better police service. Here is an example of how the effects of coaching and mentoring your officers positively impact the people they serve. The following is a letter from the students of a basic law enforcement class to Montana's Attorney General. The letter is self-explanatory. However, there is one common theme: The way the officers were treated by their academy supervisors directly influenced the way they viewed their performance as cops:

"With all due respect and consideration, the students, as a group, elected to express our thoughts regarding the training offered at the Montana Law Enforcement Academy. We hope that this letter adequately expresses our appreciation for the manner in which all academy staff members have continued to encourage and support our progress through a training program that we have found to be not only realistic and engaging but also professional and progressive.

It is fair to say that the majority of our class has found our relationship with the academy staff to be both mutually respectful and symbiotic in nature. With the support and encouragement of our training officers, we have continued to strive both individually and as a class towards a higher degree of professional development and personal growth. We feel strongly that our progress and success at the academy is highly reflective of the leadership and the challenges the Academy Training Staff have presented to us since day one.

We have been told on numerous occasions to "look in the mirror" if we are looking for someone to thank for our success. However, we realize that the vision presented in the mirror would not be possible without our instructors, who have inspired, encouraged, and challenged us to become better at what we did not know or what we thought we already knew.

We have found the training staff to be both dynamic and approachable. Disciplinary issues have been handled discretely and appropriate-ly. We also feel that our successes at the academy are, while intrinsically motivated, largely reflective of the support and encouragement of our professional mentors and leaders.

As identified in the academy basic manual, the seventh characteristic of an effective leader is "that a true leader has the confidence to stand alone, the courage to make touch decisions, and the compassion to listen to the needs of others. He does not set out to be a leader, but becomes one by the quality of his actions and the integrity of his intent. Leadership is not a title—it is a state of being" (Law Enforcement Basic Student Manual). Due to this fact, it is impossible to please everyone.

We know the training staff to call things as they see it without concern for repercussion. Such characteristics and qualities are strengths as identified in the academy student manual, and have no doubt added to the success of the Montana Law Enforcement Academy and our basic class. We feel that the success of a staff and a school is directly correlated with the leader's ability to pass on the characteristics above. And, as a class, we have observed those characteristics in our training officers and our student peers alike.

The changes at the Montana Law Enforcement Academy reflect those characteristics above, and have given the students a feeling of pride and dignity in being here. For many of us, we arrived at the Academy with a strong sense of apprehension regarding the manner in which we would be treated and trained. It is fair to say that many of us were prepared to find our days at the Academy to be the worst days of our law enforcement careers. Many of us have heard veteran officers describe the Academy as "all books," "a joke," "boot camp," "a waste of time," "fear based," or an experience that is best to be forgotten. We were, however, aware that over the past two years administrative and instructional changes have taken place at the Academy to make it a competitive, progressive, and professional atmosphere for law enforcement training and instruction.

We have found these changes to be true and thank wholeheartedly those responsible for implementing them. I assure you that it is a complete surprise to many of our departments when we return on the weekends to say that we are having a great time and learning a great deal in the progress."

The members of the basic law enforcement class personally signed the letter.

I believe it is important for you to know that the Academy Staff who were responsible for the glowing reviews stated in that letter, two years previously under different leadership, made the students perform push-ups for honest mistakes. And, even more humiliating, made the students wear a cardboard cutout of a gun around their necks that had "Barney" written on it for other academy infractions. The Academy Staff treated the students in the same disrespectful manner as their supervisor treated them. Mentoring can have a positive or negative effect–it depends on the mentor's understanding of leadership.

Mentoring Makes the Difference

Mentoring officers in properly managing the use of force incident occurs at the scene, in coaching sessions, and in the form of group discussions. The latter is the most efficient and least often-used method for mentoring officers in the proper use of force. Further, an after the incident debriefing is the most effective method for mentoring officers in properly managing the use of force incident.

The belief that a one-hour use of force update given during annual inservice training is sufficient to minimize officer and department liability is misguided at best. Training in the proper use of force needs to be ongoing and continually reinforced to be effective. The first-line supervisor is in the perfect position to make this happen. The frequency in which use of force incidents occur creates a fertile environment for conducting continuous use of force training in the form of a facilitated incident debriefing by the first-line supervisor.

The facilitated debrief is one of the most effective methods for conducting continuous use of force training for the following reasons:

- Because the debrief is conducted at the squad or team level, the supervisor has direct control over the timing of the debrief; a debrief conducted while the incident is still fresh in the officer's minds is more effective. Further, the supervisor determines which use of force incident is debriefed; consequently, the supervisor can select incidents that offer the most powerful learning lessons. Additionally, the use of force incident is reviewed, discussed, and evaluated by the members of the team, making the team members active participants in the learning process.
- Because the officers were active players in the use of force incident, they bring a personal investment to the discussion of what was done right and/or wrong in the use of force incident. Additionally, a team debrief provides the officers with an opportunity to share their individual perspectives on the use of force incident. As a result, the team functions as a Peer Jury to evaluate each officer's actions and the use of force incident as a whole.

- Through the supervisor's Socratic facilitation, the officers are guided to the proper conclusions. Conclusions that are congruent with the department's standards and philosophies regarding the use of force.
- Moreover, the diversity of perspectives and experiences that the officers bring to the discussion of the incident makes the post-use of force debriefing one of the most effective methods of use of force training.

The incident debriefing is a formalized training session that is specific to your particular team. Unlike a classroom lecture, the conversational structure of the debriefing allows all the team members to explain their roles in the use of force incident and explore how that role positively or negatively impacted the other officer's actions and the overall dynamics of the situation.

Further, the debriefing is not a formal corrective counseling session. Although, mistakes and solutions are identified as the incident is discussed, the main purpose of the debriefing is to make the officers self-aware of what was done well and what improvements need to be made to their future performances. Moreover, the debriefing is designed to provide a collective evaluation of the officer(s) actions through a peer and supervisory review of the incident.

The team debriefing has six goals:

1. To provide continuous use of force training to the members of your team.
2. To provide a timely peer and supervisory review of the use of force incident for the team's members continuous improvement in managing of their use of force incidents.
3. To reinforce the team members' proper use of force decisions and their proper management of the use of force incident.
4. To provide collective solutions to the improper use of force and the tactical mistakes that are identified during the incident debriefing.
5. To conduct a peer review of the evidence collected and the individual officers' use of force reports.
6. To minimize officer and department liability through team self-evaluation and self-improvement.

Guidelines for Conducting the Use of Force Incident Debrief

Conducting a team debriefing of a use of force incident is very similar to performing a coaching session with an individual officer. To prepare for the debriefing, the officers' reports should be reviewed and a debriefing outline developed. The outline should contain two lists: one list of the officers' proper actions and a list of the issues or problems you need to address.

After you have conducted a few use of force incident debriefings, you will develop a sense for what you additionally need to add to your outline to compliment your personal facilitation style. Additionally, you want to make a copy of each officer's use of force report for each team member and have the reports available at the debriefing.

The last step in preparing for the debriefing session is to review the following guidelines for facilitating the debriefing:

HAVE ALL YOUR DUCKS IN A ROW. Have your supporting material organized and accessible. The debriefing is a training session in properly managing the use of force incident. Subsequently, you are there to explain and reinforce your department's use of force and tactical standards, not dictate them. The strategy is to facilitate discussion and lead your officers to the proper conclusions with informative examples and persuasive arguments. Referring to your department's policies and training manuals when explaining your position on the issues gives authority and credibility to your critique.

DISCUSS THE RIGHT THINGS FIRST. This is the Golden Rule of coaching, counseling, facilitating, and teaching. Whenever an officer's performance is evaluated and critiqued during a review session, the officer goes into the session expecting a negative experience. When a cop experiences a full-blown negative evaluation of his performance, the officer bows his neck, crosses his arms, and internalizes the lyrics of a popular country western song: "I am not wrong. I am not sorry. And, it's probably going to do it again." By first identifying all the things the officer did right during the incident, you soften the officer's resistance to corrective criticism. By using this positive approach, the officers leave the debriefing acknowledging that some mistakes were made, but overall their performance went pretty well.

DO NOT PLACE BLAME. As the facilitator of the coaching session, it is your responsibility to create an environment that promotes personal accountability—not personal condemnation. An officer's personal opinions regarding the use of force and specific tactics rise to the level of a religious conversion. Consequently, attacking the officer's tactical belief system will only make the officer defensive. When an officer's defensive shields energize, the officer shuts down and tunes out. At that point, you lost the teachable moment.

IDENTIFY PROBLEMS AND SEEK SOLUTIONS. This guideline dovetails with the previous one. As the facilitator, you want to characterize officer mistakes as problems to be solved. This approach helps to depersonalize the misbehavior or mistake. For example, when addressing a mistake an officer made when he photographed a suspect's facial injury before he received medical treatment, you want to portray the mistake as a general problem to be solved: "Do you guys see a potential liability problem with the suspect's photos?" "How can we prevent dramatic photos like this?"

FRAME THE INCIDENT FOR THE OFFICERS. Providing a short summary of the incident establishes a launching platform for the subsequent discussion. The summary should include the type of call, the location of the incident, the civilians involved, the officers at the scene, and the types of force used. Framing the incident is especially important when there are members of your team present at the debriefing who were not at the scene of the use of force incident.

HAVE EACH OFFICER EXPLAIN HIS OR HER INVOLVEMENT IN CHRONOLOGICAL ORDER. Using this strategy has several benefits. First, it establishes an order for officer participation. Officers are often reluctant to participate in the evaluation of another officer's performance. This reluctance comes, in part, from knowing that the evaluation of their performance is forthcoming. Second, it allows you (as the facilitator) to focus the discussion on that specific officer's actions and force justification. Third, by having the officers explain their involvement in the sequence in which they happened, it allows the team to discuss the incident as an interconnected sequence of events. Lastly, it provides you with greater control over the pace of the debriefing.

EACH OFFICER JUSTIFIES HIS OR HER USE OF FORCE. As the facilitator, you lead the officer through his or her use of force justification in chronological order by asking a series of questions: What background information did you have regarding the incident or Threat? What was the source of that information? What did you do prior to engaging the Threat? What level of force did you initially use? Why was that force ineffective? What "Officer versus Threat Factors" and "Influential Circumstances" justified the escalation of your force? What other factors influenced your use of force decision? In retrospect, would you do anything different?

QUESTION EVERY ELEMENT OF THE OFFICER'S JUSTIFICATION WITH: "WHY IS THAT IMPORTANT?" Officers often intuitively know that their force was appropriate; however, they have a difficult time explaining their decision-making process. By asking the officer "why" the stated factor or circumstance influenced his or her use of force decision, you guide the officer to a deeper understanding of that justification. Further, by asking the officer to explain the importance of that specific factor or circumstance, you invite comment from the other team members.

DO NOT ACCEPT GENERAL TERMS, NONDESCRIPT CONCEPTS, AND UNSUBSTANTIATED STATISTICS. Officers often try to justify their use of force in general terms or with statistics they heard from an instructor. General terms like "resisted," "threatened," and "violent" generally define the Threat's behavior, but they do not specifically describe the Threat's actions. Nondescript concepts like "officer safety" or "objectively reasonable" are states of being and not definitive actions that justify the use of force. Moreover, statements involving statistical information such as "70 percent of concealed weapons are hidden in the waistband" hurt an officer's credibility in his deposition or trial testimony when the officer cannot provide the specific source of that statistic. However, if an officer can provide the specific source, the use of a statistical fact can be an effective contribution to an officer's use of force justification.

USE A PEER JURY TO EVALUATE THE OFFICER'S ACTIONS. There are a number of benefits to using a Peer Jury to evaluate an officer's performance. Using a Peer Jury depersonalizes the critique. You, as the facilitator, do not find fault in the officer's action; it is the opinion of the team that the officer made a mistake. A Peer Jury creates an active learning environment. As a result, the team plays an active role in the identification of problems and the development of potential solutions. Members of the Peer Jury vicariously learn from their evaluation of what the officer did right and wrong. And, when you offer your assessment of the officer's performance, the Peer Jury's support of your evaluation gives credibility to your critique.

I learned the importance of this last benefit while conducting scenario-based use of force training with a group of senior officers. An officer—with over twenty years of experience—shot the suspect with a handgun loaded with marking ammunition. When the officer fired the round, the officer realized he had made a bad decision and immediately holstered his weapon. I asked the officer to justify his use of deadly force. The officer looked me in the eye and said, "I didn't use deadly force." He said it with such conviction I started to doubt myself. I had facilitated more than fifty scenarios that afternoon. On this scenario did my mind wander? To make sure I hadn't made a mistake, I pushed the issue, but the officer steadfastly insisted he did not use deadly force.

Finally, I turned to the Peer Jury and asked if the officer used deadly force? Unanimously, the Peer Jury reported that the officer had used deadly force and that it was unjustified. Initially, the officer argued that he did not pull his weapon, but the pressure exerted by the Peer Jury was too much for him to resist. Begrudgingly, the officer admitted he had inappropriately used deadly force.

WHEN FACILITATING THE DEBRIEFING, YOU ARE RESPONSIBLE FOR GUIDING THE OFFICERS TO THE PROPER CONCLUSIONS. Just because the group comes to a consensus, it does not mean their assessment is correct. If the Peer Jury draws the wrong conclusion, it is your responsibility to subtly point out the flaws in their logic. Playing the devil's advocate from a civilian jury's perspective best accomplishes this. By reminding the team that jurors determine the reasonableness of an officer's actions and that the department's ultimate goal is to prevent and win lawsuits, you will guide them to the proper conclusions. Further, not correcting an ill-conceived Group Think solution can lead to liability problems in future incidents. This occurred after a post-use of force debriefing involving the use of pepper spray on a group of environmental protesters.

The protesters had chained themselves together with metal pipe sleeves over their hands and wrists. The metal sleeves prevented the officers from cutting the chains. To encourage the protesters to unchain themselves, the officers pepper sprayed the protesters' faces. The use of the pepper spray was successful in forcing the protesters to unchain themselves; however, the pepper spray contaminated the carpet and furniture and infiltrated the building's ventilation system.

In the team's post-use of force debriefing, one team member recommended that in the future they swabbed the protesters' eyes with pepper spray to prevent the contamination of the office and the building's ventilation system. This recommendation was met with unanimous agreement. Although, the team's supervisor was aware that the department's policy only allowed the spraying of a suspect's face with pepper spray, he did not veto the team's agreed-upon solution.

A few months later, the protesters again chained themselves together in a government office to protest the logging of an old growth forest. However, this time the officers applied pepper spray to cotton swabs, pried the protesters' eyelids open, and rubbed pepper spray into their eyes. This application of pepper spray did not contaminate the office or the building ventilation system. However, it was the catalyst for a FBI criminal investigation into the officers' use of force and an expensive civil rights lawsuit, which they lost.

Investigating an Excessive Force Complaint

Another important role the supervisor plays in properly managing the use of force incident is investigating citizen complaints regarding an officer's use of excessive force. This is an important obligation that a law enforcement agency has to its community. If your department does not have an Internal Affairs Division, the responsibility for investigating citizen complaints is normally delegated to the first-line supervisor.

The proper investigation into a citizen's complaint against an officer is a key factor in maintaining the public's trust. In every community, there are those who will question the validity of the investigation. It is for these reasons that the IA investigation must be conducted methodically and its results well documented. The following guidelines will assist you with this very important task.

The first step in resolving a citizen's complaint against an officer is to determine what has upset the citizen. Although you need to take all citizen complaints seriously, not all complaints are equal in their severity. Obviously, if the complaint is one of excessive force, the complaint requires a full investigation. However, not all complaints rise to that level. In fact, the majority of citizen complaints can be handled during the initial conversation with the citizen.

An officer's rudeness is the most often reported citizen's complaint. The problem with this type of complaint is that interpreting someone's behavior as rude is completely subjective. Therefore, rudeness complaints are very difficult to substantiate. Fortunately, most citizens who complain about an officer's rudeness are satisfied with an apology and a commitment from you that the officer will be counseled for the rude behavior. As I admonished previously in this chapter, never underestimate the power of an apology.

If the complaint involves more than rude behavior, it is necessary to conduct a preliminary investigation. The purpose of this investigation is to determine the nature of the complaint, the circumstances of the incident, the identity of the officer(s), and the names of any known witnesses. Although the initial complaint can be taken over the telephone, the interview of the complainant should occur at your department. Conducting the interview in a formal police setting has several advantages. First, it gives the complainant the impression that your department is taking the complaint seriously. Creating this impression is very important in the prevention of a lawsuit. Further, in a face-to-face interview, you can evaluate the complainant's credibility. Observing the complainant's body language, mental state, and emotional reactions will help you evaluate the veracity of the complainant's story. Another advantage is the ability to audio and/or video record the interview. When conducting an internal affairs investigation, the tape recording of all statements is highly recommended.

Photograph the complainant's injuries that are contributed to the alleged use of excessive force, and attempt to determine the cause of those injuries. If the complainant has no observable injuries, photograph the complainant for future identification purposes. Also, obtain a medical release from the complainant for the acquisition of the medical records that are related to the injuries allegedly inflicted by the officer(s). In addition to obtaining the complainant's medical records, interview hospital personnel for their observations regarding the injured complainant.

With the preliminary information obtained from the complainant, personally notify the accused officers of the complaint and photograph each officer for positive identification by the complainant and the witnesses. In addition, the photographs aid in eliminating the officers who were at the scene, but not involved in the alleged use of excessive force. During this phase of the investigation, the officers are not interviewed.

The next phase is the collection of the related evidence—use of force reports, photographs of the officer's or suspect's injuries, physical evidence, communication tapes, patrol car or jail video recordings, and computer-aided-dispatch printouts. The collection of video recordings, communication tapes, and dispatch information should occur shortly after the complaint is filed. This evidence is often stored for only a limited amount of time.

After the physical evidence is collected, interview all known civilian witnesses. All witness interviews should be audio and/or video recorded. During the interviews, show the witnesses each officer's photograph individually to positively identify the officer and to clarify his or her involvement in the incident.

With an understanding of the incident from the complainant's and the witnesses' perspective, interview the officer(s). As with the civilian witnesses, the officers' interviews should be audio/video recorded. If your department's policy allows, give the officer the Garrity Warning before conducting the interview. If you believe the investigation could result in a criminal prosecution and the Garrity Warning was not given, advise the officer of his Miranda Rights before conducting the interview.

The investigation is finalized with the development of your written investigative report. Your report should be written objectively. However, you may be required to state your conclusions regarding policy violations. If you believe a violation did occur, your report should state the policy violated accompanied by an explanation of the officer's actions that constitute the violation.

In this chapter, I explained the various roles the first-line supervisor plays in properly managing the use of force incident—diplomat, disciplinarian, mentor, instructor, and internal affairs investigator. No other management position plays a more prominent or influential role in the prevention of excessive force litigation. Leadership is not a title, it is a state of being. And, effective criminal justice leaders mentor their officers.

Chapter 10

MANAGING THE USE OF FORCE
INCIDENT FOR MID-LEVEL MANAGERS

Managers do things right; leaders do the right things.
–Warren Bennis, *Leaders: Strategies for Taking Charge*

So, here you are, sitting in your comfortable corner office. The top of your desk well organized and tidy. Your college diplomas, FBI National Academy diploma, and various certificates from supervisory and leadership courses are framed and placed strategically on the wall behind your desk. Impressive! You survived years of patrol. Effectively led the troops under your charge as a first-line supervisor. And, now, you have moved up the organizational ladder to middle management. You have earned it. Congratulations! So, what do you do all day long?

I am not saying you don't have responsibilities. I am just asking: What do you do all day long as a mid-level manager? I know your schedule. You get to the office between 7:30 and 8:00. You get a cup of coffee and wander through the hall, stopping to chat in different offices, like a scene from the movie Office Space. Eventually, you get to your office and check your email and voicemail.

At 9:30, you attend a meeting with the department's other mid-managers–law enforcement and civilian. At the meeting, you and the other managers sit around the conference table with your Franklin planners positioned squarely in front of you. One at a time, each manager informs the group about his or her weekly schedule, provides an update on their division or program, and complains about a personnel problem or two. After every manager has given an update, everyone checks their calendars and a date and time is set for the next meeting. Then, the meeting ends, and absolutely nothing meaningful was accomplished. It is a meeting held because that is what managers do. They hold pontificating meetings. I know; I have been there. And it

270

drove me nuts.

If you are reading this book, you are probably responsible for an operational or training division. As an operational commander, you manage a precinct or shift. As a training lieutenant, captain, or bureau chief, you manage the department's training division, an academy, or a specific training program. You may even oversee all the training activities within your department. Therefore, I am not going to ask what you do all day long. We have established that. But, I am going to ask two very important questions: What are you doing to ensure your officers are properly managing their use of force incidents? And what are you doing to minimize your department's liability? The reason why I ask is simple—if you are focused on those two issues, everything else falls into place.

If you are not focused on proactively managing use of force incidents and minimizing your department's liability, you are the captain of your own personal Titanic just waiting for the iceberg to hit. Here is an example, but it (just as well) could be a prediction.

On a dark evening, officers responded to a report of an armed and suicidal man at an apartment complex. The young man was distraught over the death of his brother, which had occurred that morning. He was at his girlfriend's apartment when he had the emotional breakdown; his girlfriend's aunt called the police to get him help.

As the tactical unit was deploying, a trained hostage negotiator spoke with the young man via the telephone. As the negotiator talked with him, the young man emphatically stated that he was not going to hurt himself or anyone else. Eventually, the negotiator was able to convince the young man to exit the apartment.

The young man came out of the apartment with his hands locked behind his head. He faced away from the officers and slowly walked back toward them. An officer ordered the young man to put his hands up, but he did not comply. As a result, the officer fired two beanbag projectiles into his back to gain his compliance. The hits from the less-lethal rounds caused the young man to run toward a parked car. As he ran toward the car, the officer fired four more less-lethal rounds, striking the young man in the back. In reaction to being hit with the less-lethal projectiles, the young man reached toward the small of his back, where the projectiles had hit. An officer providing lethal cover with an assault rifle saw the young man reach for his rear waistband. Believing the young man was reaching for a gun, the officer fired one round into his back, killing him.

The incident was reviewed by a Grand Jury. After hearing testimony from thirty witnesses, the Grand Jury declined to indict the officer. However, the grand jurors sent the District Attorney a seathing, three-page letter criticizing the police department's handling of the situation. "We feel that his death resulted from the flawed police policies, incomplete or inappropriate training, incomplete communication and other issues with the police effort," the grand jurors blasted. "We feel strongly that something must be done to correct this, and the police department should be held responsible for this tragedy."

Much to the dismay of the chief of police, this letter was released to the newspaper. This spurred hundreds of protesters to march on city hall and the mayor's office, brought Reverend Jessie Jackson to the city to protest the incident, and caused the police commissioner to call for a federal review of the shooting.

At the recommendation of the police department's review board, the officer who killed the young man was fired. The officer who shot the young man with the less-lethal rounds and the on-scene supervisor received two-week suspensions without pay. The subordinate supervisor at the scene received a one-week suspension without pay. The on-scene lieutenant and captain received written reprimands.

The incident illustrates what happens when you, as the manager of the operational or training division, do not take a proactive approach to managing the use of force incident. Just as officers and first-line supervisors are responsible for their actions during the use of force incident, you are responsible for ensuring they perform their duties properly. Accordingly, you are held accountable when they don't. Power and authority comes with a price.

I hate to be the bearer of bad news, but you can't effectively monitor what is happening in training, with your supervisors, and at ground level with your officers by sitting in your office or attending bureaucratic meetings. By sitting in your corner office, going to meetings, and working from 7:30 to 4:30, Monday through Friday, the only way you are going to proactively identify potential liability problems, poorly conducted training, or superior staff performance is if it happens in your office or during your management meeting. The likelihood of that happening is less probable than you winning the Mega Bucks Lottery. Now, I not picking on you. I am just pointing out what should be obvious.

All organizations have their own cultures. Within those cultures exist subcultures. One subculture within a criminal justice agency is the management subculture. Cultivated within the management subculture is a belief that a manager's worth comes from the position or title that the manager holds. Although authority and power comes with a management position, what a manager does with that power and authority determines the manager's value to the organization. I don't understand why the transformation occurs, but as soon as an effective first-line supervisor is promoted into a middle management position and beyond, the person loses sight of the organization's criminal justice mission and transforms into a process-driven bureaucratic. I know this well; I fought this subculture for fifteen years at two different state criminal justice academies.

Maybe I am a victim of adult ADHD, or maybe I am just allergic to bureaucracies. For whatever the reason, I could not just sit in my office and look busy and go to meetings. It is a closely guarded bureaucratic secret, don't tell anyone, but that is what bureaucrats do–not much. At the Oregon Academy, my assistant directors would have preferred that I just sit in my office, be available for their beckon call, and be perfectly satisfied with mediocrity. But, I could not do that. I did not leave active police service to become just another state drone. I accepted a position at the academy because I believed in Director Dick Roberts' progressive vision for the academy, and I wanted to help make that vision become a reality. Unfortunately, Director Robert was more visionary than politician; consequently, he was replaced with a consummate bureaucrat.

I had the same frustration at the Montana Academy. There I learned that the further you ascend up the managerial ladder the less you are supposed to do. In fact, as a high level manager, (notice I did not use the term leader) you are only expected to leave your office to go to meetings, and then return. As a high level manager, you are encouraged to assume the appearance of a cement yard gnome that has been transplanted behind your desk–dull, expressionless, and immobile.

If you read Chapter 9, you know that was not my management style. Needless to say, my very high-level bureaucrat boss would become very annoyed when he could not reach me via the telephone in my office. He would drive from his headquarters–in the marble palace–out to the academy to track me down to tell me that he had called my office, but I wasn't there. Then, my boss would ask me, "Why aren't you in your office?" I would try to explain to him that I was "managing the academy by wandering around." In an attempt to turn our conversation into a teachable leadership moment, I would explain to him that I could not identify problems or find the staff or students doing good things if I was sequestered in my office. It was like trying to explain the Internet to an ant.

I am not trying to be mean spirited or portray my bosses as dolts. They were smart professional bureaucrats. But, they thought like bureaucrats; they talked liked bureaucrats; they acted like bureaucrats, and at their worst, they were part bureaucrat and part politician. And, consequently, they really accomplished nothing noteworthy, other than maintain the status quo of their bureaucratic world.

The fear of being held accountable is the reason why most mid-managers maintain the status quo when they assume responsibility for an existing division or program. "If its not broke, don't fix it" is the mantra of the timid mid-manager. Said another way, if the way the program currently operates didn't get the last mid-manager in trouble, for God's sake don't change it. Some may even call this unproductive attitude intentional apathy. There are two flaws with this "play it safe" management attitude. Flaw Number One: When you operate in the realm of "it's good enough," at some point the planets will align, gravity will shift, and "good enough" doesn't get the job done anymore. Flaw Number Two: Brilliance, excellence, and innovation does not occur in an apathetic environment. *The status quo is the enemy of excellence and innovation.*

So, the question for you is this: As a mid-level manager what do you want to be? A comfortable bureaucrat, or a dynamic leader who makes a positive difference in your organization. If you chose the comfortable bureaucrat option, close the book—you're late for a meeting. But, if you want to make a meaningful contribution to your department read on.

Role of the Mid-Manager

Mid-level managers are responsible for everything that happens within their assigned domain. Whether it is a division, precinct, program, shift, or training academy—if you manage it, you are held accountable for what happens within it.

In an incident involving an allegation of a department cover-up, the blame for the lack of administrative oversight was placed firmly at the feet of the department's mid-managers. The incident began when a corporal's use of excessive force was recorded on a patrol car's dash camera. When the victim asked the department to investigate the incident and made reference to the patrol car video, the officers replied: "What video?" Then, fourteen months later a DVD copy of the video mysteriously appeared on a city councilman's doorstep. As a result, the corporal was fired for misconduct violations.

During a news reporter's interview of the department's chief of police, the reporter asked how was it possible that a videotape containing evidence of excessive force could disappear for fourteen months? "I don't know. All I know is it surfaced fourteen months later. It got mixed up with some other internal affairs investigations," the chief explained. When the reporter asked the chief if he was responsible for the oversight of the internal affairs' investigative process, he answered: "That's what you've got staff for. That's why you've got lieutenants, captains, and majors." Sounds like someone is going to fall on his or her sword, and its not the chief of police.

Proactively managing department and officer liability is an innovative concept. As I have explained in previous chapters the traditional approach to liability management is reactive. Historically, criminal justice agencies have stubbornly adhered to a defensive liability management game plan. The administrators wait for a lawsuit to be filed, settle it out of court if there are problems, if no problems exist—attempt to muster a defense, and then do nothing to proactively prevent another lawsuit. This is law enforcement's version of closing the barn door after the horse has escaped, except with a dysfunctional twist: We never repair the lock on the door and then continue to wonder why the horse gets out?

The role of the mid-manager in managing the use of force incident is really quite simple in concept, but more challenging in practice. Whether your area of responsibility is operational or training, the roles are the same. In purely management speak, your role is to determine *what needs to be done and then make sure that it gets done properly.* It sounds easy enough. But, it's not. If it were easy to do, criminal justice agencies would not be paying out millions of dollars in lawsuits. Here are examples of the financial tsunami: Over the last decade, the New York City Police Department has paid out nearly one billion dollars in lawsuits. The Chicago Police Department has averaged $39,000,000.00 per year over the past six years. The Los Angeles Police Department has averaged $21,400,000.00 per year in the past seven years. The Philadelphia Police Department has averaged $9,000,000.00 per year over the past four years.

Determining What Needs to be Done

In this book, I have given you the foundation for what needs to be done to proactively manage your department's liability. Now, you have to do your part. First, you need to convince your boss that the department's mindset regarding liability management and use of force training needs to change from a reactive strategy to a proactive one. Additionally, the boss must approve your plan for implementation of this new strategy. Of course there will be the seemingly endless management meetings before a decision is made. Unless, your boss is a true leader (and not a hand-wringing bureaucrat); then, a decision will be made fairly quickly. Regardless of your administrator's leadership abilities, your boss will want you to consult with your risk management division, if you have one. If you don't, the boss will want you to get your city or county attorney to sign off on the proposed strategic change. You can pitch this new proactive strategy in a couple of ways: You can spend a lot of time preparing a position paper and a PowerPoint presentation. You can give them this book to review. Or, you can do both.

After receiving the blessing from all the truly powerful people, you will experience one of two feelings: excitement—created by the opportunity to bring innovative and meaningful change to your organization or a queasy feeling in the pit of your stomach from the anxiety of trying something new. I hope you experience the first feeling. Now that you have the green light to move ahead, your first challenge will be to change the department's organizational culture regarding the proper management of the use of force incident–and that starts with briefing and training your supervisors. You could start the process by briefing your use of force instructors and revising the training curriculum, but in doing so you may be putting the cart before the horse. This happened when LAPD changed their defensive tactics-training program in the mid-1990s.

I gave a presentation at the American Society of Law Enforcement Trainers' Use of Force Training Conference in Los Angeles in 1997. While at the conference, I attended a training session conducted by the LAPD sergeant in charge of their defensive tactics/use of force training. After the Rodney King incident, LAPD completely revised their defensive tactics-training program. The training session I attended provided an overview of their new defensive tactics program. The sergeant told us that LAPD had just finished training 8,000 officers in their new forty-hour program. During the question and answer session, one of my classmates asked if the new program was being currently taught at the LAPD Police Academy? The sergeant replied that it was not and that the academy was still teaching the old program.

After the session was over, I approached the sergeant to clarify a few points about their program. I asked the sergeant if LAPD had encountered any problems with the field-training officers being trained in the new defensive tactics program and the academy graduates being trained in the outdated defensive tactics program? The sergeant stated they had encountered some field training challenges with the way that they implemented the new program. Further, the sergeant admitted that the problems could have been avoided had the operational and training divisions taught the same defensive tactics program. In their rush to implement the new program, they had put the cart before the horse, so to speak.

By briefing and training your first-line supervisors prior to changing the curriculum and providing training to your officers, you create the supervisory buy-in and support you need to ensure the officers will follow the new protocols. Additionally, as explained in Chapter 9, the first-line supervisor is essential to providing continuous use of force training to your officers through post-use of force debriefings.

After getting your supervisors on-line with the new liability management program, you then brief your department instructors and field-training officers of the changes to the department's liability management protocols. At the very least, the briefing should include the new guidelines for managing the use of force incident. From these guidelines, your use of force instructors can develop new performance objectives, lesson plans, evaluation lab sheets, and presentation materials.

With the supervisory and training personnel on-board, your use of force policies should be reviewed (and updated where necessary) to make sure they support and reinforce the new requirements for properly managing the use of force incident. Accordingly, new policies may need to be written to provide your supervisors with the authority to enforce the protocols of the new program that are not addressed under existing policies.

Finally, with all the administrative and instructional changes in place, the officers are trained in the newly adopted liability management program. To help you with that training, I offer recommendations for properly conducting use of force training in Chapter 12. Included in that chapter is a comprehensive explanation of my scenario-based use of force training model.

In the first part of this section, I explained what you should do to implement the Managing the Use of Force Incident program. However, you may feel your existing liability management program is valid, but you're not completely satisfied with its results. If that's the case, your liability problem may not be your department's use of force training program or its liability management protocols. It may be that your officers are not following their training or the department's existing liability management protocols. To make that determination, you need to perform a little research. First, you need to review what your officers are taught regarding the use of force and liability management. You can't establish whether your officers are or aren't following their training if you don't know what they are taught.

The next step is to verify that your officers are following the department's liability management protocols.

Making Sure That It Gets Done Properly

This is a never-ending process, and it cannot be accomplished from behind your desk. To be an effective mid-manager, you have to adopt the management strategy of "managing by wandering around." You have to see and hear it for yourself. "Trust, but verify," was President Ronald Reagan's admonishment regarding the Soviet Unions' commitment to nuclear arms reduction. This pithy statement should be the personal motto of every supervisor, mid-manager, and administrator. Not only does your personal verification ensure that specific tasks are being performed and department protocols are being followed, it allows you to personally clarify and reinforce your expectations to your supervisors and officers.

Managing by wandering around doesn't mean you have to spend all your time out in the field. But it does imply that you shouldn't spend every working minute cemented to your office chair. Personally, I don't think you can spend too much time finding your staff doing things right or verifying that things are being done properly. With that said, I cannot give you a recommended percentage on how much time you should spend out of your office. But I can give you an indicator that you are not doing enough wandering: Your officers seem surprised when you unexpectedly show up at the scene of a call, shift briefing, or training session. Another indicator is the continued mismanagement of use of force incidents by your officers. This should be a red flag that you are not spending enough time verifying that the right things are getting done.

Sam Walton, founder of Wal-Mart, would randomly show up at different stores and supply centers unannounced to verify the right things were being done. But more importantly, while he was there–Sam would stock shelves, move merchandise, and unload boxes on the freight dock with his employees. Not only was Sam Walton a great businessman, he was an intelligent leader. Sam's management by wandering around sent to two powerful messages: Sam cared about his organization and its employees. And, everything that happened in the organization was important. The impact of Sam's actions was not limited to only those employees who witnessed them. Walmart employees throughout the entire organization were inspired by the stories of his active participation.

As Sam Walton did at Wal-Mart, you need to check on every area of your domain. Even though it may be inconvenient, a disruption to your sleeping pattern, and an all-around pain in the butt. You need to attend a briefing on every shift. Observe training classes. Ride a shift with a patrol officer or work the line in the jail. Evaluate a post-use of force team debriefing. Randomly show up at the scene of a call. Inspect the training lesson plans, PowerPoint presentations, and training records. Whatever your officers do under your watch, you need to learn it, know it, observe it, and evaluate it. I know you are saying to yourself, "My old captain, commander, or lieutenant didn't do any of this. That is probably true–neither did mine. But, they never really made a major difference in the department either. Leader or bureaucrat? Your choice.

One mid-manager who really impressed me was the lieutenant in charge of the Atlanta Police Department's police academy. I had traveled to the Atlanta academy to conduct a forty-hour Survival Skills Instructor Course. By any standard, this course is a physical butt-kicker. Consequently, I was surprised to learn, when I arrived at the academy, that the Lieutenant in charge of training was attending the entire forty-hour course. He was in good shape, but no spring chicken.

During one of the breaks, I told the lieutenant that I have never had a mid-manager attend an instructor course with his troops. Further, I went on to tell him how impressed I was that he was participating in the course. The lieutenant's reply still resonates with me today. "I mandated that all my instructors attend this forty-hour class. They did not volunteer. They have to be here. If I mandate their participation, it is only fair that I attend the class too." Wow, a manager who leads by example and is fair. A rare breed indeed—in any sector, public or private.

The lieutenant's participation in the course inspired and motivated his instructors. I had never trained a group of instructors from one department who worked so hard and stayed on task so well. The lieutenant had taken the concept of *managing by wandering around* to the next level, and it showed in his instructors' performance.

Management By Wandering Around

"Management By Wandering Around" (MBWA) is a important management strategy for proactively minimizing department liability.

Tom Peters and Robert Waterman made this leadership concept famous in their book: *In Search Of Excellence.* In 1980, while doing research, Peters and Waterman interviewed Hewlett-Packard president John Young. Mr. Young explained that HP's hallmark management philosophy of "managing by wandering around" was responsible for the company's success.

The concept of MBWA is that managers cannot be effective if they spend most of their time in their offices. To be effective, they need to visit (note: I did not use the term "investigate") their subordinates' work environment, office, and every area of their management domain. Effective managers have informal discussions with their staff about problems. They ask questions. And, they provide positive reinforcement for a job well done. Your praise or correction is always more effective when given immediately.

There are a number of benefits to a wandering management style:

- Your supervisors and officers have face-to-face contact with you. In doing so, they understand that you are interested in how they perform their duties.
- There is a free exchange of communication. Your officers receive information from the horse's mouth, so to speak, and not filtered through their supervisor or from an impersonal department memo.
- You learn what is going on firsthand. The information you receive is not filtered, spun, or misinterpreted through another person.

- Your supervisors and officers get immediate and direct feedback from you regarding their job performance.
- Mutual respect is enhanced and relationships are created. Effective leadership is based on trust. The more interaction the troops have with you the more trust they will have in your decisions.
- Morale is enhanced and the officers' commitment to the department is bolstered. You want your officers to do more than just what they are told. As a leader, you want your officers to do the right things for the right reasons.
- You can see firsthand what needs improvement. The flatter the chain of command, the quicker you get results.

Don't confuse MBWA with micro-managing your supervisors or instructors. Micro-management is telling your supervisors how to do their jobs in minute detail. Managing by wandering around is the process of giving and receiving information from all levels in the chain of command. It ensures that your expectations are clear and duties and responsibilities are effectively and efficiently performed. MBWA empowers your supervisors and officers. When individuals are empowered to make decisions and be self-directed, they can be held directly accountable for their actions and their performance.

Criminal justice supervisors sometimes find MBWA uncomfortable because they feel their authority is being undermined by your presence and probing questions. This is the same complaint that a manager receives from an "open door policy." Supervisory insecurities are easily relieved by the outward display of your support for your supervisor's proper actions and decisions and the private counseling of his or her mistakes. As a wandering manager, you must be aware of the fine line between knowing what is going on, stating your expectations, verifying that your expectations are being met, and interfering with the performance of your supervisors' and officers' duties.

As a manager who personally used this management strategy every day, I cannot state more emphatically how effective MBWA can be in enhancing your staff's performance, solving administrative and logistical problems, and proactively identifying and correcting liability concerns and issues. At the Montana Academy, I was able to implement forty-two instructional, logistical, operational, and performance changes in a twelve-month period by "managing by wandering around."

Management By Wandering Around minimizes your department's liability by seeing firsthand what your officers do, how they do it, and what they are taught. Further, it allows you to quickly identify performance problems, informational or technical errors, and operational deficiencies and inefficiencies. Accordingly, MBWA establishes an environment where performance problems and ineffective or unsafe training methodologies can be quickly addressed.

Think Proactively

So, while you are sitting in your corner office surfing the Internet for a new desk chair, you might want to give your eyes a little relief from the computer screen and think about what you can proactively do to limit your department's liability.

Thinking proactively about the big picture of potential department liability is management's job. Although officers should think proactively in the moment to limit liability and first-line supervisors must proactively think in the short term to manage liability, it is mid-management's responsibility to think proactively to prevent department liability. To echo the point I made in Chapter 1, your officers can do everything right and still get sued. Proactive contemplation prevents your officers from being sued for doing the wrong things.

The premise for proactively minimizing liability and winning lawsuits is founded on the belief that if you can accurately identify a potential liability problem; then, you can preemptively minimize its risk or eliminate the problem altogether. Even though, the term "supervision" implies you have super vision, no manager is born with the natural ability to see the potential harm in every situation. It is an acquired skill.

To develop this important managerial talent, you must combine an inquiring mind and an innate mistrust of everything. I call this heighten state of perceptual acuity "consequent clairvoyance." Fortunately, you developed this acuity as a criminal justice officer; you just didn't realize it had an application within the management realm. All cops are born optimists; it is experience that makes us cynical.

One sunny afternoon, while on patrol as a deputy sheriff, I became acutely aware that I had developed these cognitive elements and melded them together to catch criminals. My father-in-law was on a ride-along with me that Sunday afternoon. It was a beautiful day, sunny and warm. We were driving down a country road when a truck filled with yard debris pulled out in front of us. The truck's bed was filled with brush and leafy tree branches that protruded out past the sides of the truck and shuttered as vehicles in the opposite lane passed.

After acknowledging the truck full of debris in front of us, my father-in-law (a genuinely nice guy) looked over at me and said: "That guy took advantage of this beautiful day and cleaned up his yard. Good for him." I didn't say a word, but my eyes squinted as I looked at that truck and thought to myself: "You bet, now where is that bum going to dump that crap." I realized right then and there that I had arrived; I had become a real cop.

To start the process of assessing the potential liability in an existing operational activity or with the implementation of a new use of force option, you first identify the "lowest common denominator" in your department to establish a baseline standard for liability. The lowest common denominator is defined as the officer with the least amount of common sense. You know the ones. The officers who lack the natural ability to learn from the cause and effect of their poor decisions. These officers are not malicious. However, they are (as my wise and philosophical grandfather used to say) "ate up by the dumb ass."

There are two ways to increase the level of this officer's common sense: a frontal lobe lobotomy or a turkey brain transplant. With either remedy, you are not qualified to perform brain surgery. And even if you were, the police union would file a grievance. To give these officers their due, they are often extremely intelligent, in the academic sense.

I know you have affectionately used the term "overly educated idiot" to describe these judgement impaired officers. I worked for years with one such person. Academically brilliant but did have the common sense to come off the golf course during an electrical storm. Routinely, during our conversations, he would remind me that he was the proud recipient of three Master of Science degrees and a doctoral candidate in the field of urban studies. Well, at least it wasn't in recreational activity management. That is a real degree program at the University of Montana. (As a side note, do you ever wonder what you are getting for all that money you shell out for your kid's college education? Sorry, I digress.)

During a philosophical discussion over lunch, my overly educated colleague smugly informed me that "there are not absolutes." I was taken aback by his retort. I expected a more intelligent rebuttal from a scholar with three advanced college degrees. Aware that I could not successfully match wits with such an intellectual giant, I based my lowbrow rejoinder on common sense. To rebuttal his statement, I asked him three common sense questions: "Do you think it is acceptable to sexually abuse women?" "No," he answered. "What about the molestation of children?" He shook his head to indicate he didn't. "The torture of inmates and suspects?" "Of course not," he replied, his face turning bright red as he started to realize the absurdity of his statement. I hammered home my point by rhetorically asking, with a hint of sarcasm: "So, I guess there are absolutes in life–are there not?" So much for higher education's ability to develop critical thinking skills. As many a brainwashed college student has done, my colleague mindlessly regurgitated the theoretical dribble that his liberal college professors had expostulated with conviction in their classes.

While discussing the necessity of a formal education as it relates to a person's professional success, Alistair McAlpine admonishes administrators in his book, The New Machiavelli, that to be successful a person must possess the capacity for original thought, not just the ability to repeat the thoughts of others.

The traditional solution to minimizing department liability regarding intelligent officers who have repeatedly demonstrated poor judgement is to transfer them into a position that compliments their strengths and protects them and the department from their weaknesses: detectives, D.A.R.E., training, school resource officer, or special projects. As an example of this benevolent management strategy, I provide you with the following incident:

I was using the FATS system (a computer generated, video firearms training simulator) to train officers in the proper use of deadly force. During one training session, I had an officer inappropriately use deadly force. During the video scenario, the officer was confronted with a traffic stop. As the officer approached the violator's vehicle, the driver exited the vehicle and contacted the officer next to the driver's door. As the driver was removing the driver's license from his wallet, the passenger exited and fired upon the officer. When the passenger shot at the officer, the driver fell to the ground and folded himself into the fetal position. The officer did an outstanding job firing back and neutralizing the shooter. But then the officer shot the unarmed, fetal positioned, driver twice in the back.

I asked the officer why he shot the driver? "Because he was closest to me," the officer replied. I reviewed with the officer the requirements for using deadly force stipulated in *Tennessee v. Garner.* Then, I asked the officer which one of those requirements justified shooting the driver? "The driver was an immediate threat to me," he declared. "How so?" I asked. "He was closest to me," the officer insisted. We discussed the shooting for several minutes, but the justification was always the same: "He was closest to me." Aware that he had to agree with me that the shooting of the driver was excessive force or he would not pass the required training module, the officer reluctantly admitted he had made a mistake. But I could tell by his body language the agreement was only out of a desire to graduate from the academy.

This officer was very intelligent, college educated, and did exceptionally well in his academic studies. However, the officer had a problem learning from his bad use of force decisions. Out of my obligation to the officer's department, I contacted the captain in charge of training. I presented the captain with a detailed explanation of the officer's performance during the deadly force training simulation. Further, I expressed my concerns regarding the officer's ability to make proper use of force decisions. The captain thanked me for bringing the problem to his attention, and he assured me that the department's field training officers would be informed of my concerns.

A few years later, I was having coffee with a sergeant from the same department. During our conversation, the sergeant asked me if I remembered the officer? I stated that I did. The sergeant informed me that the officer had been recently transferred from patrol to the detective division. I told the sergeant that he must have performed very well on patrol and to tell the new detective congratulations for me. "That's not why the transfer happened. He had some common sense issues with the use of force," the sergeant replied.

Apparently, the incident that broke the administrative camel's back occurred during a traffic stop. The officer took the driver out of the vehicle at gunpoint with an assault rifle for lawfully possessing a concealed weapon permit. The officer had stopped the driver for speeding. When the officer was informed by dispatch that the driver possessed a current concealed weapon permit, he overreacted.

The administrative solution for the officer's poor use of force decision was not to develop a policy for properly interacting with citizens who lawfully possess conceal weapon permits or provide the officer with more use of force training. The department's solution was to promote him out of the patrol division where the officer would not make anymore traffic stops. This may have been the most humane way to deal with the officer's poor use of force decision-making abilities, but it is administratively lazy.

Further, administrative solutions like this demean the officers who legitimately earned their promotions to detective. Another unacknowledged consequence of using a promotion to correct an officer's poor performance is that it damages the credibility of your future administrative decisions with your officers. As the sergeant lamented: "Our troops believe the fastest way to get promoted to detective in our department is continually screw up."

The ASP instructor-training program applies the lowest common denominator concept in a different way. In this commercially conducted course, the company instructor tells the instructor candidates that they need to train to the "Twos." The ASP concept is that defensive tactics instructors, SWAT officers, and officers with martial arts backgrounds because of their motivation and superior skill levels are classified as "Tens." But the average officer is classified as a "Two." Consequently, they are to gear the sophistication of their expandable baton training program for the average officer, the Two.

After you have identified your department's lowest common denominator, you overlay the officer as the actor in the hypothetical scenario. Then, you ask yourself "What are the worst possible things that can happen?" From the list of identified worst things that can happen, you develop policies, guidelines, or training programs to eliminate the problem or minimize its inherent risks.

Predicting the potential harm in every criminal justice situation is like solving a math problem. Don't panic, I can't do math either, that is why I pursued a career in criminal justice. But that is not my point. The point is that to properly solve a math problem you need to use the proper equation. There are two equations that you can use to proactively manage your department's liability. One equation for predicting potential harm and the other for identifying restrictions that minimize risk. They are as follows:

Equation for Predicting Harm: situation + lowest common denominator = the worst possible thing(s) that could happen.
Equation for Minimizing Liability: the worst possible thing(s) that can happen + the proactively developed restrictions = liability reduction.

In the following example equations, I use actual events that created department and officer liability. Additionally, I include the departments' reactively developed solutions to address the unforeseen liability problems. For instance, shortly after a department adopted the use of the Taser, an officer tasered a distraught six-year-old boy at school to prevent the child from hurting himself with a piece of glass. Two weeks later, another officer, from the same department, tasered an intoxicated twelve-year-old girl as she ran from the officer. In a press release, the Police Director stated that he could not defend the tasering of the children. Subsequently, the department had modified its taser policy to prevent similar acts from occurring.

First we will use the Equation for Predicting Harm to identify potential liability issues. Then, we use the Equation for Minimizing Risk to identify proactive protocols to minimize the risk of liability.

Equation for Predicting Harm when Deploying the Taser

The department purchases X26 Tasers (situation) + Officer Jones who is lacking common sense (lowest common denominator) = see list (the worst possible things that could happen).

Worst Possible Things: Deploys Taser probes to an elderly woman, small child, passively resisting person, visually pregnant woman, running-intoxicated juvenile, and handcuffed person. Taser probe/Drive Stuns inmate secured in a restraint chair. Deploys Taser probes to a person on the edge of a roof or atop of a bridge/fence, a person within striking distance of a cement sidewalk, or a disabled person in a wheelchair. Taser dart hits an eye. Taser is used to torture a person. Person dies after being tasered multiple times.

Equation for Minimizing Risk when Deploying the Taser

An elderly woman is shocked with the Taser probes after refusing to sign a traffic citation. (Worst possible thing that can happen) + policy against Tasering elderly people for nonviolent offenses (proactively developed restriction) = reduction in department liability.

A grade school age child is shocked with the Taser probes. (Worst possible thing that can happen) + policy against tasering grade school age children unless deadly force is justified (proactively developed restriction) = reduction in department liability.

A suspect is injured from the free fall off the top of a fence after being shocked with Taser probes. (Worst possible thing that can happen) + policy against tasering people on a fence unless deadly force is justified (proactively developed restriction) = reduction in department liability.

An intoxicated twelve year-old girl running away from an officer is Taser probed and is injured by the free fall to the cement. (Worst possible thing that can happen) + policy against tasering fleeing intoxicated juveniles (proactively developed restriction) = reduction in department liability.

A verbally abusive inmate dies after being shocked with the Taser probes. (Worst possible thing that can happen) + policy against tasering nonviolent inmates (proactively developed restriction) = reduction in department liability.

An inmate is shocked in Drive Stun Mode while secured in a restraint chair. (Worst possible thing that can happen) + policy against Taser Drive Stunning inmates secured in the restraint chair. (Proactively developed restriction) = reduction in department liability.

These equations can be used to proactively minimize liability in every activity within your department: corrections and law enforcement operations, use of force, tactics, operation of vehicles, policy and procedural development, and training.

The following is an example of using the equations for minimizing the liability in training:

Equation for Predicting Harm During Training

Use Simunitions' marking ammunition in training exercises (situation) + reserve officer (lowest common denominator) = see list. (The worst possible things that could happen). Worst Possible Things: Eye injury from projectile. Open wound caused by projectile. Duty ammo mistakenly loaded into training gun. Duty handgun mistakenly used in scenario. Protective equipment not used during scenario. Nonauthorized protective equipment used in scenario. Student mistakenly shoots the instructor. Student intentionally shoots another student during horseplay. Student demonstrates dangerous gun handling skills. Instructor shoots students with marking ammunition as a form of punishment.

Equation for Minimizing Risk During Training with Marking Ammunition

An officer, not wearing eye protection, receives an eye injury during a training scenario. (worst possible thing that can happen) + Training rule: All students will wear department issued eye protection at all times in the training area (proactively developed restriction) = reduction in department liability.

A student officer is shot during a training scenario with live ammunition. (Worst possible thing that can happen) + Training rule: all students will be physically searched by an instructor before entering the training area (proactively developed restriction) = reduction in department liability.

A student officer receives a wound to his leg during horseplay, when another student officer intentionally shot him. (Worst possible thing that can happen) + Training rule: Students will only shoot designated instructors playing the role of suspects (proactively developed restriction) = reduction in department liability.

An instructor, who was accidentally shot by a student officer, makes the student kneel down and the instructor shoots the student with a marking round as punishment. (Worst possible thing that can happen) + Training rule: Instructors will not shoot students with marking ammunition as a form of correction or as punishment (proactively developed restriction) = reduction in department liability.

A student officer in a scenario shoots at the suspect and misses and the projectile accidentally strikes and injures a member of the Peer Jury. (Worst possible thing that can happen) + Training rule: The instructor facilitating the scenario will prevent the student officer from pointing the training firearm loaded with marking cartridges at the Peer Jury (proactively developed restriction) = reduction in department liability.

An Instructor substitutes a grinding shield for a department approved protective helmet and a student receives a facial wound. (Worst possible thing that can happen) + Training rule: Only department approved protective equipment will be used during training scenarios that utilize marking ammunition (proactively developed restriction) = reduction in department liability.

Consult with Your Legal Counsel

So, you have a grasp of the whole proactively minimizing officer and department liability thing. I am going to recommend you do something that all managers dread: consult with your risk management people. I am not saying you need to go to them with your hat in your hand, asking their permission to implement a new force option or training program. Although, it is a good idea to get their prospective on any considered major operational change.

It is risk management's job to stay abreast of liability trends. Consequently, they can be a valuable resource in staying ahead of the liability curve. You should make it part of your quarterly routine to drop in and touch base with these folks. It will assist you in your proactive quest to minimize department liability. Another positive outcome of routinely consulting with this group is that you develop powerful allies. The risk management division has an incredible amount of influence with the power brokers in city or county government. Developing a partnership with such an influential force will give your proposals credibility and assist you in the implementation of liability management reforms within your department.

In addition to the risk management department, you should periodically touch base with your city or county legal department regarding liability trends. Like your risk management group, your city or county attorney monitors liability trends. Further, they are responsible for analyzing and evaluating the liability in the lawsuits that are filed against your officers. The legal division can give you an up close and personal perspective on potential liability problems within your department. Traditionally, city or county attorneys do not seek you out to discuss their concerns. Keep in mind, they are the reactive component in the litigation process. Therefore, it is your responsibility to proactively seek out their counsel regarding potential liability.

Moreover, when you are considering the implementation of a new force option, the legal department should be consulted. I know. You hate to consult with attorneys on such matters because they are in the business of saying "no." That is not necessarily a bad thing. "No" does not mean never. "No" is an attorney's way of saying slow down I have a few concerns. If, for example, more mid-managers had consulted with their legal department before implementing the use of pepper spray, less-lethal munitions, or the Taser, their departments would have encountered must less potential liability.

Further, I strongly recommend you consult with your department's insurance company or insurance authority. These institutions are a valuable resource for proactively managing liability. Because they are the ones that pay the out-of-court settlements and the jury verdicts, they have a vested interest in reducing your department's liability. Not only does their staff specialize in evaluating the defensibility of civil rights lawsuits, they work closely with the attorneys who defend officers and departments in excessive force litigation.

Accordingly, another valuable resource for you to consult with is your insurance carrier's contract attorneys. These attorneys specialize in defending criminal justice officers against allegations of excessive force. Your insurance provider will be more than delighted to provide you with the names and contact information of their attorneys. The advantage of consulting with the attorneys that work for the insurance company is that they review and litigate excessive force cases for a variety of different departments. Subsequently, they are the wellspring from which all liability management knowledge flows. Further, these attorneys are very willing to consult with you regarding liability management. Primarily because if you will take their advice, it makes defending your officers' use of force much easier for them.

The attorney who is responsible for defending your officers in excessive force litigation can be a valuable resource when implementing a new force option or during the development of new use of force policies or the revision of existing policies. Think about it. Is there a better resource available to you? I can't think of one. Furthermore, what makes consulting with the insurance company's attorneys even more appealing is that their advice is usually free. These attorneys are paid to win excessive force lawsuits. Consequently, they understand that their investment in a free consultation with you will pay big dividends when they go to trial to defend your officers.

Another resource available to you is your city, county, or state prosecutor. Although prosecutors usually have very little experience (or interest) in civil litigation, they evaluate your officers' performance every day as they prosecute their cases. As a result, deputy district attorneys, assistant city prosecutors, and assistant attorney generals can provide you with their observations of your officers' operational performance and their use of force decision-making abilities. Through their observations, you can recognize and reward your officers who are performing well. This proactively minimizes liability by reinforcing the officers' proper behavior. Further, from their observations, you can identify officers with performance and/or behavioral problems and take the required corrective action to minimize your department's liability.

Whether a criminal case is dismissed or prosecuted has a direct impact on civil litigation. When the prosecutor decides not to prosecute a case that involves an officer's use of force, the suspect almost always files a civil rights lawsuit. In addition, the failure to prosecute the case reinforces the suspect's belief that the arrest was unlawful. As a result, a civil rights lawsuit alleging a false arrest may follow. Consulting with your prosecutors on liability management can be a symbiotic relationship. By identifying why your prosecutors are not prosecuting certain cases, you can convey their concerns to your supervisors, who then make the necessary adjustments to their officers' performance. Consequently, the prosecutors receive stronger criminal cases, fewer cases get dismissed, and fewer lawsuits get filed.

What are Your Administrator's Expectations?

As a mid-manager, you answer to a higher authority. No, I don't mean a supernatural being. Although, I have worked under a few administrators who issued commandments like a deity. As the president of our deputy sheriff's association, I sent a letter to the Sheriff asking how he could justify reprimanding a corrections deputy for violating a policy that he (the Sheriff) had previously violated. The Sheriff's written reply was short and to the point– all the reply needed was a sacred mountaintop, a flaming bush, and a stone tablet. Also, it left no doubt about who was in charge of the sheriff's office. "I am the Sheriff. I make and break policy at will." As I read his response, I realized I was lucky that he did not turn me into a pillar of salt.

As a mid-manager, you are responsible for the oversight of your designated domain. Whether that domain is operational or training, it is your job to make sure the department's standards are enforced. However, as my Sheriff very bluntly pointed out, the department's administrator is the person who establishes those standards. Since the theme of this book is managing the use of force incident, there is only one question that is germane to our conversation about departmental standards: Do you know what your administrator's expectations are regarding your officers' management of their use of force incidents? When I use the term managing the use of force incident, I am referring to all the information explained in Chapters 1 through 7. I know what you're thinking: "Of course I do. They are listed in our policy manual."

Your policy manual may stipulate your administrator's tangible expectations: Whether an officer is supposed to wear long or short-sleeve shirts? What make, model, and caliber of handgun an officer can carry? But, the really important expectations don't deal with superficial requirements. The important expectations pertain to things that violate someone's civil rights, create liability for your department, and/or damage an officer's credibility or defense in a civil rights lawsuit. The policies that cover those expectations are written so broadly that you can't possibly know what your administrator's specific expectations are unless you ask him or her. And you know what happens when you assume?

An example of what happens when officers, supervisors, and mid-managers assume they know what their administrator's expectations are regarding the use of force is illustrated by the Sheriff's reaction to the use of side-handle batons on a traffic stop by two of his deputies.

The incident started with a pursuit of a man and a woman in an old truck. When the vehicle stopped, a news helicopter video-recorded the two deputies delivering two-handed strikes with their side-handle batons to the man and woman. The news camera recorded the graphic images of the woman holding on to the truck's passenger side door mirror while a very large male deputy whaled on her with his baton.

The stop was performed on a busy street during the middle of the afternoon. Based on the location and the time of day, I am led to believe that the deputy was following his training and not acting out in anger. The day after the video appeared on the nightly news, the Sheriff issued a press release: "I am shocked by the videotape of two of my deputies beating two illegal immigrants after a vehicle chase. They clearly used excessive force." Wow, who could have anticipated that reaction? Oh, ya, the department's mid-managers—if they would have asked Sheriff what he believed constituted the use of excessive force with a side-handle baton.

As stated previously, most policies regulating an officer's use of force or professional behavior are written so broadly that they really offer very little guidance. Here is an example of a broadly written nondeadly use of force policy:

> "It is the policy of this Department that officers shall use only that amount of force which reasonably appears necessary, given the facts and circumstances perceived by the officer at the time of the event, to effectively bring an incident under control. "Reasonableness" of the force used must be judged from the perspective of a reasonable officer on the scene at the time of the incident."

Now, based on that policy, tell me what are the administrator's expectations regarding the use of the baton, pepper spray, or Taser in probe or Drive Stun mode? You can't. Because the policy is intentionally too broadly written. However, if you asked the administrator: "When do you consider the use of the baton, pepper spray, or Taser excessive?" The administrator may not give you every possible situation when he or she considers that excessive force has occurred, but you would have a better set of workable expectations. And that is a lot more than you have now.

What about your policy that prohibits an officer's use of profanity, sarcasm, or demeaning terms, how is it written? Usually, this type of behavior is broadly addressed in the department's professionalism policy. Your policy probably is written something like this:

"It is the policy of this Department that officers shall conduct themselves at all times in a courteous and professional manner. An officer's behavior or language that portrays the officer or the department as unprofessional and tarnishes the image and/or the reputation of the department will not be tolerated."

So, can an officer occasionally be sarcastic? Is an officer's profanity acceptable under certain situations? Can I tell a drunk suspect in the back of my patrol car to "Shut the f . . k up" when he talks smack about my wife? Or, is it really only a problem when it's captured by a news camera team, on a witnesses' cell phone, or on the patrol car's video camera recording?

Do you know what your administrator's expectations are regarding an officer's use of profanity, sarcasm, or demeaning terms? Probably not. It is poor management practice and unfair to your officers to wait until their unprofessional behavior debuts on "You Tube" before you call them on the carpet. Further, the lack of stated specific behavioral expectations allows behaviors that damage an officer's credibility at trial and creates liability for your department to go uncorrected.

Briefing Your First-Line Supervisors

As a middle manager, you probably hold a meeting once a week or twice a month with your first-line supervisors. These meetings are necessary to share information, identify common problems, and develop collective solutions. If you have spent the past week or two performing a little MBWA, you will also have your own observations and concerns to discuss. In addition to all the administrative issues, I recommend a post-use of force debriefing become a staple of your supervisory meetings. If a major use of force incident occurred or if you have a particular concern over a specific use of force incident, you may want to facilitate the debriefing yourself. If you are going to act as the facilitator, you should follow the debriefing format and guidelines explained in Chapter 9.

If the post-use of force debriefing becomes routine part of your meeting agenda, an alternative to your facilitation of the debriefing is to assign a supervisor to facilitate. Rather than have you identify the incident to review, the facilitating supervisor brings to the meeting a use of force incident from his or her team. To allow time for the facilitating supervisors to prepare, they should be notified a week in advance. The next facilitator can even be selected at the current meeting.

I know exactly what you are thinking. This is just one more task to add to an already full meeting agenda. Well, if you are managing by wandering around, you will have fewer issues to discuss, because he will have addressed most of your concerns individually with the supervisor that it actually pertains to. As you have probably learned, general admonishments (referred to in law enforcement vernacular as "blanket ass chewings") are the least effective way to correct a performance or behavioral problem. Primarily, because the perpetrator hides in the anonymity of the group, and the other members being admonished don't care because they did not commit the offense. As a result, the offender is not held personally accountable for his or her actions; consequently, his or her behavior does not change. Furthermore, car maintenance, vacation schedules, dispatch problems, and the Christmas party should not take precedence over properly managing the department's use of force incidents.

The following are the reasons for making a post-use of force debriefing a standard agenda item:

- Discussing the use of force incident allows you to state and reinforce your expectations regarding an officer's proper use of force and/or the proper management of the use of force incident in a variety of different situations.
- The debriefing provides an opportunity to explain your administrator's expectations regarding the use of different force options and officer behavior.
- The supervisors are exposed to different supervisory points of view regarding each specific use of force incident. This is something that cannot occur doing a patrol team debriefing. Furthermore, as you know, not every supervisor is equally adept at managing the use of force incident. Routine group discussions will informally increase a supervisor's knowledge in deficient areas.
- Facilitating a post-use of force debriefing to a more sophisticated group of participants (supervisors not officers) will enhance the supervisors' skill in facilitating debriefings. This will improve the effectiveness of the supervisors' facilitated patrol team debriefings.
- Weekly discussions of use of force incidents create consistency in your supervisors' understanding of the proper use of force and the proper management of the use of force incident.
- Group supervisory evaluations of use of force incidents create an environment where problems with specific use of force options can be collectively identified and possible solutions can be explored.

Evaluating Training

The last responsibility we will discuss is the proper management of training. The ugly administrative truth about training is that managers rarely take a serious interest in it, mainly because training falls outside the operational mainstream.

Management primarily views training as a support function—as a means to an end and not an end in and of itself. As a result, there are very few permanent training positions. Most department trainers are full-time officers and part-time instructors. The full-time training positions that do exist have an expiration date—officers and supervisors are rotated in and out on an annual or biannual basis. Moreover, the full-time positions that do exist are primarily administrative; consequently, most training officers do very little training themselves.

To compound the problem, management perceives training as an evil, but necessary, money pit. They hold that view for good reasons. More workmen's compensation claims come from training activities than actual police or corrections work. Officers are paid overtime to attend training. Training equipment is very expensive, and training is instructor intensive. Consequently, training is usually the first budget to be cut during a financial crisis.

I often hear law enforcement training compared with military training. However, the honest truth is that they are polar opposites. We have the finest military in the world because our military has the best training in the world. Up until the recent wars in the Middle East, our military trained a lot and fought very little. In contrast, we have competent officers in spite of their lack of training. In the criminal justice system, officers train very little and fight a lot. It is not uncommon for criminal justice agencies not to provide defensive tactics or use of force training to their officers. The sad truth is that in many states, cosmetologists are required to attend more hours of training for their certification than P.O.S.T. mandates for criminal justice officers.

Because most managers do not understand training, many believe that by sending their officers to a one or two-day lecture seminar they are providing their officers with effective training. If you are one of those managers, I am about to pop your balloon. It is well-established in the field of adult learning that:

When a person receives information and that person does not apply that information within twenty-four hours of receiving it, the person loses 85 percent of that information over the subsequent thirty days.

This basic adult learning theory invalidates most academy and inservice lecture training. In contrast, one of law enforcement's most effective and successful training programs ever developed is based on this theory. When the improved sobriety-testing course was first introduced, its training format followed this model of adult learning. On the first day of class, officers received the information required to properly administer the field sobriety tests and the HGN examination. On the second day of class—less then twenty-four hours later—volunteer drinkers were brought in and the students practiced the sobriety tests and the HGN examination on actual intoxicated people. From a purely training point of view, it was brilliantly conceived and flawlessly executed. It is still some of the best training I have ever attended. Not the most entertaining or riveting, but extraordinarily effective. Without being aware of it, motor skills training follows this format. That is why motor skill training is so effective.

Training managers can minimize department and officer liability through the proper evaluation and oversight of the department's training programs. To properly manage the department's use of force training, a mid-manager should continually evaluate and monitor three areas of training: development, delivery, and documentation.

Before we analyze the three areas of training, it is beneficial to discuss the three specific categories of use of force training: motor, cognitive, and integrated.

In motor skill use of force training, the officer learns to properly perform a physical skill or operate a tool. Traditionally, these skills or operations are taught in defensive tactics classes. They primarily consist of the proper application of mechanical restraints, physical control holds, pepper spray, electronic control devices, focuses blows, baton strikes, and impact munitions.

Conversely, in cognitive skill development, the officer acquires an understanding of the legal restrictions on the use of force and/or the operational guidelines for using the tool; then, the officer draws upon that understanding to make proper use of force decisions. The standards that govern the use of force and the operational guidelines for the proper use and maintenance of physical control tools are primarily delivered through lecture presentations.

With the mastery of the physical use of force skills obtained and the knowledge of the restrictions on using force internalized, the officer's ability to make proper nondeadly and deadly use of force decisions is tested through the use of integrated scenario-based training. This is not merely "force on force" training. It is a training program specifically designed to evaluate an officer's use of force decision-making abilities, to reinforce the officer's proper use of force decisions, and rehabilitate poor use of force decision making.

Training Development

To properly evaluate your department's use of force training program, you should first examine the use of force decisions of your officers. If your officers are making poor use of force decisions in certain areas, it is probably caused by a deficiency in their training. The deficiency can be caused from any number of developmental missteps. Department training programs incorporate information, guidelines, and force options from a wide variety of sources: case law, academies, government-sponsored training, and private companies. The national standards for the use of nondeadly and deadly force are set forth in federal court rulings. However, recommendations from other sources are often adopted to establish de facto national standards.

While testifying as an expert in an excessive force trial, the opposing attorney asked me who develops national standards for the use of nondeadly force? I explained that federal courts established the official legal standard. Further, I explained that the companies that manufacture use of force weapons establish guidelines for the use of their products. As a result, these operational recommendations become widely accepted and implemented by law enforcement agencies. The end result of the universal acceptance of these guidelines is that the manufacturers establish nonjurisprudence-based national standards for the use of pepper spray, electronic control devices, and impact munitions.

Being an attorney, he had a hard time wrapping his head around the idea that law enforcement could have any use of force standard other than that set by the Supreme Court or a lower appellate court. Though these standards are not founded in any legal basis, they are often embraced and fanatically defended by officers, instructors, and administrators.

Here are examples of where private companies' recommendations became de facto national standards for their less-lethal weapons deployment:

When the companies that manufacture pepper spray initially developed and taught their instructor courses, they told the attending instructors that pepper spray was a harmless food additive and was less injurious to suspects and inmates than the use of wrist and arm restraints. Therefore, the use of pepper spray should be used after verbalization but before physical control holds. Accordingly, officers started spraying suspects and inmates with pepper spray in lieu of going hands-on. This recommendation became the national standard for the use of pepper spray. This application standard was accepted without question until this recommendation caused liability for departments.

In the instructor development courses offered by the makers of less lethal munitions, the companies' instructors told officers that the use of a beanbag projectile was the same level of force as a baton strike. Consequently, officers used the less-lethal impact round interchangeably with the police baton as a pain compliance tool. This recommendation became the accepted standard for the use of less-lethal projectiles by law enforcement personnel until the appellate courts placed restrictions on its application.

Regardless of the court-imposed limitation, there are still many law enforcement agencies that adhere to that standard. Consequently, their officers shoot passively resisting citizens who will not drop their video cameras, suspects who refuse to raise their hands above their heads, and struggling junior high school girls. As a result, their officers receive disciplinary action and their departments experience excessive force litigation.

Taser International provides the only nationally recognized training program for the use of their electronic subject control devices. As law enforcement agencies across the United States adopted and implemented Taser International's training program, the departments unwittingly established Taser's recommendations as the nationally accepted standard for the use of the company's electronic control device. As with pepper spray, Taser instructors told officers that the ECD was less injurious that wrist and arm locks. As a result, officers should deploy the Taser before going hands-on with inmates or suspects.

Initially, Taser International recommended deploying electric shocks to a suspect's chest. Then, after officers had followed this deployment recommendation for several years, the company revised its deployment recommendations. In a memo released to their instructors, Taser International told departments to stop shocking suspects and inmates in the chest out of a concern it may cause cardiac arrest. Of course, the company's recommended change delivered a body blow to the departments with pending wrongful death lawsuits involving a suspect who died after being shocked in the chest.

How do these recommendations by private companies become accepted national standards? You blindly adopt them as your department's operational and training guidelines. To make my point, answer this one question: Where did your department's training materials for the baton, impact munitions, pepper spray, and electronic control device come from? If you said the manufacturer's training program, you are not alone.

Commercial producers of use of force options market their products and training programs by touting that their products and programs minimize liability. However, historically, departments have experienced an increase in lawsuits by following the company's recommendations. A company's operational and training guidelines are not development to minimize department liability. They are developed to increase product sales.

Further, departments incur needless expense by following the manufacturer's self-anointed recertification requirements. Why is an officer who has successfully carried and deployed the device for a year required to fire multiple cartridges during recertification training? The company makes money on the sale of the cartridges. Think about it. For a company, it is the product that keeps on giving. If your department has one hundred officers and every officer fires two cartridges in training a year (at $30.00 each), the company receives $6,000.00 in additional sales.

Further, departments become convinced that if they don't follow the company's recertification protocols the department opens itself up to additionally liability. This is not true. A training program properly developed by an individual law enforcement or corrections agency reduces liability as effectively as a company certification program, in some cases even more so. Law enforcement agencies do not use a firearms qualification course developed by Glock, Smith and Wesson, or Colt. Departments develop their own firearms training programs. This has not resulted in additional liability.

When evaluating commercial recommendations, keep in mind a private company's first and foremost concern is profit, not department and officer liability.

I am not saying that the makers of commercially produced subject control devices do not provide useful information about their products. Their background and technical information will help you identify the possible negative consequences of their deployment. Further, it is important for an officer to understand what makes oleoresin capsicum, Taser shocks, and ballistic projectiles effective use of force options. Consequently, a manufacturer's technical information should create the foundation for a department's training programs for chemical, electronic, and impact weapons.

It has been my experience that departments which develop their own training programs in chemical, electronic, and impact weapons incur less liability than departments who mindlessly adopt a commercial program. One reason why they incur fewer lawsuits is that when a department develops a specific program it does so with specific goals and application restrictions. Another reason why department training programs are more effective in minimizing liability is that they are more adaptable.

With a department-developed program, you can quickly make adjustments based on the identified problems in the field. You are not confined by a rigid, one size fits all, monolithic program. The last reason, and probably the most important, is that when an instructor develops his or her own training program the instructor develops a deeper understanding into the program's technical applications. As a result, the instructor more clearly and effectively conveys the program's goals and application to the student officers.

In evaluating a department's training program, review the program's training materials for completeness and outdated information. The lesson plan should document the information presented and the drills and exercises performed during the training sessions. In addition, the lesson plan should state the program's safety rules and protocols. A current bibliography or at least a resource list should accompany the lesson plan. This will allow you to determine the origin and the validity of the information.

Performance objectives should drive the content of the program and the student evaluation process. Further, you should review the program's Power-Point presentation and audio/visual aides for appropriateness. A review of the training materials will give you a preliminary understanding of the program. However, a face-to-face discussion with the instructor will give you a better understanding of the instructor's training philosophy.

And, of course, there is no substitution for personally observing the training sessions. I am not saying you need to observe each and every session. But, I do recommend you evaluate each session at least once throughout the inservice training cycle. Your presence at a training session is important on two levels. First, your physical presence sends a message to the troops that you are interested in the quality of the training they receive. Second, you have to be present to evaluate the instructor's performance and the quality of the training. You cannot appreciate the high qualify of the instruction or the innovation of the program if you are not there to witness the training.

Training Delivery

The evaluation of how training is conducted is important for minimizing liability in the field and for the safety of the officers in training. All instructors who conduct training do so with the best of intentions. However, as I have mentioned previously, they are full-time officers and part-trainers. As a result, they often do not see the potential consequences of their training decisions. That is why you are there.

Liability occurs from training in two ways: The officers are intentionally or unintentionally trained to perform an action that creates liability in the field. Or, an officer or an instructor is injured during training.

Previously, I had given you an example of how improperly conducted academy training had created liability for a sheriff's department. In summary, while attending the basic academy, the deputies had received training in conducting domestic violence investigations. As part of that training, the deputies participated in a dynamic domestic violence-training scenario. During the scenario, the deputies illegally forced their way into the simulated apartment. Even though there was an instructor evaluating the deputies' performance, the deputies were not corrected on their mistake. The instructors were more concerned with tactical mistakes than unlawful actions. As a result, the deputies graduated from the academy and made the same mistake in the field. However, this time their unlawful entry resulted in a civil rights lawsuit.

The problem with this situation was not only the part-time instructors' inattention to detail or the deputies' unlawful actions. The underlying problem that caused the department's liability was the academy's lack of interest and oversight of the training program. If the lieutenant in charge of the basic training program had personally evaluated the training scenarios, he would have learned what my review of the program discovered. The concept behind the training was valid, but the delivery of the training was flawed.

In a large county correctional facility, the training officers developed a training exercise to place their deputies in a simulated hostage situation. This sounds like a valid training endeavor doesn't it? Unfortunately, the training officers did not pre-warn the deputies that the hostage situation was a simulation.

Further, the hostage situation took place in a visitation room with real inmates and civilian visitors. As the deputy in charge of the visitation room was letting in the visitors, an armed gunman took him hostage. The gunman told the deputy to kneel down. The gunman put the muzzle of his handgun against the back of the deputy's head and told the deputy he was going to be killed.

The deputy pleaded for his life in front of the inmates and visitors. Next, the deputy heard the hammer of the revolver cock. The deputy was certain he was taking his last breath. Then, he heard the click of the hammer as it fell on an empty cylinder. The hostage-taker laughed, slapped the deputy on the back, and told him it was a training simulation. The deputy filed a workman's compensation claim, medically retired, and successfully sued the department for negligence.

Proper management oversight of the department's training programs would have prevented this tragedy. The instructors' intentions were sincere. However, the development and the delivery of the training scenario were misguided to say the least. If the mid-manager responsible for the department's training division had taken an active interest in the department's training programs, the manager could have taken the necessary steps to ensure the scenarios were properly developed and conducted.

As you can see not only is the content of a training program's curriculum important, but the manner in which the training is conducted or delivered is of equal importance. When evaluating your department's training programs, keep this in mind: Training does not minimize liability. Valid training that is effectively and safely delivered minimizes department and officer liability.

Training Documentation

One area where plaintiff's attorneys probe when looking for weaknesses in an officer's defense is the officer's training. The first documents they examine are the officer's evaluation forms and inservice training records. At the training level, the officer's performance is documented on an evaluation lab sheet. Although the format and the criteria vary depending on the skill area being evaluated, there are two common lab sheet mistakes that plaintiff attorneys exploit: A numerical rating system and negative instructor comments written on the lab sheets.

A common lab sheet design problem is that a numerical or descriptive performance scale rates the officer's performance. In the numerical scale, the number "one" represents the poorest performance possible and the number "5" represents the best, with "3" representing an average performance. In a descriptive scale, the officer's performance is rated subjectively by words such as "poor," "average," "above average," "superior." The problem with using a sliding scale as a performance rating system is that it allows the plaintiff's attorney to argue that if your officer had achieved a level of skill that merited a "superior" rating and not an "average" rating the officer would not have injured the plaintiff. This common sense argument is difficult to rebuttal.

You can eliminate this problem by creating lab sheets that only document the officer's successful completion of a task or the failure to correctly perform it. Stated more plainly, the evaluation should be pass or fail. The following are examples of pass or fail lab sheet elements:

CAT-01: Correctly defend against an
   edged weapon attack.   Demo___ /No Demo___
BAT- 01: Correctly demonstrate
   a forehand baton strike.   Demo___ /No Demo___

The second common mistake made when using lab sheets is writing negative performance comments in the narrative section of the lab sheet when the officer has successfully demonstrated the skill. It is not only acceptable to describe the officer's performance deficiency in the comment section when the officer fails to properly demonstrate the skill–it is required. However, when an instructor writes negative comments on a lab sheet where the officer passed the test, the plaintiff's attorney will question the validity of the performance criteria that your department uses to evaluate the officer's performance. Here is an example:

VO-01: Demonstrate the ability to safely negotiate a curve at high-speed.
Demo: X̲

Comment: Student repeatedly failed to align the patrol car into the outside lane when setting up an outside/inside cutting of the curve's apex while negotiating a curve at high-speed.

After this officer goes back on patrol and fails to negotiate a curve and kills an innocent person in a high-speed pursuit, can you imagine the field day a plaintiff's attorney will have with that comment? Now, maybe, the officer's cornering technique was not bad enough to fail him. How is your city or county counsel going to argue that defense effectively?

An officer's inservice training record is an area that can be vulnerable to the plaintiff's attorney's attack on an officer's credibility. The issue at trial is often not that the officer did not receive the training in a specific area, but the department cannot prove that he received it. You know the old law enforcement adage: If it is not written down, it didn't happen. That saying could have been coined by a mid-manager after being cross-examined by a plaintiff's attorney regarding an officer's training records.

The problem almost always rises out of blocks of inservice training documented as "___ hours of inservice training" in the officer's training record. The way you remedy this problem is to document every topic and the topic's hours that an officer receives during a block of inservice training. Training officers are really good at specifically documenting topics that stick out as potential liability problems: firearms, SWAT, use of force, baton, pepper spray, Taser. But, they often overlook the equally important, but not as glaring, liability issues like effectively dealing with the mentally disabled, the emotional disturbed or mentally ill, the physically disabled, or crisis intervention.

Listing every topic and its hours on an officer's training record will proactively prevent the plaintiff's attorney from alleging that the officer lacked the training necessary to prevent the plaintiff's injuries or death.

As a middle manager in a criminal justice organization, you are the lifeblood of the department. First-line supervisors come to you for direction and guidance and your administrator relies on you to make sure the right things are getting done and things are getting done right.

Then, to pile more on your responsibility heap, I have told you that to proactively manage department and officer liability you are required to network with risk management, consult with civil defense attorneys on liability trends, and receive feedback from prosecutors regarding your officer's performance.

Further, I have recommended that you critically examine operational and use of force policies, evaluate existing and future use of force options, and review the department's training programs for potential liability.

I even had the audacity to poke fun at you for spending too much time in the office and not performing enough managing by wandering around. If you do all that, you will be one busy mid-manager, but your proactive efforts will pay big dividends in reducing department and officer liability and creating positive public relations.

In the next chapter we discuss the criminal justice administrator's role in managing the use of force incident. The previous chapters have outlined what is required to proactively manage the use of force incidents within your department. As the boss (or, if you are one of those stuffy blue blood types—as the chief executive officer), you are ultimately responsible for the manner in which your department manages its use of force incidents. Consequently, in the next chapter—to assist you with that task, I will explain the three administrative areas that you directly control in the proper management of the use of force incident: leadership, organizational culture, and policy.

Chapter 11

MANAGING THE USE OF FORCE
INCIDENT FOR ADMINISTRATORS

I share your fate.
−Alexander the Great, Crossing the Gedrosian Desert

A s an administrator, by the position that you hold in the organization, you are a manager of budgets, facilities, and resources. The management of things is not a difficult task and it comes with little professional or political jeopardy. An administrator's headaches, gastrointestinal problems, and public relations nightmares are not caused by things; they are caused by the people within the organization.

The reason administrators suffer from these problems is that they treat their officers as if they were chess pieces on a board. If you managed only inanimate objects and no officers, you would not have citizen complaints and civil rights lawsuits. But you don't. Criminal justice organizations are made up of people. Diverse groups of people with all the foibles and flaws that make us human. However, regardless of age, culture, education, or gender there is one intangible trait that human beings are drawn to and will rally behind: Leadership.

In my criminal justice career, I have worked under fifteen sergeants, three lieutenants, three captains, two chiefs, two sheriffs, four assistant directors, and eight administrators. They all were good managers, but only four of them were leaders: Jay Waterbury, Dick Robert, Bill Garland, and Tom Potter. I mention their names not to gain favor, but to call attention to their ability to bring out the best in their people.

The administrator's primary role in properly managing the use of force incident is to bring out the best in the troops through his or her personal leadership skills. When an administrator brings out the best in his or her officers, use of force incidents are properly managed, liability is minimized, and frivolous lawsuits are won.

There are hundreds of good leadership books (and a few great ones) available to an administrator who desires to enhance his or her leadership abilities. Additionally, private companies, government agencies, and institutions of higher learning offer criminal justice management courses and leadership seminars as well. Because of the vast amount of management information available, it is relatively easy to peruse the latest trends in leadership philosophy and wisdom. However, applying leadership theory to a real world criminal justice workplace will be one of the more challenging endeavors you will ever undertake as a public safety administrator. Many try, but very few truly succeed.

Where most leadership training falls short for the criminal justice administrator is that it is developed by civilians for civilian employees—not cops. As a criminal justice administrator, you don't herd lambs; you lead lions. To effectively lead a criminal justice organization, you must think back to what you respected as a patrol, line, or field officer: courage, dedication, technical skill, and warrior ethos. Consequently, providing effective leadership to a criminal justice organization will require you to seek out a historical heroic leader to emulate—not in accomplishments, but in character and leadership qualities. Realizing this, when I obtained a leadership position, I chose Alexander the Great as my leadership archetype.

Alexander the Great became king of Macedonia at the age of twenty. He unified Greece in less than two years after becoming king. Alexander invaded and conquered Asia Minor, Egypt, Mesopotamia, the Middle East, the Persian Empire, Afghanistan, Sogdiana, Bactria, and invaded India in a ten-year campaign that covered 10,000 miles.

By the time he was thirty-two years old, Alexander had conquered the known world. On Caesar's thirty-second birthday, he wept because he had only accomplished a fraction of what Alexander had at thirty-two. However, these accomplishments alone are not the reasons why I admire Alexander as a leader. What I find most extraordinary about Alexander the Great is that he accomplished all this with a democratic army. The Macedonian military machine was a volunteer army. His troops voluntarily walked 10,000 miles, fought major battles, crossed deserts, and braved unimaginable hardships. I believe that if Alexander can inspire that level of loyalty and commitment from his troops he has something to offer leaders of criminal justice organizations.

Alexander the Great led by example. He traveled at the head of his army. Alexander led every charge and always fought visibly from the front. He was wounded by every weapon, three times nearly fatally. Alexander shared the hardships of his troops: slept cold and ate sparingly. He insisted that the wounds of his soldiers be treated before he agreed to receive medical treatment. As equally impressive, Alexander knew the names of 10,000 of his soldiers (Kurke, 2004).

Alexander's life is blanketed with leadership examples, but there are two in particular that stand out among the others.

Midway through his military campaign Alexander's Macedonian troops refused to venture further. They had been away from their country and families for years, endured hardship, and injury. Finally, the glory of conquest had lost its allure. On a hill, they informed their leader they were headed back to Macedonia. In response to this mutinous revelation, Alexander climbed to the top of the hill, ripped open his shirt to expose the numerous scars from his battle wounds, and looked down at his army. Then, he spoke: "I have led every charge, been wounded by every weapon, refused to have my wounds treated before you were cared for, endured every hardship as you have, and asked nothing of you that I would not do myself. If you want to go back, then go. But, is this how you reward me for my bravery and sacrifice?" When Alexander had finished his oration, his troops rushed forward and begged his forgiveness. Alexander's troops went on to follow him into India before they asked to cease campaigning again.

After Alexander had defeated King Porus at the River Hydaspes in western India, his Macedonian soldiers informed Alexander that they would push no further into India and they expressed their desire to return to Macedonia. Knowing that he had pushed his troops to the limit, Alexander turned his army around and headed back to Babylon.

In an effort to gain additional geographical knowledge, Alexander took a different route home. This route took his army though the Gedrosian Desert, one of the most inhospitable deserts on earth. Halfway though the desert, the army ran out of water. At that point, it became obvious that all would die in the desert. As an act of loyalty and admiration for their leader, the soldiers emptied every last drop of water from their canteens into a silver helmet and presented it to Alexander. They would die, but there was just enough water for their leader to survive. In front of the admiring masses, Alexander poured the water out of the helmet and onto the desert's sand floor. As he did, Alexander conveyed to his troops, symbolically, that their fate was his fate. They would either all walk out of the desert together or die to together. Alexander would live or die by his leadership principles.

I can only imagine the inspiration that his troops felt from that one resolute act. But, inspire them it did. Alexander and his troops walked out of the desert nourished only by the power of his leadership.

If after reading Alexander's exploits you are considering rallying your troops and invading Canada or Mexico, you missed the leadership lesson.

The power of leading by example to motivate people to accomplish more than they believe possible cannot be overstated. Administrators of criminal justice agencies do not need to undertake epic journeys or endure life-threatening challenges to lead and motivate their troops by example. With the modern law enforcement work force, it is the subtle displays of courage, caring, and sacrifice that motivate today's modern warriors.

One afternoon as two officers were preparing to testify as defendants in an excessive force federal court trial, they received an unexpected visitor. The officers and their attorney were discussing their testimony in a conference room at the federal courthouse when their police chief entered unannounced.

The chief was new to the police department. He had recently retired as a commander from the Los Angeles Police Department to become their chief of police.

The chief walked over and shook the officers' hands. He looked them in the eye and told them that they had done everything right in the incident and, regardless of the jury's verdict, they had his and the department's complete support. Then, the chief slapped them on the shoulders and left the room.

The officers were dumbstruck. At no time prior had a police chief from their department ever expressed his or her support for an officer during a civil rights trial. This single act of compassion and support from the leader of their department bolstered the officers' morale and enhanced their performance as defense witnesses on the stand. As a result, they won the lawsuit.

Officers don't need parades, bands, banners, or banquets to feel appreciated. They need five minutes of your sincere support to make a difference in their performance. The chief, whether he was aware of it or not, was managing by wandering around. He wandered into that conference room, made a difference to those officers, and wandered out. He could not have done it better. He should not have done anything less.

Prior to accepting a position at the Oregon Police Academy, I had never experienced true leadership from an administrator. Commander Waterbury had demonstrated exceptional leadership at the patrol level. My assistant chief, chief, and sheriffs were all competent managers and fair administrators, but leaders they weren't. It was not until Director Richard Robert hired me that I experienced motivational leadership.

Director Robert was a former army officer and FBI agent. He had been the academy director for five years prior to hiring me. Dick had an expansive vision for the academy, and he understood it would take motivational leadership to turn his vision into an operational reality.

At anytime during the day, Director Robert would stop my office, inquire to how I was doing, and ask what he could do to make the academy a more effective training institution. Dick always had a few minutes to sit and talk. Then as quickly as he had dropped in, he would stand up, sincerely tell me what a great job I was doing, and disappear out the door. Dick did that to every training staff member.

On one occasion, Director Robert unexpectedly dropped by my office with a small cardboard box. The box contained a gold trimmed coffee mug with the academy logo etched on its face. Dick asked me to accept that mug as a token of his appreciation for the exceptional work that I had done for the academy. Twenty-three years later, I still have the mug and that fond memory. Then (as now) because of Director's Robert's inspirational leadership, I would gladly pour my last drop of water from my canteen into a helmet for Dick Robert. Will your troops do that for you?

After Dick Robert left the academy, a manager who had no criminal justice experience replaced him. Consequently, the academy staff and students suffered from his lack of experience and leadership for ten years. When I started at the Oregon Academy, we conducted five basic police and corrections classes of twenty-four students per class, per year. Eleven years later, we were conducting thirteen basic police and corrections classes of fifty-five students per year—with the same number of full-time staff. We were drowning, and it was apparent that our director didn't care. Don't get me wrong, I loved what I did at the academy, but it was an extremely stressful environment. Consequently, the stress started to take its toll on the training staff.

One day a corrections lieutenant made a failed attempt at humor. An overly sensitive student was offended and filed a complaint with the governor's office and a discrimination lawsuit against the academy. When the student's attorney issued a press release accusing the academy of bigotry, the news media hammered us relentlessly. The governor ordered an investigation. As a result, the director, a corrections captain, and the corrections lieutenant were forced to retire.

I still have the newspaper article reporting the investigation's findings. "Bigotry is not the problem at the Oregon Public Safety Academy, management is." The headline told the tale. Stay with me, I am getting to the leadership lesson. But, I have to lay the groundwork, first. The lieutenant and captain were not bigots. In fact, they were the most politically correct members of the staff. However, the effects of long stressful hours had made them careless. Their fate was the director's fate.

While the academy staff was being bashed about by the waves of negative newspaper articles, the governor called a meeting of the entire academy staff–janitor to deputy director. We convened in the boardroom. As we sat in our huddled mass, the governor came into the room. The governor was a former Oregon hippie who had gone to medical school, became a doctor, and then a politician. He was a very likeable guy. When he was not at the legislature, he dressed in western boots, blue jeans, cotton-collared shirt, and a sport coat. His whole casual look was topped off with seventies' collar lengthened salt and pepper gray hair.

The governor strolled in with his trademark easygoing charm. He told us that the powerful people knew that the academy's problems were the result of a stressful workload, too few resources, and not a reflection of the staff as a whole. Further, he promised that his office would find the fiscal and human resources to improve our work environment. Then, the governor looked at us and said with a completely straight face: "On my worst day, when I have been fighting with the legislature, confronted with huge budget problems, and I can't make anyone happy, I return to my office and close my door. I put my feet on my desk. I close my eyes. And I say to myself: It could be worse. I could work for the Oregon Public Safety Academy." It was hysterical. I don't think I have ever laughed as hard. It was a brilliant stroke of leadership genius. With that short, poignant, humorous antidote, the Governor demonstrated that he understood our pain.

While the governor's office was deciding what to do with the academy, the governor appointed Tom Potter as the academy's interim director. Tom is the retired chief of the Portland Police Bureau. As chief, Tom earned a respected reputation as a visionary and a progressive leader when—by the shear force of his will—he changed the Bureau's heavy-handed culture to one that embraced community policing. Tom had agreed to come out of retirement to act as our interim director for ninety days.

On Tom's first morning at the academy, he called for an all-staff meeting. As we had done with the Governor, the staff sat in a large protective mass in the boardroom waiting for his entry. The academy's deputy and assistant directors had arranged VIP seating in the front of the room for themselves and our new interim director. As the academy command staff nervously stood by their chairs, Tom strolled into the room. Chief Potter had a very confident, but affable presence. He had a warm and friendly manner, but you could tell that by the way he carried himself that he had the heart of a lion.

When Tom entered, he stopped and surveyed the room. As he did, the Deputy Director called out to him: "Here Tom, we have reserved a seat up front for you." Chief Potter looked over at the vacant seat between the directors and then looked back at us. "Thanks for the offer, but I think I will set back here with the staff," he replied. And he took a seat next to our janitor. That one statement coupled with a subtle but symbolic act sent a message to the directors and the staff that could not have been louder if it had been shot from a cannon. Our new interim director cared about everyone on the academy's staff, not just its upper echelon.

Much to our surprise at the conclusion of our first all-staff meeting, the boardroom doors opened and carts with food entered. Tom had arranged a catered luncheon for the staff at his own expense. I learned more about being a leader from Tom Potter in a two-hour staff meeting than I had in ten years from our previous director.

Overnight, the atmosphere at the academy changed from one of despair to one of excitement and motivation. You could feel the enthusiasm radiate throughout the academy. But, it was short-lived. An attorney with no management or leadership experience replaced Chief Potter as our permanent academy director.

This may not be news to you, but I discovered that attorneys (although smart people) can make lousy public sector executives. I have worked under an academy director who was an attorney and two attorney generals–they sucked as leaders. They were narcissistic and self-absorbed. Narcissist and leader are diametrically opposing states of being. Effective leaders care deeply about their followers. You will notice I used the term "followers" because true leaders have followers. Narcissistic bureaucrats have drones and subordinates and lots of union grievances.

The previous narratives illustrate two very important leadership points. First, there is a distinct difference between being a leader and being a manager. Leaders motivate their officers through their supportive actions, gestures, and genuine expressions of caring. Managers only expect compliance with the rules; consequently, they see no need to motivate their officers. (As a conversation I had with one chief of police demonstrates.) During a discussion about his officers' low morale, the chief actually told me: "If morale is low on the department, it is not my problem." Well, drones don't need high morale to follow orders. But officers do to self-initiate properly managed use of force incidents.

The second point is that if you don't take care of your officers they won't take care of you. A poorly managed, high profile, use of force incident has been the cause of more than a few administrators' forced retirement or termination. All too often, your officer's fate is your fate.

Organizational Culture

> *Either you manage your culture, or it will manage you.*
> –Roger Conners and Tom Smith, *Journey to the Emerald City*

An officer's use of force decision is directly influenced by the culture of your department. In their book, *Journey to the Emerald City,* Roger Conners and Tom Smith make the following observation about organizational culture:

> Every group of people, from street gang to a church choir, from a family to a nation, has a culture. If the group's leaders have not created it, perhaps some informal leaders or "influencers" have. Or, perhaps the culture has developed willy-nilly, for better or worse. Every organization has a culture. The only question is whether or not that specific culture is effective in creating the results those people want.

As the administrator of your organization, you are responsible for creating the operational culture within your department. Nature abhors a void. The same can be said of human nature. If you do not create the culture for your department, it will create its own.

In every corrections or law enforcement agency, there are potentially two cultures—the cultural represented by your department's mission statement, press releases, policy statements, and public relations activities; and, the culture that manifests itself in the way your officers conduct themselves. Sometimes the two cultures are one and the same; more often, they are not. In fact, it was this contrast between the two cultures that was the impetus for the creation of the national Police Corps program.

The Police Corps was enacted into law as part of the 1994 Clinton Crime Bill. The bill received national attention for putting 100,000 more police officers on the street. What received very little attention was that the bill included the creation of a new law enforcement training program based on the military's ROTC program.

Adam Walinsky initially conceptualized the Police Corps in the 1960s. At that time, Mr. Walinsky was an attorney for the U.S. Department of Justice and Robert Kennedy's speechwriter. In the early 1990s Adam wrote the Police Corps legislation and he was instrumental in getting the bill passed by the United States Congress.

In 1996, I was tasked with the creation of the first national Police Corps' academy curriculum and the management of the first Police Corps Academy program. On a July morning in 1996, I was putting the finishing touches on the Oregon Academy's new sixteen-week basic police program's curriculum when I was summoned to the director's office.

When I entered his office, I observed a manic director. He told me that we had an extraordinary opportunity: The Oregon Public Safety Academy was asked to create the prototype program for the first national Police Corps training academy. The federal government would give our academy over nine hundred thousand dollars to develop the academy's curriculum and train the Police Corps' first twenty officers. The director asked me if our academy was up to the challenge. I told him I believed we were. "But, there is a catch. The State of Virginia had been tasked first with the development of the Police Corps Academy two years ago, and they only have 50 percent of the program completed. Can we develop the program in three-months?" He asked. "Sure, if we had the right resources," I answered. "That's what I wanted to hear," he said as he shook my hand. As I left and returned to my office, I wondered how my captain, Bill Garland, would react to this new opportunity.

I had been called to the director's office because Bill was off the academy grounds. As the lieutenant in charge of the basic police program, the director believed I would be the next best person to consult. When Bill returned to the academy, the director briefed him on our new program.

A very red-faced captain appeared in the doorway of my office. I believe his first words were: "What the hell were you thinking?" I told him that we could develop the Police Corps program with the proper resources. "Ok, wise-ass. You said we could do it. The Police Corps project is all yours," he said grimly.

I discovered later that the Police Corps legislation required that the first academy class be conducted before late November. Further, I learned the reason why Oregon was selected to develop the Police Corps program: In 1994, all the states that held gubernatorial elections elected republican governors except Oregon. As a result, the Clinton administration had warm fuzzy feelings for our liberal Democrat State.

Captain Garland not only assigned me the responsibility for the development of the Police Corps academy he empowered me to do so. Without being empowered to make critical decisions over the allocation of resources and control the budget, I would not have been able to complete my assignment under the designated time constraints. Bill knew that when you empowered people they could be held more accountable for their performance or lack there of. I was fully aware that Bill had given me a professional opportunity of a lifetime, the authority to succeed, and the autonomy to be solely responsible for its success or failure.

Adam Walinsky flew out from New York and met with the command staff of the sponsoring agency, Captain Garland, and me at the academy. Adam explained that the Police Corps was conceptualized to create a more ethical and professional police officer. Adam's research discovered that it was a police department's true culture, not the public relations culture, which was at the core of police excessive force and misconduct. Further, he explained that the Police Corps was designed to make true community policing officers by inoculating them with the values of their communities.

Adam believed that by placing new police recruits in a high-stress environment that consisted of advanced physical training, mentoring by the best senior officers, leadership training, community service, and lectures given by college professors on the demographics of their communities, the Police Corps could circumvent the negative effects of a department's culture. This high-stress environment was to be created by compressing twenty weeks of training into sixteen; the students would work twelve hours a day, six days a week.

The Police Corps, in its conceptualized form, was to be initiated at the high school level. A senior in high school would apply for sponsorship to the Police Corps through his or her local law enforcement agency. As a department-sponsored Police Corps recruit, the student would receive $30,000.00 in college financial assistance. During the summer of the recruit's junior/senior college year, the recruit would attend a two-month Police Corps Academy. The following summer after graduation, the recruit would finish the last two months of the academy and return to his or her sponsoring department as an employed police officer. If the officer successfully completed five years of police service, the $30,000.00 loan was forgiven.

During our meeting, the command staff expressed their concern about hiring Police Corps graduates, employing them for five years, and then have them quit their department. The command staff told Adam that they believed it took an officer on their department at least five years before the officer was fully functional. Consequently, one commander asked: "Why would our department want to hire Police Corps officers?" Adam answered his question with a series of questions: "How many people in the United States House of Representatives have law enforcement experience?" We did not know. "None," he answered. "How many in the Senate?" "None," he answered his own question as he looked at our blank stares. "Don't you think it would be of benefit to your department if someone on your city council or county commission had law enforcement experience? What about having a Supreme Court justice who actually pulled dangerous criminals out of a car at gunpoint? Do you think that law enforcement experience would positively influence the justice's ruling on search and seizure?"

I was starting to understand, and I was in awe. Adam continued his explanation: "You think your department does community policing? This is community policing–making the community part of the police and making the police part of the community." The commanders just sat there without a rebuttal. What I treasure most about my Police Corps experience is that I had the honor and privilege to work closely with such a brilliant visionary.

Because we didn't have six years to cultivate Police Corps recruits, the decision was made to accept recent college graduates, with criminal justice degrees, from Oregon and Washington into the first two Police Corps Academy courses. In the first two academy courses, the students started their day at

0600 hours for mandatory physical fitness training. The students attended academy training from 0800 to 1700 hours. From 1800 to 1900 hours, they received advanced defensive tactics training. They finished out their last three hours with one of four training sessions: leadership training, a mentoring session, a lecture on community demographics, or a discussion of police ethics. In addition, the recruits were required to participate in community service activities on the weekends.

The students were worked so long and hard that for their safety we had medical personnel monitor their physical condition. Through this monitoring, we discovered that the students were losing dangerous amounts of weight. To ensure their nutritional needs were being met, we had specifically developed meals catered in to them.

The stress academy environment was designed to have a 25 percent failure rate. And the first two courses did. In both courses, we started with twenty students and only graduated sixteen. I had no previous military experience. The academy that I attended was run like a community college, not a boot camp. So, as I entered into this project, I was very skeptical about the benefits of a high stress, paramilitary academy. At the end of the first academy course, I was a religious convert to the benefits of a high stress academy. If I were emperor, there would only be high stress Police Corps academies. Students that I had early on identified as the better quality recruits fell completely apart midway through the academy. Those who I identified as slow starters were the ones I considered exceptional at graduation. The Police Corps taught me that anyone can play the game under less stressful conditions, but high stress causes the cream to rise to the top.

Adam's research discovered what all cops already knew. That by having a moldable police recruit ride around in a patrol car with a tainted field training officer the abusive police culture was passed on from one generation to the next. As a result, this cycle would continue on indefinitely until there is a cultural intervention. It was Adam's hope that by forging new recruits in a disciplined, ethical, and community oriented policing training environment that they would develop the character and self-discipline to resist a department's abusive culture. Unfortunately, Adam and his colleagues underestimated the level of influence that a department's culture can have on new officers.

Although the Police Corps provided its recruits with incredible training, it failed as a rehabilitative solution to a department's "us versus them" culture. It was a conversation that I had with one of my first Police Corps graduates that made me realize the Police Corps had failed in this endeavor.

Approximately two years after the officer had graduated from the Police Corps Academy, the officer was involved in a high profile use of force incident that resulted in the suspect dying in police custody. Officers responded to a report of a mentally man causing a disturbance on a street corner. The man fought with police, he was handcuffed, and laid on his stomach. The man stopped breathing and died on the corner with his neighbors watching. To make the situation worst, the officer's department had decided to stop providing CPR training to their officers prior to the incident. The news media had a field day with the mentally ill man's death.

I was teaching a defensive tactics instructor course at the same location the officer's department was holding their forty-hour inservice training session. As I walked across the parking lot one morning on my way to class, I ran into my former Police Corps Academy student. This officer had been an exceptional student. I believed, without a doubt, if any officer could resist a hyper-aggressive police culture this officer would be the one. As we stopped to talk, I asked the officer what brought him to the training center? The officer stated that he was there for his department's forty-hour inservice training. Being the flippant ass that I can be, I sarcastically asked: "Are they going to give you CPR training?" He knew exactly why I asked. A sinister smirk cracked across his face and he replied: "I tried to kill that son-of-a-bitch with my baton. Why would I want to give him CPR?" I realize at that moment the Police Corps had accomplished many great things, but inoculating young officers to a department's culture was not one of them.

Every law enforcement and corrections organization has it own culture. Subsequently, as the administrator of your organization, you can proactively create and mold that culture or let it mutate and evolve on its own. If you abdicate your leadership responsibility to mold your organization's culture, then you will be acted upon by a culture that you do not control.

To create or change an organizational culture to one that minimizes department and officer liability and properly manages use of force incidents requires the adherence to the following leadership tenants:

- Establish a vision for your department. Not just a mission statement. But, a meaningful vision for what you want your department to be. Your vision should be your legacy. Then, make that vision known to very member of your department. At any point in time, I should be able to ask any one of your officers what your vision is for the department and that officer should be able to describe it me. I don't care whether you have five officers or five thousand, every officer should be able to explain your vision for the department on demand. An administrator's articulated vision is essential for the development of a healthy organizational culture.
- Establish specific values for your department and articulate those values to your officers. If you don't define and articulate what values you

want your organization to represent, the organization's officers will establish their own. These values need to be demonstrated and driven downward from you, your commanders, and your first-line supervisory staff to the troops.

- Establish a zero tolerance for resistance to your vision and values for the department. Commanders and supervisors who do not share and foster your vision and values should be replaced with those who do. To change or develop an organization's culture requires enthusiastic support from your management staff. Lukewarm support only brings about unsatisfactory results.
- Reward those who embrace your vision and organizational values. If supporters and nonsupporters alike receive equal treatment, there is no motivation to change their organizational belief system. Change takes effort. Effort should be rewarded.
- Establish policies that reflect and support your vision and organizational values. Take swift corrective action when those policies are violated. Behavioral corrections that are delayed are ineffective in changing organizational culture.
- Manage by wandering around. See for yourself that your vision and values are being promoted by your command staff and supervisors. Always scratch below the surface. Trust, but verify. If you don't, you will discover too late that the organization's culture has not changed.
- Lead by example. Pour the water out of the helmet in front of your troops. Lead from the front. Ask no one in your department to do anything that you will not do yourself. Operating with a double standard, one for management and another for the troops, breeds a culture of contempt for management and creates saboteurs of your administration. This contemptuous culture will metastasize in the form of an increase in citizen complaints and excessive force lawsuits.

If you follow these tenets, you will positively influence the department's culture. As a result, you will have fewer citizen complaints, properly managed use of force incidents, and reduced department and officer liability.

Use of Force Policy

> *Poorly written and outdated policies are what keep me up at night.*
> −Robert Wagner, Attorney, Personal communication, 2010

Leadership, culture, policy, and training are the tools that administrators have to minimize department and officer liability. In this chapter we have discussed the importance of leadership and organizational culture in liability management. In Chapter 12, you will gain insights into the role that training plays in minimizing liability. In this last section, we will explore the role that policies play in properly managing the use of force incident.

Administrators, liability management experts, and risk management people place too much emphasis on the role that policies play in liability management, especially use of force policies. An example of this overemphasis is illustrated in the city attorney's reaction to a $1.8 million jury verdict for the family of an unarmed man who was shot and killed by two police officers. The jury found both officers liable for excessive force. The jury awarded slightly more than $1,000,000.00 to the family for their loss. Another $800,000.00 in punitive damages. With attorneys' fees, the total cost of the award will likely exceed $2,000,000.00. The city attorney's response? "Obviously there was a tragic result in this case. So, that's a continual process. And, the police department is continually evaluating their use of force policies." The city attorney's response is the traditional bureaucratic reaction to a defense loss: "It can't be that our officers made a bad use of force decision. It has to be those damned use of force policies!"

The reason for this focus on policy as the solution? Tradition. Law enforcement is a traditional institution. It has and will always be governed by a top down, command and control, management philosophy. If an administrator has an operational, personnel, or liability problem, the administrator's first inclination is to issue a policy. For an example: if an officer fails to tie his shoestrings, trips and falls, injures himself, and files a workman's compensation claim, thirty minutes after that claim has been filed a policy will appear in every officers' mailbox directing them to tie their shoestrings. Do you really think that a policy on tying shoestrings would have prevented an on-the-job injury like this? Of course not, but writing a policy is the only thing that an administrator has control over. And control is very important to policy-makers and bureaucrats.

The other reason why policy wonks place so much emphasis on use of force policies in the management of liability is that it is the easiest path to walk. It is also the least effective. Law enforcement agencies have issued use of force policies since Moses wielded a straight stick. If policies were effective in preventing lawsuits, litigation would not be at epidemic proportions. It takes little effort to sit in your office or attend a policy meeting and pencil out a policy or two. It is a lot easier than providing leadership and taking control of your organization's culture.

I know that when you read those sections you said to yourself: "Holy crap, that seems like a lot of work." Effectively leading an organization is hard work, but that is why you are the highest paid person on your department.

Just because it is a commonly held belief that the more money you make the less you do, it doesn't mean you are obligated to turn that perception into reality.

There is an old saying among academics, bureaucrats, and policymakers: "Weight is truth." The thicker and heavier the document, the truer the information contained within it. This is specifically true when it comes to department policies.

Because criminal justice agencies have a pathological need to control even the most miniscule activities of their officers, policy manuals resemble supersized astronaut training manuals. The same can be said about use of force policies. Most use of force policies contain unnecessary background and technical information, terms and definitions, and in an effort to cover all bases, information that makes the policies vulnerable to attack by plaintiff's attorneys.

There is a misconception held by writers of use of force policies that the thicker and heavier the policy the more defensible it will be. This could not be farther from the truth. A use of force policy is an administrative document, not a substitution for meaningful use of force training. The background and technical information, terms and definitions, and most of the operational information regarding a use of force option is more effectively explained in a training session.

You can drone on and on in your policy manual about everything from what color socks to wear to how many officers can take a break together; there is no jeopardy in writing voluminous policies on most operational topics. Behavioral guidelines are necessary for the effective operation of a department. However, use of force policies will be challenged at trial during a civil rights lawsuit. Consequently, use of force policies need to be focused, direct, address only the most critical issues, and written with the fewest words possible. When it comes to writing use of force policies, lean is mean to plaintiff attorneys.

Use of force policies fall into two categories: conceptual and regulatory. Conceptual use of force policies address the use of deadly and nondeadly force in general terms. Conceptual use of force policies are vaguely written to give the officer's attorney the maximum amount of defensive space to maneuver. Conversely, regulatory use of force policies place restrictions on a use of force option to minimize the risk associated with the force option's deployment. If you want to develop defensible use of force policies, criminal justice civil defense attorneys recommend you do the following:

- When reviewing, revising, and developing conceptual or regulatory use of force policy consult with your legal counsel: your city or county attorney or insurance authority/company attorney(s). They are professional litigators who are responsible for defending your policies. It is just common sense that they should be involved in the policy development or review process.

- Do not place a force continuum chart, a list of use of force options, or other specific reference material in a conceptual use of force policy. The important term is "conceptual" use of force policy. Use of force training should be specific; use of force policy should be stated in general terms. Placing a force continuum, levels of force, and lists of force options in nondeadly and/or deadly force policies do not make the policies more effective, but they do provide the plaintiff's attorney with a framework to challenge an officer's use of force decision.

- State only the restrictions mandated in *Tennessee v. Garner* in a deadly force policy and the guidelines mandated in *Graham v. Connor* in a nondeadly use of force policy. The U.S. Supreme Court recognized that there are too many variables in the use of deadly and nondeadly force by corrections and law enforcement officers for the court to mandate specific force options. You couldn't have a better example to follow than the court that actually established the use of force standards. The further you deviate from the Supreme Court's language the more rope you give the plaintiff's attorney to hang your officer. When writing deadly and nondeadly force policies resist the temptation to put your own spin on the Supreme Court's concepts and verbiage.

- Do not write more than is absolutely necessary in a use of force policy. Verbiage is to a plaintiff's attorney is as gasoline is to a flame. The more gas you feed the flame the worst you get burned.

- List only the most imperative restrictions in a regulatory use of force policy. The more requirements and restrictions you place on less-than-lethal and less-lethal force options the greater chance your officer will violate the policy. Policy violations damage an officer's defense. Accordingly, only the prohibitions that are critical to managing the liability of the force option should be placed in policy. All other requirements should be addressed in a training session.

- Do not state time frames in regulatory use of force policies. For example: Don't state, "An officer will provide medical care as soon as possible." Do state, "An officer will provide medical care." Don't state, "An officer will check on the suspect's physical condition as soon as possible." Do state, "An officer will check on the suspect's physical condition." Stating time frames in your policy allows the plaintiff's attorney to argue that the officer violated department policy by waiting too long to perform a required activity; consequently, the officer's policy violation caused the injury or further injury to the inmate or suspect.

The most important elements in a use of force policy may be stated in a section not longer than a paragraph in length. However, most use of force policies are weighted down with philosophical statements before the policy addresses the actual application of force.

This philosophical prelude is written for cosmetic reasons to appear sensitive and politically correct to the ACLU, the city council, and any paranoid schizophrenic who believes the cops are out to get him. I understand the political necessity for a warm and cuddly philosophical statement that tugs at the heartstrings, but I believe you should put most of your intellectual energy into crafting defensible policy statements for the proper use of deadly and nondeadly force.

Here is an example of a standard politically correct philosophical policy statement:

> "The use of force by this department's personnel is a matter of the utmost concern both to the community and the criminal justice profession. Throughout their day, officers are involved in numerous and varied citizen encounters and, when required, they may use force to carry out their professional duty. Officers must have an understanding of, and a true appreciation for, the appulse of their authority—particularly with respect to the civil rights of those with whom they come in lawful contact. This law enforcement agency recognizes, respects, and values all human life and dignity without bias regarding age, culture, disability, ethnicity, gender, race, religion, or sexual orientation. Further, this agency has given deep consideration to the empowerment of its personnel regarding the authority to use reasonable force to protect the community, as this authority requires a careful balancing of all human rights and community interests."

Now, doesn't that philosophical rhetoric make you feel all warm and fuzzy? Sure. But, how does it regulate an officer's use of deadly and nondeadly force? It doesn't. Because it is not written for a criminal justice audience. Philosophical pontifications like this are written for civilians to make them feel better about the use of force, which is often brutal, disturbing, graphic, and ugly.

> The following is an example of a problematic use of force policy. The vulnerable areas are italicized:
> This policy recognizes that the use of force by department personnel is of the utmost importance. Even at its lowest level, the use of force is of serious concern to the community. The purpose of this policy is to pro-

vide officers with an understanding of the objectively reasonable use of force.

It is the policy of this Department that officers shall use only that amount of force, which reasonably appears necessary, given the facts, and circumstances perceived by the officer at the scene to effectively control a situation. "Reasonableness" of the force is judged from the perspective of a reasonable officer on the scene at the time of the incident. *State law allows an officer to use physical force upon another person only when and to the extent that the officer reasonably believes it necessary to make an arrest or to prevent the escape from custody. Or, for self-defense or to defend a third person from the use or immediate use of physical force.* (This narrowly defines an officer's authority to use force. What about the use of force to detain a suspect for investigative reasons?)

Given that it is impossible to predict every possible situation that an officer may encounter, it is acknowledged that each officer must be given the latitude to use well-reasoned discretion in determining the appropriate level of force. ("Well-reasoned discretion" cannot be defined.)

While it is the main objective of every police/citizen encounter to minimize injury to the officer and the citizen alike (officers are not required to only use the level of force that minimizes injury), this policy does not require an officer to sustain an injury before applying physical force. As previously stated, the application of force by a member of this department must be judged by the standard of "objective reasonableness" and not "20/20 hindsight."

When determining what level of force to apply, an officer should consider officer versus suspect factors and influential circumstances. Those factors or circumstances should include, but are not limited to:

- *Officer versus suspects factors: age, size and strength, combat skill level, gender, and multiple suspects.*
- *Influential Circumstances: inability to disengage or confinement, close proximity to a weapon, injury or officer exhaustion, officer at ground level, terrain or environment, previous experience, special knowledge, officer disability, distance, or sudden attack.* (Some of these factors or circumstances may limit an officer's use of force when the factors are reversed.)

The department recognizes that an officer is expected to make split-second decisions under tense, uncertain, and rapidly evolving circumstances. And, the dynamics of the situation may impact an officer's decision. While an officer has access to various force options, every officer is expected to respond with only the amount of force which is objectively reasonable given the information known at the time, from the perspective of a reasonable officer at the scene, to successfully accomplish the lawful criminal justice goal in accordance with this and other related policies.

Nondeadly Force Policy: When deploying nondeadly force, an officer shall consider the severity of the crime at issue, whether the suspect poses an immediate threat to the safety of the officers or others, and whether the suspect is actively resisting arrest or attempting to evade arrest by flight. *This policy guideline applies to all use of force, including deadly force.* (This guideline only applies to nondeadly force.)

Officers have a number of force options available for use in those situations where force is reasonably necessary. The degree of force used by an officer is directly related to the facts or circumstances encountered by that officer. The force options that are available to officers on this department are as follows. (Officers use any number of force options that are not listed. Examples: head lock and football tackle):

- *Voice commands*
- *Chemical agents*
- *Physical controls*
- *Impact weapons*
- *Electronic restraint device*
- *Neck restraint*
- *Impact projectiles*
- *Deadly force*

Deadly Force Policy: An officer is authorized to use deadly force whenever it appears to the officer that there is no reasonable alternative under the following circumstances: (Officers are not required to exhaust reasonable alternatives prior to using deadly force–*Plaskas v. Drinski,* 1994.)

- To protect the officer or others from what is reasonably believed to be a threat of death or serious bodily harm.
- To prevent the escape of a fleeing violent felon who the officer has probable cause to believe will pose a significant threat of death or serious physical injury to the officer or others.
- *Prior to using deadly force an officer must also reasonably believe that all other reasonable alternatives for apprehension or prevention of escape have been exhausted.* (Not legally required under *Tennessee v. Garner.*)
- Where practical prior to discharging a firearm, *officers shall identify themselves as police officers and state their intent to shoot.* (Required to only issue a verbal warning and deadly force can occur from more than a firearm.)

At their best, deadly and nondeadly use of force polices are benign. They don't add to your officer's defense, but most importantly, they don't hurt your officer's defense. Attorneys are masters at playing word games. If you try to match wits with one, you will lose. So, the best strategic defense regarding policy composition is the less the information written into the policy, the better. The more extraneous information you place in a use of force policy, the more ammunition you give the plaintiff's attorney to shoot holes in your officer's defense.

Civil defense attorneys prefer limited and cleanly written use of force policies. The following are examples of defensively written nondeadly and deadly force policies:

> ***Philosophical Statement:*** It is the policy of this department to respect the constitutional rights of all people. As a result, officers shall only use the level of force that is objectively reasonable to control a lawfully detained person; effect a lawful arrest; prevent an arrested suspect from escaping; control a dangerous, resisting, or violent person; and to protect the officer or others from the immediate use of nondeadly or deadly force.

> ***Nondeadly Force Policy:*** An officer may use objectively reasonable nondeadly force to detain a lawfully stopped person, overcome a person's nondeadly physical resistance, effect a lawful arrest, prevent an escape from custody, and/or protect the officer or others from the immediate threat or use of nondeadly force. An officer will consider the following when determining the appropriate level of nondeadly force to employ:

> * The immediate threat to the officer or others.
> * The severity of the crime committed.
> * Whether the person is resisting arrest or attempting to escape.

> ***Deadly Force Policy:*** An officer may use deadly force to protect the officer or others from the immediate threat of death or serious physical harm.

> In addition, an officer may use deadly force to prevent an escape of a suspect when the officer reasonably believes the suspect has committed a crime involving the use or threatened use of serious physical harm or death.

When reasonable, an officer must issue a verbal warning before using deadly force.

Use of force policies that are written in this fashion are based on federal law, easy for an officer to understand and apply, and impervious to a plaintiff attorney's attacks and challenges.

In addition, if your department policy regulates the firing of warning shots, shooting at occupied and/or moving vehicles, or the shooting of injured animals, I recommend you place those policy restrictions in your firearms' section of the policy manual. This keeps the focus of your use of force policies on the federal standards governing the use of deadly force.

Regulatory use of force policies are developed to establish operational guidelines and restrictions for the department approved deployment of a specific use of force tool or option, such as: baton, chemical agents, pepper spray, electronic control device, impact munitions, concussion munitions, neck restraint, and the police dog. It is not uncommon for criminal justice agencies to have regulatory use of force policies that exceed ten pages in length. Obviously, the developers of these lengthy policies failed to recognize that the average officer is required to remember and apply all that information on demand in the field. Taking this into account, I will caution you as a purveyor of policy to restrict your regulatory use of force policies to two component parts: restrictions on the application and the operational procedures.

The importance of a properly developed regulatory use of force policy can be seen in a lawsuit that settled out of court for $2,000,000.00. The suspect died after being shocked for 54 seconds with a Taser. The attorney for the slain man's family, said the size of the settlement shows that the city understands "that there are serious and significant issues with respect to the department's policies and training."

In determining what information to include in a regulatory policy, you should ask yourself the following exploratory questions:

- Is the inclusion of specific terms and their definitions required for the accurate interpretation of the policy?
- Are there different applications for the force option? If so, do they need to be defined?
- What restrictions on deployment are necessary to limit liability?
- Is it necessary to mandate training or a certification?
- Are there specific care and handling requirements?
- Are there specific post-deployment requirements?
- After deployment, are their specific evidence collection protocols?
- How is the deployment be documented?
- What are the supervisory responsibilities, if any?
- Are there any specific consequences to a policy violation?

The following are two examples of regulatory policies. Each department utilizes its own policy format. Consequently, the headings that are contained within the body of the policy are used for illustrative purposes only.

Electronic Control Device

Policy: It is the policy of this department to authorize the use of an electronic control device (TASER®). An electronic control device (ECD) is a neuro-muscular disruption weapon that provides subject control through neuromuscular incapacitation. The ECD is considered a nonlethal use of force. This department only authorizes the use of the TASER" X-26 electronic control device.

Officers are not authorized to draw or display the ECD, except during authorized training or on duty, where the circumstances create a reasonable belief that it may be necessary to deploy it.

Application: There are six separate types of ECD application that require documentation:

Spark Test: An approximate one-second test of the ECD's ability to conduct electricity and to verify that it is functioning properly. The test is conducted with the air cartridge removed.

Spark Display: A noncontact demonstration of the ECD's ability to discharge electricity. This demonstration is conducted with the air cartridge removed. The spark is displayed in an attempt to convince the subject to comply with a lawful order and avoid the application of the ECD.

Probe Deployment: The deployment of the two ECD probes, resulting in the partial or total neuromuscular incapacitation of the subject.

Drive Stun: The application of electricity through the direct contact with ECD electrodes to the subject's body, after the air cartridge has been expended or removed. The Drive Stun is effective as a pain compliance technique only.

Drive Stun Intimidation: The direct contact with ECD electrodes to the subject's body (after the air cartridge has been expended or removed) in an attempt to convince the subject to comply with a lawful order and avoid the application of the ECD.

Visual Deployment: The pointing of the ECD at a subject, with or without the laser sight activated, in probe deployment mode. The ECD is displayed in an attempt to convince the subject to comply with a lawful order and avoid the application of the ECD.

Target Areas: Rear torso, lower abdomen, limbs. The ECD should not be intentionally deployed to the head, neck, face, groin, or upper chest.

Duration of Application: The ECD may be deployed when a subject is actively resisting arrest or displaying threatening or violent behavior. Officers should not deploy the ECD for more than five seconds per cycle.

Restrictions on Deployment: The ECD will not be used:

- On a passively resisting subject, in probe mode.
- To subdue a subject who is fleeing a misdemeanor offense, unless the subject has shown a propensity for violence or is an immediate threat to the officer or others.
- When the subject is in a location or position where a fall may cause substantial injury or death.
- When a subject is restrained in mechanical restraints (handcuffs, nylon restraints, restraint chair or similar device), unless the subject is harming him/herself or another; or lesser force options have been ineffective.
- Sadistically, maliciously, as punishment, or for coercion.
- To escort a subject.
- To awaken an unconscious or intoxicated subject.
- On a visibly pregnant female subject or if informed the subject is pregnant, unless deadly force is justified.
- On an elderly subject, unless deadly force is justified.
- On a physically disabled subject, unless deadly force is justified.
- On a child under fourteen years of age, unless deadly force is justified.
- In an environment that contains flammable material or vapors or when the officer knows a subject has come in contact with flammable liquids.
- For crowd control, to disperse a group of individuals, or deployed indiscriminately into any group.

The ECD should not be used under the following circumstances, unless there are compelling reasons that justify its deployment.

- When the subject is operating a motor vehicle or other dangerous equipment.
- When the subject is holding a firearm.
- When deadly force is clearly justified and then only when Lethal Cover is available to protect the officer and others.

Training: Officers must successfully complete a departmentally approved ECD training program before being authorized to carry and deploy an ECD. Officers must annually attend a departmentally approved ECD update training session to maintain their authorization to carry and deploy an ECD. Officers are required to possess a current CPR and first aid certification prior to being authorized to carry an ECD.

Equipment: Officers who are authorized to carry and deploy the ECD shall be issued a Taser® X-26, two cartridges, a department approved holster, and alcohol wipes and bandages. Supervisors shall issue replacement cartridges as needed. An inventory of available and issued cartridges will be maintained by cartridge serial number.

Maintenance: At the beginning of the officer's shift, the ECD shall be inspected for damage and cleanliness and the batteries and cartridges will be replaced as needed. Officers will conduct a spark test at the beginning of their shift outside of public view. ECDs that fail the spark test or that have 20 percent or less of a battery charge will require the battery pack to be changed.

Carriage: Uniform officers will carry the ECD in a department-approved holster. The holster will be carried on the duty belt, on the opposite side of the duty firearm. The ECD may be carried in a drop holster on the strong-side thigh, with department approval.

Record Keeping: The ECD's internal record program will be synchronized with the department computer's date and time. If ECDs are assigned by shift and not to specific officers, each officer will document the ECD carried at the start of each shift: paper log, notebook, CAD, as designated by the department. Each time the ECD is activated the activation will be documented in a report, notebook, or CAD entry, as designated by the department.

The department will establish an ECD download schedule–the length of time between downloads is dependent on the frequency of use. The administrative supervisor will maintain a file for each ECD's activation log.

Probe Removal: Officers shall remove ECD probes from a subject in manner consistent with their training. Recovered probes shall be treated as biohazard sharps and packaged as evidence in the manner described in the evidence section of this policy.

Medical Treatment: Officers shall summon medical personnel when:
- More than three cycles of the ECD were effectively deployed to a subject.
- The ECD probes are embedded in the subject's face, neck, groin, or a female subject's breast area.
- The ECD probes appear broken off and possibly embedded in the subject.
- The subject was injured or rendered consciousness.
- The subject appears dazed, confused, or incoherent.
- The subject requests medical attention.

Evidence Collection: Officers shall collect all available forensic evidence after an ECD deployment. The areas where the electrodes or probes contacted the subject's body–whether there are or aren't visible marks–will be photographed. The spent air cartridges, blast doors, or AFID tags will be photographed in the location where they were found and collected as evidence. The probe wires in the condition and location where they were found will be photographed. To protect the condition of the probe wires, officers will not coil the wires around the cartridge, but fold the wires into six to eight-inch lengths and package them as evidence. The ECD's activation record will be downloaded and printed out. A copy of that record shall be submitted with the officer's written report.

Documentation: Every time the ECD is deployed (Spark Display, Probe Deployment, Drive Stun, Drive Stun Intimidation, Visual Deployment) a report shall be written. The report will state:

- The method of deployment: Spark Display, Probe Deployment, Drive Stun, Drive Stun Intimidation, or Visual Deployment and why the officer chose that method of deployment?
- The location(s) of the probes on the body or area(s) Drive Stunned, or touched. How many times the subject was shocked and why?
- The factors or circumstances that were considered prior to the deployment.
- The other levels or types of force that were used prior to the ECD.
- The composition of the surface the person hit after the free fall and objects impacted. If medical was called? The names of the EMTs.

Supervision: Supervisors will evaluate their officers' ECD deployments to determine if it was within policy guidelines. Supervisors are to ensure that their officers' reports are complete, the required photographs were taken, and the ECD evidence was collected and properly packaged.

The information contained in the previous example policy was developed from a sampling of contemporary TASER® policies and my litigation experience involving the use of the TASER®.

It is very interesting to observe the evolution in ECD policy development. In the early days of the Air Taser's deployment in the field, departments' ECD policies primarily focused on the operation and maintenance of the device. There was little, if any thought given to restrictions on its application. Nor did policies address documentation and evidence collection. The contrast between the early ECD policies and the policies of today is a testimonial to the importance of proactively identifying potential liability and operational problems prior to the implementation of a new force option. The evolutionary changes that have occurred to departmental ECD policies are reactionary responses to unanticipated liability problems.

Even though every negative consequence cannot be foreseen, the actions that were the impetus for the restrictive changes in contemporary ECD policies could have been forecasted if administrators had followed the recommendations presented in the previous chapters.

Another predictable liability issue that looms on the horizon is the lack of department policy regarding an officer's carry and use of a tactical folding knife. If you allow your officers to carry tactical folding knives on or off-duty, you should have a policy that regulates its carry and usage.

If an officer possesses a weapon, it is just a matter of time before that weapon is deployed. Consequently, to minimize your department's liability, you should have a tactical folding knife policy and provide your officers with legal and technical training in the deployment of the tactical folding knife as a law enforcement weapon.

To assist you in proactively minimizing your department and officer liability regarding the carry and deployment of the tactical folding knife, the following example knife policy is provided.

Knife Policy

Policy: Officers are authorized to possess and use a fixed blade and/or tactical folding knife on-duty. It is recognized that an officer may have many needs for such a tool while on-duty: general work and as a defensive weapon. While not an optimal weapon in a lethal force situation, an officer may use a fixed blade knife or tactical folding knife to defend himself or herself or others from immediate serious physical harm or death.

Blade: An officer may carry a tactical folding knife, fixed blade knife, or both types of knives. The blade length is defined as the sharpened edge of the blade. Any tactical folding knifed carried on-duty will not have a blade length longer than five and one-half inches. Any fixed blade knife carried on-duty will not have a blade length longer than seven inches. The blade of a tactical folding knife and a fixed blade knife may have a double-edged cutting surface.

Mechanism: An officer may carry on-duty an automatic, spring-assisted, or manually opened tactical folding knife.

Carriage: A fixed blade knife carried on-duty by an uniformed or non-uniformed officer must be housed in a sheath and carried concealed.

A tactical folding knife carried on-duty by an uniformed or nonuniformed officer must be carried in a manner that obscures the presence of the knife. In addition, the tactical folding knife must be carried in a location where the officer can access the knife with either hand and from any position.

This policy does not apply to a tactical folding knife or fixed blade knife that is carried by an off-duty officer. However, off-duty officers are required to conform to all local and state laws and/or ordinances that apply to the carrying of edged weapons.

Special Units: Special investigative, enforcement, and tactical units may have specific needs for different or larger cutting tools. Therefore, at the discretion of the appropriate supervisor, an officer of a special unit may carry specialized edged weapons or cutting tools while performing his/her duties. This supervisory exemption must be granted in writing and the document granting the permission must be placed in the officer's personnel file.

The tactical folding knife has become standard carry equipment by criminal justice officers. As a result, you should take the deployment of the knife as a defensive weapon as seriously as you do the officer's firearm. Because the edged weapon is not viewed by the public as a traditional law enforcement weapon, it is predictable that an incident involving an officer's use of an edged weapon in self-defense will receive sweeping media attention, criticism from civil rights activists, and scrutiny from city, county, federal, or state officials. Proactively having your administrative ducks in a row, will help stave off a potential public relations and liability catastrophe.

As an administrator, the information provided in the previous chapters is pertinent to your efforts in evaluating potential liability and establishing and implementing the policies and protocols for properly managing use of force incidents by your officers.

In the next and final chapter, we will discuss the role that training plays in reducing department and officer liability. In addition, the chapter will provide an overview of the first nationally recognized scenario-based-use of force training model–a program that may reduce your citizen complaints by 85 percent and lawsuits by 80 percent.

Chapter 12

USE OF FORCE TRAINING

Traditionally, criminal justice use of force training has been conducted as academic endeavor. Normally, but not always, the instructor is an attorney, and the presentation mainly consists of an explanation of appellate court case law, Supreme Court rulings, and state statutes. Although an intellectual discussion of federal and state law is necessary to establish a foundation for the proper application of force, it is not very effective in minimizing officer or department liability. Primarily because the discussion of the legal restrictions placed on police use of force is theoretical in nature.

Officers do not use force in a theoretical hypothesis; they use real force, on real people, in the real world. Consequently, to train officers to properly manage use of force incidents, minimize liability, and win lawsuits, academies and departments need to change the methodology by which they train their officers. Stated more succinctly, they need to stop treating use of force instruction as a purely academic endeavor and teach it as an integrated applied science.

Effective use of force training consists of three component parts:

KNOWLEDGE. To properly manage the use of force incident, an officer must have a complete understanding of the federal court rulings that regulate the use of nondeadly and deadly force. I know you are saying duh! But you may be surprised to learn that it has been my experience, as a use of force instructor, that very few officers truly have a comprehensive understanding of the real world application of *Tennessee v. Garner* and *Graham v. Connor*. Further, federal case law is not static. It is constantly evolving to address the changes in use of force application and technology.

Consequently, to minimize liability, officers must be updated when the rules regulating the use of force change. Knowledge is not limited to only case law. To properly manage a use of force incident, an officer must have an understanding of the actions and behaviors that create officer liability and damage an officer's defense against allegations of misconduct and/or excessive force.

Further, an officer must possess the specific knowledge necessary to properly collect, document, and photograph the evidence of a use of force incident.

Additionally, an officer must have the knowledge that is required to properly explain and justify the officer's use of force in a written report, during an internal affairs interview, in a deposition, and on the witness stand.

INTEGRATION. In order for use of force training to be effective, it must be holistically developed and conducted. A major cause of officer liability is the segregation of use of force training into isolated training components. Baton, pepper spray, physical control techniques, electronic control devices, impact munitions, and force-on-force simulations are all taught as separate unrelated skills.

The effect of this fragmented training methodology is the production of officers who stubbornly stay with a force option that is clearly ineffective, then panic, and jump directly to the use of deadly force. The result of this unintentional conditioning is an increase in wrongful death litigation. To prevent panic induced liability, officers should be taught to transition from one nondeadly force option to another until the appropriate nondeadly force options have been exhausted and deadly force then becomes necessary to stop an unarmed Threat.

Further, the integration of handcuffing into baton training, pepper spray training, Taser training, and force-on-force simulations should occur. In the real world, the use of force does not end after the instructor gives the command to "stop." Ultimately, the use of force incident ends with the Threat handcuffed. Many a lawsuit could have been avoided if the officers would have quickly transitioned to handcuffing after the Threat had been temporarily incapacitated through the use of nondeadly or deadly force.

SIMULATION. Excessive force lawsuits are not filed, lost, or settled because the officer used a specific level of force; lawsuits are filed, lost, and settled because the officer made a bad use of force decision. Based on this simple, but poignant truth, it is strategically smart to conduct training that focuses on an officer's use of force decision-making abilities. The most effective way to evaluate and improve an officer's use of force decisions is to conduct scenario-based use of force training.

The most common simulation training methods are conducted one dimensionally: force-on-force with AirSoft, paintball, or Simunition®; video firearms training simulators; baton and weaponless technique training utilizing the Redman or Hitman simulation training suits. Although these simulation methodologies have value, most offer little in the way of improved use of force decision-making, properly managing the use of force incident, and officer and department liability management.

For a training program to enhance an officer use of force decisions, promote the proper management of the use of force incident, and minimize officer and department liability, the program must be three dimensional, integrate simulated nondeadly and deadly force options, and be scenario based.

The previous eleven chapters have explained in detail the knowledge that is required for criminal justice officers, of any rank, to properly manage the use of force incident. In the following three sections, we will discuss training safety considerations, how to properly develop and conduct integrated use of force simulations, and the benefits of a scenario-based use of force training program.

Training Safety

As a criminal justice instructor, I have a personal philosophy regarding the training of officers: The training will not benefit the officer if he or she does not survive the training. Accordingly, when I develop a training program, I always weigh the potential training value of an exercise against the potential harm to the officer. Harm to an officer can occur in a training exercise from poor supervision, carelessly conducted training, or the direct application of force.

There is a trend in less-than-lethal technology training to expose officers to the effects of the force option. Officer exposure simulations gained acceptance with the adoption of pepper spray by criminal justice agencies. There are legitimate and compelling reasons for exposing officers to the effects of pepper spray. An officer may have to fight through the effects of pepper spray after being accidentally sprayed by an officer, exposed to an O.C. contaminated environment, or disarmed and sprayed by a Threat during a violent encounter. For officer survival, officers must know that they can fight through the effects of pepper spray to control a suspect or inmate, transition to other nondeadly force options, and fire their handgun accurately—if required for the officer to survive a violent attack. By any standard, these are compelling reasons for spraying officers during training.

However, the positives must be weighed against the negatives. Officers have received chemical burns to their faces and suffered detached retinas to their eyes from pepper spray exposures during training. These injuries are infrequent but, nevertheless, they occur. Most chemical burns from pepper spray do not cause permanent skin damage, and the eye injuries that do occur are the result of the violent tensing of the officer's facial muscles that cause a detachment of a weak or partially torn retina. When the potential for an officer injury is compared to the potential benefits of a pepper spray exposure during training, I believe that officer survival trumps the possibility of a superficial injury or an aggravation of a pre-existing condition.

The other training program that integrates an officer exposure exercise is Taser International's electronic control device training program. In my opinion, there are no legitimate, compelling reasons for shocking an officer in probe mode during training. The theoretical justification offered is that the exposure bolsters an officer's defense during excessive force litigation. Theoretically, an officer's testimony that he was not injured after receiving a Taser shock during training demonstrates the noninjurious nature of the electronic control device. It is an erroneous argument that being shocked is a legitimate excessive force defense for the following reasons: When the officer received the shock during training, a probe didn't hit the officer in the eye. The officer wasn't shocked multiple times. At the time of the shock, the officer was not a chronic drug abuser, under the influence of narcotics. In addition, the officer didn't free fall and hit his or her head on the cement. So, you can see the folly in this ridiculous justification for shocking officers during training.

The primary reason for shocking officers during training is marketing, and it has been a brilliant sales pitch. It did not take a vast amount of marketing research to discover cops love this stuff. We get paid to come together as a group, see everyone grimace, wet their pants, and fall over. As a bonus, we videotape the exercise–for a future showing at our Christmas party. Then, when the class is over, we have a beer together and laugh about being shocked. What could be better? Sure, it is a great time if you survive the training. However, officers sometimes do not survive the shock unscathed. Here are a couple of examples:

In one training accident, the officer fell off the mat and banged his head on the cement floor after being shocked. As a result of the training injury, the officer suffered short-term memory loss.

In another training-related accident, an undersheriff was shocked during training. When the undersheriff received the shock, he was kneeling on a training mat and supported by a deputy on each arm. The Taser shock dislocated both his shoulders, broke his shoulder sockets, and broke both humus bones in his upper arms. The physician who treated his injuries told him that his injuries were classic electrocution injuries.

The undersheriff had been shocked before during training. He volunteered to be shocked again as a leadership example. The undersheriff wanted to demonstrate to his troops that he would not ask them to endure anything that he was not willing to undergo himself. The undersheriff was in good health, early thirties, physically fit, and one of my defensive tactics instructors at the Montana Law Enforcement Academy.

His department sent the X-26 unit back to Taser International for evaluation. They determined the Taser did not malfunction.

It was first believed that he would be medically retired. However, he was able to return to active police work a year after his physical rehabilitation.

So, give me a compelling reason that justifies the potential medical retirement of even one good officer. I didn't think you could. But, for those of you who are dyed-in-the-wool believers in shocking officers during training, here are safety protocols that may minimize the potential for an injury:

- Tape the probes to a leg and pass electricity from the thigh to the calf. This will expose the officer to the neuromuscular incapacitation effect of the Taser, while minimizing the electrical current that is passed through the officer's body.
- Have a spotter on each side of the officer to prevent a free fall to the floor.
- Shock the officer in the center of a large matted area.
- Shock the officer in a kneeling position. This minimizes the potential for injury should the spotters be unable to prevent the officer from falling.
- Have medical personnel on stand-by at the training site.

Training injuries are not limited to an officer's exposure to chemical and electronic weapons. An officer became permanently blind in one eye during a baton training exercise. The officer was using a foam training baton to block the instructor's foam baton strikes. Even though the officer was wearing a protective helmet, a strike hit him in the eye.

Similarly, a deputy was blinded in one eye when he was shot with a paintball during a building search exercise. The deputy was wearing a makeshift protective visor.

In a patrol tactics class, a reserve officer received a thigh injury when another officer shot him at point-blank range with a blank cartridge. The shot blew a large hole in his thigh and exploded the keys in his pocket, driving shrapnel into his hip.

While practicing a neck restraint in defensive tactics class, an officer suffered a stroke. Pressure to the neck broke free a piece of plaque in an artery. It traveled to his brain and caused a stroke.

All the above incidents resulted in litigation against the instructor, the department, and/or the equipment manufacturer.

When I was a member of the Macho Redman Advisory Board, I traveled to conferences representing Redman®. Countless times while standing at the display booth, I would be approached by officers who would tell me: "We used to have a Redman suit, but the city manager took it away from us. We had too many training injuries." The injuries were not the result of using the Redman suit during training. They came from training with the suit that was poorly developed, improperly executed, and/or reckless.

Many training accidents can be avoided and officer injuries prevented through the liability evaluation process explained in Chapter 10:

Equation for Predicting Harm: situation + lowest common denominator = the worst possible thing(s) that could happen.

Equation for Minimizing Liability: the worst possible thing(s) that can happen + the proactively developed restrictions = liability reduction.

However, some training injuries are unforeseeable and not preventable. There are variables that an instructor has no control over: the level of the participants' physical fitness, pre-existing conditions that make a participant prone to injury, equipment failure, and freak accidents. Regardless of the variables you can't control, a common sense evaluation of a proposed training exercise can pay dividends in preventing officer training injuries and workman compensation claims.

Integrated Simulation

Because departments are prone to sending officers to instructor development training courses sponsored by companies that produce the force options, most departments adopt several individual training courses and teach them as unrelated training modules. Accordingly, ASP baton-training focuses only on baton training. Taser training covers only electronic control device application. Pepper spray training consists only of the application and decontamination of O.C. In arrest and control tactics training, only on the application of control holds and handcuffing are practiced. During counter assault tactics training, only hand, elbow, and knee strikes and kicks are taught and practiced.

With this compartmentalized training methodology, it is mistakenly assumed that an officer can take all these isolated skills and properly integrate them together under the pressures and stresses of the use of force incident. Of course officers cannot. Therefore, liability occurs in one of two ways: Under stress the officer fixates on the use of only one nondeadly force option. Then, after its repeated failure to control the Threat, the officer panics and escalates to deadly force. Or, the officer fixates on the use of only one nondeadly force option, but it only partially incapacitates the Threat. Having never practiced transitioning to another less-lethal force option or handcuffing a partially incapacitated Threat, the officer repeatedly applies the force option until the Threat dies or is seriously injured from its excessive application.

Not convinced you need to take an integrated approach to your use of force training? Here are three examples of what happens when you don't:

The Eleventh Circuit Court of Appeals ruled that the officers used excessive force when they tasered an unarmed man eight to twelve times in two minutes, causing his death. "We agree with the district court's determination that the force employed was so utterly disproportionate to the level of force reasonably necessary that any reasonable officer would have recognized that his actions were unlawful," the court concluded. The officer reported that she might have tasered the suspect eleven to twelve times. In her justification, the officer stated she kept pulling the trigger until the suspect stayed on the ground. The Taser activation log showed eight applications in two minutes. Each application lasted five seconds. At the hospital, the suspect was pronounced dead as a result of "being struck by a Taser," according to a forensic pathologist.

In another incident, the city settled a $2,000,000.00 lawsuit filed by the family of a man who died after being tasered. The suspect died after being shocked for fifty-four seconds. The officer reported that she inadvertently held down the trigger for forty-nine seconds. Then, shocked the suspect again for five seconds more. The medical examiner's office ruled the suspect's death as a homicide. The suspect's family filed a lawsuit against the officer and the police department, alleging the officer was improperly trained, and as a result, used excessive force.

A TriMet surveillance video camera recorded the shooting of a twelve-year-old girl with a beanbag shotgun by an officer. The video showed the primary officer take the resisting girl to the ground. Then, as the girl was pinned to the floor by the primary officer, the cover officer shoots her one time with a beanbag round. The girl was hospitalized from the shooting. After reviewing the video, the chief of police called the incident "troubling and not consistent with my expectations and what I believe are the community's expectations for a police officer."

Integrated use of force training can prevent excessive force complaints and wrongful death lawsuits. And, of equal importance, in incidents where deadly force is used, the transition to multiple nondeadly force options before using deadly force on an unarmed suspect creates a more defensible use of deadly force. It is not rocket science. It is just common sense.

Effective use of force training integrates the transition from the primary less-lethal weapon to other force options and handcuffing. This concept can be applied to all nondeadly force option training. We even integrated the transition to other force options in our law enforcement ground defense training program.

I first started the integration of force options when I developed the Oregon Academy's pepper spray training program. In fact, I titled the program:

Integrated Pepper Spray Training. In the original course, the officer was exposed to pepper spray and then engaged an instructor in a Redman suit. Under the influence of pepper spray, the officer delivered three knees, five practice baton strikes, and then high-risk handcuffed the instructor. After the instructor was handcuffed, the officer was led to the firing line where he or she fired six shots from a handgun into a target, preformed a tactical reload, and fired six more shots. Throughout the simulation, the officer was required to use the appropriate verbalization.

The reasoning behind the integration of focused blows, baton strikes, and the application of deadly force was based on a study that stated pepper spray is only 86 percent effective in controlling a Threat and field reports stating that officers are often contaminated during the use of pepper spray. As experience has shown, pepper spray is much more effective on cops than it is on crooks. Consequently, I wanted to train officers to transition to other nondeadly force options when pepper spray was ineffective in controlling a Threat under the worst conditions possible: respiratory impaired, partially blind, and experiencing extreme pain. Further, I wanted officers to know that they could—when nearly incapacitated—effectively deploy their handgun under the influence of pepper spray to protect themselves.

With the development of the Hitman suit, I was able to replace the live-fire component of the transitional simulation with the use of Simmunition® marking cartridges. The Hitman suit was the first simulation training suit developed for use with marking ammunition. The introduction of marking cartridges into the program made the training more realistic and effective. No longer was the transition to deadly force performed as a separate task. With marking ammunition, the officer could smoothly and realistically transition through all the force options.

I have used that program as a template for the integration of force options into all my nondeadly force training programs: arrest and control tactics, baton, counter assault tactics, electronic control device, extended range impact weapon, and ground defense. Regardless of the force option being trained for, the training methodology is the same:

Phase One: The training session begins with a discussion of the case law that regulates the application of the force option and where the option fits into the continuum of force. Next, the guidelines for evidence collection and documentation of the specific force option are reviewed. Finally, an overview of the motor skills aspect of the training program is given and the safety rules and protocols are explained.

Phase Two: If the officers are being trained on a new force option, the motor skill is taught in a building block fashion and practiced to build skill proficiency. If the training session is a review of a previously learned force option, its proper application is demonstrated, practiced, and the officers are evaluated for proficiency. At this phase, the application of handcuffing is taught and practiced after the use of force option has been applied. Further, multi-officer control and handcuffing is taught and practiced.

Phase Three: The transition from the primary force option to other nondeadly force options and the escalation to the officer's handgun is practiced. The officer practices to develop proper form, smooth transition, and to build muscle memory. Each transitional routine ends with the Threat handcuffed.

Phase Four: The officer transitions from the primary force option through the other nondeadly force options to the use of the handgun in a dynamic simulation. The officer engages an instructor in the simulation-training suit. The officer applies the simulated primary nondeadly force option and that option fails to stop the Threat. Finding that force option ineffective, the officer transitions to another nondeadly force option and that option fails. Then, the officer transitions to another nondeadly force option. When all available less-than-lethal options have proven ineffective, the officer escalates to deadly force via his or her handgun. After the Threat has been shot, the officer or the cover officers high-risk handcuff the Threat.

The following example will provide you with a clearer understanding of the transitional process in the integrated use of force simulation:

TASER SIMULATION. The officer pulls the Taser and orders the instructor to "Get on the ground!" The instructor continues to advance and the officer simulates deploying the Taser. The Taser malfunctions: a barb misses, the Threat breaks the wires, etc. The officer transitions to inert pepper spray. It is ineffective. The officer transitions to focused blows. The instructor is knocked to the ground, gets up, and advances on the officer. The officer transitions to the practice baton and delivers three to five baton strikes. The baton blows fail to cause the instructor to comply. The officer transitions to his or her handgun and simulated deadly force is deployed. The officer high-risk handcuffs the incapacitated instructor.

Your officers should complete several simulations. In some of those simulations, the instructor (role-player) should randomly comply after the officer has transitioned through one, two, or three force options. You want your training to mirror the real world application of force. In the real world, some suspects comply after the transition to another force option has occurred. Also, they comply when faced with the threat of deadly force. Officers should be trained to smoothly transition from one force option to the other as the circumstances dictate, not just follow a pre-scripted escalation of force.

Law enforcement officers and trainers have said for years that "the way you train is the way you react." However, for some reason, that admonishment has become just a hollow slogan for many trainers. For if law enforcement had truly embraced that concept, officers everywhere would be participating in integrated use of force training. Those of you that have embraced the concept of the integrated force option training are the exception and not the rule. Keep up the good work. It is a common misconception that training minimizes liability. The simple truth is that training does not minimize liability; effective training minimizes department and officer liability.

Confrontational Simulation

Scenario-based use of force training is the most effective training methodology for improving an officer's use of force decisions. Furthermore, it is the most effective training method for minimizing department and officer liability, reducing excessive force complaints, and winning excessive force lawsuits. Confrontational Simulation (Con Sim) was the first nationally recognized scenario-based use of force training model. When Confrontational Simulation was created and implemented at the Oregon Public Safety Academy and adopted by Oregon criminal justice agencies, excessive force lawsuits were reduced in Oregon by 80 percent. Furthermore, Oregon officers won more than 98 percent of the excessive force lawsuits that went to trial. When the Burbank (California) Police Department adopted the Confrontational Simulation program as their use of force training model, the department experienced an 85 percent drop in citizen complaints the first year. Do I have your attention?

Development

Twenty-three years ago I was hired by the Oregon Board on Police Standards and Training to manage the Oregon Police Academy's defensive tactics and use of force training programs. By accepting that position, I became the academy's chief defensive tactics instructor and the State of Oregon's use of force expert. As the state's use of force expert, I was responsible for reviewing excessive force lawsuits involving Oregon criminal justice officers and consulting with the officers' attorneys. Additionally, I was tasked with defending the officers' actions and use of force as an expert witness in state and federal courts and labor relations hearings.

After spending a year reviewing excessive force lawsuits and consulting with civil defense attorneys, I realized that in the majority of the use of force incidents that I reviewed the officers did not use excessive force. However, in 99 percent of the cases, the officers were unable to effectively explain their justification for their use of force. The officers intuitively made the right use of force decision. They just couldn't effectively articulate the reasons for it. Further, to make the evaluation process even more difficult, the officers wrote their use of force reports like incident reports. Consequently, their use of force reports contained simply who, what, and when—with little or no "why?" Unable to determine whether the officer's use of force was appropriate based on the information contained in the written report, the officer's attorney sent me the officer's deposition to review.

I found it extremely interesting that the officer would write a two-page use of force narrative report, but it would take over one hundred deposition pages for the officer to explain his or her use of force justification. In addition, I discovered that officers do not suffer excessive force litigation for using the wrong tactic or technique; they were sued for mismanaging perceptions at the scene and/or for making bad use of force decisions.

It was from these revelations that I realized the academy needed to change the way we taught use of force. I had already revised the academy's use of force curriculum. So obviously, it was not the content of the training that was the problem, but rather the way the training was delivered. It became crystal clear to me that putting officers in a classroom and discussing federal guidelines, force justifications, and the levels of force was not effective. I needed to think outside the conventional box to find an instructional methodology to improve our officers' use of force performance in the field. But, thinking outside the box is easier said than done. Then, I attended two training seminars that changed the way I view and conduct criminal justice training.

Dave Smith taught the first seminar. In his presentation, Dave told us that an officer's training experience directly affects his or her performance. And he used a brilliant example to illustrate his point: "If I told you that we are going outside and jog two miles on the next break, how many of you would be excited to do it?" Dave asked. No one raised his or her hand. "Your first response was—why am I being punished, right?" Dave went on to explain that we learn to associate running with punishment from school sports. When we made a mistake or did not put forth 100 percent effort, we were punished by running laps. Dave went on to explain that when officers have negative training experiences like being killed during training scenarios we condition them to fail in the real world. When I heard Dave's critique of contemporary law enforcement training, I thought to myself, "I've been there, and taught that." However, I never realized until that moment that I was doing more harm than good to the officers that I trained.

The second seminar dealt with adult learning theory. The presenter discussed several valuable concepts of adult learning theory. However, one struck a chord with me, and it would become the genesis for my scenario-based use of force training program. The research on adult learning had shown that when an adult learner receives information that is not applied within twenty-four hours of receiving it–the adult learner will lose 85 percent of that information after thirty days. This research explained why the academy's use of force instruction was ineffective. At that moment, I realized that officers needed to apply the use of force information that they received in the classroom within twenty-four hours in scenarios for the training to be effective. However, the challenge was how to make scenario-based use of force training effective, positive, and safe.

Around this time, Macho Martial Arts Supply had released its new Redman suit for purchase by law enforcement agencies. The Redman suit had been developed at the request of the U.S. Secret Service. The Secret Service wanted a protective suit that they could use for simulation training. With the development of the Redman® equipment, Macho expanded their market into law enforcement training. At that time, a law enforcement agency could buy a complete Redman suit for $300.00.

When I received an advertisement for the Redman® equipment at the academy, I knew I had found the solution to my safety concerns with scenario-based use of force training. However, I was not about to go to the Academy Director and ask for a $1,000.00 to buy Redman® equipment for a nonexistent training program. I believed, at that particular point in my career, it was easier to be forgiven than get permission. So, I asked my part-time defensive tactics instructors to pitch in fifty dollars each, and we purchased the Redman® equipment ourselves.

The academy had previously conducted training scenarios in domestic violence investigation and vehicle stops. In both those classes the manner in which the scenarios had been conducted caused liability for law enforcement agencies in the field. Furthermore, I had attended scenario-based training courses throughout my law enforcement career and I found them to be negative, inefficient, and ineffective.

In the courses that I attended, five things occurred: I spent most of my time waiting for my turn to participate in one scenario. When I did get to participate, a skilled instructor (who had previous knowledge about the scenario) killed me. I was only told what I did wrong, but not instructed in how to perform the task properly. I was not given the opportunity to correctly perform that task in the scenario. Therefore, I left the scenario as a loser and not a winner.

In my new scenario-based training program, these flaws would be corrected. There would be no time wasted waiting for a scenario; the students would be actively involved in each scenario through "observational learning." Students would not be intentionally set up for failure; the student would be corrected after each mistake, the scenario would be restarted, and the student would practice performing the behavior correctly. The student would have a positive learning experience with each scenario; the student would finish the training as a winner and not a loser. Additionally, in this new scenario-based training program the student would use simulated force in confrontational scenarios and be evaluated on the appropriateness of his or her use of force decisions. Accordingly, I decided to title this new program Confrontational Simulation.

By now, I was managing the Basic Police Program as well, so I had control over the basic police program's curriculum and schedule. However, I still had not informed the Academy's administration of what I was about to do. During this time frame, in the basic police curriculum, we were not providing the students with a hands-on building search exercise, primarily because the class was too large. In order to provide building search training, the class would have to be split in half. My new scenario-based use of force training program would be perfect for dividing the class into two groups. On a Friday morning toward the end of the basic police course, after the students had received defensive tactics, firearms, and vehicle stops training, I sent one-half of the class out to practice building search tactics and the other half to Confrontational Simulation.

The academy had a small isolated gym that the training staff referred to as the "utility classroom." It was never used, making it the perfect place to conduct a covertly developed training program. I asked my most trusted defensive tactics instructor (Don Oliver) to act as the first role-player (Redman). On that fateful morning, I grabbed the Redman® equipment, brought the students into the utility classroom, and started running confrontational scenarios. At the end of the day, having put fifty basic police recruits through the one hundred and fifty scenarios, I could see the benefit to what we had stumbled onto.

We had been conducting Confrontational Simulation for approximately six months. By that time, we have refined the program and our role-playing and evaluation skills to the point where the results had exceeded my wildest expectations. All this time, the academy administration had no idea that I was conducting this training. Then, one afternoon I received a telephone call from a television news station in Portland. The Portland Police Bureau had recently experienced a string of police shootings. Even though the shootings were justified, the shootings had tweaked the interest of the news media. Channel Eight wanted to do a news story on police training, with a focus on the use of force. Since I was the academy's use of force instructor, the reporter wanted to come to the academy and conduct an interview. In addition, she asked if the academy had any training that was visual and dynamic that they could videotape and use in their story. She was in luck, I told her. "We have a new use of force training program that is scenario-based and utilizes a red protective suit," I added. Three days later, the reporter and her cameraman were videotaping Confrontational Simulation.

The following week the story aired on the nightly eleven o'clock news. At 11:45, I received a telephone call at my home from the academy's deputy director. The conversation went like this: "Howard, I saw the new academy training program on the news tonight. It looks good. Hey, I just got a call from the director. He thought it looked good too. But, he wanted to know how long the academy has been offering that training? How long have we been doing that training?" The deputy director asked. "Not long," I replied. "That's what I told him. Good job! Keep up the good work." And, with that, the Confrontational Simulation program became the crown jewel of Oregon Public Safety Academy.

The program was added to the academy's corrections and parole and probation curriculums, as well. As the demand for the program grew, it because obvious that I needed to develop a Confrontational Simulation instructor program. Eighteen months from the day the first covert, experimental, Confrontational Simulation scenario was conducted, the Oregon Academy offered its first scenario-based use of force instructor course. One of the instructors who attended that course was Mike Janin, a training sergeant from the Beaverton Police Department.

Mike was an accomplished defensive tactics instructor and ASP baton instructor trainer. About a year after he attended the Con Sim instructor course, Mike was sent to Australia to teach an ASP instructor course. While preparing for his trip, the Australians asked Mike what other training programs he could teach in addition to ASP? Mike asked me if he could teach my Confrontational Simulation program to the Australians? I told him I would be honored to have the Con Sim program taught overseas. When Mike returned from Australia, he told me that my program was a huge hit. In fact the Australians liked it so much that, before he had left to return to Oregon, the Aussies had purchased $10,000.00 worth of Redman® equipment.

Aware that my Confrontational Simulation program created a demand for the Redman suit, I sent Macho Products a letter explaining that I had a training program that was increasing their sales. Further, my letter explained that the Con Sim program could market the Redman® gear as Monadnock and ASP marketed their batons through baton instructor courses.

Macho Products responded to my marketing proposal by stating that the company was not interested in providing training. However, they were in the process of establishing a Redman Advisory Board, and they offered me a position on it. The new board was to make improvement recommendations for the Redman® equipment. Also, as an advisory board member, I would travel to national law enforcement conferences to promote their training gear.

During my time as a member of the Redman Advisory Board, Simunition® introduced their marking ammunition to American law enforcement trainers. Believing that marking ammunition was the next innovative improvement to law enforcement training, I recommended to Macho Products that they change the covering of the Redman suit to allow it to be shot with marking projectiles. Or, at least, develop a protective jumpsuit that could be placed over the Redman suit. As with my marketing proposal, Macho Products did not see the value in modifying the Redman suit to allow for the integration of marking ammunition into Redman® simulation training.

With Macho Products' blessing, I started conducting Confrontational Simulation instructor courses outside of Oregon. As I traveled to other states to introduce my program, I was surprised at the number of agencies that had experienced officer injuries during what they termed "Redman® training." As part of my introduction to the Confrontational Simulation program, I told the attending instructors that I had personally trained over 5,000 officers using the Con Sim program without injuring a single student. At a Con Sim instructor course held at the Phoenix Police Department's academy, I had a Burbank Police Department defensive tactics instructor in attendance. During the first break, Brian Arnspieger introduced himself. Brian told me that his department had purchased over thirty Redman suits, and they had just concluded their "Redman® training." During our conversation, Brian told me that during their recent Redman® training sessions they injured fourteen officers and permanently disabled two. So, naturally, he was interested in how I had prevented officer injuries from occurring in my use of the Redman suit.

I explained to Brian that the Con Sim program was not a defensive tactics-training program. It is scenario-based use of force training. Consequently, when the officer has made his use of force decision and deployed it, the scenario is stopped. Officers are not allowed to struggle on the ground. Further, Con Sim instructors are trained to allow the officer to "win" in the scenario. The training is restricted to use of force decision-making and justification, only. And the safety protocols are strictly enforced. As a result, the training is extremely safe.

Brian is an extremely talented instructor. Consequently, after completing the instructor course, he implemented the Con Sim program in its entirety at the Burbank Police Department with spectacular results. According to Brian, the department experienced an 85 percent drop in citizen complaints within a year of the implementation of the Con Sim program. Because of the program's success, the Burbank Police Department went on to sponsor several Con Sim instructor courses.

A few years later, Macho Products sent a Redman® brochure to DHB Armor Group. DHB Armor is the parent company of Point Blank and Protective Apparel Corporation of America (PACA) body armor companies. Further, DHB owned NDL Products. NDL manufactured snowboard and inline skater protective equipment. In addition, NDL made Hitman boxing equipment. DHB is short for David H. Brooks. David's brother Jeffery Brooks was an executive in the company. It was Jeffery Brooks who received the Redman® brochure.

Jeffery reviewed the brochure and summoned the company's research and development specialist to his office. Jeffery showed Alan the brochure and asked, "Can we make a suit like this?" Alan stated they could. "Can we make one better?" "Ya, we can, but we will need a consultant to work on the project," Alan replied. Jeffery turned over the brochure, and on the back of the brochure, the names of the Redman Advisory Board members were printed alphabetically in a text box. Out of the grace of the training gods, dumb luck, or fate, Jeffery started reading at the bottom of the list. The last board member listed was "Howard Webb, Oregon Police Academy."

I received a call from Jeffery Brooks at the academy. Jeffery explained his connection to DHB Armor and he asked me if I would be interested in developing my own tactical training suit? While trying to keep my excitement under control, I stated that I would be interested in developing my own suit. As we discussed the project, I explained to Jeffery that Simuntion® marking ammunition was the next innovative advancement in law enforcement training. Therefore, the suit needed to be designed for use with marking ammunition. Being a businessman and not a law enforcement trainer, he had no idea what marking projectiles were. So, Jeffery agreed to rely on my experience and training expertise for the suit's design.

Within a week, Jeffery had sent me samples of padding and covering materials for the suit. A day or two later, I faxed him a sketch of my proposed design. Two weeks later, I flew to NDL Products in Fort Lauderdale, Florida to evaluate the prototype suit. At NDL Products, I met with Jeffery and Alan (the R & D specialist) in Jeffery's office. The suit turned out better than I had hoped it would for our first attempt at a design. However, the suit needed more padding in the chest, thigh, and groin. Also, it needed a helmet. When

Alan donned the suit, I could see it provided excellent coverage and mobility. I reminded Jeffery that the suit needed a marking cartridge shield for its chest and helmet.

Aware that Jeffery had no idea what marking cartridges were, I had brought six 38 caliber Simunition® rounds to our meeting. I pulled them from my pocket and handed them to Jeffery. "What do these shoot from," he asked. "Any 38 caliber revolver," I replied. Jeffery opened a drawer in his desk, removed a snub nose revolver, emptied its cylinder, and started loading marking cartridges into it. "What are you going to do with that?" I asked. "I am going to shoot him," Jeffery replied, as he pointed to Alan. "You don't want to do that. Alan is not wearing a protective helmet," I cautioned. "Ya, you don't want to do that," Alan nervously stammered. Jeffery opened another drawer and removed a Fort Lauderdale telephone book. "Place this in front of your face and stand against the wall," Jeffery told him, as he handed Alan the phone book.

Again I warned Jeffery, "You shouldn't do that. It's not safe." Alan voiced his agreement. "It will be fine," Jeffery said consolingly. Then, he fired five marking projectiles into Alan's chest at a distance of ten feet. The projectiles left five pink stars on the suit. "That is very cool. We will add the shield," Jeffery said with a grin. As a result of that meeting, the Hitman suit was to become the first simulation-training suit developed for use with Simunition® marking ammunition.

As we discussed the suit project, Jeffery told me that the suit would be offered through their Hitman boxing line of training equipment. Consequently, the suit would be sold as the "Hitman" simulation-training suit. Before the suit hit the market, the name was shortened to the "Hitman Suit."

Within two months of our meeting, Jeffery recruited and hired Redman's national sales manager, Steve Parker, to manage the Hitman sales program. Steve understood the positive role that training could play in marketing law enforcement products. Consequently, Steve was the driving force in the establishment of "Hitman Training Systems" (HTS). HTS became the official training division for the Hitman equipment. Because I had developed the Hitman Suit, Steve asked me to be the director of training for HTS. As the director, I developed instructor development training programs for the Hitman Suit and conducted instructor development courses nationally.

In 1996, DHB Armor sent a group of my instructors and me to the Olympics in Atlanta, Georgia to provide Confrontational Simulation training to the 2,000 member Olympic Security Team. The Olympic Security Team was comprised of a mosaic of volunteer criminal justice officers from fifty-four countries. Teaching use of force to international police officers was a rewarding experience. To fully recount those experiences would require me to write another book. I will, however, tell you that cops are the same no matter which country they call home. But, their arrest protocols, search and seizure laws, and use of force guidelines are a little frightening. Thank God for our Bill of Rights.

Prior to the development of the Hitman training equipment, I was unable to integrate simulated deadly force into Confrontational Simulation. While using the Redman suit in Con Sim, we had to use inert training guns. Because the guns did not fire, I had to develop scenarios that did not require the officer to pull the trigger and say "bang." Because of the way an officer is trained is the way he or she will react under stress, I believed (and still do) that having an officer say "bang" to simulate shooting a suspect is a counter-productive training practice. Fortunately, the development of the Hitman suit made Confrontational Simulation the first truly integrated, scenario-based, use of force training program.

Integrated Scenario-Based Use of Force Training

Confrontational Simulation is an integrated scenario-based use of force training program. To understand what the program is, you must first learn what it isn't. It is not a defensive tactics-training program. The officers are not evaluated on the correctness of their technique application. Even if you wanted to critique the technique, the protective suit prevents the proper application of control holds.

It is not "force on force" training. The "Threat" does not only deploy simulated deadly force. The Threat's confrontational actions cover the entire spectrum of inmate and suspect behavior: despondent, static resistant, verbally abusive, menacing with and without a weapon, physically combative, attempt to disarm the officer, and firing a handgun.

It is not a one-dimensional training system, like a "shoot/no shoot" firearms training simulator. The officer can realistically apply all force options, starting with the officer's presence and escalating to deadly force.

It is not a "tough guy" contest where the officer learns that a trained instructor can defeat an undertrained officer. The officer finishes the scenario as a "winner" with more confidence and a greater appreciation for the training.

Confrontational Simulation is the most effective training program developed for teaching proper use of force decision-making, defensible use of force justification, articulate use of force report writing, and effective witness and juror perception management.

In addition, Con Sim can inoculate an officer to the negative effects of stress and therefore minimize department and officer liability. Stress inoculation is an important factor in creating better officer use of force decisions.

A training program that is designed to give officers realistic experiences enhances confidence, reduces the heart rate during the confrontation, and minimizes the potential of hypervigilance (panic) from occurring (Siddle, 1995).

It is no coincidence that the percentage of attorney Robert Franz's excessive force lawsuits dropped from 90 percent of his litigation case load to 10 percent after Confrontational Simulation was implemented at the Oregon Academy. Robert was Northland Insurance Company's main Oregon trial lawyer. Nor was it by accident that Oregon's criminal justice officers won over 98 percent of their civil rights trials during the same time period.

Although the instructors that I have trained conduct Confrontational Simulation by pulling one or two officers, at a time, from patrol to undergo Con Sim training, the program is designed to be (and is most effective when) conducted as a group exercise. In Con Sim learning occurs in two ways: The officer learns directly from the experiences encountered in the scenario, and the officer learns vicariously by observing the proper actions and mistakes of other officers in their scenarios. Further, the officer learns how to properly manage witness perceptions by observing and experiencing the use of force incident as an uninvolved third person.

The Confrontational Simulation program consists of two training modules: a comprehensive use of force presentation and a series of integrated use of force training scenarios.

USE OF FORCE PRESENTATION. It is unfair to evaluate an officer's use of force decision-making skills without first providing him or her with the information necessary to make valid use of force decisions. Consequently, the preparatory use of force presentation includes the federal guidelines for using nondeadly and deadly force, an explanation of the continuum of force, Officer v. Threat Factors and Influential Circumstances, the requirements of a properly written use of force report, and the guidelines for properly managing a use of force incident. Additionally, the proper use of Hard and Soft Cover is discussed as it relates to preventing the necessity to use force.

INTEGRATED TRAINING SCENARIOS. Depending on the time allotted and the number of students to train, each officer will receive between three to five consecutive scenarios. The officer is evaluated by an instructor designated as the "Evaluator" and a Peer Jury comprised of the officers waiting for their series of scenarios. Each officer is evaluated on the behaviors that create or minimize officer liability: his or her use of force decision, the ability to articulate the justification for the use of force, proper verbalization skills, and the proper use of Hard and Soft Cover.

A concept that is unique to the confrontational Simulation program is its emphasis on the use of physical and psychological barriers to minimize the need to use force and/or assist in the justification of it.

THE PROPER USE OF COVER. Most officers understand the traditional definition of Cover: any natural or man-made object that will stop, deflect, or slow down bullets. Unfortunately, this narrow definition does not take into account the use of lesser objects as physical and psychological barriers for suspect control and officer safety.

There has never been a police officer that has been told in advance that his or her *butt was about to be kicked* and it actually happened. Police officers have a tactical advantage: An officer is armed with a baton, aerosol restraint, Taser, and firearm. When pre-warned, the officer will almost always win. It is the Eleventh Commandment. Police officers who are successfully assaulted are caught off guard (surprise attacked).

A Threat will only attack if he or she believes that the attack will succeed. Any physical or psychological barrier that places the Threat at a disadvantage will create an element of doubt and that uncertainty is likely to prevent an assault on the officer. However, in the event that an assault does occur, the barrier will impede the Threat's ability to harm the officer. Furthermore, the act of the Threat coming around or over the barrier demonstrates his or her intent to harm the officer, which adds another element to the officer's use of force justification.

When an officer properly uses Cover, the Threat is not afforded the opportunity to escalate the encounter, thereby minimizing the necessity for the use of force and maximizing the officer's and the Threat's safety.

The Confrontational Simulation program utilizes two definitions of Cover: Hard Cover is any natural or man-made object that will stop, deflect, or slow down bullets. Soft Cover is any natural or man-made object that can be used as a physical or psychological barrier to impede the Threat's ability to harm an officer. Examples: vehicles, furniture, fences, ditch, etc. Even the Threat's position or contacting the Threat from the rear is defined as Soft Cover. Basically, the Con Sim definition of Cover is "any action or object that makes it hard for the Threat to hurt you."

How important is the use of Cover to officer safety? Of the officers who are killed investigating suspicious person calls, 64 percent of the officers did not use Cover or left Cover to contact the suspect (AIMS Media, Suspicious Person Calls: An Analysis of Officers Killed).

Safety Equipment

The safety of the officers and the instructor acting as the role-player is paramount. Confrontational Simulation training must not occur without the proper safety equipment. The following equipment is required to conduct safe and effective Con Sim training:

ROLE-PLAYER. A complete protective simulation-training suit (Hitman, Redman, or FIST) is required to safely conduct Confrontational Simulation training. Needless to say, I prefer the Hitman suit. Regardless of which suit you use, the suit must provide neck protection and its helmet must have a clear protective shield that provides full-face coverage or the helmet must accommodate a Simunition® or paintball mask. Most simulation suits include a "C" collar neck protector, and they provide good protection against marking projectiles.

Since the integration of marking cartridges into the Con Sim program, I have used good quality paintball masks as marking cartridge shields on the Hitman helmets. They have provided excellent protection against marking projectiles. In addition to the suit's exterior groin protector, I recommend the role-player wear a protective athletic cup. When it comes to role-player protection, it is better to be too safe then painfully sorry.

STUDENT. Each student officer who participates in the scenario must wear a protective helmet and eye protection inside that helmet. Because in Confrontational Simulation the Role-Player does not shoot projectiles at the officers, the students' helmets do not require a clear shield or a paintball mask. However, the helmets are required to have a protective cage. Protective eyewear that fits comfortably inside the helmet must be worn as well.

Although to safely conduct confrontational scenarios, only two student helmets are required. You will find that the use of four helmets makes the training more efficient: While two students are participating in the scenarios, two more students can be suited up. Having four complete sets of student safety equipment minimizes the downtime between scenarios.

In addition, I recommend that each officer wear protective elbow and kneepads. Redman® offers very functional elbow and kneepads; however, any good quality adult inline skating elbow and kneepads will adequately protect the students. The extra protection that elbow and kneepads offer is required when conducting Con Sim training on a carpeted floor. Even if you are conducting the training on mats, I would recommend that the students wear the additional padding until the Evaluator and the Role-Player become competent at conducting the scenarios.

FIRST AID. When conducting Confrontational Simulation training, a stocked first aid kit, bio-hazardous material clean-up kit, and a reliable communication source to request emergency medical personnel is required. Although I have never had an officer seriously injured during Con Sim training, officers and the Role-Players have received minor scrapes and cuts from training guns, belt buckles, and finger nails. As you are aware, blood (no matter how slight) must be cleaned up and disposed of in a safe manner. Also, open cuts and scrapes must be covered and dressed before the officer is allowed to participate in the scenario. In the worst case scenario (no pun intended), an older officer could suffer a heart attack or stroke during the training, requiring emergency medical services to be summoned.

Training Props

Training props are divided into three categories: The student props, Role-Player props, and simulated Cover. Props add realism to the scenarios and enhance the effectiveness of the training. The more realistic the scenario the more effective the training. Confrontational Simulation is designed to balance the need for realistic use of force training with officer and instructor safety. To conduct effective Confrontational Simulation training, you will need the following training props:

STUDENT PROPS. A minimum of two marking cartridge handguns are required to conduct Con Sim scenarios for law enforcement officers or corrections deputies/officers who perform prisoner transports. Simunition® offers a specific 9mm blue frame FX marking cartridge pistol and conversion kits for some makes and models of semiautomatic pistols.

For those who carry revolvers, each Simunition® box of 38 caliber marking cartridges comes with two sets of cylinder safety rings: 38 Special and 357 Magnum. When using a revolver, make sure you insert the 38 Special rings only into 38 Special revolvers. The 357 Magnum safety rings are longer. Consequently, if they are inserted into a 38 Special revolver, they will prevent the marking cartridges from being fully seated in the cylinder.

Of course, your officers will require marking ammunition in two different colors. I prefer pink and blue: pink for girl officers and blue for boy officers. Just kidding–for those of you who are overly gender sensitive, you need to toughen up. Bad guys try to kill you, harmless jokes about gender should be the least of your concern. Just a little Uncle Howie advice. Sorry, I digress. Using two different colors of projectiles during two officer scenarios allows the Evaluator to determine where each officer's projectile hit on the Role-Player.

If your officers are issued beanbag, less-lethal shotguns, you may want to consider adding a Simunition® converted shotgun to the Con Sim program. The shotgun conversion kit consists of a bushing that inserts into the chamber and specifically designed shotgun shells that act as a chamber for the 38 caliber marking cartridges. The shotgun loads and functions like a real less-lethal shotgun. In addition, Simunition® offers submachine gun, rifle, and carbine conversion kits.

The only downside to using Simunition® training guns and marking ammunition is the cost. The cost of a specifically designed marking cartridge pistol is on par with a good quality handgun. The marking ammunition can cost almost a dollar per cartridge. This may not seem like a lot of money. But, if each officer fires a full magazine of marking cartridges per scenario, it could cost over ten dollars per officer per scenario. However, the financial, political, and public relations benefits of providing effective use of force training will pay for the cost of conducting the scenario-based training a hundred times over. When conducting use of force training, resist the temptation to be penny wise and lawsuit foolish.

For departments with a limited training equipment budget, good quality AirSoft pistols, shotguns, and assault rifles can be used in lieu of Simunition® training products. When purchasing AirSoft guns for use in Con Sim, select guns that fire the pellets at marking cartridge speeds (approx. 400 fps) and cycle like a real firearm. I have trained with AirSoft pistols and assault rifles, and I found them to be accurate, reliable, and realistic.

If your officers carry a Taser on-duty, it needs to be a force option available to them to use in the scenario. With Taser lawsuits on the rise, I cannot think of a more important force option available for deployment in a scenario-based use of force training program. Not to beat a dead horse, but officers are not sued for deploying the Taser. Officers are sued for making bad decisions as to when to deploy the Taser. Confrontational Simulation is the perfect medium for conveying the department's expectations and restrictions on Taser usage. It is also the perfect program for evaluating an officer's ability to make proper Taser deployment decisions.

The Taser can be integrated into a Con Sim scenario in two ways. The Taser can be used with the shell of a spent cartridge with the wires removed. With this deployment simulation, the officer simulates a probe deployment by causing the Taser to cycle. When the Role-Player hears the Taser cycling, he or she acts out the designated response. To simulate a Drive Stun deployment, the officer holds the Taser electrodes off the Role-Player's body six inches and activates the Taser. Again, when the Role-Player hears the Taser cycle, he or she performs the appropriate response.

The alternative is to use Taser training cartridges. They provide a more realistic Taser deployment simulation in the scenario. Again, the downside is cost. Training cartridges cost nearly, if not, as much, as a standard probe cartridge. Regardless of which method you choose to use for the simulated Taser deployment, you should have specifically designated Tasers for use in the Con Sim training. Because the Tasers will receive some abuse during the scenarios, you do not want officers using their duty Taser.

If your officers are issued an aerosol restraint, inert aerosol restraints are realistic props to use in Con Sim scenarios. The major manufacturers of pepper spray offer "inert sprays." They are fairly inexpensive and effectively simulate the use of pepper spray. When selecting an inert pepper spray, pay particular attention to the inert fluid. Some manufacturers use alcohol as the substance ejected from the canister. When sprayed at close range, the alcohol can burn the eyes of the Role-Player or damage the clear shield of a helmet. I actually had the fluid ejected from an inert pepper spray canister damage the plastic facemask of the paintball helmet the Role-Player was wearing.

In the days prior to the commercial production of inert pepper spray, we used empty pepper spray canisters and simulated canisters made from PVC pipe. If you are on a tight budget, these low cost substitutions work well as props to simulate the deployment of pepper spray.

Of course, no simulated force option toolbox would be complete without the inclusion of training batons. A minimum of two foam training batons and baton holders are required to conduct Con Sim scenarios. However, four training batons are better. Having four complete sets of officer safety equipment and training props allows you to have two officers participating in a scenario and two other officers in the bullpen waiting to go. When the participating set of officers finish their scenario, the next set of officers seamlessly start their scenario. The previous set of officers remove their gear, and the next pair of officers suit up. This assembly line approach to student preparation eliminates the dead time between scenarios.

Because the officers will participate in nighttime scenarios, two (fully charged) department issue flashlights are required as training props. The use of a flashlight in a low light environment adds realism to the training. Further, it demonstrates to the officer how effective blinding a Threat with a flashlight can be in a confrontation.

Also, simulated portable radios or four lapel microphones will add realism to the scenario when the officers simulate calling dispatch for a driver's status check or running the Role-Player for wants and warrants.

The last consideration regarding student-training props is the officers' holsters and utility belts. If your officers have uniformity in their holsters and duty belts, it is preferable to have each officer wear his or her duty belt during the scenarios. However, if your officers wear a mixed assortment of duty handguns, pepper spray, and Taser holsters, you may want to consider providing duty belts and holsters with the simulated force options. This will prevent an officer from using a holster(s) in the scenario that compromises the security of the simulated weapon.

ROLE-PLAYER'S TRAINING PROPS. In the Con Sim scenario, the officer makes his or her use of force decision—and then justifies that decision—based on the Role-Player's actions. An important consideration when evaluating the dangerousness of the Role-Player's actions and behaviors is the possession of a weapon, or the Role-Player's close proximity to a weapon or other dangerous object. As a result, simulated conventional and environmental weapons play an important role in the confrontational scenario.

One important difference between the Confrontational Simulation program and other "force on force" simulation models is that the officers are not shot with marking projectiles or AirSoft pellets by the Role-Player. In Con Sim when a Role-Player shoots an officer, the officer is shot with a blank pistol. I designed the Con Sim program to use blanks (only) for the following reasons.

First, the Confrontational Simulation program is a scenario-based use of force training model, *only*. The program's complete focus is on teaching an officer to make correct use of force decisions and how to properly manage the use of force incident. If you are in the market for a Special Forces–"Kill them all and let God sort it out"–type of scenario-based training program, this program is not for you. Con Sim is not a building search, defensive tactics, fight to survive, ground fighting, or gun fighting training program. By design the program's total focus is on the officer's use of force, not the Role-Player's ability to shoot the officer.

When students and instructors engage in simulated gunfights, the focus (no matter how well intended) always shifts from the evaluation of the proper use of force to gun fighting tactics. Cops don't experience civil rights litigation for shooting the suspect too dead. But, they are sued for making a suspect dead from a bad use of force decision.

Second, the shooting of an officer with a plastic projectile is an intentional act by the instructor to cause the officer's failure (simulated death). There is nothing positive about being shot with a marking projectile. Being shot with a plastic bullet during a scenario indicates (no matter what spin you attempt to place on it) the officer failed.

When new or inexperienced officers are shot during training scenarios, it damages their self-confidence, makes them paranoid, and sets the stage for a panic-induced use of excessive force.

When veteran officers experience an intentionally caused failure during a training scenario, they withdraw mentally from the training experience. This withdrawal is usually expressed by the phrase: "This is bullshit!"

Third, a major component of the instructional methodology of the Confrontational Simulation program is the Peer Jury. At any given time in the training room, there will be between five and fifty officers sitting in rows observing the scenarios. It is impossible to cost effectively protect the members of the Peer Jury from the marking projectiles that may unintentionally miss the officers participating in the scenario.

I am aware that some academies and departments have viewing windows in their facilities for officers to safely observe "force on force" training with marking ammunition. However, any barrier that protects a Peer Jury from being shot with a plastic bullet will eliminate or impair the Peer Jury's ability to effectively convey their critique to the officer. Further, it will unintentionally create a psychological barrier between the Peer Jury and the scenario, thus degrading the effectiveness of the observational learning process.

It is for these reasons that the Role-Player, in Con Sim, is armed with a starter revolver and blanks. I recommend using a starter revolver, in lieu of a real gun with blanks, because the barrel is plugged. This prevents a separated blank casing from being fired from the barrel.

A secondary reason is that during the scenario the Role-Player will drop the handgun and the officers will throw or kick it out of the way. I personally don't want an expensive gun abused or damaged. The starter pistols and the blanks they fire are inexpensive. Also, starter revolvers are also very durable. I have used the same starter revolver for the last fifteen years. Its grip is wrapped with electrical tape and the barrel and cylinder are blotched with pink and blue marking material. It has been a training trooper. When I purchased that rugged little bugger fifteen years ago, it was the best thirty dollars that I ever spent.

Additionally, the Con Sim program utilizes other simulated conventional and environmental weapons: Rubber knife, baseball bat, six-foot staff, foam nunchucks, plastic liquor bottles, plastic beer mug, cellular phones, pipe bomb, and a syringe with the needle removed. You want to draw from your own experience and incorporate simulated weapons that your officers encounter in the field or the facility.

HARD AND SOFT COVER. During the scenarios, officers are critiqued on their use of physical and psychological barriers for officer safety, to minimize the necessity for force, and as part of their use of force justification. So naturally, you will need noninjurious objects to use as "Cover." If you have a sufficient number of accordion training mats, they can be stacked to represent the front of a patrol car, tables, chairs, fences, or generic physical barriers. They can be stood on end and used to represent a vertical barrier or to create a doorway.

If mats are not an option to use as Cover, then, large and medium size cardboard boxes make excellent simulated Cover. They can be stacked to make different sized barriers, and they are easily obtained from retail and appliance stores at no cost. The Oregon Academy had Crown Mat Company produce specific foam blocks to be used as Cover. The academy even had Crown Mat create a foam holding cell to use in the corrections Con Sim program.

Whatever you chose to use as simulated Cover, the officers and the Role-Player must be able to fall or be thrown against it without being injured. Objects just as tables, desks, metal trash cans and wooden boxes have sharp corners and edges, making them dangerous to use as Cover in the scenarios. One of the reasons why I have never injured a student in Confrontational Simulation is because I only use training mats and/or cardboard boxes as Cover.

Training Personnel

To conduct safe and effective Confrontational Simulation training, the program requires two instructors: an Evaluator and a Role-Player. The two positions have completely separate responsibilities; however, the instructors must work together as a team to conduct meaningful scenario-based use of force training.

ROLE OF THE EVALUATOR. The Evaluator is responsible for the logistics of the program and the facilitation and evaluation of the confrontational scenarios. The logistical responsibilities include the procurement, storage, and maintenance of the simulation equipment, training props, and safety equipment. Additional logistical responsibilities include the development of the confrontational scenarios and the Role-Player's responses.

ROLE OF THE ROLE-PLAYER. I do not recommend using students as Role-Players. Effective role-playing in confrontational scenarios is a skill that is acquired through preparation, knowledge, and experience. Putting an untrained person in the protective suit and throwing that person into a series of Con Sim scenarios at its best will make the training ineffective. At its worst, it will get the Role-Player or an officer injured. Consequently, the most efficient way to develop the necessary evaluation and role-playing skills is to attend a Confrontational Simulation instructor development course.

The Role-Player is the most important component of the confrontational scenario. It is the Role-Player's actions and behaviors on which the officers base their use of force decisions. Further, it is the Role-Player's skill level and attention to detail that will make the training scenario a success or a frustrating experience for the Evaluator and the officers. To maximize the effectiveness of the confrontational scenario, the Role-Player should do the following:

- Create a positive learning experience by allowing the officers to "win" in the scenario. This does not imply that the officers do not make mistakes. Winning is a reward for performing properly, and it promotes the reoccurrence of those behaviors in the field.
- Draw out the proper officer response through clearly demonstrated actions and overt behaviors. Ambiguous actions and behaviors create frustrating and ineffective scenario-based use of force training.

The Role-Player, also, is used in the evaluation of the officers' performance. For example: When the Role-Player's response was to assault the officer but the officer's use of Cover was so effective that it prevented the attack, the Evaluator should call upon the Role-Player to explain his intended response. As part of the explanation, the Role-Player tells the officer (from a suspect's perspective) why the officer's use of Cover was so effective. Providing an officer with the suspect's perception of what the officer did right is an excellent way to reward and reinforce the officer's proper behavior.

Developing Confrontational Scenarios

Confrontational scenarios must be reality based and discipline specific: deputy sheriff, city police, county and state corrections, state trooper, etc. The scenarios must be open-ended. An open-ended scenario, by design, does not have a predetermined outcome. The outcome is determined by the officer's use of force decision.

Scenarios that contain too many specifics become restrictive and limit the realistic aspects of the Con Sim training. The information contained in the scenario should mirror what an officer receives when he or she is dispatched to the call. In essence, when the Evaluator explains the scenario to the officers, the Evaluator is dispatching the participating officers to a call for service. If conducting corrections scenarios, the Evaluator establishes the reason for the officer's contact with the inmate or parole and probation client.

Confrontational scenarios should only contain the following information:

- Time of the incident.
- Location of the incident.
- Nature of the complaint, problem, or situation.

Examples:

Police–It is 11:00 in the evening (time) and you receive a report of an unwanted person (problem) at a tavern (location).

Corrections–It is 3:00 in the afternoon (time) and you receive a call from an officer who attempted to change the location of an inmate (problem), and the inmate refused to leave his cell (location).

Parole and Probation–It is 1:00 in the afternoon (time) and you're conducting a home visit on a convicted drug dealer (situation) at his rural residence (location).

Base your confrontational scenarios on the common situations and complaints that routinely occur in your community, facility, or work environment. You should also develop scenarios based on real-life incidents that have created controversy or liability in your department or region.

I develop my Confrontational Simulation scenarios based on my personal experience as a police officer, the use of force incidents that I review, and from the scenarios developed by instructors who attend the Con Sim instructor courses. In the Con Sim instructor course, each instructor candidate is required to develop ten scenarios for use as the Evaluator. Many of these instructor-developed scenarios are excellent. The following is a sampling of the scenarios that I use when conducting law enforcement Confrontational Simulation training:

- It is 2:00 A.M., and you receive a citizen complaint regarding a suspicious person in the parking lot of an apartment complex.
- It is 11:00 P.M., and you respond to a complaint of an unwanted person in a tavern/lounge.
- It is 3:30 in the afternoon, and you respond to a complaint of a transient bothering people at the city/county park.
- It is 10:00 A.M./P.M., and you respond to a complaint of a panhandler bothering the patrons at the entrance of a local mini-mart.
- It is 12:30 A.M., and you receive a report of a prowler in the backyard of a house where a sixteen-year-old girl is baby-sitting.
- It is 3:30 A.M./P.M., and you respond to a suspicious person complaint. You arrive and find a person sitting next to the wall behind a store.
- It is 3:00 P.M., and you respond to a report from a concerned neighbor that a mentally handicapped adult is walking down the street with a large hunting knife. The adult has the intelligence level of a four-year-old child. *Training Goal: To have the officer trade something for the knife and not react in a manner that panics the handicapped person.* A Los Angeles County Sheriff's Department instructor, who attended the Con Sim instructor course, developed this exceptional scenario.

The program does not require a large number of scenarios. The Evaluator can recycle the same scenario multiple times with different Threat Responses. Here is an example:

The first set of two officers are dispatched to this call:

Scenario: It is 2:00 A.M., and you receive a citizen complaint regarding a suspicious person in the parking lot of an apartment complex.

Response: **Verbally Abusive:** No threatening gestures.

The officers successfully complete this scenario and participate in two more different scenarios.

Four more pairs of officers are cycled through the program with different scenarios; then, the sixth pair of officers receive the same scenario as the first set of officers, but with a different Threat Response:

Scenario: It is 2:00 A.M., and you receive a citizen complaint regarding a suspicious person in the parking lot of an apartment complex.

Response: ***Initially Compliant–Close In And Grab The Officer's Gun:*** appear to cooperate, act intoxicated, fake illness, attempt to shake hands. Any ruse to close the distance with the officer.

The sixth pair of officers successfully completes their three scenarios, and additional sets of officers cycle through the training.

Then, the tenth set of officers receive the same scenario as pairs one and six with a different Threat Response:

Scenario: It is 2:00 A.M., and you receive a citizen complaint regarding a suspicious person in the parking lot of an apartment complex.

Response: ***Pull The Gun and Shoot The Officer:*** Drop the gun after being shot.

As you can see, even though the other officers (Peer Jury) have witnessed the same call for service three times, the change in the Threat Response makes the scenario uniquely different each time it is given to a different set of officers.

There are two benefits to using this approach to scenario-based use of force training: First, it reinforces that there are no routine calls. Second, it prevents the officers from anticipating the role-player's response. If you have ever received training with a video firearms training simulator, you know that with each scenario it will be either a "shoot" or "no shoot" situation. In Confrontational Simulation training, the officer is required to select the proper use of force from the full spectrum of force options, dependent on which Threat Response the officer encounters.

Threat Responses
(Role-Player Reactions in the Confrontational Scenario)

One problem often encountered with scenario-based training is that role-player's behavior quickly spirals out of control. The challenge in conducting effective scenario-based use of force training is to reach a balance between maintaining control of the scenario without retarding the realism of the suspect or inmate response. I achieved this balance through the development of specific Threat Responses that designate the Role-Player's type of resistance, but not the Role-Player's specific verbalization or animation. In other words, the Role-Player does not follow a written script; his or her role-playing performance is an improvisation.

As an example: When I tell my Role-Player to be *"Verbally Abusive and Physically Menacing: Advance on the officer, but do not strike,"* I want the Role-Player to draw from his or her personal experience as an officer to emulate how suspects actually verbally abuse and physically menace officers. Because each Role-Player brings his or her unique confrontational experiences into the Threat Response, the realism of the confrontational scenario is maximized. The following are the Threat Responses used in the Confrontational Simulation program:

Static Resistance: Verbalize, but refuse to move.
Despondent: Do not acknowledge the officer's presence. May scream for no reason when touched.
Verbally Abusive: No threatening gestures.
Verbally Abusive And Physically Menacing: Advance on the officer, but do not strike.
Immediately Combative: Push, choke, or deliver multiple punches to the body, arms, or shoulders.
Initially Compliant–Close In And Grab The Officer's Handgun: Appear to cooperate, act intoxicated, fake illness, attempt to shake hands. Use any ruse to close the distance with the officer.
Initially Compliant–Sucker Punch The Officer When The Opportunity Presents Itself: Only strike the sides of the helmet, no direct face punches.
Produce A Knife: Menace Only. Do not advance or stab the officer: Pace side-to-side.
Produce A Knife: Advance very slowly making verbal threats and threatening gestures with the knife, but do not stab the officer.
Hold A Walking Stick, Cane, Baseball Bat, Pipe Bomb, Or Nunchucks: Do not menace or threaten, display the weapon only.
Threaten To Commit Suicide: Cut wrists, hold the knife to your throat, or point the gun to your head.
Threaten To Commit Suicide: Point the gun to your head and then shoot the officer.
Pull The Gun And Shoot The Officer: Drop the gun after being shot.
Pull The Gun And Shoot The Officer: Keep the gun after being shot, fall to the ground (hesitate), and shoot the officer again.

Produce A Knife: Menace Only–do not advance or stab the officer. Drop the knife and walk away. This is a fleeing dangerous felon scenario.

Verbally Abusive And Physically Menacing With A Club, Staff, Baseball Bat, Or Nunchucks: Advance slowly on the officer, do not strike.

Verbally Abusive And Physically Menacing: Fight through the effects of pepper spray and/or Taser–comply if hit with the baton, struck with focused blows, or shot with the handgun.

Produce A Knife: Stab a third person, drop the knife, and walk away–fleeing dangerous felon.

Produce A Knife: Stab a third person, sit down on the ground, and refuse to drop the knife.

Pull A Cellular Phone And Point It At The Officer: Hold the phone with your hands concealed. When ordered to do so, show the officer your hands.

As you reviewed these Threat Responses, you probably noticed that they were specifically designed to give the officer every opportunity to "win" in the scenario. For example, in the Threat Responses where the Role-Player shoots the officer, he or she only fires a blank pistol. Using a blank pistol replicates a suspect shooting at, but missing the officer. The officer returns fire and shoots the suspect with marking projectiles, replicating the effective use of deadly force to stop the Threat. If the officer makes a tactical mistake, he or she learns from that mistake, but still "wins" (lives) in the scenario.

To ensure that the Role-Player's behavior compliments the designated Threat Response, the Role-Player and the Evaluator should review and clarify the Evaluator's expectations for the Role-Player's actions and reactions before conducting Confrontational Simulation training.

Training Area

To properly conduct Confrontational Simulation training, there are specific requirements for the size and set-up of the training area. The floor plan of the training area can have a negative or positive influence on the scenarios. Consequently, experience has demonstrated that the following room set-up will enhance the efficiency and quality of Con Sim training:

- At least a 20′ x 30′ training area. A scenario training area at least 20' by 20' covered with a training mat is recommended; however, a carpeted floor is acceptable to use, in lieu of a matted area, with student elbow and kneepads.
- Centrally locate the Peer Jury's seating, approximately six feet away from the area where the scenarios will be conducted.

- If using a large room, locate the training area in a corner and use the two walls to contain the scenario. If you conduct the scenarios in the middle of a large room, the officers and the Role-Player will wander outside of the designated training area, thus, increasing the risk an officer will fire a marking projectile into the Peer Jury.
- Line the officers' seating along the open side (facing the wall) of the training area. This "U" shaped configuration gives you more control over the scenario and more effective communication with the officers when discussing theirs actions and decisions. This set-up, furthermore, provides better communication with the Peer Jury when discussing the officers' use of force justification.
- Arrange at least three stacks of training mats or cardboard boxes in a loose pyramid-shaped figuration. Each stack should be approximately five feet long and three feet tall. Against one wall place two sets of stacked boxes or two accordion mats placed on their ends to simulate a doorway.
- Place a table with the officers' safety equipment near the officers' seating. This will facilitate the smooth transition from being a Peer Jury member to an officer ready to participate in the next series of scenarios.
- Conceal a second table, from the officers' view, for the Role-Player's props. An accordion mat can be stood on its edge to create a screen to conceal the Role-Player's preparation. Or, you can use an adjoining room or hallway. If possible, locate the Role-Player's prop table near the room's light switch, so it is conveniently accessible to the Role-Player to darken the room for nighttime scenarios.

Safety Rules

All criminal Justice training activities and programs have their own established safety rules. Safety rules may vary (depending on the activity or the environment), but they all have one singular purpose: to prevent officer and instructor injury. The following safety rules were developed for the Confrontational Simulation program. They have been successful in preventing officer injuries for over two decades.

- No live firearms or ammunition allowed in the training area.
- Everyone must be searched for weapons and ammunition prior to entering the training area. If a person/officer/instructor leaves the training area, that individual must be searched again before being allowed to reenter the training area.
- Officers must remove all injurious items from their persons and duty belt (wrist watches, earrings, handcuffs, batons, aerosol restraints, mag-

azines, pens, tactical folding knife, flashlight, Taser). In addition, they must remove their footwear. It is unsafe to kick the Role-Player with shoes or boots. However, the wearing of wrestling shoes during the scenario is acceptable.

- When the Evaluator gives the command to "Stop" all activity must stop immediately.
- Officers must notify the Evaluator of all pre-existing conditions that may affect the officer's ability to fully participate in the program.
- No confrontational simulation training will occur without the direct supervision of the Evaluator.
- Absolutely no intentional strikes to the Role-Player's head, groin, or spine.
- Strikes and kicks against the joints are prohibited.
- Strike full power with the training baton.
- Strike full speed (but with only 3/4 power) when punching, striking, kneeing, or kicking.
- Control Holds may be applied lightly to the joints: wrist, elbow, and shoulder.
- Do not make contact with the Role-Player's body when applying a "Drive Stun" with the Taser. Keep the electrodes at least six inches from the Role-Player's body.

Safety Note: The Evaluator will stop the confrontational simulation when the Role-Player is taken to the ground with a takedown technique. Participants will not be allowed to struggle on the ground. Confrontational Simulation is an integrated use of force evaluation and training program. It is not a defensive tactics-training course.

Facilitating the Scenario

Even in the largest of law enforcement agencies, an officer can find him or herself in a confrontation without back-up. Consequently, I recommended that single officer scenarios be conducted first. Then, after all the officers have participated in three single officer scenarios, advance to two officer scenarios.

In a series of three to five scenarios, two to four of the scenarios should require a nondeadly force response and one to two scenarios should involve a deadly force response. This combination of nondeadly and deadly force scenarios prevents the officer(s) from anticipating the "shoot" scenario.

To aid in the efficient facilitation the Con Sim program, I recommend that the training scenarios and the Threat Responses be bound together in a three-ring notebook. This ensures the scenarios are conducted in order. It also allows the Evaluator to quickly select the appropriate Threat Response and secretly brief the Role-Player. It is very important for the integrity of the training scenario that the participating officers and the Peer Jury are unaware of the forthcoming Threat Response.

After the Role-Player has been notified of the Threat Response, the Evaluator explains the scenario to the officer(s) and the Peer Jury. The scenario is given verbatim off the list of scenarios. When explaining the scenario, speak to both the officers and the Peer Jury as one group. A common mistake made during the scenario explanation is the Evaluator only directly communicates with the officers.

The scenario is a learning exercise for all the officers in the class. Therefore, all the officers need to feel included in the explanation, student evaluation, and the use of force justification. This is accomplished by speaking directly to, and making eye contact with, the Peer Jury members. While the Evaluator is announcing the scenario, the Role-Player obtains the appropriate training props.

When the Role-Player is in position, the officer(s) are sent into the scenario. The scenario should not be allowed to go longer than a minute before the officer(s) and the Role-Player have serious interaction. The entire confrontational scenario should last no more than three to five minutes at the longest. When conducting scenario-based use of force training, the Evaluator must always keep in mind that the more scenarios an officer experiences the more training the officer receives.

The number of mistakes an officer makes determines the amount of time that is required to conduct a scenario. As the officers' performance improves, the less time the scenarios will take to facilitate.

With experience comes efficiency. I can facilitate three scenarios per officer, for fifty officers, in four hours. However, a lesser-experienced Evaluator may only be able to facilitate twenty officers through three scenarios within the same time frame.

Role-Playing in the Scenario (Being the Inmate or Suspect)

The Role-Player is the most critical component of confrontational simulation. The officer selects his use of force option by evaluating the Role-Player's actions. Consequently, it is vitally important that the Role-Player does not send mixed signals to the officer.

For example, a very fine line exists between a suspect who is verbally abusive and a suspect who is verbally abusive and physically menacing. However, the use of force responses for the two are radically different. The

Role-Player must recognize the difference between the two and eliminate any gray area as the role is played. In other words, the Role-Player's intentions must be exaggerated and clearly discernable to the officer. An objective of Confrontational Simulation is to develop an officer's ability to recognize actions, behaviors, and verbal cues that justify the use of force. The more obvious the threatening behaviors and verbal cues, the easier they are for the officer to identify.

Furthermore, the Role-Player can reinforce proper or improper behavior with his or her responses to the officer's actions. Here are two examples:

Proper Response. An officer delivers firm, effective strikes to the Role-Player with a training baton. With each strike, the officer orders the Role-Player to "Get down on the ground" and the Role-Player complies. The Role-Player's compliance reinforces the officer's proper use of the baton and proper verbal commands.

Improper Response. An officer lightly strikes the Role-Player with the training baton and fails to give the Role-Player the proper verbal commands, but the Role-Player goes to the ground and complies. Through his compliance, the Role-Player has inadvertently reinforced the improper use of verbal commands and the baton.

The following are Confrontational Simulation's role-playing guidelines:

The Officer Always Wins:

- Never place the officer in a "No Win" situation.
- Never stab or club an officer–Menace Only.
- Never tell the officer "Your Dead" or "You have just been killed."

Violations of the above listed rules will make the officer defensive, damage his/her self-confidence, and shut down the learning process.

Effective Confrontational Role-Playing:

- Make your actions and intentions obvious.
- Don't crowd the officer, keep your distance–this allows the officer time to make a quality use of force decision.
- Exaggerate your movements. This makes it easier for the officer to observe your actions and evaluate your intentions.
- Advance slowly with a weapon: move back, pace side-to-side, or stand in place and inch forward.
- When menacing without a weapon, advance slowly with exaggerated threatening gestures and bellicose verbal threats. Give the officer every

opportunity to perceive the threatening behavior and hear the verbal threats.

- When about to be struck with the training baton, give the officer a target. If you don't, the officer will strike the unprotected areas of the suit.
- Do not resist being controlled, the more resistance you offer the greater chance you or the officer will be injured. The protective suit prevents the officer from applying effective control techniques: arm bar, wrist lock, etc. So, when the officer applies a comealong technique, submit. When the officer applies a takedown technique allow the officer to take you down, then comply.
- Expect the unexpected–be prepared for any officer overreaction or rule violation.
- Use your forearm guards to protect your body against knee strikes.
- When being grabbed by the officer(s) pull your arms into your body, this minimizes the leverage the officer(s) can apply to your arms and shoulders.
- When striking the officer, hit lightly on the sides of the officer's helmet.
- Comply after the appropriate verbal commands have been given. If the commands are improper, wait for the Evaluator to intervene.
- Comply if the use of force is appropriate. If the use of force is improper, wait for the Evaluator to intervene.

The Role-Player and the Evaluator must work as a team to safely and effectively conduct Confrontation Simulation training. During the scenario, the Evaluator will communicate nonverbally with the Role-Player to increase or decrease the level of the Role-Player's aggressiveness. It is the Role-Player's responsibility to watch the Evaluator for the following nonverbal commands:

Thumb Up–Increase the intensity, become more aggressive.
Thumb Down–Decrease the intensity, tone down the confrontation.
Head Nod–Doing fine, maintain this level of intensity.

In addition, a code word is needed for the Role-Player to give if he or she is being hurt. For the Role-Player's safety, this word or phrase must be different from what an actual inmate or suspect may say during a real confrontation. If the Role-Player wants the scenario to stop for whatever reason, he or she must shout "Yield." This term has not been used in the common english language for over three hundred years.

Do not rely on words or phrases like "stop," "it hurts," "let go" as indicators that the Role-Player is in distress. These are the things real suspects or inmate say; consequently, you do not want to condition the officer to release control of the Threat prematurely. Furthermore, the use of common words or phases make it difficult for the Evaluator to differentiate between effective role-playing and the Role-Player in real distress.

Branching the Scenario

The Evaluator controls the intensity and duration of the scenario. As previously explained, the scenario should not go longer than sixty seconds without serious officer versus suspect interaction. Often officers are reluctant to make contact with the Role-Player. This wastes precious scenario time. Other times, the officer is doing such an effective job at keeping a barrier between himself and the Role-Player that the Role-Player cannot gain access to the officer to carry out the Threat Response. In either situation, the Evaluator can facilitate officer versus Role-Player interaction by "Branching" the scenario. Scenario branching can occur through the injection of additional information, assuming a third person role, or by commenting on a basic procedure.

BRANCHING THROUGH ADDITIONAL INFORMATION. This form of branching occurs when the Evaluator interjects additional information into the scenario to force the officer to take action. The following are examples of informational scenario branching:

The officer responds to a call of a suspicious person in the parking lot of an apartment complex. The designated Threat Response is for the Role-Player to disarm the officer of his handgun, if given the opportunity. The officer contacts the Role-Player at a distance and asks for identification. However, instead of approaching the Role-Player and reaching for his ID card, the officer tells the Role-Player to place his ID on the hood of the patrol car. This effectively prevents the Role-Player from grabbing the officer's gun.

Now, the Evaluator has two options: He can reward the officer for his effective use of Cover. This is accomplished by stopping the scenario, explaining that it was the Role-Player's intention to disarm him, but because of his effective use of Cover he prevented the assault. This is an effective way to reinforce positive behavior. Keep in mind not every scenario must end with a use of force greater than verbalization.

The other option is to change the dynamics by branching the scenario. To branch the scenario, the Evaluator informs the officer that the Role-Player has a nonviolent misdemeanor warrant. This forces the officer to engage the Role-Player. This change in dynamics provides the Role-Player with an opportunity to grab the officer's gun.

If the officer calls for a Cover Officer, the Evaluator can branch the scenario again by informing the officer that there is a major accident and traffic has been stalled or (if you work in a small to medium size agency) the other officers on shift are involved in another incident(s).

As another example of branching the scenario, the officer responds to a complaint of a panhandler bothering patrons in front of a mini-mart. The designated Threat Response is for the Role-Player to be verbally abusive to the officer. To give the scenario more depth, the Evaluator assumes the role of the mini-mart manager. As the manager, the Evaluator tells the officer that he wants the panhandler removed from the store's property.

When the officer contacts the Role-Player, the suspect is verbally abusive, but cooperative. The officer obtains the Role-Player's identification card and runs him for wants and warrants. The Evaluator, acting as the dispatcher, branches the scenario by informing the officer that the suspect has an outstanding arrest warrant for armed robbery. This information should force the officer to escalate his or her force; therefore, hastening the conclusion of the scenario.

BRANCHING BY ASSUMING THE THIRD PERSON ROLE. With this method of branching, the Evaluator plays the part of the complainant, store owner, bartender, relative, etc. to expedite the scenario by making a citizen's arrest or provoking the Role-Player to attack. Here are two examples:

The officer responds to a complaint of an unwanted person in a tavern. The designated Threat Response is for the Role-Player to offer "Static Resistance." The officer contacts the bartender played by the Evaluator. The bartender tells the officer that the Role-Player is bothering the other patrons by being loud and obnoxious. Further, the bartender states that he has asked the Role-Player to leave, but he refused to go. The bartender wants the Role-Player to leave on his own or be arrested.

The officer contacts the Role-Player and attempts to convince him to leave the tavern. The Role-Player verbally and physically refuses to leave. As a result, the interaction between the officer and the Role-Player bogs down into a fruitless exercise in Verbal Judo. To force the officer into action, the Evaluator reassumes the role as the bartender, expresses his dissatisfaction with the officer's results, and places the Role-Player under citizen's arrest. This forces the officer to take action.

In this next example, the officers responds to a reported violation of a restraining order/order of protection where the victim has locked herself in the residence. The Threat Response is for the Role-Player to be despondent toward the officers. The officers contact the Role-Player, who is sitting in the front yard of the residence. The officers (acting as the primary officer and cover officer) attempt to verbally communicate with the Role-Player. The Role-Player does not acknowledge the officers. At this point, the scenario comes to a standstill because the officers are reluctant to physically engage the Role-Player.

To force the officers to act, the Evaluator assumes the role of the victim's new boyfriend who lives next door. The boyfriend comes into the yard and start yelling threats at the Role-Player. This causes the Role-Player to attack the new boyfriend. As a defense, the boyfriend hides behind the officers. This forces the officers to act in defense of the boyfriend.

BRANCHING BY COMMENTING ON A PROCEDURE. This branching method works best with recruit and reserve officers because they often do not respond like an experienced officer. Inexperienced officers will contact a suspect and play twenty questions without asking for personal identification. This time-consuming officer response burns up scenario time and accomplishes nothing meaningful.

To intervene, stop the scenario and ask the Peer Jury: "What would normally happen in a contact like this?" The Peer Jury's response is always, "Ask for ID." With the solution identified, start the scenario over again. When the officer obtains the Role-Player's identification, the scenario can be branched further if necessary by having the Role-Player wanted on a warrant. The following is an example of branching by commenting on a procedure:

The officer responds to a report of a homeless man bothering people in the park. The Threat Response is for the Role-Player to offer "Static Resistance." The officer confronts the Role-Player and tells him to leave the park. In response, the Role-Player sits down and tells the officer, "I can stay here. It is a public park." Instead of immediately asking for identification, the officer wastes scenario time with a prolonged tactical communication session. To salvage the scenario, the Evaluator stops the scenario and asks the Peer Jury for a recommendation on how to properly handle the situation. With the proper procedure identified, the scenario is restarted from the beginning. The officer obtains the Role-Player's ID and runs the homeless man for warrants. The Evaluator informs the officer that the Role-Player has felony warrant for assault on a police officer, which forces the officer to take action.

An additional advantage of branching the scenario by commenting on a procedure is that it teaches inexperienced officers that running the suspect for a warrant can often solve complaints and problems.

Although branching a scenario is a valuable facilitation technique, 90 percent of the confrontational scenarios that are conducted will not require a branching of the scenario by the Evaluator to force an officer to take action. Of the nineteen Threat Responses used in this program, only five Threat Responses may need to be branched.

Another consideration is the officer's effective use of Cover. It has been my experience that after the first five or six scenarios the officers learn to use Cover so well that often force beyond the use of handcuffing is not required. In these situations, it is sometimes best to let the scenario play out to simu-

lated handcuffing. This rewards the officer for the use of Cover that eliminates the need to escalate the force. Acknowledging an officer's proper use
of Cover that prevents an assault is another aspect of allowing the student to
"win" during the scenario.

Justifying the Use of Force

An important goal of the Confrontational Simulation program is to produce officers who can effectively articulate their justification for their use of
force. This is accomplished by having the officer explain his or her justification for the use of force at the end of the scenario. The Evaluator segues into
the justification by simply asking the officer, "Justify your use of force?" With
this question, the Evaluator purposefully draws out the Officer v. Threat
Factors and/or Influential Circumstances that justify the officer's use of force.

However, you want more than just the factor or circumstance that justifies
the officer's use of force. You want the officer to demonstrate that he or she
understands the reasons why the factor or circumstance justifies the officer's
use of force choice. Consequently, after the officer has identified the factor
or circumstance, ask the officer: "Why is that important?" Here is an example of how the facilitation technique works:

> "Why did you taser the suspect?" The Evaluator asks. "The suspect
> was in close proximity of a weapon," the officer replies. "What weapon?"
> "The beer mug on the table," the officer answers. "Why is that impor-
> tant?" "Because I was afraid that if I tried to grab his arm to apply a con-
> trol hold he would hit me with the mug," the officer explains. "Any other
> reasons?" "The suspect had an altered mindset," the officer adds. "Why
> is that important?" "Well, the bartender said he was drunk and angry
> over being cut off from the bar." "So, why is that important?" "Suspects
> who are drunk and angry have higher pain tolerances. So, I was afraid if
> I pepper sprayed him it would not be effective and he would attack me
> with the glass mug."

As you can see from the example, the officer not only properly identifies the
factors that justify the use of the Taser, the officer also demonstrates an understanding of why the factors create an immediate threat. Additionally, the officer demonstrates the ability to effectively explain his use of force justification.

At some point during the "Why is that important?" discussion, the officer
will have covered all the pertinent factors and circumstances that justify his
use of force. At that point the Evaluator turns to the Peer Jury and asks: "Was
the officer's use of force justified?" When the individual members of the Peer

Jury answer, "yes or no." The Evaluator facilitates discussion further by asking, "Why?" When the peer juror identifies the factors or circumstances that justify the use of force, the Evaluator draws the justification out of the juror with, "Why is that important?" This cycle of questioning keeps the Peer Jury actively involved in the observational learning process.

Critiquing the Officer

The critique can make or break the officer's learning experience in Confrontational Simulation. The Evaluator acts more as a performance coach and an officer advocate than a traditional law enforcement trainer. An effective Con Sim Evaluator does more than just critique the officer's use of force, verbalization skills, and use of Cover. An effective Evaluator critiques the officer in such a way that the officer not only accepts the criticism, he or she embraces it. Criminal justice officers do not embrace negative experiences. Do you follow me on this?

Being aware of this, Con Sim was designed to create an officer's successful completion of the scenario. In the thousands of officers I have trained in Con Sim, I have only failed one officer. And I only failed him after several scenarios convinced me that he lacked the intellectual capacity to learn from his poor use of force decisions. Put another way, he was just plain stupid. Even a blind hog finds an acorn every now and then. This officer couldn't even reach that level of success.

Based on the concept that under stress a person can only retain three pieces of information in the conscious mind, the officers are not allowed to make more than one mistake at a time before being corrected. Performing in front of their peers causes most officers stress. So, if the maximum number of corrections that an officer can remember is three, it just makes sense to me to correct one mistake at a time.

So, based on this one mistake and one correction rule, the scenario continues uninterrupted until the officer makes a mistake:

Doesn't Use Available Cover:

- Fails to use Cover at all.
- Uses Cover, then, moves away.
- Uses Cover, then, inches forward away from Cover.

When evaluating an officer's use of Cover, keep in mind the Confrontational Simulation's definition of Cover is "any action or object that makes it hard for the Threat to hurt you." There will be situations when the officer must leave the protection of a physical barrier to control the Role-Player. In those situations, approaching the Role-Player from the rear makes it harder for the Role-Player to harm the officer. Therefore, by Con Sim's definition of Cover, approaching a suspect from the rear is considered a proper use of Cover. I know that this concept takes some of you out of your "Cover" comfort zone. But this thinking outside the box definition of Cover maximizes an officer's safety and minimizes liability.

Because you want to train the officer to use available Cover, every Con Sim scenario should have objects in the training area that can be used as physical and psychological barriers. A common mistake made by lesser-experienced Con Sim instructors is that they tell the officer: "In this scenario there is no available Cover. So, ignore the objects in the training area." To tell officers to ignore physical and psychological barriers when you are trying to train them to use Cover is a dumb idea. It occurs when the instructor strays beyond the three goals of the Con Sim program: proper use of force, proper verbalization, and *proper use of Cover.*

Uses improper verbalization:

- Commands lack projection and authority.
- Verbalization is too aggressive for the situation. Or, not aggressive enough.
- Commands are too wordy, not clear and concise.
- Makes an unenforceable threat.
- Uses vulgar language or sarcasm.
- Does not identify him/herself as a police officer.
- Does not utilize verbal commands when deploying force.

The use of proper verbalization during a use of force incident cannot be emphasized enough during Con Sim training. As I have explained a number of times in this book, an officer's verbalization can enhance an officer's defense or damage it. The use of the Peer Jury as a student evaluation method works at its best when evaluating an officer's verbalization skills during the scenario. The members of the Peer Jury hear the officer's verbalization from a witness's perspective. Consequently, they bring this unique perspective to the officer's attention during the critique.

Selects an improper use of force option:

- Did the officer under-react or overreact for the situation?

To conduct Confrontational Simulation training, the Evaluator must have a comprehensive understanding of the use of nondeadly and deadly force for his or her discipline: county or state corrections, law enforcement, and parole and probation. The first half of this book is dedicated to the concepts, guidelines, principles, and standards that provide for the proper evaluation of an officer's use of force decisions during the confrontational scenarios. Even more importantly, the information presented in this book provides the Evaluator with the knowledge and background to explain and justify his or her evaluation of the officer's use of force performance.

It has been my experience that criminal justice officers often will not accept a negative critique based on the Evaluator's opinion. Conversely, I have found that those same officers are willing to accept an Evaluator's critique when the correction is explained from a liability management, juror, and witness perspective.

Be positive with your critique:

- *Don't use negative words or terms.* The negative phrasing of your critique will make the officer defensive and shut down the learning process. The following are examples:
  Positive: "How can we improve this situation?"
  Negative: "What is wrong with this?" "How did Officer Smith screw-up?"
- *Have the officer critique himself or herself.* Officers become more receptive to criticism when they are part of the problem-solving process. Here are examples:
  Positive: "How could you improve your situation?" "Are you using Cover?"
  Negative: "What's wrong with you?" "Are you trying to get yourself killed?"
- *When delivering the critique, find something right first.* Then, comment on the deficiency. This is a very important evaluation tool. I recommend that an Evaluator comment on as many positive actions as possible before delivering the correction. Since only one correction is made at a time, the positive comment to correction ratio should be–when possible–two or more to one. This makes the evaluation overwhelmingly positive. Because the bulk of the comments are positive, the officer views the corrective comment as an anomaly. In other words, the officer says to himself or herself: "Ok, I made a mistake, but overall I did a good job." This positive approach makes the criticism much more palatable, therefore more effective. Here are examples:
  Positive: "You had strong verbal commands. You made an effective tac-

tical approach, and you did a good job coordinating your efforts with the Cover Officer. But, you didn't use cover." "Let's try it again from the beginning."
Negative: "Hold it." "You didn't use cover." "Now, start using your head, and do it right this time."

- *Peer Jury* (the observing officers): The Peer Jury works well because the critique becomes depersonalized. No longer is the critique Evaluator to officer. The correction becomes a group evaluation. If an officer has difficulty admitting he or she has made a mistake, call on the Peer Jury to provide credence to your comments and apply peer pressure for acceptance.

The Peer Jury also involves the whole class in the learning process. The major benefit of using the Peer Jury as a teaching model is that the officers experience "Observational Learning." Even though an officer may only physically participate in three or five scenarios, that same officer will continue to learn by observing the other officers in their scenarios. As a result, the entire training session becomes an active learning experience for the officers.

THE OFFICER MUST CORRECTLY COMPLETE THE SCENARIO. The officer is not allowed to fail. The scenario is stopped each time the officer makes a mistake. The officer is corrected and the scenario is started over from the beginning.

By stopping the role-play immediately after observing a mistake, the officer can focus on that single error and its correction. This prevents the officer from feeling overwhelmed and promotes a positive learning experience.

The officer repeats the scenario (with the same Threat Response) until he or she successfully completes the role-play. The fundamental principle of Confrontational Simulation is that the officer always wins. If the officer puts forth honest effort and is not a safety risk, the officer is not allowed to fail the scenario.

At the end of the scenario, the Evaluator summarizes the officer's proper use of force, proper use of Cover, and proper verbalization. The Evaluator only facilitates the dialog. It is really the Peer Jury who summarizes the officer's performance. Directing a series of questions to the Peer Jury facilitates the summary: Was the officer's use of force justified? Why? How was the officer's use of Cover? Why was it good? How was the officer's use of verbal commands? What was good about them?

A summary of the officer's positive performance reinforces the proper use of force, the proper use of Cover, and the proper verbal commands to the officer and the Peer Jurors. Further, it allows the officer to be recognized for his or her positive performance and to finish the scenario as a winner.

Additional Benefits of Confrontational Simulation Training

During the first year that the Con Sim program was in full swing at the Oregon Academy, I identified two unanticipated benefits of the program. The first unanticipated benefit was that the officers who formed the Peer Juror started to see the officer's use of force in the scenario from a witness's point of view. From a managing the use of force incident perspective, this is very valuable. If an officer can experience what a witness sees and feels during a use of force incident, the officer can more effectively manage witness perceptions while using force.

After realizing this was occurring, I incorporated this "witness perspective" into my critique of the officer's verbalization. When an officer did not verbalize while using force, I would turn to the Peer Jury and say, "You're witnesses on the street, what did you see and hear?" "A beating," they would answer. Then, I would have the officer start the scenario over, but this time with verbalization while applying the force. "What did you see and hear, this time?" "An officer controlling a suspect and the suspect resisting the officer's commands," the members of the Peer Jury would reply.

As an instructor, you can explain the importance of verbal commands while using force until your hoarse, but most officers really won't understand the importance of proper verbal commands until they experience an officer's proper and improper verbalization for themselves from a witness's perspective.

The second unanticipated benefit was that the Con Sim program provided us a mechanism for determining what the students retained from their defensive tactics training. Prior to the Con Sim program, we put the students through hours of defensive tactics training, they demonstrated the required techniques, and then they graduated. The training staff had no idea if our training methodology effectively prepared the students for the street or the facility.

By observing the students spontaneously apply their techniques and tactics during the scenarios, it allowed us to identify the weaknesses in our defensive tactics techniques or the flaws in the way we taught the techniques.

For example, during the Con Sim scenarios, the officers would leave Cover while giving verbal commands to the suspect at gunpoint. I would correct the mistake and have the officer start the scenario over. Ninety percent of the officers would creep away from Cover on their second and third remedial scenarios. I could not understand why this was happening. We discussed the use of Cover when we taught the officers high-risk handcuffing. Then, it came to me. We taught the officers high-risk handcuffing in an open gym, without using cover.

With the next defensive tactics class, we demonstrated and taught high-risk handcuffing from behind Cover, only. During the next Con Sim class, 100 percent of the officers used Cover correctly when giving verbal commands to the suspect at gunpoint. We never would have discovered that the manner in which we taught high-risk handcuffing was detrimental to the officer's survival tactics without the Con Sim training.

As another example, we changed our handgun retention techniques based on what we observed during Confrontational Simulation. As you have learned, one of the Threat Response's is to disarm the officer of his or her handgun. While watching this Threat Response unfold during the scenarios, we made two very important observations:

First, the Role-Player did not stand in front of the officer and reach out and grab his gun with one arm, as the officers' practiced in defensive tactics training. The attempted disarming always occurred in the form of a grapple with the Role-Player's arms wrapped around the officer's waist. Consequently, the handgun retention tactics that we had previously taught were ineffective.

Second, because our handgun retention tactics were based on false assumptions and practiced unrealistically, the officers did not realize the Role-Player was trying to disarm them. As a result, when the officer was asked what he or she thought the Role-Player was trying to do during the assault, 99 percent of the officers replied: "The suspect was trying to wrestle me to the ground." From these revelations, we developed weapon retention techniques that were designed to defeat a grappling-disarming attempt. Further, we adopted and taught the philosophy that any time a suspect grappled with an officer, with his or her arms around the officer's waist, the officer is to assume that his or her gun is being grabbed and a disarming is being attempted.

Another benefit of Con Sim training is an improvement in an officer's use of force report writing skills. Although I developed the program with this goal in mind, I was surprised at how quickly it produced results. In a fairly short period of time, the officers had gone from writing use of force reports that stated: "I saw, I came, I kicked his butt" to writing reports that did a good job of explaining their use of force justification. I knew, intuitively, that having the officers' explain their justification during the scenarios would somewhat improve their use of force report writing. But I was very surprised to observe how much their use of force reports had improved over such a short period of time.

Further Con Sim Application

When I became Director of the Montana Law Enforcement Academy, I met with many of Montana's chiefs and sheriffs. From those conversations, I learned that only about 10 percent of Montana's law enforcement agencies had formal field training programs. Further, I became aware that the vast majority of law enforcement agencies expected their officers who graduated on Friday to function as effective law enforcement officers on Saturday morning. This was an unrealistic expectation, considering that 85 percent of the academy's training consisted of classroom lecture.

To meet this challenging expectation, I would have to incorporate a simulated field training program into the basic law enforcement training program. In other words, I would have to create a complete scenario-based police academy curriculum. To accomplish that formidable task, I used Confrontational Simulation as the basis for the new scenario-based law enforcement academy training program. I reduced classroom lecture hours by over 50 percent, and added an eight-hour scenario-based simulation-training lab to every classroom topic. I designated the last week of the basic law enforcement course as a scenario-based, simulated, field training officer program. And I conducted a job task analysis to ensure that the new curriculum was based on the tasks currently performed by Montana's law enforcement officers.

The Montana Academy occupies the site of a former girls' school that was built at the turn of the twentieth century, on two hundred acres. I had struck scenario-based training gold. I had buildings and space galore. To provide the training facilities that I needed, I had my wonderful maintenance staff turn every unoccupied space into apartments, a mini-mart, and a fully functional tavern.

When I was finished, I had created the first scenario-based law enforcement academy curriculum and training program. The academy's new training program did not just add training scenarios to the last few weeks of the training schedule. Scenario-based training was the basis for the new curriculum, training philosophy, and training methodology. And it all started with a covertly developed scenario-based use of force training program called Confrontational Simulation.

Conclusion

I have given you a comprehensive overview of the Confrontational Simulation program and its benefits and virtues. To explain all the complexities and nuances of conducting scenario-based use of force training would require a separate book devoted to the subject. It is my hope that after reading this chapter that you have gained a deeper understanding of the positive effects that simulation and scenario-based use of force training can have on officer and department liability. As we close the last chapter my life's work,

I leave you with my personal use of force training mantra: *Training does not minimize liability; effective scenario-based use of force training minimizes liability.*

In closing, I would like to recognize and offer my sincere thanks to the following former Oregon Public Safety Academy instructors who were instrumental in the development and the success of the Confrontational Simulation program: Don Oliver, Richard Dague, Jack Burright, Mark Yoshihara, Gary Dahl, John Black, Scott Dye, Ken Herbst, and Mike Espinoza.

In addition, I would like to thank the national and international instructors that I have trained in Confrontational Simulation for their contributions to the program. You are too numerous to mention individually; nevertheless, your insights and contributions have had a positive impact on scenario-based use of force training.

In addition, I must thank the following Montana Law Enforcement Academy Staff and part-time instructors who made the transformation of the Confrontational Simulation program into an effective scenario-based academy law enforcement training program: Deb Butler, John Spencer, Dale Aschim, Rick Lang, Rae Ann Forseth, Tom Higgins, Dave Ogle, Jim Summers, Alan Guderjahn, Josh Rutherford, Tim Coleman, Roy Tanniehill, and Jeff Kraft. Thank you all for your dedication and service to the training of Montana's law enforcement and corrections officers.

FINAL THOUGHTS

America's criminal justice officers are entrusted with the authority and power to deprive a man of liberty, seize his property, injure his body, and end his life: robbing a parent of a son, a sister of a brother, a wife of a husband, and a child of a father. I hope you truly understand the honor and the privilege that has been bestowed upon you. For no other in our country is entrusted with such utter and complete power. Further, I pray that God gifts you with the strength to use your power and authority with restraint and wisdom. For what you do on-duty reflects on every one of us who wears or has ever worn the badge.

It is said that we are a nation of laws and not of men. But, the truth is that those who purport this noble virtue do so from behind the protection of the men and women in uniform who are tasked with the protection of those who write and live under the law.

For a nation and its laws are only as resolute and righteous as those who brandish the shield and wield the sword. For those who have sworn to protect and serve are the warrior guardians of a free society. For without the courage and dedication of those who answer to a higher calling, evil prevails, society collapses, and the laws of nations become only hollow words written on gilded paper.

For regardless of the eloquent oration of the ruling class, the philosophical rhetoric of learned men, or the impassioned ranting of the heretic, in the end, it is force that rules the day.

This book is dedicated to the men and women of law enforcement and corrections who willingly place their personal and professional well-being on the line every time force is deployed in the performance of their public safety mission. It is my most sincere hope that the information contained in these pages will be of assistance to you, as an officer, supervisor, or administrator, in properly managing the use of force incident.

TRAINING RESOURCES

Howard Webb is the Executive Director of the American Council on Criminal Justice Training (ACCJT). The ACCJT is a 501(c)(3) nonprofit criminal justice and public safety training organization. The ACCJT offers the following training seminars and instructor development courses to criminal justice organizations and officers:

Training Seminars

Managing the Use of Force Incident for Officers–eight-hour presentation
Managing the Use of Force Incident for Supervisors–eight-hour presentation
Managing the Use of Force Incident for Mid-Managers–eigh-hour presentation
Managing the Use of Force Incident for Administrators–eight-hour presentation
Confrontational Simulation–eight-hour scenario-based training course
Writing an Effective Use of Force Report–eight-hour presentation
Forty-Two Rules of Officer Survival–eight-hour presentation
Success Without Promotion–eight-hour presentation

Instructor Development Courses

Confrontational Simulation Instructor Course–twenty-four-hour course
Counter Assault Tactics (CAT) Instructor Course–sixteen-hour course
Law Enforcement Ground Defense Instructor Course–sixteen-hour course
Weapon Retention and Disarming Instructor Course–sixteen-hour course
Community Awareness violence-Resistance Education (CARE) Instructor
    Course–twenty-four-hour course
Survival Skills Instructor Course–forty-hour course
Defensive Tactics Instructor Course–forty-hour course
Criminal Justice Instructor Development Course–forty-hour course
Additional seminars and instructor courses are available through the ACCJT.

Criminal Justice Organizations who are interested in an ACCJT training seminar or instructor development course can contact Howard at the ACCJT website: www.accjt.org.

BIBLIOGRAPHY

Americans with Disabilities Act (1990), Public Law 101-336,101st Congress of the United States.

An Analysis of Officers Killed: Burglaries (training tapes). Aims Media, 9710 DeSoto Avenue, Chatsworth, California 91311.

An Analysis of Officers Killed: Man With Gun Calls (training tapes). Aims Media, 9710 DeSoto Avenue, Chatsworth, California 91311.

An Analysis of Officers Killed: Handling Prisoners (training tapes). Aims Media, 9710 DeSoto Avenue, Chatsworth, California 91311.

An Analysis of Officers Killed: Suspicious Person Calls (training tapes). Aims Media, 9710 DeSoto Avenue, Chatsworth, California 91311.

An Analysis of Officers Killed: Traffic Stops (training tapes). Aims Media, 9710 DeSoto Avenue, Chatsworth, California 91311.

Bennis, W., & Nanus, B. (2007). *Leaders: The strategies for taking charge.* New York: Harper Collins.

Boyle v. City of Tualatin, Circuit Court of the State of Oregon–No. C95 0232 CV

Carl Bryan v. Brian McPherson, No. 08-55622 (2009), United States Court of Appeals for the Ninth Circuit.

Canton v. Harris, 489 U.S. 378 (1989), U.S. Supreme Court.

Connors, R., & Smith, T. (1999). *Journey to the Emerald City.* Upper Saddle River, NJ: Prentice Hall.

Garrity v. New Jersey, 385 U.S. 493 (1967), U.S. Supreme Court.

Graham v. Conner, 490 U.S. 386 (1989), U.S. Supreme Court.

Kurke, L. B. (2004). The wisdom of Alexander the Great: Enduring leadership lessons from the man who created an empire. *AMACOM,* xxii, xxiii.

Law Enforcement Officers Killed and Assault. (2008). U.S. Department of Justice, Federal Bureau of Investigation, October 2009.

Los Angeles County Sheriff's Department Psychological Services Unit. (1991). A View of Force, 1.

Malaika Brooks v. City of Seattle, No. 08-35526 (2010), United States Court of Appeals for the Ninth Circuit.

McAlpine, A. (1989). *The new Machiavelli: The art of politics in business.* Hoboken, NJ: John Wiley & Sons.

Plakas v. Drinski, No. 93-1431 (1994), U.S. Court of Appeals for the Seventh Circuit.

Pistorius v. City of Medford, U.S. District Court–No. 93-2260-13.

Richard Leo Deorle v. Greg Rutherford, No. 99-17188 (2001), United States Court of Appeals for the Ninth Circuit.

Siddle, B. K. (1995) *Sharpening the warrior's edge.* PPCT Research Publications, 46–49, 106, 107.

State of Oregon v. Daniel Beugli, District Court of the State of Oregon–91D- 103499.
State of Oregon v. Jerry Walton, District Court of the State of Oregon–No. 96D 105792.
Tennessee v. Garner, 471 U.S. 1 (1985), U.S. Supreme Court.
Terry V. Ohio, 392 U.S. 1 (1968), U.S. Supreme Court.

INDEX